TAJIKISTAN

CHINA

Hindu Kush

Indus River

N

Bagram
KABUL
A1
Khyber
Pass

Jalalabad

Peshawar

Srinagar

Islamabad

Tora
Bora

5

Shah-i-Kot
Valley

K
I
S
T
A
N

Lahore

INDIA

Jacobabad

Indus River

N

0                                    300 miles

0                                    500 Km.

Chazaud

# One Bullet Away

# One Bullet Away

## THE MAKING OF
## A MARINE OFFICER

## Nathaniel Fick

HOUGHTON MIFFLIN COMPANY
BOSTON · NEW YORK
2005

For information about permission to reproduce selections from
this book, write to Permissions, Houghton Mifflin Company,
215 Park Avenue South, New York, New York 10003.

Visit our Web site: www.houghtonmifflinbooks.com.

*Library of Congress Cataloging-in-Publication Data*
Fick, Nathaniel.
One bullet away : the making of a marine officer / Nathaniel Fick.
p.   cm.
ISBN-13: 978-0-618-55613-7    ISBN-10: 0-618-55613-3
1. United States. Marine Corps—Officers—Training of.
2. Fick, Nathaniel.  I. Title.
VE23.F53 2005  359.9'6'092—d22  2005010332

PRINTED IN THE UNITED STATES OF AMERICA

Book design by Robert Overholtzer

QUM 10 9 8 7 6 5 4 3 2 1

TO

CAPTAIN BRENT MOREL

*Bravo Company, First Reconnaissance Battalion,*
*First Marine Division. Killed in Action 7 April 2004,*
*Al Anbar Province, Iraq*

AND

THE BRAVE MOTHERS
OF UNITED STATES MARINES

# Contents

# PART I

# Peace

We should remember that one man is much the same as another, and that he is best who is trained in the severest school. — THUCYDIDES

# 1

FIFTEEN OF US climbed aboard the ancient white school bus. Wire mesh covered its windows and four black words ran along its sides: UNITED STATES MARINE CORPS.

Dressed casually in shorts and sandals, we spread out and sat alone with our bags. Some sipped coffee from paper cups, and a few unfolded newspapers they had brought. I found a seat near the back as the bus started with a roar and a cloud of smoke blew through the open windows.

A second lieutenant, looking crisp in his gabardine and khaki uniform, sat in the front row. He had just graduated from Officer Candidates School, and would escort us on the hour's drive to the Marine Corps base in Quantico, Virginia. Shortly after we pulled away from the recruiting office, he stood in the aisle and turned to face us. I expected a welcome, a joke, some commiseration.

"Honor, courage, and commitment are the Marines' core values," the lieutenant shouted over the engine. He sounded scripted, but also sincere. "If you can't be honest at OCS, how can the Corps trust you to lead men in combat?"

Combat. I glanced around the bus's gunmetal interior, surprised to see people reading or pretending to sleep. No one answered the lieutenant's question. He stood there in the aisle, glaring at us, and I sat up a little straighter. The lieutenant was my age, but he looked different. Shorter hair, of course, and broader shoulders. It was more than that. He had an edge, something in his jaw or his brow that made me self-conscious.

I turned toward the window to avoid his gaze. Families drove next to us, on their way to the lake or the beach. Kids wearing headphones gawked, surely wondering what losers were riding a school bus in the summertime. A girl in an open Jeep stood and started to raise her shirt before being pulled back down by a laughing friend. They waved and accelerated past. I thought of my friends, spending their summer vacations in New York and San Francisco, working in air-conditioned office towers and partying at night. Staring through the wire mesh at the bright day, I thought this must be what it's like on the ride to Sing Sing. I wondered why I was on that bus.

I went to Dartmouth intending to go to med school. Failing a chemistry class had inspired my love of history, and I ended up majoring in the classics. By the summer of 1998, my classmates were signing six-figure contracts as consultants and investment bankers. I didn't understand what we, at age twenty-two, could possibly be consulted about. Others headed off to law school or medical school for a few more years of reading instead of living. None of it appealed to me. I wanted to go on a great adventure, to prove myself, to serve my country. I wanted to do something so hard that no one could ever talk shit to me. In Athens or Sparta, my decision would have been easy. I felt as if I had been born too late. There was no longer a place in the world for a young man who wanted to wear armor and slay dragons.

Dartmouth encouraged deviation from the trampled path, but only to join organizations like the Peace Corps or Teach for America. I wanted something more transformative. Something that might kill me — or leave me better, stronger, more capable. I wanted to be a warrior.

My family had only a short martial tradition. My maternal grandfather, like many in his generation, had served in World War II. He was a Navy officer in the South Pacific, and his ship, the escort carrier *Natoma Bay,* fought at New Guinea, Leyte Gulf, Iwo Jima, and Okinawa, often supporting Marine invasion forces ashore. At 0635 on June 7, 1945, so the family story went, only two months before the end of the war, a Japanese kamikaze crashed into the *Natoma Bay*'s flight deck. The explosion tore a hole in the steel twelve feet wide and twenty feet long. Shrapnel peppered my grandfather's body. My mother remembers watching him pick pieces of metal from his skin twenty years later. He had some of that shrapnel melted into a lucky horseshoe, which was shown to me with great reverence when I was a child.

My father enlisted in the Army in 1968. When most of his basic training class went to Vietnam, he received orders to the Army Security

Agency. He spent a year in Bad Aibling, Germany, eavesdropping on Eastern bloc radio transmissions and waiting for the Soviets to roll through the Fulda Gap. He completed OCS just as President Richard Nixon began drawing down the military, and took advantage of an early out to go to law school. But my dad was proud to have been a soldier.

The Army sent me a letter during my junior year at Dartmouth, promising to pay for graduate school. The Navy and Air Force did the same, promising skills and special training. The Marine Corps promised nothing. Whereas the other services listed their benefits, the Corps asked, "Do you have what it takes?" If I was going to serve in the military, I would be a Marine.

A few months before, I'd seen a poster in the dining hall advertising a talk by Tom Ricks. Then the *Wall Street Journal*'s Pentagon correspondent, Ricks had recently written a book about the Marines. I sat up most of one night reading it. I arrived early to get a good seat and listened as Ricks explained the Corps's culture and the state of civil-military relations in the United States. His review of the Marines, or at least my interpretation of it, was glowing. The Marine Corps was a last bastion of honor in society, a place where young Americans learned to work as a team, to trust one another and themselves, and to sacrifice for a principle. Hearing it from a recruiter, I would have been skeptical. But here was a journalist, an impartial observer.

The crowd was the usual mix of students, faculty, and retired alumni. After the talk, a young professor stood. "How can you support the presence of ROTC at a place like Dartmouth?" she asked. "It will militarize the campus and threaten our culture of tolerance."

"Wrong," replied Ricks. "It will liberalize the military." He explained that in a democracy, the military should be representative of the people. It should reflect the best of American society, not stand apart from it. Ricks used words such as "duty" and "honor" without cynicism, something I'd not often heard at Dartmouth.

His answer clinched my decision to apply for a slot at Marine OCS during the summer between my junior and senior years of college. I would have laughed at the idea of joining the Corps on a bet or because of a movie, but my own choice was almost equally capricious. Although I had reached the decision largely on my own, Tom Ricks, in an hour-long talk on a cold night at Dartmouth, finally convinced me to be a Marine.

But even joining the Marines didn't seem as crazy as it had to my parents' generation. This was 1998, not 1968. The United States was cashing in its post–cold war peace dividend. Scholars talked about "the end of history," free markets spreading prosperity throughout the world, and the death of ideology. I would be joining a peacetime military. At least that's the rationale I used when I broke the news to my parents. They were surprised but supportive. "The Marines," my dad said, "will teach you everything I love you too much to teach you."

The Marine Corps base in Quantico straddles Interstate 95, sprawling across thousands of acres of pine forest and swamp thirty miles south of Washington. Our bus rumbled through the gate, and we drove past rows of peeling warehouses and brick buildings identified only by numbered signs. They looked like the remnants of some dead industry, like the boarded-up mills on the riverbanks of a New Hampshire town.

"Christ, man, where're the ovens? This place looks like Dachau." Only a few forced laughs met this quip from someone near the back of the bus.

We drove farther and farther onto the base — along the edge of a swamp, through miles of trees, far enough to feel as if they could kill us here and no one would ever know. That, of course, was the desired effect. When the air brakes finally hissed and the door swung open, we sat in the middle of a blacktop parade deck the size of three football fields. Austere brick barracks surrounded it. A sign at the blacktop's edge read UNITED STATES MARINE CORPS OFFICER CANDIDATES SCHOOL — DUCTUS EXEMPLO. I recognized the motto from Latin class: "Leadership by Example."

I hoped a drill instructor in a Smokey Bear hat would storm onto the bus and order us off to stand on yellow footprints. Pop culture has immortalized the arrival of enlisted Marine recruits at Parris Island, South Carolina. But this was OCS, and the lack of theatrics disappointed me. A fresh-faced Marine with a clipboard took the roll by Social Security number and then handed a pencil to each of us, saying we had a lot of paperwork to fill out.

For two days, we shuffled from line to line for haircuts, gear issue, and a battery of physical tests. Candidates who had returned after being dropped from previous OCS classes explained this routine: the schedule was designed to minimize the number of us who flunked out for high blood pressure. On day three, with physical evaluations completed, the hammer would fall.

We slept in squad bays with fifty bunks per room. There, on the evenings before OCS really started, I got my first lesson in esprit de corps. OCS is competitive. Since the peacetime Marine Corps needs a fixed number of officers, a certain number of candidates are earmarked to graduate while the rest are destined to fail. I thought this put us in competition with one another, but the candidates who had been dropped before, or who had served as enlisted Marines, shared their knowledge with the rest of us.

The Corps is a naval service, with nautical vocabulary. Doors are hatches, walls are bulkheads, and floors are decks. Signs at Quantico, miles from the sea, read WELCOME ABOARD. They also taught us the more arcane language of the Marines. Running shoes were called go-fasters. Our flashlights, worn on the hip at OCS, were moonbeams. When we looked confused, one of the prior-service Marines laughed. Just wait till you get to the Fleet, he told us. Three different pieces of equipment were known as a "donkey dick" — a radio antenna, a brush for cleaning mortar tubes, and a funnel for fueling Humvees.

In the beginning, my strongest impression of Quantico, apart from its isolation, was its timelessness. Looking around the squad bay, I could imagine Franklin Roosevelt in the White House. No plastic, no advertising, no bright colors. Just two-high metal racks, as our bunks were called, a green linoleum floor, brick walls, and bare bulbs overhead. The only decoration was a sign of two-foot-high letters stenciled along an entire wall: HONOR, COURAGE, COMMITMENT. I already had the feeling that the Marines were a world apart, that what we did at OCS would be separate from the rest of my life.

When another candidate dragged a wooden footlocker next to mine and sat down, I was glad of the company.

"I'm Dave Adams." He stuck out his hand.

Dave was a football player at William and Mary. His brother had gone to Dartmouth. His easy smile made me like him right away.

"So what do you think?" I tried to ask the question with less trepidation than I felt.

Dave smiled and said, "I think we're in for a shitty summer. But I've wanted to be a Marine since I was a kid. What's that saying? 'Pain is temporary. Pride is forever.'"

"I saw a bumper sticker in the parking lot that said 'Nobody ever drowned in sweat.'" I was nervous. Not scared or intimidated — that would come later — but apprehensive. The Marine transformation is one of American life's storied tests. I knew its reputation was earned.

We had the barest taste of it at the supply warehouse on the morning of the ominous third day. All the candidates lined up and moved from bin to bin, selecting green camouflage blouses and trousers, nylon belts with two olive-drab canteens attached, and odd items such as bug spray labeled "Repellent, Arthropod." Two young Marines in the warehouse took advantage of the chance to hassle a group of future officers.

"Get at parade rest!"

It was an alien command. I clasped my hands in front of me and tried to look respectful.

"You gonna gaff us off? Get at the position of attention."

The candidates around me stood a little straighter, with their hands at their sides. The two Marines told us there were only two ways to stand at OCS: parade rest — feet shoulder-width apart, hands clasped in the small of the back, eyes straight ahead; and at attention — heels together, back straight, hands at your sides with thumbs along the trouser seams.

Later, we assembled for lunch in a Word War II–era Quonset hut. Baking in this sun-beaten aluminum oven, we munched processed meat sandwiches and apples — a prepared lunch the Marines called a "boxed nasty" — as the school's commanding officer (CO) outlined his expectations of us. The colonel's lantern jaw, craggy nose, and graying hair were straight from a recruiting commercial. He looked as if he could wrestle any of us to the floor, and authority ran deep in his voice.

"We seek to identify in each candidate those qualities of intellect, human understanding, and moral character that enable a person to inspire and to control a group of people successfully: leaders," he said. "A candidate's presence under pressure is a key indicator of leadership potential. In trying to identify Marine leaders who may someday face combat, we want to see who can think and function under stress. Stress at OCS is created in many ways, as you will see."

When the colonel concluded, he called forward the school's staff, introducing each Marine. All had served as drill instructors. At OCS, though, they were called "sergeant instructors," and we would address them by that title, their rank, and their name. The staff marched smartly down the aisle and stood at attention before us. Khaki uniforms with splashes of colored ribbons, eyes focused over our heads on the back wall of the room, no smiles. They were sergeants, staff sergeants, and gunnery sergeants, mostly men with ten to twenty years in the Corps. I saw scars and biceps and tattoos. With introductions complete, the colonel turned to the staff and uttered ten words that ended our civilian lives: "Take charge and carry out the plan of the day."

Tables turned over, chairs clattered to the floor, and I forgot all about the half-eaten apple in my hand. The staff charged us. We ran out the back door of the Quonset hut. I wanted to keep running, to disappear into the woods, make my way out to the highway, and hitchhike home. But pride trumps most other impulses in young men, and I fell into a ragged formation with my new platoon-mates.

"Stop eyeballing the freakin' area, maggot." My eyes were locked to the front. I didn't think he was talking to me. Warm, wet breath on my cheeks. If not me, then someone right next to me.

"Lock your body!"

Spittle across my eyes and lips. The Marine strutted up and down our crooked ranks. He spoke to the group, but in a way that made it personal for each of us.

"If you so much as *breathe*, I'll hear it and rip your freakin' windpipe out. Now grab your freakin' trash and move with purpose. Pretend for me that you want to be here."

We shouldered our bags. Candidates with foresight had brought hiking packs. They stood comfortably, looking ready to strike out down the Appalachian Trail. The truly lost labored with their leather brief bags and suitcases. I fell somewhere in between, striving mightily to be inconspicuous with an oversize duffel bag.

I snuck a look at the instructor's nametag. Olds. Three stripes on his shoulder. Sergeant Olds. He was yelling, veins popping, eyes bulging. His arms waved from broad shoulders that tapered to his waist with all the menacing grace of a wasp. I looked at Sergeant Instructor Sergeant Olds, sensing he had just become a fixture in my life.

"Don't eyeball me, candidate. Do you want to ask me out on a date? You look like you want to ask me out."

"No, Sergeant Instructor Sergeant Olds."

"Go ahead, candidate. Keep whispering. And keep looking deep into my eyes." His voice dropped to a whisper, and he moved in close. I watched a vein throbbing in his temple and struggled not to make eye contact. "I dare you to ask me out. Your chucklehead classmates here might get a laugh out of it, but I swear it'll be the last thing you ever do."

This is theater, right? I had seen *Full Metal Jacket*. It's all a joke. But it didn't feel like a joke. When Olds spoke to me, icy adrenaline washed through my chest. My legs shook. The worst part was that Olds knew he'd gotten to me. He would, I feared, increase the pressure.

For now, Olds pivoted on a spit-shined heel and struck out across the parade deck. Lacking better options, we followed him. Large raindrops splotched the dark asphalt. The splotches grew bigger and closer together until they finally merged into a single, dark stain. I dragged my duffel bag along the pavement, struggling to keep its strap from biting into my shoulder. The bag had felt lighter when I'd hefted it the night before. I had packed only the required list: three sets of civilian clothes, running shoes, a toiletry kit, and the combat boots mailed weeks before so I could break them in. I folded the clothes crisply, careful to crease each trouser leg and keep the shirt fronts smooth.

Sergeant Olds had opened a gap of fifty yards between himself and the straggling platoon. He stood facing us with his hands on his hips. "Dump your trash. I want to see who's trying to sneak naked pictures of his boyfriend into my squad bay."

I hesitated, unsure whether he actually meant for us to dump our belongings onto the puddled pavement. Steam rose as the rain hit the ground.

"What are we, deaf? I said dump your trash. Do it now. *Move!*"

I unzipped my bag and placed the boots on the blacktop. Then I stacked my clothes on them and put the toiletry bag on top to deflect the rain. Olds's attention landed on my carefully constructed pile. He kicked it over and put a boot print on the chest of my neatly ironed shirt.

"What's in here?" He grabbed my toiletry bag. "Drugs? Booze? Maybe a tube of K-Y jelly and a big cucumber?"

One by one, my toothbrush, toothpaste, razor, and shaving cream fell to the ground.

"You must have hidden it pretty well, candidate," Olds growled. "But I'll find it. Oh, yeah, I'll find it. And when I do, I'll run your ass out of my Marine Corps before you can even call your congressman."

Olds moved on to his next victim, and I hesitantly began to piece my life back together, wondering again why I was at OCS. Next to me, Dave caught my eye with a smile and mouthed, "Semper fi."

# 2

AT EXACTLY FIVE O'CLOCK each morning, candidates roaming the squad bay on the night's rotating guard threw the switch on the fluorescent lights. It was like shooting the day from a cannon. The instructors burst out of the office at the head of the long room. We had five seconds to launch from our racks, slide into our black rubber flip-flops (referred to as "shower shoes" in the Marines), and assume the position of attention with our toes along a black line that ran the length of the squad bay. No head starts. No wearing shower shoes in the rack. Don't yawn, don't wince, and don't be late.

Olds was always the loudest. "I'm looking for morning wood. I want to find the candidate who was thinking dirty thoughts about me in his sleep." He prowled up and down the line, bent at the waist to stare at our crotches. The other two instructors were Staff Sergeant Carpenter and Staff Sergeant Butler. They were the ultimate masked men. In ten weeks, we never learned a thing about them. They dominated our every waking hour, but the interaction was almost purely animal.

A favorite morning ritual of theirs was getting dressed by the numbers. With the candidates toeing the line, we began a screamed, scrambled version of Simon Says. "Put your left sock on now." We had three seconds to take the shower shoe off and slip on a black boot sock.

"Too slow! Take it off!" Olds howled in cadence, as if to a drumbeat.

We returned to the starting position, holding a sock loosely in each hand. In the corner of my eye, I noticed Candidate Dunkin next to me. I had been cursing the alphabetical arrangement of the racks, since Dunkin had become a lightning rod for hate and discontent. He was overweight and undermotivated. While the rest of the platoon played along with the sergeant instructor, Dunkin was slowly getting dressed on his own. Olds noticed, too.

"We have an individual." Olds spat the word like it was a synonym for child molester. "Candidate Dunkin, what are you doing?" The drumbeat again.

Dunkin didn't answer. He removed his socks and returned to the starting position, staring blankly at the wall across the squad bay. Olds levitated two inches in front of his nose, hissing in a whisper only those of us closest to him could hear.

"I got you pegged, boy. But you're gonna suffer before I send you home." Dunkin blinked, and Olds inhaled before bellowing at the platoon. "Right sock!" This time, he didn't even wait to see how quickly we moved. "Too slow!"

After ten repetitions with the socks, we ended up with our boots on our hands, clomping around the squad bay on hands and knees, "marching" to cadence. Olds explained that orders slowly executed meant advantages lost. My OCS fear had subsided, to be replaced by frustration. I didn't understand the point of the games. It seemed like fraternity hazing, and I expected more from the Marine Corps. I crawled in a circle with my boots on my hands and fantasized about quitting, about going home and spending the rest of the summer as a lifeguard. This wasn't the warrior rite of passage I was looking for.

When Olds declared the games over, we got dressed and piled outside to form up on the physical training (PT) field.

The centerpiece of the PT field was a red wooden platform. Atop it, silhouetted against the rising sun, stood a British Royal Marine color sergeant. He was on exchange from the U.K. and clearly enjoyed beating platoons of aspiring American officers into shape. "Ah, good morning, candidates. Your steady diet of Big Macs and Jerry Springer has surely prepared you for this morning's activities. Remember, nothing proves your effort to me like projectile vomiting."

I already had a history of Corps-induced vomiting. A few weeks after Tom Ricks's talk, I had walked into the Marine recruiting office in Lebanon, New Hampshire. Above the government-issue metal desk were posters with slogans such as "Superior thinking has always overcome superior force" and "We're looking for a few good men." I liked it. The crisp sergeant behind the desk looked me up and down and laughed. Sure, he said, he'd sign me up right now, and I'd be on a bus to Parris

Island by the end of the week. But since I was a college student, he thought I'd prefer an officer program, and his office only handled enlisted Marines. I confessed that I barely knew the difference. He handed me a business card and wished me well. Sitting in the car, I looked at the card. Captain Steven Ettien, Officer Selection Office, Portsmouth, New Hampshire.

Three weeks later, I made the trip to Portsmouth. The office was hidden in a nondescript professional center. An efficient receptionist greeted me and sat me on a couch. The waiting room was neutral, softly lit, almost corporate — not what I expected. I stood when the door to the inner office opened. Captain Ettien was trim and fit, looking in his dress blues like every recruiting poster Marine in my mind.

"So you think you have what it takes to be an officer in my Corps." It was a statement, almost an accusation, not a question.

My first hurdle would be passing the Marines' physical fitness test. Three hundred was a perfect score, and officer candidates were expected to score better than 275. There were three events: pull-ups, crunches, and a three-mile run. A score of 300 required doing twenty dead-hang pull-ups without dropping off the bar, followed by one hundred crunches in under two minutes, and then completing the run in under eighteen minutes. Like a triathlon, none of the individual events is especially difficult, but in combination they test overall fitness. I had played football and lacrosse in high school and was a strong bicycle racer at Dartmouth, so I left Portsmouth that afternoon intent on conquering the fitness test.

Captain Ettien greeted me on my next visit by asking in what order I'd been training for the three events. Grateful that he was taking my preferences into account, I told him I relied on pull-ups, crunches, run.

"Great." He grinned. "Then we'll start you with the run, followed by crunches, and then pull-ups." It was my introduction to the Marine Corps way.

I must have blanched, because he added that he'd come on the run to motivate me. Two minutes later, I sprinted out of the parking lot with Captain Ettien behind me at the wheel of a government van, honking the horn and shouting to pick up the pace. I ran three miles in 17:30. Moving over to the grass, I lay on my back with the captain on my feet. At his whistle, I started crunching. Ninety-eight, ninety-nine, one hundred. Ten seconds to spare. Another perfect score. I was rolling. We moved over to the pull-up bar. Every breath formed a cloud of condensation. My body was sore from the run and the crunches, but my arms felt good. Jumping up to the bar, I started curling my chin over the metal pole as Captain Ettien counted aloud.

"Thirteen, fourteen, fourteen, fourteen." *What am I doing wrong?* "Stop kipping — fourteen, fourteen." *What the hell is kipping?*

By now, I'd done twenty pull-ups but his count stuck at fourteen. My arms shook, and despite the cold, sweat dripped into my eyes. I dropped off the bar, buckled at the knees, and poured my breakfast into the grass. When the heaves stopped, I asked, "What's kipping, and why did you stop counting at fourteen?"

"Swinging your body back and forth. You have to move up and down in a straight line. I'm tempted to give you one for effort because of the puke." Ettien paused and looked at his clipboard. "Two-seventy — not bad. Just keep working on it and you'll qualify for OCS."

By the time I stood in front of the color sergeant that morning, I was a machine. I could run three miles in sixteen minutes and do twenty-five dead-hang pull-ups. Unfortunately, OCS rarely tested what we'd already trained for.

"This morning you will do the log run. Give me a squad to demonstrate."

Twelve candidates jumped up and jogged to the front of the group. In unison, they snapped to parade rest.

"Pick up the log."

The candidates hoisted a full-size telephone pole onto their shoulders. It was twenty feet long and weighed six hundred pounds. The pole reeked of creosote and rubbed off brown on their hands and shoulders.

"Now run," the color sergeant ordered.

They trotted in a circle around the field.

"See, it's simple. Even you wankers should be able to figure this one out. Each squad grab a log. Catch me." He took off down the trail.

We strategized. "Tallest to shortest — otherwise the short guys won't be bearing any of the weight. Tall guys in front will keep the pace high." Dave and I were the tallest guys in our squad, so he stood at the front of the pole, with me a foot behind.

A dozen squads of a dozen men each struggled off down the trail, looking like millipedes beneath their logs. Legs moved quickly, but progress was slow. We slopped over muddy roots and banged between trunks. Once or twice, the log threatened to roll off our shoulders and crush our feet. I wrapped one arm up over the log and used the other to wipe sweat from my eyes.

Ahead of us, the color sergeant bounced along in his running shoes and white tank top, bemoaning the future of the Marine Corps. "Your Corps has been around for two hundred twenty-three years, right? Not a bad run. A respectable try, really. The Army will pick up your slack." He reached a fork in the trail and turned left.

"He's headed toward the ford. I wonder how we're gonna do that." The voice came from behind me, where candidates were struggling with the weight and the slippery footing.

The ford was a deep pool of stagnant water sitting in the middle of the trail. Stopping at the water's edge, the instructor picked up a rock the size of a bowling ball. He waited for the squads to pant into position all around him before heaving it into the ford. When it splashed into the water and sank out of sight, four little heads popped up.

"You're doing a good job, so I'm showing you where the snakes are. Go get wet."

We joined the snakes in the ford, splashing out to the deep water and swimming next to the log like tugboats pushing a barge. Our boots filled with water and threatened to drag us to the bottom. I had grown up on Chesapeake Bay, a strong swimmer, but being trapped underwater was my private terror. A short candidate at the back of the log was yelling encouragement when his hand slipped off the muddy pole and the words turned to gurgles as his head went under. I hardly heard him because I was focused on keeping my own hands on the log and my own head above water.

"Let's go, fellas. Just a little farther. Good job." Ahead of me, Dave was pushing the log and looking back at the rest of the squad. He was soaked, red-faced, and squinting to see. I could tell he was in pain, but he was turning his energy and attention outward, pulling the rest of the squad behind him.

An hour after we'd started, Dave led us back onto the sunny field where we had begun. He was singing cadence, and we echoed with all the breath we had left. "Born in the woods. Raised by a bear." Dave jogged easily under the log. "Double set of dog teeth. Triple coat of hair." The pain started to subside for me, too. "Two magazines and my

M-16. I'm lean and mean." By suffering together, we could spread the hardship around until it almost disappeared. "I'm a U.S. Marine."

Olds was waiting to march us back to the squad bay. "Cut that trash out. You ain't Marines." I thought I saw a glimmer of satisfaction beneath his dismissal. "PT showers. You have four minutes. We're already late for chow." It wasn't even seven A.M.

PT showers were one of OCS's many small indignities. They were cold, soapless soaks with forty of your closest friends. The staff turned on all the nozzles in our communal bathroom while the platoon stripped. Then we walked in single file, "nuts to butts," past the spraying shower-heads. It was enough water to turn dusty limbs muddy, but never enough to get clean. We toweled off, dressed, and marched across the parade deck, still breathing hard from the log run.

The platoon marched in three columns of about a dozen candidates each. In addition to marching everywhere we went, we usually spent an hour or two each evening on the parade deck. Olds called it "driving the bus." We would march from one end to the other, about-face, march back, and repeat. We carried M-16s on our right shoulders, gripping the buttstock with a hand extended parallel to the deck. In the beginning, Sergeant Olds had called our cadence, but he slowly shifted the responsibility to us. It wasn't words so much as a haunting wail, rising and falling like a plaintive southern spiritual. But the wail had a beat, and our heels struck the pavement in unison. Halfway across the parade deck on our way to the chow hall, Olds pulled me from the formation to take over calling the cadence.

I screwed it up from the first note. My lefts were rights, my rights were lefts, and the tempo surged and sagged. The platoon worked not to expose me, but it was too confusing. They collapsed into a pitter-patter of mismatched heels, like a group of tourists out for a morning stroll. Olds lit into me.

"Daggone it, candidate. You know what happens to lieutenants who can't even march a platoon?"

I croaked, "No, Sergeant Instructor Sergeant Olds."

"They get their Marines killed in combat." This fate, at OCS, was promised not only to candidates who couldn't march but also to those who failed to blacken their boots, polish their brass belt buckles, or put on their socks quickly enough. "You want to get your Marines killed?"

"No, Sergeant Olds." I realized my mistake the second it left my lips.

Olds shrieked, "*What* did you call me? You think we're drinking buddies? You want to date my sister?"

"No, Sergeant Instructor Sergeant Olds," I yelled as loudly as I could.

"Candidate, I think you're a soft one." Olds dropped his voice to a low snarl and put his face inches from mine. "And I run the soft ones out before they can get Marines killed. You just remember that."

Olds rattled me. I slunk back into the platoon, where my buddies whispered encouragement, saying everyone got his day in the sun. But I was nervous. I wanted to be there, and I tried hard. For the first time in my life, desire and effort wouldn't be enough. I was learning that in the Marines, the only easy day was yesterday. Success the day before meant nothing, and tomorrow might never happen. I woke up each morning at Quantico wondering whether I'd still be there that night.

The candidate chow hall was in a low-slung building on the banks of the Potomac River, across a set of railroad tracks from our squad bay and the parade deck. We crossed the tracks on a footbridge, winding up and down the ramps twice for each meal, three times a day. Three hundred seventy-eight crossings during the course of the summer. OCS didn't allow candidates to wear wristwatches, and wall clocks were intentionally few. We measured time from meal to meal.

I shuffled through the food line holding my tray in front of me and parallel to the ground, elbows bent ninety degrees, thumbs and forefingers touching in small circles. Sergeant Olds demanded this posture because it mimicked the way we held our rifles at shoulder arms while marching. Those with the best muscle memory, he said, will graduate. Those without can join the Army. A gauntlet of screaming instructors lined the path from the chow line to the tables. After my ass-chewing on the parade deck, I was desperate to avoid being singled out. I ducked my head and plunged through, not wanting to waste my precious meal time at the position of attention listening to a spittle-laced lecture on the virtues of endurance or loyalty. The harassment, I suspected, wasn't random. The staff pulled candidates they thought needed punishment or a challenge. Apparently, I'd had my dose for the morning because I slipped among the tables untouched.

I sat at a Formica table with my back straight and my heels together at a perfect forty-five-degree angle. The genteel posture was a façade.

There were no manners here, no conversations with tablemates. I shoveled food into my mouth, dripping flecks of syrup and gravy down my camouflage blouse. My mission for the next three or four minutes was to consume enough calories for my body to recover from the log run and make it through the morning.

Classes filled most of each day between morning PT and evening drill practice on the parade deck. We marched to the classrooms, usually Quonset huts or converted aircraft hangars, and filed silently down the rows of tables. We couldn't sit until Olds gave the command. When the whole platoon stood at attention by its chairs, Olds would roar, "Ready. Seats!"

"Kill!" we shouted in response. It was an early step toward acclimating us to violence. We had one second to drop into our chairs, or else we'd stand and do it again. Each candidate carried a binder filled with loose-leaf paper and outlines of the classes. The instructors were mostly officers, captains and first lieutenants, and they stuck to the Marine Corps's formulaic teaching method. We memorized the names and dates of famous battles and the exploits of renowned Marines. We learned the fourteen leadership traits, the eight principles of camouflage, and the six battlefield disciplines.

The curriculum seemed ridiculous at first. My liberal arts education had valued discussion, debate, and nuanced interpretations of complex ideas. But in combat, we were told, there's rarely time for discussion and debate. Complex ideas must be made simple, or they'll remain ideas and never be put into action. The leadership traits were bearing, courage, decisiveness, dependability, endurance, enthusiasm, initiative, integrity, judgment, justice, knowledge, loyalty, tact, and unselfishness. We drilled them, and every other list, over and over again. I memorized them in the classroom, in line at the chow hall, and in my rack at night. The purpose, we were promised, was to make them instinctive. They would become innate to our decision-making process and infuse everything we did without even a conscious thought.

One of the captains stood at the front of the classroom and read a quote from T. E. Lawrence, leader of the Arab revolt against the Turks in World War I. "Nine-tenths of tactics are certain, and taught in books: but the irrational tenth is like the kingfisher flashing across the pool and that is the test of generals. It can only be ensured by instinct, sharpened by thought practicing the stroke so often that at the crisis it is as natural as a reflex." He said we would be taught one tenth at OCS and another five or six tenths at The Basic School (TBS). If we were lucky, we'd pick up an additional one or two tenths in our first platoons. The final tenth could be learned only in combat. That tenth, for us, seemed impossibly remote.

During the first three weeks, I slept in five different racks, since we continually shifted to fill the gaps left by dropped candidates. Their transgressions varied. Two fell out of three runs in a row. "Not physically qualified." Another couldn't grasp the concepts in our written work. "Academic failure." They were kicked out, taunted by the staff as they emptied their footlockers, and then ridiculed after they had gone. The fourth, though, was treated more solemnly.

Candidate Dunkin had been struggling since the first week when Olds had singled him out as an individual. The accusation proved true. I was learning that the staff valued enthusiasm and loyalty above all else. They wanted candidates with heart who could work as a team. A struggling candidate could redeem himself by trying harder, wringing performance from effort. Dunkin chose a different course.

Dietary supplements were strictly forbidden. We drank water, not Gatorade, and ate chow hall food, not laboratory-engineered performance bars. Every candidate was warned that being caught with a supplement of any kind would be an honor violation, meaning instant dismissal from the course.

As we toed the line one evening, ready for taps, the staff announced a footlocker inspection. Hidden in Dunkin's shoeshine kit was a bottle of ephedrine. He stood there, blubbering, as Staff Sergeant Carpenter calmly told him to pack his bag and go stand in the hallway. No screaming or theatrics, just a stern dismissal, a clear statement that he was not Marine officer material. The platoon stood at attention, watching in silence as he packed. No one said a word as he shouldered his seabag and walked between the rows of racks.

Dunkin had broken the cardinal rule — the bond of trust between leaders and led. The leadership traits were more than a list to memorize for a test. Dependability. Integrity. Judgment. That evening, I understood for the first time the relationship between the sergeant instructors and the officer candidates: learn to obey before you command. For ten weeks, the staff owned us. They could yell and scream, make us put on and take off our socks fifteen times each morning, and harass us from reveille to taps. But after commissioning, the authority would shift. The candidates would become lieutenants, then captains and colonels. They would be the commanders leading enlisted Marines in battle. The staff had a very real, vested interest in killing bad candidates before bad officers killed Marines.

# 3

H ALFWAY THROUGH OCS, I was in the spotlight. I couldn't march, failed to appreciate the importance of aligning the right edge of my belt buckle with the right edge of the top button of my trousers, and had a masochistic reaction to being screamed at: I stared into my assailant's eyes, prompting a whole new round of abuse. Olds had singled me out so many times that he stopped using my name. He'd say, "Well, well, well, look who it is," or "What a surprise." I was in danger of dismissal for "failure to adapt."

On a Friday afternoon, we lined up our folding campstools in the back of the squad bay and sat at attention, backs straight and hands on our knees, waiting for a speech by our platoon commander, Captain Fanning. I later learned that OCS platoon command is just a holding tank for young captains returning to Quantico for advanced training. It's a cushy job to decompress after a Fleet tour — easy hours, little supervision, and no real responsibility. OCS is run by sergeants, staff sergeants, and gunnery sergeants — the notorious "gunnies." But the truth was still hidden from me in the summer of 1998, and the captain was power personified. He walked down the aisle, and we jumped to our feet.

Captain Fanning was a soft-spoken helicopter pilot. I stared at the silver bars on his collar and the gold aviator wings pinned above his left breast. He held a single piece of paper and told us to sit down. Fanning looked at us with a mixture of empathy and disdain.

"Five weeks down. The mission of OCS is to train, evaluate, and screen. Mainly screen. We want to see who has Marine officer potential. It's a game. You have to play by the rules. Our rules, the Marine Corps's rules. Most of you are probably college athletes." Candidates nodded, grateful for the human connection. Fanning went on, "This is no different from football: learn the rules and play the game. Trust me, this isn't the real Corps. Just do what you have to do here, and then you can get on with your career and your life. Four more weeks till the Crucible starts."

The Crucible was our final exercise. We'd all heard rumors about three or four days of running through the woods with no food and no sleep. I was distracted thinking about it when Fanning looked down at his paper and changed the subject. "I want to talk with you today about leadership — five of the Marine Corps's leadership principles that helped me in the Fleet."

I uncapped my pen, thinking it futile to reduce such complex ideas to a list. But Fanning didn't only run through the five principles. He told us what they meant and how he, as an officer, had used them. "First," he counseled, "you must be technically and tactically proficient." There was no excuse for not knowing everything about the weapon, radio, aircraft, or whatever else it was you were trying to use. "Being a nice guy is great, but plenty of nice guys have gotten half their Marines killed because they didn't know their jobs.

"Second, make sound and timely decisions." According to Captain Fanning, one of the gravest errors was waiting to have all the information before making a decision. In the fog of combat, you'll never have all the information. A good plan violently executed now, he urged, was better than a great plan later. Be decisive, act, and be ready to adapt.

Fanning's third piece of advice was simple: "Set the example." As officers, all eyes would be on us. We would set the tone, and the unit would take its cues from our attitudes — good and bad. "Why do we care here about how your uniform looks?" Fanning asked us. "Because your Marines will care." Sloppiness begets sloppiness, and small inattentions would set us on the slippery slope to large ones. That, according to the Marine Corps, was the causal link between the alignment of my belt buckle and the survival of my future platoon.

"Fourth, know your men and look out for their welfare." Fanning smiled as he remembered Marines he'd served with. They will, he said, follow you through the gates of hell if they trust you truly care about them. "This is not about you." Fanning spoke the sentence slowly, emphasizing each word. He explained that the Corps existed for the enlisted infantryman. "Everyone else — you aspiring infantry *officers* included — is only support.

"Finally," Fanning exhorted us, "train your men as a team." A unit's good morale and esprit de corps depend on each man's feeling part of it. Marines need to know one another's jobs. "That includes you and your platoon sergeant," he added. A new lieutenant and his enlisted second-in-command had to share their responsibilities. Too often, Fanning said, platoon commanders focused on the mission while platoon sergeants focused on troop welfare. "Each of you has to do both." Fanning drove the point home with a question: "What's the difference between you and your platoon sergeant?" He paused and then answered it himself. "One bullet."

Captain Fanning wasn't General George S. Patton in front of an American flag. He didn't rant and rave and wave a pistol in the air. Because of that, his words resonated with me. He gave us a glimpse beyond the fantasy world of OCS. We began to see the connection between practicing and playing, between fake pressure and real pressure. Captain Fanning had explained the purpose of the game.

From that afternoon on, I accepted the rules and lived by them. When getting dressed by the numbers, I tried to move faster and yell louder than anyone else. When Olds made me call cadence, I did it with heart and never backed down. He stopped caring that my calls confused the platoon. Marching didn't matter. It was about cool under pressure. It was about detachment. We had to retain our ability to think when the world was crumbling around us. Not for ourselves, but for our Marines.

Starting the next afternoon, we got twenty-four hours off. My dad picked me up at Quantico's gate and took me to Annapolis for the day. I tried to describe OCS, but the stress and the chaos were laughable, a million miles away. It embarrassed me to seem too affected by them. After all, this was training, really nothing more than a summer job. But it *was* more. The bullets were blanks, and the screaming was an act, but the test was real. By the Marine Corps's own admission, I was being screened to see if I had what it takes to be a combat leader. It was a rite of passage, my generation's chariot race or duel. I wanted to pass that test more than I had ever wanted anything in my life.

Growing up, I'd tested myself on the athletic field. A bad football play or a lost lacrosse game could be shaken off — commiserate with teammates and look forward to next week. In college, I was never truly challenged. I worked hard to do well but never doubted the outcome. I knew from the first day of freshman year that I would graduate. At OCS, my commission was mine to lose. And I could lose it at any moment.

The future disappeared, and my selfish motives went with it. I existed only in the present. The one thing keeping me going was being part of a group, knowing each mistake made my comrades a little weaker. Group punishment, shunned in most of American society, was a staple at OCS. Platoons fight as groups. They live or die as groups. So we were disciplined as a group. The epiphany struck one morning the next week as I locked my body in the leaning rest — the "up" pushup position. Sergeant Olds put the whole platoon in that posture while he berated a candidate at the far end of the squad bay for having scuffs on his boots. The message wasn't in Olds's words; it was in recognizing that this wasn't about how much we could take, but about how much we could give.

As we moved into the last month of the summer, the days seemed to accelerate. Riding the bus through Quantico's gates felt like a long time ago. I thought of my early mistakes and laughed. At least they'd kept me around long enough to learn from them. The Crucible was only a week away. We would put together all the classes and PT in one final test. There were rumors of a ceremony after the Crucible. We would receive an Eagle, Globe, and Anchor, the traditional symbol of the Marine Corps: a token of our survival.

During the final week, each day ended as it began, with our platoon toeing the line along the length of the squad bay. We stood at attention in brown T-shirts, green shorts, and shower shoes. The sergeant instructors strutted past, berating us mostly, but then including a few nuggets of praise.

"You candidates are the worst we've seen yet. The slowest. The dumbest. The most selfish." Olds pointed at a different candidate with each pejorative tag. I exhaled when he moved on without pointing at me. "We may still send most of you back to college. Back to playing tennis and mixing martinis and thinking you're better than the men who defend your freedom." He wasn't bluffing. We had lost another platoonmate earlier that week — this time to a stress fracture. "But a few of you have heart. And we'll make those candidates into Marines. They'll go out and kill communists for Suzy Rottencrotch." Suzy was a Marine

Corps metaphor for every cheating wife and girlfriend we'd left behind. Nothing in our lives was sacred to Olds except our ability to lead Marines. He finished with one of his most often repeated pieces of advice: "A little heart will get you a long way in the Marine Corps."

We took it as praise.

At the end of each night's monologue, we hydrated. "Hydrate" is another entry in the Marine lexicon. Marines don't drink; they hydrate. Many of our platoon's casualties spent their last hour as Marine officer candidates sprawled in a tub of ice, getting jabbed with a rectal thermometer called "the silver bullet." Heat stroke in July in Virginia does not discriminate between tall and short, black and white, or good candidate and bad candidate. It knows only hydrated and dehydrated. So there was no resistance to the nightly command to hydrate. We tilted our heads back and poured a whole canteen of water down our throats, holding the empty canteen upside down over our heads to prove it was empty. Some candidates had a hard time keeping so much liquid down, heaving streams of regurgitated water across the aisle to pool around the feet of the men on the other side, who kept their eyes stoically to the front to avoid the wrath of the stalking instructors.

Olds pointed to the puddles, deeply offended. "This is my house. That water better be cleaned up by reveille. And none of you maggots better get out of your racks tonight either. The Marine Corps Order says sleep, so sleep."

At the command "mount the racks," we clambered into our bunks. But even then the day wasn't over. We lay at the position of attention, arms at our sides with fists clenched and thumbs on our imaginary trouser seams, heels together with feet at a forty five-degree angle, eyes on the ceiling.

Olds stood in the center of the squad bay with his hands on his hips.

"*Reeeaaaaddddy!*" The word came not from his mouth, or even from his lungs, but from someplace deep inside known only to drill instructors and Italian tenors.

"*Sing!*"

"From the halls of Montezuma, to the shores of Tripoli." Forty-five voices in the first week, then forty-one, then thirty-eight as the summer progressed, bellowed "The Marines' Hymn." Not "The Marine Corps Hymn" but "The Marines' Hymn," the song that belonged to the Marines.

"First to fight for right and freedom, and to keep our honor clean."

All the pride, all the striving, all the heart was there in those lyrics being shouted at the ceiling.

"If the Army and the Navy ever look on Heaven's scenes, they will find the streets are guarded by United States Marines."

That moment at the end of the hymn, when silence roared in our ears and I could hear my fellow candidates catching their breath, was my favorite time of the whole day.

"The more we sweat in peace, the less we bleed in war. Good night, candidates." Sergeant Olds always said "we," never "you." He flipped out the lights, leaving us at attention in the darkness with the airfield's rotating beacon flashing across the walls.

I woke up early on August 7. Normally, I was so exhausted I slept until the lights came on. But I was excited. The Crucible would start that night. Only one week left before graduation. We sweated through our morning workout and marched to chow. The platoon functioned as a single organism now, humming along under its own power. We strutted across the parade deck, calling our own cadence. As we crossed the bridge, I saw Staff Sergeant Carpenter watching us from the concrete pad outside the chow hall. He looked stern.

Holding up a hand to interrupt our march, he motioned us toward him.

"Candidates, bring it in and listen up." I expected to be berated for some imaginary transgression, such as leaving dirt on the squad bay floor.

"Terrorists have attacked the American embassies in Kenya and Tanzania. Blew 'em up. Marines guard those embassies. Some of my brothers — your future brothers — are probably dead. Oughta get your blood up. Y'all are about to be in a growth industry. Go eat chow."

We lived in an information vacuum — no weather forecasts, no baseball scores, certainly no analysis of the destruction of two American embassies.

Candidates whispered urgent conversations in the chow line.

"What does this mean?"

"War."

"Bullshit. It don't mean anything. Not for us at least. The guys in the Fleet might get some play, but not us."

"Maybe eventually."

"No way. This ain't World War Three. Just a couple of bombings.

We'll lob some missiles at 'em, and that'll be that. Damn. They burned the pancakes again."

The Crucible started at ten o'clock. After a full day, Sergeant Olds had us sing the hymn as usual. But instead of turning out the lights afterward, we shouldered our packs and left the squad bay for a ten-mile hike through the dark woods. Olds didn't scream much anymore. He just told us what to do, and we did it. We started off down a gravel road in two columns. I walked next to Dave. He smiled and whistled, relentlessly upbeat. I half expected him to start skipping. When we turned off the road, the platoon stretched out in single file along a narrow dirt path. We paralleled the swamp I'd seen from the bus and passed the airfield where the president's helicopter, Marine One, was based. Quantico didn't feel like a prison anymore.

In the dawn light, Sergeant Olds said it was time for the Quigley. I had heard about the Quigley. We had all heard about it. Most of OCS was successfully kept under wraps, so each day brought unwelcome surprises, but this muddy trench had become an icon of Quantico's training, the sort of thing generals recalled in speeches.

We jogged down a trail through the woods. After a night of hiking without sleep, we stumbled along at half speed. The temperature was already ninety degrees, and sweat soaked my uniform. Canteens thudded against my hips with each step and the pack straps cut into my shoulders. Candidates strung out along the trail, urging one another on. I panted into a clearing and saw the trail disappear into a bog. A wooden pier extended across it, clearly not intended for me. My path lay in the mud beneath strands of barbed wire next to the pier.

I dove under the first strand into the stinking beige water, eager to impress the instructors with my gung ho. It was deeper than I expected, and I sank beneath the water. I recovered and began to crawl, scratching my way forward beneath the banks of mud.

Another candidate struggled along in front of me, and I made it my goal to close the gap between my hands and his boots. Suddenly, he stood straight up, shouting and waving. Something long and black hung from his upper arm: a snake.

*Christ,* I thought, *there are snakes in here.* I started to stand.

A boot heel between my shoulder blades drove me, face-first, back beneath the water.

"What do you think you're doin', boy? Crawl."

"Aye-aye, Sergeant Instructor." It came out garbled because mud stuck to the roof of my mouth like peanut butter. I continued pulling myself forward, past the candidate with the snake on his arm. The instructor who had kicked me was waiting as I climbed out of the Quigley.

"You can't compromise a mission and get men killed for a harmless little snake. Not even for a poisonous big snake. Discipline always. Now get out of my sight."

His message was clear: you need discipline most when it's hardest to muster — when you're tired, hungry, outside your comfort zone. I struggled for the next two days to stay alert, stay disciplined, and keep my focus on the candidates around me. We worked in squads of twelve, rotating as squad leader and attacking through acres of humid woods. Our tactics were unsophisticated: walk as quietly as possible to the objective and then charge it, wildly firing blanks from our M-16s. The mission of OCS was more to gauge spirit than to teach us skills.

It rained through both nights, and we slept in Korean War–era pup tents seemingly designed to collect water and channel it onto us. The rain and the gnawing hunger (we received only one meal per day) conspired to keep us awake. By the third afternoon, the dirt-encrusted faces of the candidates around me reflected the countless attacks and long runs with all our gear that we had endured. Just a few hours before the Crucible's end, I was digging a hole to stay awake.

"What the hell are you doing, Candidate?" Olds's voice suggested that whatever I was doing was not what I ought to be doing.

"Digging a foxhole, Sergeant Instructor Sergeant Olds."

"Digging a *what*?"

"A foxhole." I paused, trying to stand at parade rest while holding a shovel and pushing my helmet up so I could see him more clearly.

"Foxes dig holes to hide in. Marines dig fighting holes to kill the enemy from. Are you planning to hide in your hole or to use it as a weapon to kill the enemy?"

In the Marines, anything can be a weapon; it's a whole new way of thinking. My plastic MRE (Meal, Ready-to-Eat) spoon was a weapon if I used it as an insulator on a radio antenna so that I could talk to jets and call in air strikes.

"Weapon, Sergeant Instructor."

"Right. Now who's providing security for you while you dig this weapon?"

I looked into the brush, searching for the other three candidates in my fire team. They were snoring.

"Candidate, Marines do everything in pairs. We fight in pairs. We patrol in pairs. We dig in pairs. Go to Thailand on deployment, and you'll see that we even fuck in pairs. A Marine alone is easy to kill. A Marine with a buddy is hard as hell to kill. Don't let me catch you alone again."

Train your men as a team. I cursed myself for letting fatigue get to me.

Later in the morning, we packed our gear and hiked down to the parade deck. Hulking gray CH-53 Super Stallions, bigger than school buses, waited to ferry us over to TBS. It was my first helicopter ride. We sat on nylon benches along the sides of the cargo bay, and I looked past the tail ramp as the parade deck and our barracks fell away beneath us. Crossing I-95, I looked down at the cars filled with commuters. Clean people, well-fed, rested, in control of their days. I realized I wouldn't trade places with any of them.

Candidates were grouped in fours as we gathered at the edge of the TBS landing zone. A second lieutenant met each group. These men had been on the Crucible not long before and knew to take us straight to the chow hall. We filled our plates with macaroni and pizza and ate slowly. No sergeant instructors lined the paths to our seats. No one threatened us for looking around the room or failing to keep our boot heels together. It felt rebellious. We went back for seconds.

Outside the chow hall, the platoon assembled in a formation. We were filthy but stood straight. Our rows and columns were perfectly aligned. Sergeant Olds made his way down each row, stopping before every candidate to shake his right hand and press a cold piece of metal into his left. I hoped Olds would say something encouraging to me, maybe note my improvement or say he had enjoyed having me in the class. Instead, he locked me with unblinking eyes and said, "You ain't done yet."

But we were done. I held the coveted Eagle, Globe, and Anchor. I snuck a look when Olds moved on to the next candidate in the formation. One inch across and anodized in black, it was a pin, eventually for wearing on a dress uniform. It was the symbol of the Marine Corps, immortalized on bumper stickers and baseball caps across America. With it in hand, I could go back to college for my senior year. When I returned to Quantico, it would be as a second lieutenant.

# 4

O N JUNE 12, 1999, in Dartmouth's Baker Library, I raised my right hand to take the oath of office as a Marine Corps second lieutenant. "I do solemnly swear that I will support and defend the Constitution of the United States against all enemies, foreign and domestic."

My mother pinned the gold bars on my epaulets, and my father presented me with the Mameluke sword. I knew from my summer at Quantico that the sword was a reminder of Lieutenant Presley O'Bannon's expedition against the Barbary pirates in 1805. But I had no idea what it meant to be a Marine. Wearing my dress blues for the first time, I felt like an impostor in a Halloween costume.

After OCS graduation, I could have walked away from the Marines with no obligation. The Marine Corps liked the program because it attracted people who might not sign up for four years otherwise. Candidates liked it because we could return to school for a year and debate whether we wanted to go back to the Marines for a longer stay. For me, it was no decision at all. OCS had planted the hook. I hadn't suffered through ten weeks at Quantico for nothing.

My classmates would soon be marching off to their graduate schools and consulting jobs, but our paths had not yet diverged. We still lived in the same world. Walking together out into the sunlight on the Hanover green, I felt the first twinge of impending separation. I had already noticed a subtle change in my worldview. My tolerance for abstract theories and academic posturing had evaporated. Instead of classes in philosophy and classical languages, I gravitated toward national security and current events. When the Marines went into Kosovo, Macedonia, and Liberia, I followed their progress every day. The world's problems felt closer and more personal.

I had orders to check into TBS on a Sunday in November 1999. On the way down to Quantico from my parents' house in Baltimore, I detoured off the highway in Rosslyn, Virginia. It was a spontaneous decision. High on a hill above the Potomac stood the Marine Corps War Memorial. My last visit had been as a child, and I wanted to see it again.

The night was starry and cold, and Washington's monuments glowed across the river. Floodlights bathed the statue. An American flag flapped above five faceless Marines and a Navy corpsman, modeled on Joe Rosenthal's Pulitzer Prize–winning photograph of the flag-raising on Iwo Jima in 1945. The anonymity of the statue appealed to me. Six men. No names, ranks, or distinguishing features. They were Marines.

As I circled the memorial, I read the roll of battles burnished in gold on the granite base. Revolutionary War, when a newspaper ad had sought "a few good men" for the new Marine Corps. Spanish War, when correspondent Richard Harding Davis had reported, "The Marines have landed and have the situation well in hand." Belleau Wood, where, in 1918, First Sergeant Dan Daly had led his men over the top, yelling, "Come on, you sons of bitches. Do you want to live forever?" Iwo Jima, where nearly 6,000 Marines had died and 17,000 had been wounded capturing an island one-eighth the size of Washington, D.C. Admiral Chester Nimitz had had the last word on that campaign: "Uncommon valor was a common virtue." Korea's Chosin Reservoir, where the First Marine Division had fought its way out of a Chinese trap in weather so cold that gasoline froze. Lebanon, where an early shot in the terror war had been fired on October 23, 1983. A truck bomb had ripped through the Marine barracks, killing 241 Americans.

The carved band of campaign names stirred me. But it wasn't the past that gave me pause. It wasn't the names already engraved. It was all the blank space next to them for battles still unfought. I looked at the expanse of smooth black stone flecked with gold and tried to imagine the names to come. On that quiet night in 1999, it seemed inconceivable that I might be part of them.

The TBS campus, called Camp Barrett, looks more like a dilapidated community college than the cradle of the Marine officer corps. On that first Monday morning, I watched lieutenants hurrying back and forth between classes. They carried brief bags and plastic coffee mugs, like graduate students. Camp Barrett's dozen anonymous buildings include two barracks, several classrooms, a pool, a theater, and an armory, all surrounded by flat expanses of grass that double as playing fields when not being used as helicopter landing zones.

The compound's only distinctive feature is Iron Mike, a bronze statue of a Marine holding a rifle in his right hand and waving on unseen men with his left. The name is a misnomer because the figure is actually Lieutenant Colonel William Leftwich. In 1970, Colonel Leftwich had commanded the First Reconnaissance Battalion in Vietnam. We new lieutenants knew nothing of First Recon, except that it boasted the best unit insignia in the whole Marine Corps: a skull and crossbones superimposed on the blue diamond of the First Marine Division, surrounded by the words "Swift, Silent, Deadly."

Colonel Leftwich had ridden along on every emergency extraction of his reconnaissance teams. These were the most dangerous missions of all — teams calling for emergency extract had usually been compromised and suffered casualties and were being chased by larger enemy forces. After rescuing a team called "Rush Act" on a stormy day, the helicopter carrying Leftwich and his Marines had flown into a mountainside, killing everyone aboard.

It was next to Iron Mike that our class assembled that morning. I stood by the statue, conscious again that I was being intentionally steeped in the history of the Corps and its heroes. Around me stretched the six platoons of Alpha Company, 224 newly commissioned second lieutenants. A lanky guy with a wry smile stood next to me, and I turned to introduce myself.

He took my hand, saying, "Jim Beal. Tennessee."

I couldn't know that morning how much Jim and I would share in the coming two years. I knew only that his laid-back confidence was reassuring, another indicator that TBS would be different from Officer Candidates School. Jim's barracks room was next to mine. Platoons of forty lieutenants were divided into squads of thirteen or fourteen, and the squads were further divided into fire teams of four or five. Jim and I were half our fire team. We would spend the next six months at Camp Barrett, learning all the basic skills we would need as Marine officers. The Corps's mantra is "Every Marine a rifleman." Its corollary is "Every Marine officer a rifle platoon commander." In the Marine Corps, jet pilots, clerks, and truck drivers are all infantrymen first. TBS would teach us those basic infantry skills, plus all the rules, regulations, and administrative requirements that are part of a peacetime military. The greatest topic of conversation at TBS was MOS selection. Military occupational specialties are the specific jobs in the Corps — aviator, artillery, logistics, tanks, infantry, and others — and they're competitive. We would be assigned to the various specialties according to class rank. The most coveted of them was infantry.

President Harry Truman once said that the Marines had a propaganda machine second only to Stalin's. He was right. My impression of the Corps, even as a newly commissioned officer, was one of a lean, mean fighting force, all teeth and no tail. I was shocked when my platoon commander, Captain McHugh, told his assembled lieutenants that only 10 percent of us would be infantry officers. The rest would go to the other combat arms — artillery, amphibious assault vehicles, and tanks — or to support jobs such as supply, administration, and even financial management.

McHugh urged us to keep an open mind and learn about each job before deciding which to compete for. I nodded but knew that only one thing would satisfy me: infantry officer. I wanted the purity of a man with a weapon traveling great distances on foot, navigating, stalking, calculating, using personal skill. I couldn't let a jet or a tank get in the way, and I certainly wasn't going to sit behind a desk. I wanted to be tested, to see if I had what it takes. The Marine Corps had recently unveiled a recruiting campaign using the motto "Nobody likes to fight, but somebody has to know how." It was dropped because Marines *did* like to fight and aspiring Marine officers wanted to fight.

The grunt life was untainted. I sensed a continuity with other infantrymen stretching back to Thermopylae. Weapons and tactics may have changed, but they were only accouterments. The men stayed the same. In a time of satellites and missile strikes, the part of me that felt I'd been born too late was drawn to the infantry, where courage still counts. Being a Marine was not about money for graduate school or learning a skill; it was a rite of passage in a society becoming so soft and homogenized that the very concept was often sneered at.

During our first week at TBS, Captain McHugh asked us to prepare a list of our MOS choices from first to twenty-fourth. He said he would use the lists while evaluating us over the coming months and would do his best, while remembering the paramount "needs of the service," to assign us to one of our top three choices. I turned in a paper listing my top three choices as infantry, infantry, and infantry.

"Lieutenant Fick." The captain had scanned through the sheets and called me to the front of the room. He sounded pained. "Don't be a smart-ass. Put down three choices."

"All I want is to be an infantry officer, sir."

"We don't always get what we want, Lieutenant. Half the men in this class want to be grunts. The Marine Corps will put you where the Marine Corps needs you. The only way to have your pick of jobs is to graduate first in your class. Do you think you can graduate at the top of this class?"

Remembering my struggle just to graduate at all from OCS, let alone at the top, I chose amphibious assault vehicles and tanks as my second and third choices.

I loved TBS as much as I had hated OCS. Jim joked that the acronym stood for "The Bleeding Sphincter," but the pace was high, the material was clearly relevant, and we were finally being trained instead of screened. We spent our first month on the rifle range, learning to shoot the M-16 and the Beretta 9 mm pistol. Some of my classmates had been hunters since they'd learned to walk, but I had fired a gun only two or three times in my life. The Marine Corps is a gun club, the infantry most of all, and I realized I was starting with a deficit. I had three weeks to pay attention and learn how to shoot. On the last morning, Qualification Day, we would shoot for score, and the score would determine what shooting badge we wore on our uniforms. Those who barely qualified would be Marksmen, above them were Sharpshooters, and the best riflemen would be Experts.

"It's like condoms," Jim explained. "Large, extra-large, and extra-extra-large."

I laughed, but in my mind no self-respecting infantry officer could stand in front of his first platoon with anything less than an Expert shooting badge.

The Marines' known-distance shooting course features slow and rapid shots at human-size targets from two hundred, three hundred, and five hundred yards. Slow shots work out to about one round per minute from the sitting, kneeling, and standing positions. Rapid shots emphasize firing, re-aiming, and firing again — ten rounds in a minute. We aimed through "iron sights," not scopes, and learned that good shooting is a matter of discipline. There is no Zen involved, and hardly any luck. Do what you are told, and you will hit the target.

The Corps teaches three fundamentals of marksmanship: sight picture, bone support, and natural point of aim. Sight picture is lining up the rifle's front and rear sights with the target — a simple enough proposition. Bone support means resting the rifle on the steadiest surface available: bone. Muscles and tendons waver and shake, but bone resting on earth is like a tripod for a camera. The third element, natural point of aim, is the most important. With each of the shooter's breaths, the rifle muzzle rises. It settles with exhalation back to a natural resting point between breaths — the natural point of aim. Make the bull's-eye your natural point of aim, squeeze the trigger near the bottom of your breath, and you'll hit the target.

For two weeks, we ran through the fundamentals, arriving at the range in the predawn darkness and staying until midafternoon. I learned that consistency is key, and I was maniacal about it: same (light) breakfast each morning, same layers of clothing, same method of cleaning my rifle at the end of each day. The weather was gorgeous, cool mornings giving way to warm sun with almost no wind. It was perfect shooting weather.

We began firing for score in the third week, but only Thursday would count. There were 300 possible points on the course, and I needed 220 to qualify as an Expert. On Monday, I shot 180. Tuesday, 210. Wednesday, 220. Hovering at the cusp, I went to bed Wednesday night thinking about consistency. I had to replicate everything perfectly. The only element out of my control was the weather.

I woke at 0400 on Thursday and pulled open the blinds on my only window. Rain streaked the glass, and naked trees danced in the wind. A cold December morning. Damn. We drew our weapons from the armory and formed up in the parking lot outside Graves Hall for the three-mile hike to the range. Less than an hour after crawling out of my warm bed, I was chugging up the aptly named Cardiac Hill, a steep climb from a creek bed made more difficult by the mud, my heavy pack, and a line of vomiting lieutenants whose breakfasts had been heartier than mine.

It was still dark when we reached the range. I could barely make out the red wind flags through two hundred yards of blowing mist. They snapped parallel to the ground, the strongest wind I had ever shot in. I sat on my ammo can in the dark, shivering and waiting for enough light to start. I thought about the fundamentals as I rubbed a clear spot on the frosty ground at the two-hundred-yard line. Sight picture, bone support, natural point of aim. *Do what you've been taught, and you'll hit the target.*

Chills shook my body. I had a sweater and jacket in my pack but fought the urge to put them on. Consistency. I hadn't worn a jacket on the warm days earlier in the week. That extra millimeter of fabric on my arm now would have an outsize effect on the little black disk five football fields away. I willed myself warm.

"With a magazine of ten rounds, load!" The range master's voice echoed through the fog from his perch in the tower above and behind us.

"Make ready!" I racked my charging handle to the rear and chambered a round.

"Shooters, you may fire when your targets appear."

I settled my breathing, letting the muzzle rise and fall naturally. I centered the rifle's front sight post in the aperture of the rear sight and put it on the black target. I pulled my elbows in tight to my body, squirming in the mud to make one connection between rifle, bone, and dirt. Breathing naturally, I made little adjustments until every exhalation put the target in the center of my sights. Then I squeezed the trigger.

Wide to the right. I dialed in a click of windage to correct for the gusts and fired again.

Wide to the right.

Relax. Easy breaths. Back to the basics. Ignore the distractions. No cold, no rain, no wind. Do what they taught you. Line it up. Good support. Easy trigger pull.

Bull's-eye.

My next twenty shots were all in the black. Shooting was mechanical, rote. The key, as we'd heard so many times, was practicing the stroke and making it instinct. The only skill involved was learning the lessons of those who'd gone before. By the time I walked off the five-hundred-yard line, I had shot a 231.

Learning institutional lessons is the overarching theme of the classes at TBS. Our instructors were fond of pointing at the pile of tactics manuals on each of our desks and saying, "These books are written in the blood of lieutenants and captains who went before you. Learn from their mistakes; don't repeat them." The Marine Corps adheres to a crawl-walk-run philosophy, so we spent much of our time in the classroom before going out to the woods to practice what we'd learned. In the beginning, that learning was formulaic, just like OCS.

We learned the six troop-leading procedures by the acronym BAMCIS. Begin planning. Arrange for reconnaissance. Make reconnaissance. Complete the plan. Issue the order. Supervise. We used METT-T to estimate a tactical situation in order to complete the plan: mission, enemy, terrain, troops and fire support available, time. Most of all, we began to issue orders. Not yelled commands in mid-assault, but multipage written orders built around the five-paragraph format called SMEAC: situation, mission, execution, administration and logistics, command and signal. We wrote dozens of them.

Instruction at TBS goes far beyond rote memorization, growing into some amalgamation of chess, history, boxing, and game theory. We studied the fog and friction of war, how the simplest things become difficult. During our written test on the subject, the instructors cranked Metallica at full volume, hurled tennis balls at our heads, and sprayed our faces with water pistols. The lesson was focus: ignore the distractions and do your job.

We learned about warfare's dynamism. We wouldn't be fighting wax men in castles. In our instructors' words, "The enemy has a vote, too." When confronting an opposing will, we fight people who are also fighting us. They will learn as we learn. Their tactics will evolve as ours do. The key consideration in any tactical move is "to turn the map around." Look at your own situation from the enemy's perspective. What are your vulnerabilities? Where will he hit you, and what can you do to defeat him?

Speed, we were taught, is a weapon. Be aggressive. Keep the tempo high. The Marine Corps's hallmark is maneuver warfare, slipping around the enemy's hard surfaces and into his open gaps. Never attack into the teeth of the guns. We learned that indecision is a decision, that inaction has a cost all its own. Good commanders act and create opportunities. Great commanders ruthlessly exploit those opportunities and throw the enemy into disarray.

The focus on commanders recognized that war is a human enterprise. Even in the twenty-first century, wars are fought by people, not machines. Commanders must command from where they can influence the action. Marine officers, we were told, lead from the front. They thrive on chaos. We learned that the Corps relies on mission-type orders: "Tell me what to do, not how to do it." Decentralize command and allow subordinates to operate freely within the framework of the commander's intent. Train them as a team. Develop trust, loyalty, initiative.

This is the art of war. Some of the terms were new, but the principles had been recorded by Thucydides, Sun Tzu, and Clausewitz. We wanted to get out in the woods and apply them.

# 5

OUR EVALUATION AT TBS was in three columns: leadership, academics, and military skills. The last was the most significant, and first among those skills was tactical command. We spent much of the winter in the woods and fields surrounding Camp Barrett, practicing tactics as squads and platoons. We attacked and defended, ambushed, raided, patrolled, and did reconnaissance. Lieutenants rotated as leaders of the missions. Before every operation, the leader wrote and delivered a formal order. Sometimes the orders stretched into dozens of pages, accounting for every detail of navigation, communication, resupply, and actions upon running into the enemy.

We bitched and complained about the onerous process of writing orders. Would we have time for this in combat? Of course not, and that was the point. We wrote so many orders in SMEAC format that its components became ingrained. In December, when I was given a tactical problem and one minute to identify key considerations, I may have come up with five. By March, I saw thirty. In May, fifty. Our assessment process sped up, and with it our actions. We learned to use speed as a weapon, to create opportunities and exploit them.

But the learning process was painful, sometimes humiliating. One snowy afternoon, I was chosen to lead the squad in an attack against a defended hilltop. I got disoriented in the white ravines, lost track of our position on the map, and led my twelve Marines up the wrong hill. Sheepishly, I followed an exasperated captain to the correct hill, and we resumed the attack. A few weeks later, after resolving never to screw up my navigation again, I was chosen by Captain McHugh to lead the platoon in a daylight ambush patrol. I picked a trail where we guessed our enemy was operating and split the platoon in half to ambush any traffic from two directions instead of one. We hid in the snow for hours, watching the path. Near sunset, a four-man fire team walked slowly toward us. I sprang the ambush, and the woods erupted with the pops and roars of blanks fired from thirty-five rifles and machine guns. Just as I began to feel smug, Captain McHugh called me over. "Your geometry's all fucked-up. That half of the platoon," he pointed at the group across the trail, "would have killed this half if you guys had real bullets. I sat here for two hours waiting for you to notice."

One of TBS's most important training evolutions was a five-day field exercise called O&D Week, short for offense and defense. It took place just before MOS selection, so the staff used it as a final vetting of the lieutenants who wanted infantry slots. Captain McHugh turned up the heat on me. On our last full day in the field, he pulled me aside. We stood on a low hilltop and could see through the budding trees for a hundred yards in every direction.

"Lieutenant Fick, I have a mission for you." McHugh reminded me of the Civil War hero Joshua Chamberlain — a tall, austere New Englander. His smile hovered between mischievous and sadistic. "The Marine Corps fights at night. This evening, for the first time, your platoon will fight at night. I want you to be platoon commander for our first night attack."

Captain McHugh ran through the scenario, using METT-T. Intelligence assets reported an enemy platoon somewhere in the area. They were static, guarding a cache of supplies. My job was to locate and destroy the platoon before midnight. McHugh smiled and added, "The terrain will be Quantico-like." It had become a running joke that all our missions, in hypothetical countries around the globe, were conducted on Quantico-like terrain.

Bird-dogging me on the mission would be one of the staff instructors, Captain Gibson. Gibson was a tight-skinned little infantry officer. I had first noticed him in his dress blues in Camp Barrett's bar. He wore the only combat valor award I had ever seen in real life. One of the lieutenants asked him how he'd earned it.

"I did my job," he replied.

Now Gibson stood next to me, watching a helicopter drop into the landing zone behind us.

"That smell . . . that smell." Gibson closed his eyes as if remembering a particularly delicious meal. "The smell of jet exhaust pumping out the pipes of a helicopter waiting to take you and your Marines to kill the enemy. I love that smell."

I was unsure what to make of him, so I focused on the mission. A night attack. Thirty-five people. Unfamiliar terrain. I clicked through the checklist of tactical considerations we had learned in the classroom. First we had to locate that enemy position. Turn the map around. I unfolded the laminated sheet from my cargo pocket. Supplies meant supply lines — roads. There were only two road intersections in our zone, and we had patrolled within a hundred meters of one of them earlier in the day. It hadn't been occupied. I was willing to bet my shot at infantry on the enemy platoon being at the other intersection. Begin planning, arrange reconnaissance, make reconnaissance.

"Sir, I want to recon this road intersection." I pointed at the spot on the map. "And I want to leave now so I can get there before sunset."

I settled the platoon into a loose perimeter. They would guard the hilltop until we returned. I gathered three other Marines and we set off toward the intersection, with Captain Gibson shadowing a few meters behind. We were racing the sun. I wanted to reach the intersection in time to see the terrain in daylight and then return to brief the platoon before it was completely dark. Following trails, rivers, or other "natural lines of drift" is a lazy Marine's death wish, a tactical sin we had been taught never to commit. I led us straight down a creek bed, imagining Captain Gibson crossing out "infantry" in his notebook and replacing it with "supply." But the risk was calculated, not a gamble. We had to hurry, and this little valley would be a comfortable feature to steer the platoon in the dark. Fog. Friction. Keep it simple.

For the first time all week, I was grateful for Virginia's humidity. Moisture in the air muffled our whispered voices and dulled the clanks of rifles and gear vests on branches. Sodden leaves deformed compliantly underfoot, and we padded along as if on pile carpet. Draws cut into the hillside to our left. According to my map, the third one we passed would lead us up to the road intersection. I counted them, trying to match the lines on the map to the rolling terrain. When we reached the third notch in the hillside, I knelt down next to an oak tree and motioned the Marines around me.

"This is our turn. Take a good look and remember it for later. I'm taping an IR chem light to this tree so we have a guide in the dark."

I unwrapped an infrared chemical glow stick, visible only through night vision goggles, and cracked it. Using a roll of electrical tape looped around a carabiner on my web gear, I taped the chem light to the tree trunk at knee level, positioning it to be visible from down the valley we would approach from, but not from higher in the draw near the road intersection.

Slowly and silently, we began to move up the draw. Less than three hundred meters from the tree where I'd taped the chem light, I dropped to a knee again. The human eye notices movement and contrast. Up ahead, through the dense leaves, I saw a color lighter than anything around us. Too light. Man-made light.

We crept forward, inching along on our hands and knees and moving diagonally out of the draw to the high ground on the side where we could take a better look. The color was dirt — freshly turned, piled, reddish orange dirt. Fighting-hole dirt, dug by the enemy platoon. I eased down onto my stomach and debated whether to move closer. We had found them. Now, with a little more snooping, I could figure out how they were set up, maybe even locate the end of their lines so we could come back with the whole platoon and turn their flank. Rather than attack into their defenses, we could go around and hit them from behind. Maneuver. Captain McHugh would be impressed.

But I fought the urge. This reconnaissance mission had already been a success. We located the enemy and marked a route by which to return. Greed could cost me all my gains. We would probably be compromised if we tried to get closer in daylight. The smart thing to do was to back away and be thankful. I remembered the "80 percent solution" — a good plan now was better than a perfect plan later. We had crossed the threshold of action. This was enough information to do the job; now the task was to do it. We backed slowly down the side of the draw. The other Marines fell into formation around me, and we looped back up the river valley to the waiting platoon, careful not to retrace our steps.

In the fading light, I briefed my squad leaders. There wasn't time for a full operations order. I was thankful for all those months of repetition. Mission. Enemy. Terrain. Signal plan. Casualties. Navigation. Fire support. We huddled under a poncho to hide the red-lens flashlight. I ran through the plan. The other lieutenants nodded, confident that we had covered the most likely contingencies. We would step off one hour after sunset.

*     *     *

I guided the point man through the trees with silent glances and hand motions. A quarter-moon shone overhead, bright enough to see the outlines of Marines among the trees but not enough to cast shadows. I scanned ahead with my night vision goggles, hoping the infrared chem light was making good on its advertised eight-hour burn time. Every Marine is a cynic, and every cynic knows our equipment is made by the lowest bidder. I cursed myself for not taping two lights to the tree. For the cynic, two is one, and one is none.

Just when I began to worry that we had passed the turn, I saw the light ahead. I steered the platoon up into the draw and signaled for them to stop. Each Marine dropped obediently to a knee, turning the moving column into a stationary, cigar-shaped perimeter. I peered over the hill and saw the faint outlines of turned dirt. A dim red-lens flashlight bounced along in the hand of a person walking the lines of the enemy position. They were still there, and apparently they didn't know that we were again here.

I grabbed Jim Beal, who was in charge of our machine guns. "Take the guns to the top of this hill. Set up quietly. I'm taking the platoon around to the right." Jim nodded, and I whispered, "We'll initiate with a radio call, green star backup, and then you suppress all along the ridgeline as we sweep across from right to left. Consolidate on the objective. Got that?"

Jim flashed a thumbs-up. I planned to start the attack with an order on the radio. If that didn't work, I would fire a green flare into the sky as a signal to open fire. The machine guns would shift their fire across the enemy position in advance of our attacking Marines, hopefully mowing down resistance like a scythe.

As Jim crawled up the hill with his machine gunners in tow, the squad leaders took their Marines around its base to set up for our assault. We had to move quickly. This was the time of maximum danger — lots of people moving close to the enemy position. Conventional doctrine says that attackers should outnumber defenders by three to one. We were about one to one. To be compromised would rob us of our only advantage: surprise. The guys up near the road intersection were Marines, too, trained in the same school as we were. They would have security patrols out, and avoiding them in this darkness would be largely a matter of luck. I hoped ours would hold.

We reached our assault position without any shouting or gunfire disturbing the dark woods. I took a deep breath and a last look at my compass. It would be unforgivable to begin firing the machine guns and then charge off in the wrong direction.

"Machine guns, begin your suppression," I whispered into the radio.

Jim's only answer was the rat-a-tat-tatting of the guns. Even shooting blanks, the things sounded formidable. Ripping, guttural roars shattering the night.

"Let's go," I shouted. No more whispering now. Trying to strike my best Colonel Leftwich pose, I pointed my rifle at our targets and waved the platoon forward. Marines streamed up the hill, lit in the eerie, swaying light of overhead flares. Our positioning was perfect. We hit the enemy position squarely on its eastern flank. The goal of every attacker, and the fear of every defender, is enfilading fire — shooting along a position's length so that more bullets have a better chance of hitting a target. We fired straight down the enfilade of the trenches. Marines in their sleeping bags struggled to find weapons in the dark and were shot point-blank.

Not everything went our way, though. Through the smoke and noise, I saw Captain Gibson and Captain McHugh moving across the hillside like angels of death. "You're dead. You're dead." They pointed to my Marines and the defenders alike, pushing shoulders and backs to the ground, personifying the fate and caprice of the battlefield. "You, get down. You're dead."

To my left, the machine guns sparkled, shooting fake bullets but firing real tongues of flame from their muzzles. Standing in the center of the enemy position, with Captain Gibson at my side, I yelled to the Marines on the hillside, "Consolidate!"

Dark shapes appeared from fighting holes and clumps of trees, forming a loose circle around the crown of the hill. With a lot of luck and some good reconnaissance, we had accomplished one of the hardest infantry missions: locating and capturing a fortified position in the dark. I was elated.

"Lieutenant Fick, come with me." Captain McHugh led the way back down the hill toward the trench lines. "Good attack. Well organized, fast, and accurate. But I want you to take a look around." He reached into his cargo pocket and launched a white flare up through the trees. It hissed overhead, swinging in its parachute, casting moving shadows across the hill. Crumpled on the ground were the bodies of my fallen Marines. Eleven of them from a platoon of thirty-five.

"Even when you win, you lose. By the books, these are great numbers. You captured a fortified position, outnumbered, and lost less than a third of your people. But that's eleven letters to eleven mothers, eleven funerals, eleven names you'll never forget for the rest of your life. Nice job tonight, but you paid a price for it."

I looked around at the bodies as the flare flickered out.

Captain McHugh smiled. "Dead Marines, rise. You are healed. Go forth and conquer."

The lumps rose, dusted themselves off, and jogged up the hill.

McHugh motioned for me to follow them and put a hand on my shoulder. "This was an easy attack. No air to coordinate, no artillery, no other units to your flanks. We're gaming the game: your enemy was stationary, and you knew where he was. It'll be a lot harder at the Infantry Officer Course." I froze and looked back at McHugh. "It won't be official for another month," he said, "but I'm going to make you a grunt."

TBS graduation was a big deal for everyone except the grunts. Jim, the laconic Tennessean I had met six months earlier, moved to Oklahoma for artillery school, and our other classmates left for places like Pensacola or San Diego. We carried our few belongings to a row of rooms along an upstairs hallway in the barracks. The Infantry Officer Course (IOC) was just across the street. Its single brick building had an aura of mystery. The sign in front read DECERNO, COMMUNICO, EXSEQUOR — "Decide, Communicate, Execute." None of us called it IOC. It was "the Brick House" or "the Men's Club." IOC was, in our terms, all balls, men only. If the Marine Corps was a last bastion of manhood in American society, IOC was its inner sanctum. Just before graduation, the twenty-eight future infantry officers in Alpha Company were called over to IOC for a meeting.

We went as a group and pushed hesitantly through the glass doors. Awards from Marine units and foreign militaries covered the walls: Ka-Bar knives and colorful patches on plaques with mottoes such as "Death on Contact" and "Whatever It Takes." The building was cool, dark, and quiet. A sandy-haired captain bounded down the stairs and pushed us all into a classroom. His chest and shoulders threatened to burst through his camouflage uniform, and he grasped the sides of the podium with hands that could palm basketballs.

"Gents, I'm Captain Novack, your class adviser. I've got a task for you."

We all looked at one another, wondering what our first mission at IOC would be.

"The class ahead of you is going to the field this week." We had heard that our barracks rooms would be little more than storage lockers. Classes went to the field all week, every week. "I need you to mow the lawn and weed the beds while we're gone." Novack looked back over his shoulder as he turned to go. "And welcome to IOC. It's not what you think."

# 6

IOC'S MISSION WAS to train the best small-unit infantry leaders in the world. It was a tall order for ten weeks. If we crawled at OCS and walked at TBS, then IOC was a full-out sprint. Classes built on what we'd already learned, adding nuance and complexity. We studied the full spectrum of Marine operations — not only conventional combat but also the countless gradations of peacekeeping and nation-building that had occupied the military since the end of the Gulf War.

It was the summer of 2000, before the October 2000 attack on the USS *Cole* in Yemen and before 9/11. The U.S. military, from our perspective as fledgling officers, was equipped to fight the Soviets and training to fight another Somalia. But the Marine Corps was innovating. The whole institution was leaning forward, trying to feel out the next fight. The summer's buzz phrase was "low-intensity conflict." We learned that the interventions of the 1990s had taught the Marines a lesson: "low-intensity conflict" was not "combat light." The unspoken assumption among earlier groups of officers was that a platoon that trained to attack a fortified position knew how to hand out MREs. A platoon that ran a good ambush patrol could figure out how to build a school. The IOC staff acknowledged that this was mostly uncharted territory and promised only that we would do our best to prepare for it. Their candor made sense to us. We had grown tired of attacking wooded hilltops. The world, we knew, was more than Quantico-like terrain.

Low-intensity conflict put special demands on young officers and their Marines. We learned about the concept of the "three-block war." In this model, Marines could be passing out rice in one city block, patrolling to keep the peace in the next, and engaged in a full-scale firefight in the third. Mental flexibility was the key. A second concept we labored over was the "strategic corporal." Twenty-first-century warfare places massive destructive power in the hands of even the junior-most Marine and then beams his image in real time to living rooms around the world. A single Marine's actions could have strategic repercussions, good or bad. With no major conflict looming, we trained to do riot control and humanitarian missions and to work with the media.

Infusing all this was a strong dose of moral reflection on the nature of our job. I was learning that most Marines, behind the tough-talking façade, are idealists. Captain Novack, a TV-perfect infantry officer, told us earnestly that our responsibilities as leaders would be three: to be ready when called, to win every time, and to return our Marines to society better than they were when we got them. We learned that moral courage is as important as physical courage. Leaders have an ethical responsibility to serve as buffers, protecting their subordinates, and a moral obligation to act from the courage of their own convictions. The moral courage of their leaders is what separates combat units from armed mobs.

Captain Novack had pinned a quotation on the classroom wall from Steven Pressfield's *Gates of Fire*, about the Spartans at Thermopylae:

> This, I realized now watching Dienekes rally and tend to his men, was the role of the officer: to prevent those under his command, at all stages of battle — before, during, and after — from becoming "possessed." To fire their valor when it flagged and rein in their fury when it threatened to take them out of hand. That was Dienekes' job. That was why he wore the transverse-crested helmet of an officer.
>
> His was not, I could see now, the heroism of an Achilles. He was not a superman who waded invulnerably into the slaughter, single-handedly slaying his foe by myriads. He was just a man doing a job. A job whose primary attribute was self-restraint and self-composure, not for his own sake, but for those he led by his example. A job whose objective could be boiled down to the single understatement, as he did at the Hot Gates on the morning he died, of "performing the commonplace under uncommonplace conditions."

Novack sometimes interrupted class to point at the paper on the wall. "Gents, it's all there. We don't carry swords, but our job's the same." I wrote the quote in my notebook to take with me to the Fleet.

\*　　\*　　\*

Despite the heady classroom sessions, IOC is a war-fighting school. During most of our three months there, we left Camp Barrett on Monday morning and returned on Friday evening, spending our weeks shooting machine guns and mortars, calling in artillery and close air support, and training for urban combat in a mock city of cinderblock buildings called Combat Town. There I learned one of my training's crucial lessons on a hot July morning.

I was the acting platoon commander, tasked with assaulting a building in the center of town. A rebel warlord and his cadre were holed up inside, and the streets for blocks around teemed with bands of armed supporters. Given ten minutes to plan the mission, I briefed the staff that we would advance methodically from block to block toward the target building, covering the platoon's movement with mortar fire and support from armored vehicles. It was the kind of incremental approach that had worked so well for me during the night attack at TBS.

Novack threw his clipboard into the dirt, shouting, "Your mindset's all wrong! No good tactical plan grows from a timid mindset." He calmed down, and the earnestness returned. He wanted me to learn. "Execute every mission with speed, surprise, and violence of action."

He explained that Americans, especially young American men, exhibit posturing behavior. Two guys in a bar bump chests, get up in each other's faces, and yell. If a fight follows, it's about honor, saving face. That's posturing. Marines on the battlefield must exhibit predatory behavior. In that bar, a predator would smile politely at his opponent, wait for him to turn around, and then cave in the back of his skull with a barstool.

The new mission plan had us rappelling from helicopters onto the roof of the target building itself. No bluster, no incrementalism. Predators.

Near the end of IOC, our focus shifted to a Marine's most deadly weapon — his mind. Novack had taught us about the combat mindset, both the tactical need to be a predator and the moral imperative to know where to draw the line. Thus primed, we were deemed ready for a formal introduction to society's ultimate taboo.

I slid into the classroom early one morning with the other lieutenants, tracking wet boot prints across the floor. Rain drilled against the windows. We were loud and happy to be inside with Styrofoam cups of coffee and cheese danishes instead of getting soaked in Combat Town. A single word in block letters covered the chalkboard: KILLOLOGY.

Spending a morning talking about death and calling it work felt illicit. Around me, the class pretended to banter about baseball scores and weekend adventures, but our eyes kept flickering back to that solitary word on the chalkboard.

The door opened, and Captain Novack led an anonymous man to the podium. "Good morning, gents," Novack said. "You've heard me run my mouth about speed, surprise, and violence of action. Violence of action doesn't start with weapons and tactics. It starts in your head." Novack turned to the man by his side. "This is Dr. Clete DiGiovanni. Dr. DiGiovanni — we call him Dr. Death around here — is a psychiatrist. Before he started shrinking heads, he was an officer in the CIA's Directorate of Operations and the Special Operations Group in Vietnam. He speaks your language."

Novack started to turn the podium over to Dr. DiGiovanni but leaned back toward the microphone.

"One more thing. Lieutenant Fick, the doctor is a Dartmouth grad, too. You can trade squash tips after class."

"Good morning, Marines." Dr. DiGiovanni spoke with solemn control. "My nickname is unfortunate, because my job is to help keep you and your troops alive."

He defined "killology" as the study of healthy people's reactions to killing. Its corollaries are the factors that enable killing and the maintenance of psychiatric health during prolonged exposure to mortal danger. DiGiovanni explained that an infantryman's effectiveness is more fundamental than his ability to shoot a rifle or carry a heavy pack. All else is predicated on psychiatric health. He identified five things an infantry leader can do to help maintain the psychiatric effectiveness of his men in combat: minimize fatigue by sleeping whenever possible, build confidence as a team, encourage communication, use spare time to practice emergency medical training, and do after-action critiques to address the shock of combat and killing.

"And trust me, gentlemen, it *will* be a shock," he said.

A slide projector whirred to life, casting a square of blank light on the screen at the front of the room. DiGiovanni explained that the first step toward understanding the topic was exposure to violent death.

"The pictures you are about to see are very graphic. Young infantry officers, like yourselves, in Vietnam."

The photos were indeed of young men like us, but after suffering horrific trauma to their heads and torsos. I had to squint and tilt my head to separate the victims' eyes from mouths from cheekbones. High-velocity rifle bullets tear through bone and flesh, destroying all vestiges of animate humanity. I could not help but contextualize the pictures. Platoon commanders, recent graduates of this same school, who shipped off to take their first commands. They woke up one morning, pulled on their boots, ate breakfast, and never guessed that nightfall would find them as exhibit A in the killology curriculum of other lieutenants.

Like most Marine training, hands-on experience followed DiGiovanni's class. The closest battlefield to Quantico was the Anacostia neighborhood of southeastern Washington, D.C. On Friday night, two other lieutenants and I stood discreetly against the wall in D.C. General Hospital's emergency room, waiting for the casualties to pour in.

The doctors and nurses welcomed Marine observers on nights filled with drug and gang violence that sometimes spilled into the hospital itself. For us, the program was a chance to see gunshots and stabbings in a sterile place, without the additional stresses of combat, command, and dying friends.

A young surgical resident escorted us. We must have looked bored, hugging the wall and watching a steady stream of sore throats and twisted ankles.

"Don't worry, guys," she said. "It's a hot summer night. After ten or eleven o'clock, the ambulances will be backed up outside. You'll see plenty."

She was right. The first trauma patient of the evening was a teenage girl with a dozen knife wounds in her back. Her lungs had been punctured, and she blew little pink bubbles with each faint breath. Next came a guy our age whose legs had been broken by an attacker with a hammer. Bones sticking out of his skin reminded me more of a roast chicken than a human being. Sometime after midnight, we noticed the doctors scrambling to meet a gurney at the door. They hadn't done this before. We asked what was coming.

"Gunshot to the head."

The man on the stretcher looked as if he was made of wax. Powder burns surrounded the entry wound — a point-blank shot. It was small caliber, maybe a .22, and there was no exit wound. The bullet had just bounced around inside his skull, turning brain to mush. This was the first dead man I had ever seen, and it was, as Dr. Death had promised, a shock.

We left the following Monday on a major field exercise. I was sitting on my pack at the edge of the landing zone, waiting for a helicopter, when Captain Novack appeared, calling my name and three others. We scrambled over to him, and he led us into the trees, out of sight and hearing of the rest of the class.

"Gents, when you get back over there, tell the class I had to counsel you for failing the last written test."

I must have looked surprised.

"You didn't really. I have a secret task for each of you. Your squads will be operating independently out there this week. Starting tomorrow, each of you will become progressively more withdrawn. You'll be uninvolved, uninterested, and, eventually, uncooperative. The missions culminate on Thursday with a night attack. Confusing as hell. By then, you have to be in full revolt."

A lieutenant asked Novack why we would be doing this.

"Feigning psychiatric casualties. Giving your buddies a taste of the chaos of not being able to trust one of their own. They'll think you're an asshole, but we'll debrief it Friday afternoon with Dr. Death, and they'll understand you were playing a role." He glanced up at the approaching helicopters. "Here come the birds."

I sat near the door, enjoying the cool slipstream and dreading our plunge back into the steamy woods. Our acting squad leader, VJ George, gave the two-minute warning, and I clicked a magazine into my M-16.

I had first met VJ on the pull-up bars outside Graves Hall during TBS. He had been shirtless, cranking his arms like hydraulic pistons. A lieutenant next to me had turned and whispered, "That guy's the best athlete in Alpha Company." Big praise in the Corps. VJ was an unlikely Marine. His parents, Indian immigrants, wanted him to go to med school, and his brother was a Silicon Valley programmer. His main interests were classical music and libertarian economics. VJ had gone to the Naval Academy, where he competed as a powerlifter and developed a distaste for military customs such as short hair and addressing people by rank. After IOC, we were going to the same infantry battalion in California and planned to be roommates.

VJ led us off the landing zone and through our first two days of patrolling. I tried to distance myself slowly from the work of the squad — carrying less of our common load of radio batteries, ammunition, and water; participating only halfheartedly in digging our defensive positions when we stopped; and abstaining from conversations and decision making. On Wednesday, just before sunset, we halted on a hillside above a gravel road. It was a bad position, visible from the road and at the mercy of a commanding ridgeline above. A voice was screaming inside me to move higher on the hill, to get into a defensive position where we would be less visible and more able to control the ground around us.

"So, Nate, I'm planning to stop here for a few hours. What do you think?" VJ crouched next to me, eyes lost beneath the brim of a floppy bush hat.

I shrugged.

"Man, I'm asking your opinion."

He was testing me. The position sucked. He knew it. I knew it. He knew I knew it.

"Whatever. Your call."

VJ swore under his breath and moved back to the rest of the squad, leaving me sitting alone next to a fallen tree. I could hear them speaking together in low voices. About me. About what an asshole I was. Unreliable. Self-centered. Dead weight. VJ moved the squad to a better position, and I followed silently.

By dawn on the day of the final attack, the distance between me and the rest of the squad had become personal. I could tell they were questioning how they could have misjudged me, concerned that we had orders to the same battalion in the Fleet. The squad took a security halt, dropping quietly to the ground for fifteen minutes to make sure we weren't being followed, and I refused to go any farther. The other Marines stood to keep moving, but I stayed on my stomach.

"Yo, Nate." A scuffed boot kicked me gently in the hip.

I looked up but didn't respond.

"C'mon, man. We're moving."

I kept quiet. VJ walked back to me, half-stooped under his heavy pack.

"What the fuck, Nate? Are you sick?" I shook my head. "Then why are you being a bitch? I thought you were a fucking Marine, a fucking infantry officer."

I no longer cared about Captain Novack or the training. VJ plucked my strings, appealing to my duty and my pride. I couldn't let my friends down, couldn't be seen as the weak link, even knowing it would all be cleared up on Friday afternoon. My will collapsed.

"It's an act. Dr. Death set me up to be a psychiatric casualty. I was supposed to be withdrawn, give you guys a chance to deal with someone losing his shit. I can't take it anymore."

They looked as if they didn't believe me.

"Goddamn it. I'm telling the truth. Give me some of the extra batteries and water. We've got a long way to go still." I opened my pack to fill it with gear. "And VJ, that position yesterday fucking sucked."

VJ's smile glowed white from his dirty, black-painted face. "Good to have you back, man."

But I was less enthusiastic. The more I thought about it, the more unhappy I was with what I'd done. Captain Novack had given me an order. I understood it, acknowledged it, and disobeyed it. In doing so, I chose my short-term emotional comfort over the long-term benefit to my buddies of dealing with a psychiatric casualty in training. We never talked about it again and slid through the debrief with everyone implicitly knowing what not to say. But it gnawed at me. After a full year at Quantico, impulse could still overcome training.

We graduated from IOC on a Friday morning in September. My father came down to Quantico for the ceremonial breakfast, and I was proud to have him sitting there next to me. Camouflage poncho liners covered the tables. We ate steak and eggs, the traditional preinvasion breakfast. In slow succession, each of our twenty-eight men shook Captain Novack's hand, received his diploma conferring the coveted 0302 MOS — Infantry Officer — and faced the room to deliver a martial quote.

I chose the creed of the Spartan infantry: "When you return from battle, you will either bear your shield or be borne upon it."

VJ picked a line from former Navy secretary and Marine infantry officer James Webb: "I wouldn't cross the street to watch Jane Fonda slit her wrists."

After coffee, Captain Novack rose. He congratulated the class on completing one of the most challenging small-unit leadership courses in the world and passed on some last-minute advice. "Your Marines will expect four things from you: competence, courage, consistency, and compassion." Taking a notebook from his pocket, he flipped open its spiral-bound cover. "Historically, about four of you will one day be colonels, and point-five will be a general."

Novack paused, looking to the empty place setting at the head table. Every Marine dining hall keeps an empty place in honor of Marines missing in action. "One of you will die in the line of duty.

"No more blank ammunition, gentlemen," he continued. "From now on, when this country dials 911, it's calling you."

# 7

STARING AT MY REFLECTION in a car window, I straightened the shooting badges on my chest and wiped fingerprints from the gold bars on my shoulders. I'd worn this uniform only once before — at the tailor's shop. After IOC graduation, I drove across the country to Camp Pendleton, north of San Diego. VJ and I rented a house near the ocean and got ready to report to the First Battalion of the First Marine Regiment, known as 1/1. Being "the first of the first" sounded good to me, but I was anxious. This wasn't just another school. It was my first command in the Fleet. I hoped I knew enough to avoid embarrassing myself or getting someone hurt.

I walked across the gravel parking lot, dust settling in a thin layer across my spit-shined shoes. A sign over the door of the battalion headquarters proclaimed: FIRST BATTALION, FIRST MARINES — FIRST ON FOOT, RIGHT OF THE LINE. "First on foot, right of the line" was the position of honor in a military formation, so I guessed it was an accolade bestowed on the battalion for some past triumph. A list of those exploits hung next to the door, a series of red wooden slats painted with yellow names. I stopped on the steps to read them. Guadalcanal, Peleliu, Okinawa, Inchon, Chosin Reservoir, Da Nang, Dong Ha, Hue City, Quang Tri, Khe Sanh, Desert Shield, Desert Storm. Empty hooks, ready for the next addition, hung from the lowest slat and reminded me of the Marine Corps War Memorial's blank granite.

Marines in boots clomped back and forth down the halls. I tried to blend in, but a cherry lieutenant is obvious. Their eyes rolled from my shoes to my hair before settling back onto my face with a reserved "Good morning, sir." I found the battalion's admin office and dropped my stack of records on a desk just inside the door. "Good morning, Sergeant. I'm Lieutenant Fick — new guy checking in."

"We have you slated for Bravo Company, sir." He tore the orders from my record book and handed it back to me. "Captain Whitmer. Downstairs and to your left."

I took a deep breath and rapped three times on the cinderblock wall outside the door marked COMPANY COMMANDER.

"Come on in."

"Good morning, sir. Lieutenant Fick, reporting as ordered." I snapped to attention in front of the metal desk, with my eyes locked on the rear wall.

Captain Whitmer stood to shake my hand. He looked like the actor Ed Harris, chiseled and gray.

"Rich Whitmer. Welcome aboard. Grab a seat." He pointed to the small sofa in front of his desk. A helmet and flak jacket lay on the floor next to it, and I tried to absorb other details in the room without his noticing my wandering gaze: a Michigan State mug, a photo of a little boy, and engraved awards from an infantry platoon and a counter-narcotics unit in Thailand.

Captain Whitmer's defining feature was calm. He spoke slowly, choosing every word, asking about IOC, my family, my background. His office felt soundproof, and the bustle in the hallway receded. Answering his questions, I thought I sounded loud and inarticulate. But it wasn't an interrogation. Whitmer laughed easily and soon put me at ease.

Once we got down to business, he seemed to know exactly what was on my mind. Each of an infantry battalion's three rifle companies has a primary means of getting to and from its objectives: helicopters, amphibious assault vehicles called "amtracs," and rubber Zodiac boats. At IOC, we'd learned that most Marines go ashore by helo. Our consensus was that if we were stationed near the relatively warm Atlantic, boats would be impractical but fun. In the cold Pacific, boats would be miserable. Now Whitmer said, "Hope you don't mind freezing — Bravo Company is boats."

Next he told me that I would command Bravo's weapons platoon. Each infantry company has four platoons — three rifle and one weapons. Leading a rifle platoon, forty Marines with M-16s, is a new lieutenant's typical first job. But weapons platoon is different. Its forty-five Marines are divided into sections for machine guns, assault rockets, and mortars, the bulk of the company's firepower. Since employing the weapons platoon is complex, its commander is usually a senior first lieutenant who's already led a rifle platoon. Captain Whitmer asked if I was comfortable taking weapons on my first day in the Fleet.

"Yes, sir. Absolutely." In fact, absolutely not.

Whitmer nodded with a smile that said he understood my reservation but expected me to figure it out. "Go ahead and get settled. The company's in the field until this afternoon." Standing to shake my hand, Whitmer said, "I do things a bit differently, as you'll see."

Bravo Company's four platoons shared an office down the hall from Captain Whitmer's. Lockers filled with tactics manuals and gym clothes lined the walls, and Marine posters covered the empty spaces between lockers. The smell reminded me of my high school football coach's office — rancid sweat, stale coffee, and disinfectant. Eight desks were pushed together to make an island in the center, one each for the four platoon commanders and platoon sergeants. I carried my gear from the supply warehouse and piled it in an empty locker. Then I grabbed a manual about weapons platoon from a shelf near the door and sat down to read.

IOC primarily trained rifle platoon commanders. Weapons platoons, unlike their rifle counterparts, don't fight as units under a single commander. The machine gun and assault sections frequently beef up the rifle platoons to augment their firepower. The mortar section provides mortar fire for the whole company, usually controlled by the company commander and the rifle platoon commanders. With all his Marines working for other people, the weapons platoon commander serves as the company's fire support coordinator. This means controlling artillery, air strikes, and bombardment from naval ships — complicated missions I had never practiced; missions that would kill many people if I screwed them up. I had a lot to learn and little time to do it.

When Bravo Company hiked onto the parade deck that afternoon, I went outside to watch. I hoped to catch a glimpse of my platoon, but the Marines were indistinguishable in two long lines of dusty green. A lieutenant smeared with camouflage paint separated from the mass of troops and walked toward me. He stooped beneath body armor and a vest festooned with smoke grenades, flares, a knife, and canteens. His rucksack stuck out on both sides of his body, and a whip antenna swayed above his head.

"You must be the new weapons guy," he said as he lumbered right past me. Without stopping, he added, "I'm Patrick English, First Platoon commander. Come into the office. I have to drop this gear."

Inside, Patrick's ruck thudded onto the floor, and he shrugged out of his web gear. Sweat soaked the uniform beneath. "Sorry. Didn't mean to be rude." He stuck out his hand. "Welcome to Bravo Company." Patrick cracked open a Gatorade bottle and sat on one of the desks. He was a New Yorker, sharp-featured with close-cropped hair. Patrick had played lacrosse at Holy Cross and worked in the district attorney's office in Manhattan before starting OCS.

It seemed as if we should be talking about work, but I barely even knew the right questions. "So what's coming up on the calendar?" I asked, trying to sound nonchalant.

He replied that the company would spend the next four months on conventional infantry skills such as shooting and patrolling. Then in February, the battalion would be attached to the Fifteenth Marine Expeditionary Unit (Special Operations Capable) as its ground combat element. A MEU (SOC), I knew from TBS, is a seaborne task force of two thousand Marines built around an infantry battalion and a helicopter squadron. At any given time, one is deployed from the West Coast and one from the East Coast. We would hone our MEU skills for six months, mostly raids in the boats. Then in August 2001, the Fifteenth MEU would sail from San Diego to cruise the Indian Ocean and Persian Gulf for six months, training with foreign forces and acting as first responders in case of a crisis.

Every few minutes, Marines came into the office to update Patrick on the count of his platoon's weapons, the status of missing equipment, or the progress of paperwork for people's promotions and other training exercises. He bantered with me and gave them instructions without even pausing. I was surprised to learn he'd been at 1/1 for only two months.

He talked fast, describing the battalion and its key personalities, and starting with what I most wanted to hear: "Captain Whitmer's fucking solid — best CO in the battalion." He then assured me that "the LPA gets together for beer and tacos every Thursday night up near San Juan Capistrano." I knew about this venerable tradition: every unit has an

informal Lieutenants' Protective Association. "Some guys," Patrick confided, referring to the battalion's other platoon commanders, "have to
lean on each other since they have weak platoon sergeants. I don't have
that problem, and you won't either."

Every young lieutenant remembers meeting his platoon sergeant. The
relationship between a fresh officer and his salty second-in-command is
almost as mythic as boot camp. Patrick and I were still talking when
Staff Sergeant Keith Marine walked into the office. The first thing I noticed about him were his ears, sticking out from his regulation haircut
like fins on a fish. The second thing I noticed was his remarkable name.
I didn't comment on it, figuring he'd heard too much already on that
score.

Marine quickly dispelled any mythic overtones our first encounter
might have had: "Sir, you're sitting in my chair." He insisted we go out
for coffee — "it's a tradition for officers to buy" — to talk about tactics
and training plans for the platoon. We traded autobiographies on the
walk across the parade deck to the chow hall.

Staff Sergeant Marine had grown up in the coal country of West Virginia. Even without his name, Marine's background seemed to destine
him for the Corps. His grandfather had served as a Marine in the
bloody campaigns of Bougainville, Iwo Jima, and Okinawa. His grandfather's brother had been killed at Leyte Gulf, where my grandfather
had fought. Marine had already served ten years in the infantry. Before
that, he had been stalking deer with a rifle while I had been playing with
blocks. He had spent the last year working for the gunner, the battalion's weapons expert, and knew every detail of every infantry weapon
in most of the world's militaries.

"So," I asked, "how do you think the M-16 stacks up?" Most Marine
grunts carry M-16s. The Corps instills in a young Marine an intense, almost obsessive attachment to his rifle.

"I don't know what dickhead designed the M-16, but it shoots a var-
mint round. You don't want a fucking squirrel gun in your hands in a
firefight."

I paid for our coffee, and we slid into a booth near the window. Marine took a can of Copenhagen tobacco from his pocket and snapped it
between his thumb and forefinger. After cramming a wad inside his
lower lip, he offered the can to me. "Dip, sir?"

"No, thanks."

"I won't hold it against you." Marine sounded as if it was a major concession. "At least you're drinking coffee. Your illustrious predecessor didn't even do that. He was a shitbird." Marine paused, lost in thought, and shook his head. "The road to hell is paved with the bleached bones of second lieutenants who didn't listen to their staff NCOs. The one before him got shot in a porta-shitter out at the rifle range. So at least you got small boots to fill."

Sipping my coffee, I asked Marine to tell me about the platoon. I expected a continuation of his earlier sarcasm, but he turned serious. Instead of talking about the Marines' performance, he focused on their personalities, families, and interests.

"You gotta care about 'em for real, sir. If the Marines trust you, you can order 'em to yank Satan off his throne by the balls. Almost anybody can do this job. You want to make the Marines care enough to do it well."

I sat quietly, happy to listen as long as Marine cared to talk. He must have sensed it because he paused, sizing me up, and asked bluntly how I saw my role in the platoon. For a second, I was taken aback. I hadn't expected a quiz on my command technique, and I certainly wouldn't have asked the same question of Captain Whitmer earlier. But his directness impressed me. I thought for a moment and told Marine I didn't want to roll in like the new sheriff in town, changing the rules before I knew how things worked. I told him I tended to give people the benefit of the doubt and then nail them to the wall if they took advantage of me. Without using Captain Novack's words, I tried to promise him competence, courage, consistency, and compassion.

In return, I expected that Marine would back me up in front of the troops. We would disagree behind closed doors. He nodded. Marine was a new staff noncommissioned officer (NCO), but I sensed from the start that he was of the old school and knew that seasoning me was a primary, if unspoken, part of his job. As if to affirm this, Marine told me about Chris Hadsall, his platoon commander in 1/1's Charlie Company two years before. Hadsall had apparently become the yardstick by which he judged officers. "We'll get you up to speed like Lieutenant Hadsall in no time, sir," he assured me.

By the time we'd finished our third cup of coffee, Marine and I had staked out our respective roles in the platoon. My greatest fear had been clashing with a platoon sergeant I didn't like or couldn't trust. But I liked Marine, and I trusted him instinctively. Most platoon sergeants, I suspected, feared an overeager and domineering young lieutenant. I pledged to be neither. On our way to the door, Marine said the words I'd been waiting to hear since OCS: "Time for you to meet the platoon."

I thought I'd be nervous. The new lieutenant meeting his first command was supposed to be like first love or losing your virginity. Staff Sergeant Marine called the platoon from the armory, where they were cleaning weapons after the field exercise. I watched them walking in groups of two or three across the parade deck, hands blackened with carbon, wearing green T-shirts and camouflage trousers. This was my platoon. I would train them, deploy with them, and maybe even go to war with them. Their performance would directly reflect my leadership. I wasn't nervous at all.

The forty-five Marines fell into a formation of three ranks, one for each section. They were so young. Half of them looked under twenty. I was only twenty-three, but that small gap cast me in the role of coach or big brother. So the authority came naturally. Staff Sergeant Marine stood six paces from the center of the front rank. He took reports from each of the section leaders and about-faced toward me.

He saluted and called out, "Good afternoon, sir. Weapons platoon, all present."

I stood at attention in front of him and returned his salute. Marine stepped off smartly, leaving me alone in front of the men.

The last thing they needed was a Pattonesque monologue from a newborn lieutenant, so I introduced myself and said I was happy to be the newest member of the platoon. I told them I wanted to meet with each man individually over the coming week and asked if they had any questions for me. There were none. Staff Sergeant Marine dismissed them, and they headed back to the armory. I thought I heard approval in his voice as we walked back to the office. "No bullshit, sir. Marines appreciate that."

The next ten months were a graduate seminar in infantry tactics, our last chance to learn before doing it for real. Captain Whitmer was the professor, and his style was unlike anything I'd seen at Quantico. Many of my buddies in 1/1's other companies complained that their commanders kept a thumb on them. They shunned boldness for fear of making an attention-grabbing mistake. The prevailing culture of 1/1, at least among the officers and senior NCOs, was careerist: laugh at the colonel's jokes, don't get anyone hurt, and stay under the radar.

Not Captain Whitmer. The standard Marine Corps brief before live-fire training began with the words "Safety is paramount."

"If safety were paramount," Whitmer declared, "we'd stay in the barracks and play pickup basketball. Good training is paramount." Whitmer's idea of good training reminded me of something I'd read about the Roman legions — their exercises were bloodless battles so that their battles were bloody exercises.

He drove the point home one night on a windy ridge above the Pacific. The battalion's three rifle companies were moving independently toward a cinderblock town. Our mission was to link up near the town no later than 0100 and capture it for follow-on forces to use as a staging base. A reconnaissance team was observing the town, and the battalion's plan of attack kept changing as the team updated its reports on how the defenders were set up.

Bravo Company had come ashore from a Navy ship a couple of hours before. We stumbled along a ridgeline in thick mist, still a mile away from where the battalion planned to link up. Wind blew the fog in whorls and eddies across the trail and down into the darkness that fell away to either side. Behind me, machine gunners and mortarmen carried their heavy weapons as quietly as they could, stifling the grunts and groans and clanking metal. Every few minutes, Captain Whitmer passed the battalion's updates over the radio to his platoon commanders. I cursed in the dark, trying simultaneously to navigate, keep track of the changing plan, and inform my section leaders of the updates as we pressed closer to the linkup point. Staff Sergeant Marine must have walked twice as far as the rest of us, moving back and forth through the column to pass word and keep tabs on the Marines. The platoon rolled with the changes. No complaints. No hesitation. We arrived at 0045, exhausted and disoriented, but on time for the attack. The other companies reported over the radio that they were still an hour away.

Whitmer's lieutenants converged on him while we waited. He circled us close, soaked and shivering, and pointed out the night's lesson. "The other company commanders stopped moving each time a change came over the radio. They called their platoon commanders in and showed them the new plan on their map. Now look — they're fucking late." He paused, and I looked at Patrick, seeing the lesson crystallizing in his mind as it was in mine.

"You guys were probably cursing me for briefing changes on the fly." We nodded in confession. "But I did it because you have to learn to operate that way. Any one of you," he whispered with emphasis, pointing at each of us, "is one bullet away from commanding this company. You need to learn it here, not in Iran or Somalia or wherever."

I looked at my watch and saw that the other companies were still more than half an hour away. Captain Whitmer must have done the same, because he followed up with a question: "So what should we do now?" He wasn't looking for advice; he wanted to critique our decision making.

"We should attack, sir." I said it with a confidence I didn't feel. "We have a whole company here. Recon reports only about a dozen guys in the town. The battalion set its timeline for a reason."

Captain Whitmer replied that we, as infantry officers, had been trained to be aggressive. Nods all around. "But there's a fine line between aggressive and foolish." Good commanders, he explained, could operate right at that line, without crossing it. We had to know the difference between a risk and a gamble. All commanders take risks. They are calculated decisions to make gains in a dangerous environment. Gambles are pure chance — closing your eyes and running the gauntlet. "Attacking that town right now, Lieutenant Fick," he said with renewed intensity, "would be a gamble. Don't ever be in a hurry to get your Marines killed."

When the other companies arrived, the battalion attacked the town and secured it. I watched proudly as my platoon moved confidently through our sector of cinderblock buildings. They were having fun. With the overwhelming force of three companies, we suffered no casualties, and the slight delay to the battalion's timeline didn't matter. I felt chastened.

We took a more direct route back to the boats, eager to be far from the beach before daylight. The moon was a fuzzy spot behind the clouds, and the wind had picked up, flecking spray through the air and blasting us with sand. Waves thundered onto the beach in sets of three. The company's coxswains had remained behind with the boats. They had them near the water's edge when we arrived, ready to launch.

Staff Sergeant Marine and I knelt together in the sand, struggling into our wetsuits. I noticed that his was twice as thick as mine. "Why the polar bear suit, Staff Sergeant?"

He looked smug and replied, "I been in boat company before, sir."

I looked out at the wind-whipped ocean. "I'm gonna freeze my tits off tonight, aren't I?"

"Just remember that there are two kinds of people in the world," Marine said sagely. "Those who piss in their wetsuits and those who lie about it."

After we got dressed, Marine ran from boat to boat, counting the troops and making sure weapons were tied to the aluminum deck plates. He gave me a thumbs-up. The platoon was on its game.

My six-man boat crew dragged its Zodiac into chest-deep water, holding the ropes that ran along the gunwale tubes. My breath caught in my throat. Each surging wave raised the water to my neck. I floated off my feet, struggling to keep the boat's bow pointed into the breakers. It would broach if it turned sideways, dumping our gear into the water and forcing us back to the beach to try again.

The coxswain clambered aboard and started the engine, yelling, "All in!" We struggled up over the sides and fell into the bottom of the boat in a tangle of legs and rifles. "Get some weight in the bow," he shouted. Ahead, a line of white, five feet above eye level, raced from the darkness — the foaming crest of a wave. The coxswain opened the throttle, and we streaked toward the wave. We climbed its base and teetered at the top. I tried to will our center of gravity over onto the back side of the wall of water threatening to throw us up onto the sand.

The engine shrieked as the propeller broke out of the water. Then our bow settled, and we were through. Surf passage complete. We steered for the bobbing shapes of the company's other boats, and I took my radio from its waterproof bag.

"Pale Rider, Pale Rider, this is Oden. Touchdown. I say again, touchdown." "Touchdown" was our code word to the ship for "mission complete." Had something gone wrong, we would have said "foul ball."

"Pale Rider copies touchdown. Be advised we're tossing pretty hard out here. May be unable to recover you aboard. Do you have fuel for alternate extract?"

The waves had grown over the course of the night, and the ship's crew doubted that they could pick us up safely. Alternate extract meant a long, cold, punishing ride down the coast to the Del Mar Boat Basin at

Camp Pendleton. My wool watch cap, soaked with salt water, kept slipping over my eyes. I pushed it back to look at Captain Whitmer.

He squinted through the blowing spray. I imagined him hearing the siren song of warmth and rest for his troops on the ship and the satisfaction of running a mission as briefed. But this was training, and Captain Whitmer would do whatever challenged the company most, forcing it to improvise, adapt, and overcome.

"Run the alternate," he ordered.

The trip took two hours. Icy spray stung my exposed skin like needles as we crashed down the waves. In every trough, I thought we were about to be swamped by the next roller. Headlights crawled along I-5 to our left. I imagined the drivers on their early commutes, warm, listening to the radio, sipping coffee. In the bow of the boat, one Marine slipped into hypothermia. He stopped shivering, and his lips turned pale with bluish edges. We wrapped around him to share body heat and shelter him from the frigid spray. Through it all, Captain Whitmer sat on the gunwale tube. He betrayed no discomfort, no concern, no rush to get back.

When we pulled into Del Mar shortly after sunrise, I confronted Whitmer; his rationale was still unclear to me. "Sir, why didn't you at least try to get aboard the ship? Why make the Marines suffer? We'll never use these boats anyway."

Captain Whitmer looked at me for a long moment, as if surprised I didn't get it. "Nate, it's not about the gear. Not even about the mission. It's about the people." He looked around at the Marines, now laughing and cleaning the boats in the morning sunlight. "When this company suffers, we're not wasting time or abusing anyone. The Marines are learning to hang together when things get bad, and that'll come back to us in spades. If there's ever a real mission for this battalion, Bravo will get the call, and we'll be ready."

Shortly before we deployed, I arrived at the office one morning to find Jim Beal, my friend from Quantico, sitting at my desk. We hadn't seen each other since TBS graduation. I dropped my duffel bag and grabbed his hand. Jim explained that he'd been sent to 1/1 as an artillery forward observer, or arty FO. This man works hand in hand with the weapons platoon commander in a MEU to run the company's fire support. I couldn't believe my good luck and asked Jim how he'd ended up in Bravo Company.

"I asked which weapons platoon commander was the most fucked-up, and they sent me to you."

"Whatever. They probably match the shitbird FO with the shit-hot platoon commander."

My happiness was short-lived. A note on my desk announced that a senior gunnery sergeant would be joining the platoon later in the week. I knew what that meant. I would have to demote Staff Sergeant Marine from platoon sergeant to leader of the mortar section. I stormed into Captain Whitmer's office, but he could only shake his head. Out of his control. I tried the first sergeant, responsible for personnel changes in the company. Same reaction. The bureaucracy had deemed Bravo short one gunny and that was that. These more experienced Marines knew better than to waste too much time and emotion fighting the machine.

It hurt. Why mess with a good platoon just before it deployed? Why did the platoon commander, and even the company commander, have no say in the matter? Marine and I had bonded. We worked well together. When I called him into the office to break the news, I was ready for a fight.

But I should have known better. Staff Sergeant Marine ended up consoling me, saying that the new gunny was a good Marine and that he would enjoy working with mortars, even if they had a low CDI factor.

I took the bait. "What's CDI?"

"Chicks dig it, sir. Football team: high CDI. Chess club: low CDI. Platoon sergeant: high CDI. Mortar section: low CDI. Doesn't matter that mortars have all the firepower. Life's unfair. Didn't they teach you that in college?"

# 8

EELING LIKE AN ACTOR on a movie set, I stood at the ship's rail in my khaki uniform. On the pier far below, throngs of people cheered and waved American flags as two tugboats pushed us away. A breeze rippled the water of San Diego Bay. At precisely ten A.M. on August 13, 2001, the USS *Dubuque* slid beneath the graceful span of the San Diego–Coronado Bridge, turning west past Point Loma for the open Pacific. On the flight deck, Marines and sailors lined the rails, hands clasped behind their backs and eyes straight ahead. The only sound was the wind as each man soaked up his last view of the city skyline, the beaches, California.

The *Dubuque* and two other ships, the USS *Peleliu* and the USS *Comstock,* made up an Amphibious Ready Group. The ARG's three ships carried the Fifteenth MEU (SOC). Two thousand Marines were in the MEU, including our infantry battalion, a helicopter squadron reinforced with four Harrier jets, and attachments such as a recon platoon, four tanks, and logistical support units. For the next six months, we would be America's "force in readiness" for half the globe.

Staff Sergeant Marine joined me at the rail as I watched the coast turn misty and gray in the distance.

"Congratulations, sir. This is your first step toward becoming an old campaigner like Lieutenant Hadsall."

"I'll have to land on a few foreign shores before I feel like much of a campaigner," I replied, but I smiled at the thought that I might be catching up with the ideal in his head. "What're your predictions for this float?"

Marine leaned on the rail with his hands out over the water, and the mischievous gleam faded for a moment. "Well, I heard a gunner in Fifth

Marines say something real smart once. We had just come home from months of sitting in the desert after Saddam kicked out the U.N. inspectors back in '98. Lots of missed birthdays, anniversaries, births, and all that crap. Marines were a little discontent about not doing anything. This gunner said to us, 'Never regret not doing a real mission. Now you can have all golden memories and no ghosts.' I try to remember that when the war fever takes over."

The *Dubuque* had been commissioned in 1967 and served off the coast of Vietnam. Five hundred sixty-nine feet long and displacing sixteen thousand tons, the ship carried its four hundred crew members and five hundred Marines at about fifteen knots. A five-story superstructure covered the forward third of the ship, and a flight deck stretched across the rear two thirds to the stern. Below it, the *Dubuque*'s dominating feature was a well deck, a sort of garage for boats that could be flooded and then pumped dry again. At the stern, a huge clamshell door provided entrance to the well deck. In accordance with the Navy's hierarchy, enlisted Marines and sailors lived beneath the deck of the ship in catacombs of narrow passageways lined with steam pipes and electrical wiring. Officers, both Navy and Marine, lived in staterooms in the superstructure.

Life aboard a warship at sea, especially one nearly forty years old, is like moving between a small closet, an apartment building boiler room, and a machine shop. The dominant features are movement and noise. The ship pitches and rolls constantly, throwing food from tables and men from bunks. As it moves, the steel creaks and groans. Engines throb, boilers hiss, and the ocean gurgles beneath the hull. Metal hatches must remain closed in case of flooding, so traffic, day and night, is marked by the rasps and clangs of closing and locking doors. Whistles, buzzers, and bells announce the events of the day — reveille, meals, drills, and taps. The ship's intercom and constantly buzzing telephones round out the cacophony. Newcomers quickly learn to carry earplugs.

The *Dubuque* was configured to serve as a fleet flagship, which meant there was a second bridge for the admiral and extra officer berthing. Since the *Peleliu* was, in fact, the flagship of our small flotilla, the *Dubuque* carried far fewer officers than it was equipped to handle. So I had a four-man stateroom to myself. The price I paid for this luxury was that my living space doubled as a storage room for everyone else's things. A glance into my stateroom revealed the intentions of the *Dubuque*'s Marines: three surfboards, four bags of golf clubs, four guitars, and a pile of Hawaiian shirts for liberty ports. Absent were maps of central Asia, down parkas, and Pashto and Dari translation guides. We still lived in a peaceful world.

Every western Pacific cruise starts with a trial period — the five-day steam to Hawaii. It's a time to get used to the rhythm of life at sea before pulling into a safe harbor. I settled into a comfortable daily routine, waking up at five-thirty to run on the flight deck before the day grew hot. Then I took a tepid, vaguely salty shower and ate breakfast in the officer's mess, called the wardroom. I dedicated the morning to work — planning training, cleaning weapons, and slogging through administrative paperwork. My favorite pastime was teaching classes to the Marines. I used my IOC manuals to keep our tactics fresh and reached back to my college courses to teach about famous battles. Patrick did the same, but he had studied economics. The company's office in the superstructure often overflowed with Marines learning about efficient markets and elasticity.

Training was limited by our tight confines, but we held races to assemble and disassemble machine guns while blindfolded, shot off the ship's stern at targets on the flight deck, and rappelled down elevator shafts into the well deck. Lunch was the day's high-water mark, followed by an afternoon slide of naps, reading, and lifting weights in the small triangular gym wedged into the bow. The old shipboard adage was "Sleep till you're hungry, then eat till you're tired, and repeat for six months."

My favorite time of day was the early evening. After leaving the gym, I'd climb to the *Dubuque*'s highest outside deck, just below the towering mast of radio antennas. There, on a rubber mat, Rudy Reyes led his trademark conditioning workouts — stretching, abs, breathing, and more stretching. Rudy was a sergeant in the MEU's recon platoon. Recon is the Corps's special operations force, trained to collect information behind enemy lines. But Rudy's demeanor in this gung-ho world was so decidedly nonmilitary that his platoon-mates called him "the Associate." Even the colonel stopped calling him Sergeant Reyes. He was Rudy. Afterward, I would lie on my back and watch the sky turn pink as the rocking ship made the clouds appear to swing overhead.

\*      \*      \*

The morning we pulled into Pearl Harbor, I woke early to watch our approach to Oahu. I wanted to see this fabled port from the deck of a Navy warship. As the sun began to light the sky, we rounded Diamond Head and glided west along Waikiki to the harbor entrance. The narrow channel cuts north past Hickam Air Force Base before turning hard to the right at Ford Island.

A carpet of manicured lawns and stands of swaying palms flanked Hickam's lush waterfront. The green was startling after five days of empty sea. I stood at the rail, looking down at the ship's crew at work on the bridge below. It was fully light by the time the *Dubuque* made the turn at Ford Island. The previous evening, at the ship's nightly operations/intelligence brief, the navigator had said that this turn would be preceded by one long blast from the ship's whistle to ensure no traffic came barreling through from the other direction.

"Oh, hell no!" A salty, prior-enlisted officer was quick to disagree. "The admiral and chief of staff live on the point right near that turn. A wise captain" — this punctuated with a glance at the CO — "will make a radio call in advance to be sure the channel's clear."

The *Dubuque* slid silently past the point and the homes of the sleeping admiral and chief of staff. Rounding the turn, we looked directly down the barrels of the USS *Missouri*'s sixteen-inch guns. Off her bow, gleaming white in the morning sun, floated the delicate span of the USS *Arizona* Memorial. It sags in the middle to symbolize initial defeat but stands firm at the ends in testament to resolve and ultimate victory. Above it, an American flag snapped in the breeze against a smudged backdrop of mountains, with piles of clouds threatening to pour across and drench us.

When the gangplank dropped, Patrick and I escaped to catch a launch out to the *Arizona*. We spent our allotted fifteen minutes on the memorial watching oil still bubbling from the wreck after sixty years. Among the names on a bronze tablet listing the ship's casualties, we noted a lone Marine lieutenant. After leaving the memorial, the launch passed the *Dubuque* at its pier. Patrick and I watched the other tourists snapping pictures of the ship.

"What would they think if we went to the parking lot and took pictures of their cars?" Patrick mused.

Although we blended into the crowd in T-shirts and sandals, I didn't really feel part of it. "Do you feel different?" I asked him.

"We are different. They're going back to hotels on Waikiki, and we're staring at six months in that big gray box." Patrick paused and looked around Pearl Harbor. "But different in a good way, too. Especially here."

We sailed the next afternoon for the two-week steam to Darwin, on Australia's north coast. Life fell once again into the easy shipboard routine of training, working out, and reading. I spent the evenings after Rudy's workouts in a chair at the ship's rail, watching our bow wave push toward the setting sun and reading Ernest Hemingway's *A Farewell to Arms.* "The world breaks everyone and afterward many are strong at the broken places," Hemingway wrote. "But those that will not break it kills. It kills the very good and the very gentle and the very brave impartially. If you are none of these you can be sure that it will kill you too but there will be no special hurry."

Steaming southwest at fifteen knots, we were in no special hurry either.

At six o'clock on a Friday evening, two weeks and six thousand miles from Camp Pendleton, we sailed south of Guadalcanal. I had learned a few days before that we would be passing by the island and worked to prepare a presentation about the Marines' first great battle of the Second World War. When I gathered the platoon on the upper deck, a reddening sun cast streaks above our heads. Guadalcanal's green mountains climbed from the sea and disappeared in a ring of clouds.

In the late summer and fall of 1942, the entire First Marine Division, including 1/1, had battled the Japanese army for control of Guadalcanal. I saw the Marines looking at the island while I spoke, probably imagining, as I was, the lines of landing craft, geysers of water where Japanese shells fell, machine guns raking the beach. Infamously, the Navy had abandoned the Marines ashore after four of its ships were sunk. With limited supplies, the Marines had pried the island from Japanese control at a cost of more than a thousand dead and four times that many wounded. They had killed twenty-five thousand Japanese.

History is the Marine Corps's religion. I'd seen it throughout my training and felt it at the Marine Corps War Memorial, as I read the list of battles outside 1/1's headquarters at Camp Pendleton, and even when I saw the name of the lone lieutenant killed aboard the *Arizona.* Past deeds are a young Marine's source of pride, inspiration to face danger, and reassurance that death in battle isn't consignment to oblivion. His buddies and all future Marines will keep the faith. Some people in my life would call that naiveté, but I was coming to know it as esprit de corps. My platoon lingered at the rail that evening, talking softly and watching Guadalcanal fade in the gathering darkness.

A week later, we pulled into Darwin for two days of training in the outback. Half the platoon joined the company for live-firing exercises, while the mortar section and Jim and I rode a bus three hours inland to a desolate training area, where we planned to drop mortars, artillery, and bombs. We arrived after dark and found the battalion combat operations center (COC) fully outfitted with lights, running water, tents, and showers. They were courteous enough to direct us several miles down a dirt road to our bivouac site in a burned-out field full of termite mounds the size of telephone booths.

We settled in uncomfortably, remembering the battalion surgeon's warning that Australia is home to nine of the world's ten deadliest snakes, including the death adder and taipan, which can render a man, in his words, "completely fucked." We were briefed that even the cute mini-kangaroos called wallabies can grab a person with their little hands and try to kick off the person's head with their powerful hind legs. The Marines around us snored as Jim and I opted to stand by the Humvee and talk rather than take our chances on the ground.

After two days of shooting, we returned to Darwin for a day off before our departure. Jim, Patrick, and I drove to the Adelaide River and spent the afternoon feeding crocodiles from a riverboat and swimming in waterfalls. That evening, we found a bar for dinner and drinks. Our ships were scheduled to leave at nine o'clock the next morning.

I sipped a Victoria Bitter and looked at my watch, trying to calculate the time on the East Coast of the United States. Ten-fifteen P.M. in Darwin made it eight-fifteen A.M. the same day in Maryland. I couldn't remember the date, but it was Tuesday, so maybe I could catch my dad at his desk.

I walked across the street to the pay phones in a hotel lobby. My dad and I talked for ten minutes, he asking about our trip and I asking about news from home. Neither of us had anything interesting to tell. I said I'd send him an e-mail soon from the ship and hung up. As I walked out, I saw Patrick talking on a phone farther down the wall.

"What's the word, bro?" Jim pushed a fresh beer my way and asked what was happening in the States.

"Nada. Pretty morning in Baltimore. Nothing to interest you guys." I had barely settled back onto my stool when Patrick burst through the door.

"Fucking terrorists flew planes into the World Trade Center and the Pentagon."

"Relax, bro. Have a beer." Jim and I laughed. Then we saw that Patrick was serious. Abandoning our drinks, we filed out the door and across the street to join a growing crowd around the lobby's big-screen TV.

Slowly, we realized the impact this would have on us. Jim summed it up best: "Fellas, history just bent us over." We had to get back to the ship.

Marines and sailors mobbed Darwin's streets, all streaming down the hill to the docks. As we joined the crowd, a car pulled up, and a young Australian couple asked if we needed a lift. We gratefully accepted and piled in the back seat. Minutes later, the car skidded onto the pier, where floodlights lit the three ships and armed sentries already stood along the rails. The driver shook our hands and said, "Guess you blokes are headed for war."

PART II

# War

Archidamus gave a great defeat to the Arcadians, in the fight known by the name of the Tearless Battle, in which there was a great slaughter of the enemy without the loss of one Spartan . . . The old men and the women marched out as far as the river Eurotas, lifting up their hands, and thanking the gods that Sparta was now cleared again of the disgrace and indignity that had befallen her, and once more saw the light of day. — PLUTARCH

# 9

MARINES CROWDED THE FLIGHT DECK. Only an hour after the attacks half a world away, most of the *Dubuque*'s sailors and Marines were already back aboard and far more restrained than usual this late on a night in port. My platoon milled around, clad in sandals and Hawaiian shirts. No one spoke. On the stern, two sailors manned a machine gun. They trained it on the cars depositing passengers at the gangplank. The ship rumbled and smoked from its funnel. The *Dubuque* was making steam, getting ready to sail.

I climbed up to Captain Whitmer's cabin, to let him know his officers were all aboard. I found him sitting at his desk, wearing sweatpants and looking relaxed. His incense burner smoldered, and acoustic guitar played softly in the background. This was Captain Whitmer at his best, embodying the line from Rudyard Kipling's poem about keeping your head when all around you are losing theirs. Yes, he knew about the attacks. Yes, he expected we'd be sailing earlier than planned. No, he saw no need for concern. We would hold a company formation at 0100 on the flight deck. Standing there in flip-flops and a T-shirt, I wanted to salute him but only nodded and closed the door.

At 0100, the flight deck looked like a party that had been halted in midstream. Marines, mostly drunk but acting very sober, bobbed and weaved in a rough formation. The ship was at THREATCON DELTA, wartime footing. I counted my men and found them all present. In fact, every sailor and Marine on the *Dubuque* returned to the ship within two hours of hearing the news from the States. Just as people at home were gathering together to absorb the blow, we did the same.

Even on the flight deck in the middle of the night, I recognized the pivotal moment. It was like a weight settling on my shoulders. I scanned the platoon's three ranks of faces. They looked worried, disoriented, uncertain — the same way I'd felt before I saw Captain Whitmer. They would take their cue from me just as I had taken mine from him. A dumb-ass lieutenant banging on his war drum would be of no help.

"Fellas, get some rest," I said evenly. "I'm sure the ship's e-mail will be shut down pretty soon, so try to get a message off to let your families know you're OK. I don't know how this affects our plans, but I'm sure we'll have more information tomorrow."

Captain Whitmer's calming effect was contagious. I could see that my reaction surprised them. Already, the worry lines began to disappear. Before dismissing the platoon, I turned it up just a little bit. "When the shock wears off, we're gonna be pissed. Maybe, if we're lucky, we'll be the ones to get revenge for this."

It resonated with them, and I saw a flicker of resolve. My emotion surprised me. Looking at the Marines, I saw football stars and thugs and baby-faced eighteen-year-olds. Black and white and Hispanic. They were my platoon, my men, my responsibility. Ruefully, I remembered Staff Sergeant Marine's comment about golden memories and no ghosts.

"Semper fi. Dismissed."

I stood on the dark deck and looked out over the lights of Darwin for a minute before slowly climbing the superstructure to my stateroom. There was an e-mail message from my dad. "Stand tall," it read, "but come home physically and psychologically intact." When I woke at six, we were already out of sight of land, three hours before our scheduled departure.

The ARG was ordered to "proceed at best possible speed" and join the U.S. Fifth Fleet in the Arabian Sea. Fifteen knots crept to eighteen and then to twenty, as fuel consumption became unimportant. Our scheduled stops in Singapore and Hong Kong were canceled. But the MEU interrupted its sprint for a daylong humanitarian mission in East Timor, the former Indonesian province then struggling for independence. I rode to the beach in Dili aboard a landing craft filled with lumber, grain, medicine, and, inexplicably, a crate of ThighMasters. Apparently, someone far up the chain of command wanted us to extend an olive branch to one nation before blowing the hell out of another.

Energy on the ship began to build. I learned that one of my Dartmouth classmates had died on the 104th floor of the North Tower. Marines had fathers and brothers in the New York City Fire Department, and sailors swapped the *Dubuque* baseball caps they normally wore with their uniforms for hats emblazoned with FDNY or NYPD. One Marine captain played bagpipes for the New York City Police Department band. He led a sunset memorial service on the flight deck, piping the mournful notes of "Amazing Grace" out over the empty ocean. Patrick, another New Yorker, received a note from a classmate whose boyfriend had died in the towers. She had been on the telephone with him when the line went dead. Patrick's father, a doctor, had waited for the injured at St. Vincent's Hospital in Manhattan. On a wall in the gym, a Marine painted a mural of a bald eagle sharpening its talons with a file.

Lacking a definitive mission, the MEU prepared to do everything. Captain Whitmer spent most of our westward transit aboard the flagship *Peleliu*, where he could more easily keep up with the ever-changing plans. Consequently, Patrick and I camped out in TACLOG, the ship's radio room for Marine communications, living on scraps of information passed back to us. "Great concern about possibility of multiple noncombatant evacuations. May want to focus on such an operation in and around Pakistan."

Over the next two weeks, reams of information flowed to the MEU in preparation to evacuate up to nine thousand Americans from Pakistan. Bravo Company was tasked with flying to Islamabad to secure the U.S. embassy and ready its staff and their families for movement out to the ships. The ship's executive officer wondered aloud how many people we could squeeze onto every available inch of deck space: four hundred? six hundred? What if the ambassador wants to bring her cat? Central Command gave us detailed blueprints and aerial photographs of the embassy and its grounds. Common features of American embassies and consulates are lovely soccer fields and lawns that double as helicopter landing zones. Patrick and I scoured the pictures looking for light poles, electrical wires, or anything else that would hinder our approach. We studied the buildings and surrounding gardens so we would waste no time with maps while rushing through them in the dark. By the end of the week, I knew the American embassy in Islamabad as well as I knew my parents' backyard in Baltimore.

\*     \*     \*

After reaching the Arabian Sea south of Pakistan, the *Dubuque* steamed in circles. The ocean had been carved into six boxes, named along a 9/11 theme: Pentagon, Pennsylvania, WTC North, WTC South, NYPD, and FDNY. The ships moved continuously but stayed within the boundaries of their assigned boxes in order to avoid collisions. It was a legitimate concern. By early October, dozens of American ships steamed circles in the same small patch of ocean.

The MEU slowly pulled back from its plans to evacuate civilians from Pakistan. Marine security guards at the consulate in Karachi and the embassy in Islamabad reported the situation well in hand. Nonetheless, we shared the general expectation that American strikes against Afghanistan would prompt a virulent anti-American backlash in neighboring countries. So we kept the evacuation plans on ice and began to focus more intently on Afghanistan.

After dinner on a typical Tuesday evening in the north Arabian Sea, I climbed to the upper deck and slid through the blackout curtains to the rail outside. The ship rocked gently on the dark ocean. Without visual reference points, the stars seemed to sway back and forth overhead. Far below, I saw and heard the white foam of the bow wave slide along the hull as the ship sliced through the water.

So much for a peaceful world. I remembered the day at OCS when the embassies in Africa had been bombed. I had been so naive. That afternoon, I'd still believed in the so-called peace dividend. Now my generation had its own Pearl Harbor, and I was an infantry lieutenant in the Marines. I could have been in medical school or wearing a suit to work. How could I have done this to my family? I wondered how many Marine infantry lieutenants in December 1941 had survived to see 1945.

I always did my best thinking outside on the deck. Fresh air, wind, and a view — even of only a dark horizon — brought me back to reality. Skippy peanut butter and CNN in the wardroom were of great comfort but disarmingly artificial. The wardroom was, for me, always in San Diego. Ten thousand miles from home, I would eat dinner and then open the hatch, fully expecting to see the lights of Coronado off the stern. But tonight there were no lights at all. I imagined the dozens of blacked-out American warships and, beyond them, the coast of Pakistan. A few hundred miles beyond that, across the mountains and deserts, was America's newest target: Afghanistan.

\*      \*      \*

Afghanistan was not only landlocked but time-locked as well. I sat on a metal chair in the TACLOG and flipped through printouts of a CIA analysis of the country. Patrick sat across from me, reading about Taliban battle tactics.

"Listen to this," I said. "Population of twenty-five million people, but only thirty-one thousand telephones and one hundred thousand televisions. Thirty percent literacy, eight hundred dollars GDP per capita, life expectancy of forty-five years, and the biggest exports are opium, nuts, carpets, and animal pelts. It sounds like we'll be fighting guys armed with clubs and slingshots."

"And Stingers. They bled the Soviets white," Patrick said without looking up from his reading. The Stinger is a shoulder-fired, heat-seeking, surface-to-air missile.

"Yeah, and the ragtag Chechens just kicked that same army in the teeth because the Russians' tactics and training and leadership suck. I don't think the comparison with us stands up."

"Maybe not. I'm just saying we need to remember the history." Patrick ran through a sketch of the foreign powers that had come to grief in Afghanistan's mountains.

"In 327 B.C., Alexander the Great comes through the Khyber Pass and gets hit by an Afghan archer's arrow. He nearly dies. Almost a thousand years later, Genghis Khan imposes his will over this whole part of the world. Who are the only people to pry concessions from him? The Afghans. And then there're the British. I wouldn't be surprised if Tony Blair wants no part of this operation. They lost three fucking wars to these people."

Patrick flipped back through his sheaf of papers and held one up. "Check this out. January 1842. The Brits withdraw from Kabul in a column of 16,500 soldiers and civilians. They're trying to get to safety at a garrison in Jalalabad, 110 miles away. Guess how many made it?"

"None."

"No, *one*. The Afghans slaughtered all of them except one. They let him live to tell the story.

"Christ, and the Soviets," he continued. "They *admitted* to fifteen thousand dead in the 1980s, plus at least ten times that number wounded and thousands dead from disease. And that's only what they admitted. So my point is just that this place has been a graveyard for a lot of guys like you and me, and we owe it to ourselves at least to learn from their mistakes."

I turned to a report on Taliban tactics. Their technique for moving through a minefield, according to the brief, was to put the unit in single file with the man at the front holding a large sandstone rock. Before each step, he drops the rock in front of him. If it falls on a mine, it will explode in a puff of dust, with the soft sandstone absorbing most of the blast. The point man may be stunned and temporarily deaf, but he will just go to the back of the line while the next guy takes over with a new rock.

The brief also said the fighters never carried any of their own gear — women and mules did that. If there were no women or mules available, they'd do without that particular equipment. The briefer finished with a note that Westerners who worked with the mujahideen in the 1980s said it was almost impossible to launch a coordinated attack with them; they quickly abandoned support positions in order to join in the glory of the assault.

"Death before dishonor."

"Say again?" Patrick looked up. I hadn't realized I had spoken aloud.

"Death before dishonor. Marines tattoo it on their forearms, but these fuckers *live* it."

Any cavalier bravado I might have had — what Captain Novack would have called my "posturing behavior" — was ebbing away.

"Gents, the order we've all been waiting for is on the street." It was October 7, and I stood at the back of the nightly brief in the wardroom, listening to the ship's operations officer. He shook a stack of papers and went on. "This is the night's theater air-tasking order. This document is usually one page of resupplies and medical flights. As you can see, this one looks more like a telephone book. Our neighbors this evening will include B-1 and B-2 bombers, B-52s, and every type of carrier air. Lots of it."

I had learned earlier in the day that Charlie Company had flown off the *Peleliu*. Their mission was to secure an airfield in Jacobabad, Pakistan, for use by combat search-and-rescue aircraft. That could mean only one thing: American pilots would soon be in the sky over Afghanistan.

The operations officer continued. "The phased air campaign against Afghanistan begins in about an hour. Tomahawks from the *Philippine Sea* will be part of the first wave. Now I want to wrap this up so we can all get on deck to watch the show."

Word had spread quickly through the ship, and dozens of Marines gathered in the dark on the upper decks. One level below, two sailors strummed guitars and sang Bob Dylan's "Shelter from the Storm."

Patrick saw it first. A distant glow resolved itself into a small orange ball, rose vertically to the top of a haze layer about one finger above the horizon, and then flattened to horizontal flight as the Tomahawk missile disappeared to the north.

We'd been waiting for this moment for weeks. September 11 had been an act of war, but we couldn't really say we were at war until the United States responded. Now all ambiguity disappeared. As if to confirm my thoughts, the ship's captain made an announcement over the shipwide loudspeaker that all scheduled events for the next two days were canceled "in anticipation of operational taskings." We were at war.

# 10

HIGH ON THE SUNLIT DECKS a week later, just below the signal bridge where the old Navy traditions of flags and blinker lights lingered into the twenty-first century, my troops were kicking my ass on a blue rubber mat. I may have been the platoon commander, but many of my Marines were bigger than I was and better fighters. We passed idle time on the ship by training in the Marine Corps Martial Arts Program, universally known as "semper fu." My machine gun section leader, Staff Sergeant Law, was instructing.

"OK, listen up, all you pussies who've never been in a fight. If you can fuck or play baseball, you can fight. It's all in the hips." Law looked more like a librarian than a Marine machine gunner. He described himself as "skinny but fat," tall and thin but soft. He was one of the platoon's only combat veterans, with a handful of Balkan firefights in his past. His "skinny fatness" didn't inhibit his skill as a semper fu artist.

The Marines mimicked Law by slamming someone, preferably of higher rank, to the mat. Having been stomped two or three times in the past hour, I was relieved when one of the company clerks came rushing up the ladder with a message. "Lieutenant Fick, the skipper needs you in TACLOG right away. Important message traffic."

Captain Whitmer waited in front of a computer. "Nate, I've just been called over to the *Peleliu* for mission planning. I want you and Patrick to come with me. No time for questions right now. Pack a bag for two or three days and be ready to go in five minutes."

A dry-erase board hung on the wall behind Captain Whitmer. Our current list of missions, under the heading "Be Prepared To," was written in blue marker: "BPT reinforce USEMB Islamabad, BPT secure forward airfield at Zhob, BPT reinforce Jacobabad." This mission didn't sound like any of those. I ran down the passageway to my stateroom and threw my planning paperwork, some workout clothes, and a paperback copy of Wallace Stegner's *Angle of Repose* into my waterproof bag. After closing the door, I realized I had forgotten my plastic *Dubuque* coffee mug and went back for it. Mission planning meant late nights. I climbed back to the top deck and told the platoon I'd be gone for a couple of days but would be in touch as soon as I knew more.

Captain Whitmer and Patrick were waiting for me. "No helos flying. We're going by RHIB."

The *Dubuque* carried two eleven-meter rigid hull inflatable boats. They were small black craft, grossly overpowered, and usually used to insert SEALs on clandestine missions. We climbed down narrow ladder wells to an open cargo door in the ship's side. Ten feet below, the ocean foamed past. One of the RHIBs maneuvered off the ship's beam, and beneath us dangled a rope ladder.

As the boat slid beneath the ladder, we swung our way down and clambered aboard. The RHIB crew seemed intent on showing off their boat's performance to a group of Marine officers, and we shot away from the *Dubuque* as if it were steaming in reverse. Open ocean lay ahead. We rocketed along at forty knots for ten minutes before the *Peleliu's* hulking profile loomed in the haze. Coming alongside, we reversed the earlier process and climbed up a rope ladder into the cavernous hangar bay. The *Peleliu's* flight deck stretched from bow to stern, like an aircraft carrier, and the MEU's whole squadron was aboard. Inside the hangar bay, helicopters and Harrier jets crouched on their landing gear in the dim light, while maintenance crews scurried around and a group of Marines practiced semper fu on a blue rubber mat.

The Battalion Landing Team (BLT), composed mostly of infantry Marines from 1/1, planned its missions in a room the size of a Manhattan studio apartment. Computers lined one wall, and a huge map of Pakistan and Afghanistan covered the opposite bulkhead. Exposed pipes and fluorescent lights hung from the ceiling, and some wag had taped a drawing of Osama bin Laden to the door. Its caption read, "You can run, but you'll only die tired." Battalion officers and staff NCOs filled the scattered chairs.

When Captain Whitmer, Patrick, and I walked in, the battalion's executive officer called the room to order. He freed up chairs by dismissing several Marines from the room. "We're keeping details on this one close to our chest, gents. Sorry."

They walked out, looking hurt, and the door was closed behind them. This was starting to sound interesting.

"Welcome, Bravo Company," he said with a nod in our direction. "What I am about to say will not leave this room. You will do your planning, theorizing, and bullshitting within these four walls — not on the mess deck, not in the wardroom, and not in the gym. Is that clear?"

We all nodded as he continued. "As you know, the United States has been dropping bombs on Afghanistan for the past nine days." He explained that there was a small CIA and Army Special Forces presence on the ground, mainly in the north. There was as yet no ground presence in the country's south. The executive officer paused for effect. "That is about to change. On Friday evening, October 19, Task Force Sword will conduct a mission into southern Afghanistan to seize an airfield and attempt to capture a high-value leadership target." Pause. "We have been tasked with providing a Bald Eagle for that mission." Pause, and a slow turn to face Captain Whitmer, Patrick, and me. "Bravo Company, you're it."

The three of us glanced at one another. A Bald Eagle was a company-size reserve element, ready to help in case a raid force ran into trouble. The question on all our minds was "Why Bravo?"

Captain Whitmer was too self-effacing to say it, but I knew the answer. Among the battalion's company commanders, he was the iconoclast, the outcast stepchild who trained his Marines to *be* good instead of *look* good. He pushed us hard, questioned authority, and couldn't even feign obsequiousness. But when the first real mission called, the battalion turned to him.

"Task Force Sword is composed of SOF currently embarked on the *Kitty Hawk*," the executive officer continued. The aircraft carrier *Kitty Hawk* was being used as a floating base for special operations forces working in and around Afghanistan.

"Here's your mission statement." He handed us a sheet of paper marked SECRET in bold red letters. I read, "On order, Task Force Bald Eagle launches from PEL in 4 x CH-53 to OBJ RHINO, links up with TF SWORD mobile reserve, and conducts relief in place. Defend RHINO with Bravo Company for up to twenty-four hours. O/o turn over OBJ

RHINO to TF SWORD and withdraw to ARG shipping." This prompted more questions than it answered.

After a more comprehensive brief, I thought I had a good idea of the plan. On Friday night around dusk, elements of Task Force Sword, mostly Army Rangers and Special Forces, would launch from the *Kitty Hawk*. They would fly into Pakistan, securing a small airfield near Dalbandin, code-named Honda, to use as a refueling and rearming point. From Dalbandin, part of the force would parachute into a desert airstrip in southern Afghanistan code-named Rhino, while the other part would raid Taliban leader Mullah Omar's residential compound outside Kandahar. We would serve as a reserve in case something went wrong during any part of the mission. This sounded complex, I thought, and a lot could go wrong.

Bravo Company flew over from the *Dubuque* the next morning. While the NCOs settled the troops in their temporary berthing and began distributing ammunition and gear for the mission, Captain Whitmer, Patrick, and I continued with planning. Every MEU mission ran through three planning stages. First came a warning order from some higher command notifying the MEU to "be prepared to" execute a given task. That task may have been distributing food to the people of East Timor, evacuating the embassy in Islamabad, or serving as the quick reaction force for a mission into Afghanistan. Once the warning order was received, the MEU staff went into overdrive, developing a course of action for how the MEU would accomplish the mission.

It is a central tenet of the Marines' war-fighting philosophy that each subordinate must provide options to his boss — tell him what you can do, rather than what you can't. Depending on the situation, two or three or four courses of action would be developed and then roughed out into basic operational plans. For the Sword mission, helicopter pilots calculated distances and fuel burn, charting different paths through the mountains. Infantry officers studied maps to memorize the layouts of Rhino and Honda and decided how many men they'd need in different scenarios. All the hypothesizing came together in the final construction of three possible courses of action — put the Bald Eagle on the ground at Honda in case it was needed, keep it airborne over the ocean until called, or keep it on the *Peleliu*, ready to launch on a few minutes' notice. The MEU commander reviewed the options and decided to keep the quick reaction force aboard the *Peleliu*. Its response time would be almost as fast and at greatly reduced risk. With a course of action chosen, the MEU fleshed out a detailed concept of operations for accomplishing the mission.

The wheels spun madly again. Numerous small planning cells, each focused on a different aspect of the mission, convened in coffee-fueled debate sessions. Pilots plotted their courses and picked the mix of Super Stallion transport helicopters and Cobra gunships. Grunts finalized their manifests, picking platoons and dividing them among the helicopters so that one crash wouldn't wipe out all the machine gunners or all the officers. Other cells focused on communications, requesting dedicated satellite radio channels and preparing encryption codes to scramble the transmissions. Logisticians brought ammunition up from the ship's magazine. Medical teams prepared the ship's operating rooms and thawed blood for the Marines to take with them. All the details of the plan were then presented to the MEU commander in a concept of operations brief.

Preparing a concept of operations during training had always frustrated me. The briefs were PowerPoint presentations held in the *Peleliu's* wardroom. Captains and majors fought over font size, background color, and whether to include cute graphics of moving helicopters. The purpose, though, was sound: to air the plan publicly, criticize it, test its assumptions, focus on the friction points where something was likely to go wrong, and strengthen it. Finally, after the appropriate changes and refinements were made, the plan was rehearsed from start to finish in a confirmation brief, with each key player explaining his role to the MEU commander. According to MEU (SOC) standards, the whole process, from warning order to confirmation, had to be done in less than six hours.

Only after the plan was approved did I feel comfortable briefing the Marines. I wanted to insulate them from the confusion of changing details in the mission.

"Weapons platoon, circle it up," I said, standing in the hangar bay with my notebook and a photocopied map.

The Marines stopped loading ammo and programming radios, pressing close to hear the word. I quickly outlined the mission to low whistles and nods of approval.

"It's important right now that we stick to our timeline. We have a lot to do. The rest of this evening is your time to prep individual and platoon gear. Get some rest tonight — tomorrow's a busy day." I tore a page from the notebook and taped it to the bulkhead above the platoon's gear. "Here's the schedule: 0600 breakfast; 0630 to 0800 draw weapons, issue ammo, and stage equipment; 0800 to 0900 helo drills; 0900 to 1000 formal platoon order issued; 1100 to 1200 final gear staging; 1200 to 1300 rules of engagement brief; 1300 to 1600 rehearsals; 1630 test fire; and 1700 call away and final load rehearsals. After 1730, Sword is airborne, and we're on alert 10 — that's ten minutes from notification to launch."

I looked around at the crowd of faces. "You're it, fellas. A hundred million American men would like to be in your shoes right now. We have the honor of fighting back."

On Friday, I got my first look at the wartime military. While the platoons ran through the schedule, Patrick and I gathered equipment for the mission. I was used to signing for a roll of duct tape and accounting for each individual MRE we ate. But now gear seemed to materialize from nowhere — Javelin antitank missiles, iced coolers full of blood, atropine injectors for defense against chemical nerve agents, and two laser marking systems for guiding smart bombs in the dark.

By 1700, our packs, ammunition, and medical equipment were staged in the helicopters, which sat, fueled and waiting, on the flight deck. The evening was balmy and clear, with dry air seeming to throw the ship's features into high relief. I sent the platoon to its berthing area with orders to stay together — no trips to the gym or the late-night chow line. At last, I joined the company officers in TACLOG, where the Sword mission was unfolding over the radio speaker.

We listened as the Rangers on the ground in Afghanistan vectored AC-130 Spectre gunships in on targets. Feeling helpless and wanting to be rested in case we got the call, I climbed five levels down from the *Peleliu*'s tower and then up into an empty bunk, turning off the light and drawing the privacy curtain around me. Fatigue won out over excitement, and I fell asleep.

The battalion executive officer yanked back the curtain. "One of the Sword helicopters crashed. Get up and stand by."

I leaped from the rack and pulled on my boots, laces still flapping as I ran down the passageway to the battalion planning room. The clock read 3:45 A.M.

The Sword mission was still under way, and information was incomplete and contradictory. The helo had been shot down in Afghanistan, or it had crashed in a cloud of dust while landing in Pakistan. No casualties, or everyone aboard had been killed. Rescue would launch immediately, or the Rangers would attempt to do their own recovery. Our default setting was to wait and let the situation develop. I picked up a phone to wake the Marines and then thought better of it. Each adrenaline rush is followed by a crash. Each time we prepped to launch but didn't go would leave us a little more tired, jaded, and frustrated. It would be better, I thought, to protect them from as much of that as possible. With dawn an hour away, we didn't have enough darkness to launch and reach the crash site before sunrise.

The parachute jump into Rhino had been successful, and the Rangers had overcome limited resistance. The Sword mission to capture Mullah Omar failed because he hadn't been there when the raid force had arrived. The Americans had narrowly avoided disaster when their helicopters came under fire while taking off. One Chinook had clipped a stone wall, knocking off one of its landing gear, but escaped safely.

The crash had occurred at a staging base along the Pakistani border. Two Rangers had been killed when an MH-60 special operations Black Hawk rolled over after the pilots got disoriented in swirling dust. The dead men had been pulled out, and the survivors had been evacuated on other aircraft, but the helicopter was still where it had crashed.

Despite the Pakistani government's nominal alliance with the United States, it had only loose control over the border regions, where Taliban sympathies were strong. After one attempt to recover the helicopter was thwarted by heavy hostile fire, reaching the Black Hawk became a high priority. This was partly because of the sensitive nature of its avionics, and partly because of its propaganda value to our enemies. But mostly it was because the Marines weren't going to let a few Pakistanis with rifles chase them away. Planning began for a beefed-up recovery force to go in, shooting if necessary, to bring back the Black Hawk. It would be built around Bravo Company.

Again, we staged our gear, issued briefs, and coordinated the countless details of air support and communications. At 2030, word came to stand down. The U.S. ambassador to Pakistan was afraid we'd end up killing Pakistanis and damage the fragile American alliance with President Musharraf. Pakistani security forces would surround the airfield at Panjgur, where the Black Hawk sat, before we went in. The mission was on hold until the next night.

The MEU commander, Colonel Thomas Waldhauser, scheduled the confirmation brief for four o'clock on the afternoon of the mission. Colonel Waldhauser had the tall, spare looks of a combat Marine. He had served as a young officer in the infantry and recon and had a reputation for letting his subordinates do their jobs.

Patrick and I arrived fifteen minutes early to get a seat. Too late. Every table was full, and more people were crammed along the back wall. Only two platoons were going on this mission, but there must have been fifty officers in the room for the brief. I was exasperated but also reassured that so many people had a hand in it.

The MEU operations officer began the presentation, speaking from the projected slides and talking mainly to the MEU commander and the Navy commodore in charge of the ARG, seated together at a table in the front row. They had sole veto power over any part of the plan. In succession, each key player, and many peripheral players, briefed his portion of the night's mission. Air, intelligence, operations, communications, logistics, medical, weather, even the chaplain said a few words.

Finally, Captain Whitmer stood up. He would be the leader on the ground in the dark. Looking rumpled and speaking softly, he had none of the perkiness of the earlier briefers, those who would stand on the ship and watch the helicopters fly away. He flashed a sympathetic smile at Patrick and me, as if acknowledging the necessity of this circus, and talked the commanders through our plan. Whitmer's brief was thorough and confident, running through each of the mission's decision points, from deciding whom to bring to deciding when to abort.

Throughout the confirmation brief, Colonel Waldhauser had been pushing power down the chain of command, authorizing his subordinates to make the critical decisions at each point in the mission. When Captain Whitmer said he would be leaving his mortars behind due to space limitations on the helicopter, the colonel nodded. Abort criteria were no different. The colonel ordered only that we would abort the mission if we came under fire while approaching the landing zone. After landing, whether to abort would be a command decision by the men on the ground. When he was comfortable with the details, Colonel Waldhauser stood, faced the room, and said, "This mission is confirmed. Good luck, gentlemen."

After the brief broke up, Captain Whitmer, Patrick, and I had an appointment with Colonel Waldhauser in his cabin. Captain Whitmer rapped on the door, and the colonel himself opened it. He invited us to sit on two sofas and poured coffee for four before sitting in a chair opposite us.

"Gentlemen, I invited you up for this private talk because I need you to understand the importance of this mission. General Musharraf has put himself way out on a political limb in order to support Operation Enduring Freedom." The colonel leaned toward us for emphasis and went on. "What's the most important thing you can do tonight?"

Patrick and I looked at each other and said in unison, "Recover the Black Hawk."

"Wrong. The most important thing you can do tonight is not kill any Pakistanis. The Pakistani army has a security cordon around the airfield. Several hundred armed men will be out there in the dark. You might hear them, you might see them, but you must not shoot them. I don't want a nervous young trigger-puller losing his cool and sparking an international incident. That, not recovering the helicopter, is the most important part of your mission tonight.

"But," he added with a smile, "I expect you'll recover the Black Hawk, too."

I walked down through the Marines' berthing area to check on my platoon and answer any final questions. Staff Sergeant Law was briefing his machine gunners, drilling the pyrotechnic signal plan and call signs for what must have been the hundredth time. "All right, warriors, once more. Red pyro means emergency extract. Green pyro is a squad pulling back — don't shoot 'em. White is for illumination only, and smoke of any color is solely for concealment. Everybody got that?"

Leaning against the wall, I listened as he ran through the call signs. "Mission commander is Proud Tiger, the forward air controller is Neck, and the escort Cobras are Swordplay." When eyes began to glaze over, Law cut it short and turned to me.

"Well, LT, we're about as ready as we'll ever be," he said. "Let's hope this mission actually goes tonight." Law's eyes were red behind his glasses. "Too much of this up-and-down crap and even my sharp edge gets dull."

"I think this time it's a go," I said. "Don't forget to get some rest yourself."

I was pulling the metal hatch open at the base of the ladder well when Law called out, "Hey, sir. Don't worry 'bout machine guns. We're locked and cocked. These are good motherfuckers. They're ready to go."

Suppressing a smile, I paused and nodded before climbing the ladder.

# 11

I SET MY ALARM for twelve-thirty A.M., but trying to sleep was futile. I tossed and turned in my bunk for three hours, finally giving up and reading a month-old *Sports Illustrated* while listening to Metallica's *Ride the Lightning*. Unable to stand the waiting any longer, I grabbed my plastic coffee mug and walked through the dark passageways toward the wardroom.

The ship was quiet. Most people were sleeping soundly, unaware of the drama unfolding in our lives. A light shone under the wardroom door, and I opened it to find Captain Whitmer and Patrick sitting at a table. They looked up at me with sympathetic smiles. Across the room, a group of pilots nursed steaming coffee and talked quietly over a map. I filled my mug and sat down at the table. A few minutes later, our three watch alarms went off simultaneously. At least I wasn't the only one who couldn't sleep.

We walked down to the hangar bay with a nonchalance I doubt any of us really felt. I know I didn't. This was it. A real mission. A combat mission. I thought back to all my training and the instructors who had combat experience. They had seemed better than us, calmer, more assured, more capable. I didn't feel that way now. I was just a boot lieutenant caught up in something beyond my control. The weight pressed down again, the burden of responsibility and the hope, above all else, that I wouldn't do anything stupid and get people killed.

I sat on my pack beneath the fluorescent lights and opened cardboard boxes of rifle ammunition. Live rounds. My hands were shaking as I loaded the magazines. Each bullet weighed about an ounce, a wide brass casing tapering to a lethal, copper-jacketed point. I had loaded thousands of live rounds in training but had never really examined them. They looked dangerous. I wondered whether any of mine would end up inside another human being before the night was over.

We filed past the open elevator shaft to test fire our weapons out over the dark ocean. My rifle cracked and jumped in my hands. The purpose of a test fire isn't to make sure the gun fires that first time, but to ensure that the next bullet is seated in the chamber, ready to go. The sound of shots reverberated off the metal walls, and acrid cordite hung in the air.

The platoon lined up on the nonskid floor of the ramp leading to the flight deck. Each Marine sat in the order in which he would board the helicopter. That order, when reversed, was how we would hit the ground at Panjgur. Fire teams and machine gun squads sat together. I sat alone at the back, first man off the bird.

Captain Whitmer, bulky in his body armor, called the lieutenants and sergeants over to where he stood in a corner. I expected a last-minute change to the plan or maybe a final reminder of our rules of engagement.

"If any of you screw up and get a Marine killed tonight," he said without preamble, "I will personally put a bullet in your head."

I caught Patrick's eye and we mustered a quiet "Aye-aye, sir." Captain Whitmer walked off. The hangar bay was too crowded to talk privately with Patrick, so I returned to my place in the line of Marines waiting on the ramp. Whitmer's comment gnawed at me. Did he not trust us? Did he think we weren't taking the mission seriously? If it had been an attempt to motivate us, it failed. I tried to put it out of my mind and focus on getting ready to go.

I fitted a rubber life preserver around my neck and pulled on a pair of green Nomex shooting gloves. The life preserver had a carbon dioxide cartridge and a strobe light that would activate upon hitting the water. The gloves would keep my hands from being burned in a fire and allow me to grab weapons hot from shooting.

After all the training, all the classes at Quantico and patrols at Camp Pendleton, I had a picture in my mind of how it would be. Momentous, significant, high drama. But grandiose phrases such as "in harm's way" and "Godspeed" just didn't fit. Around me sat a few dozen Marines waiting to launch. I saw ordinary guys doing a job. I didn't think about the sweep of history, about the Afghan people or protecting America. My mind was on call signs and radio frequencies and the satellite pictures of the Black Hawk. Any fear or reservation disappeared in the task at hand. Sitting there in the dark with my rifle suddenly seemed to be the most natural thing in the world.

Staff Sergeant Marine snapped me back to the hangar bay. "You'll regret not bringing the mortars, sir, about the time the hajis are overrunning your perimeter." He was walking along the line of troops, talking to the Marines waiting to leave.

His tone was joking, but I knew he wished he was joining us. I did, too. Before I could answer, the intercom announced, "Call away, call away!" — our signal to board the helos.

Marine clapped my shoulder. "Stay safe tonight."

We shuffled to the flight deck and turned our heads against the deafening roar of three Super Stallions, snorting jet exhaust and tossing us sideways with their rotor wash. The Marines around me shone dimly blue in the subdued lighting. I led a column to the lead helicopter, painted with the name "Creeping Death," and counted thirty men aboard before taking the last seat near the tail ramp. Two other CH-53s roared farther down the flight deck. One would carry thirty more Marines, while the third would fly empty to lift the crashed Black Hawk and ferry it back to the *Kitty Hawk*.

I donned a helmet attached to the helo's internal radio and got a comm check with the pilots. The Marines squeezed onto webbed nylon seats around a pallet of spare ammunition and a pallet of medical supplies. Across from me, Staff Sergeant Law flashed a slight smile. My platoon and Patrick's were mixed up, spread-loaded between the two CH-53s in case one of them crashed. Patrick's first squad leader, Sergeant Tony Espera, sat next to Law. Espera had joined the Corps after working as a repo man in L.A. He looked unfazed and smiled when our eyes met.

The engine noise increased, and we lurched sideways off the *Peleliu's* deck. Climbing over the ocean, I listened to the pilots' routine chatter — fuel, power, altitude, and navigation. The other two helicopters were dimly visible to our rear through my night vision goggles. The pilot called "Feet dry" over the intercom to let us know we'd crossed the Pakistani coast. I gave a hand signal that was relayed through the helicopter, and we took off our life preservers. The bird dropped to low altitude. Beyond the tail ramp, the ground flashed past almost within reach, but I saw no lights. Below us was Baluchistan, one of the least hospitable parts of the earth. With nothing to see and too much noise to talk, each man was alone with his thoughts.

All through my training, I'd heard sports analogies. OCS was a game. Taking advantage of unrealistic details on field exercises at TBS was "gaming the game." Winning. Losing. Code words like "touchdown" and "foul ball." But sitting in that CH-53, racing north into Pakistan, it didn't feel like a game. It felt like the most serious thing I'd ever done.

The pilot passed the five-minute warning over the radio — five minutes to touchdown in the landing zone. I turned my backpack radio to high power and rechecked all my gear. Night vision goggles adjusted, seat belt unbuckled, last sip of water. The engine pitch changed as the pilots wrenched the big helicopter through a series of evasive turns approaching the landing zone. The landing gear thumped down, and the ramp dropped. I ran out, turning left to avoid the spinning tail rotor, and crouched at the edge of the runway to get a radio check as the helo thundered away in a cloud of dust. Staff Sergeant Law and his machine gunners disappeared to the north without a word. They would secure a perimeter around the crashed Black Hawk.

I jogged across the runway to the spot we'd picked to set up a command post, passing the hulk of the helicopter. Over my headset radio, one of Patrick's teams reported muzzle flashes in the distance. The lights of a Navy P-3 communications relay aircraft winked high overhead — too high even to hear.

A group of Marines clustered in the darkness, and I ran toward them. Captain Whitmer stood with a Pakistani officer. They were laughing, standing lightly as if at a cocktail party. I felt rude approaching them with my rifle, crouched under a heavy pack.

"Lieutenant Fick, this is Major Magid."

"Pleased to meet you, sir." I shot a glance at Captain Whitmer, who smiled placidly.

The major was slight, bedecked with ribbons and huge braided epaulets. His orderly stood nearby with a silver tea tray.

"Do not be afraid. We have three layers of defense and you are in very good hands," the major said, bowing slightly. "Would you care for a cup of tea?"

The orderly poured into a chipped china cup. The tea was dark and sweetened with goat's milk. My gloved hand was clumsy, so I cupped it like a softball. I drank the tea quickly so that I could get back to work without offending the major. My first two missions couldn't be delivering ThighMasters and drinking tea. An unearthly wail broke the silence as a muezzin called the faithful to morning prayer. Panjgur wasn't hostile, but it wasn't quite friendly either. We were a long way from the *Peleliu* wardroom.

Staff Sergeant Law had his Marines in place, and Patrick's platoon manned positions all around us. The teams on the perimeter called back and forth on the radio, pointing out Pakistani army positions. I scanned the horizon through my night vision goggles, looking for the telltale flashes of firing rifles. Nothing. I spoke to the Cobra gunship pilots who orbited farther out past the airfield fence. They, too, saw nothing amiss.

With Bravo Company's perimeter in place, an explosive ordnance disposal (EOD) team moved cautiously to the Black Hawk, dropping red chem lights behind them to mark a safe path of retreat. After they checked the helicopter for booby traps, a specially trained suspension team got the wreck ready to move. They wrapped long nylon straps around the fuselage, joining them at the top with a loop and a hook. If the Black Hawk couldn't be lifted out, we planned to use incendiary grenades to burn holes in the cockpit and transmission, then blow the tail boom off with a strip of explosives. But the straps were attached without trouble, and the empty Super Stallion came in for the pickup.

The pilot slowed to a hover over the Black Hawk, and a cloud of talcum-like dust engulfed the CH-53 — the same sort of brownout that had caused the initial crash. Every few seconds, a rotor or piece of fuselage would peek from the cloud to reassure us that it was still flying. After a tense minute in a hover, the CH-53 went around while Marines untangled the sling, which had been twisted by the rotor wash. On his second pass, the pilot lifted the CH-53 out of the dust cloud with the Black Hawk hanging beneath it and lumbered off to the south. The eastern sky was just beginning to lighten.

I made a radio call and Law's Marines collapsed their perimeter. Patrick's platoon also pulled back, and we all converged on the runway. The Cobras made a low pass down its length to remind us we weren't alone. With lowered gray noses, they looked like sharks slashing through the dawn sky. The two Super Stallions roared in low and settled on the pavement. Patrick and I did a final sweep to ensure that we had all our men and were the last aboard the helicopters. The tail ramp was already rising as we threw our packs in and scrambled behind them. I looked at my watch. It was five A.M.; we had been on the ground exactly forty-two minutes.

In the light of the rising sun, we flew over a snow-white desert studded with piles of red stone. Jagged mountain ridges rose straight up, so that the helicopter alternately seemed to soar and then to scrape past with rocks just outside the open doors. When the pilot called "Feet wet" over the Arabian Sea, we pulled the magazines from our rifles and relaxed. Ninety minutes after takeoff, we settled onto the *Peleliu*'s flight deck — just in time for an omelet in the wardroom.

I slept through the afternoon, exhausted more from the adrenaline than from missing a night's sleep. Around four o'clock, Patrick shook my shoulder. "The commandant's flying out to the ship to have dinner with us tonight. You may want to clean up and get ready."

I sat up, momentarily lost in the whirlwind of the past twenty-four hours. General James L. Jones was the four-star general in charge of the whole Marine Corps. I didn't think he'd come from Washington to congratulate us for picking up the Black Hawk. Instead, he'd probably come for a pep talk. Some future mission, but what? The only uniform I had aboard was the desert camouflage I had worn all night, so I climbed from the bunk and wore it into the shower to scrub out some of the grime.

A few minutes before six, Patrick and I walked to the wardroom together. The officers around us were nattily dressed in freshly starched uniforms with polished rank insignia. By comparison, we looked ratty in dirty field cammies with dull brass. Our only consolation was that we'd been earning our combat pay while the other guys had been ironing and shining.

The wardroom lights were dimmed. A long head table lined the far wall, with a dozen round tables in front of it and name cards at each place. The tables were set with silver, china, and maroon tablecloths. The BLT platoon commanders sat together at the front center table. Since alcohol was forbidden on the ship, we sipped apple juice and talked while waiting for the commandant to arrive. Conversation centered on the absence of Alpha Company's lieutenants, who were ashore at the airfield in Jacobabad.

"That place is a shit hole," VJ proclaimed, having just returned from ten days there. "Hot, dusty, smoky, no chow, no showers. Fucking spies everywhere. The security situation is a joke — we're covering with a company what a battalion could barely handle. If someone wants to hit us there, they can." Patrick and I leaned in to listen. We were next in the rotation to take over security at the base.

"Attention on deck!" Conversation ceased, and everyone sprang to their feet.

"At ease, gentlemen. Please take your seats," General Jones said. He and Colonel Waldhauser sat together at the head table. Throughout the dinner of steak and shrimp, we stole glances at the general. He was tall, easily the tallest man in the room, and wore the Marine Corps's new digital-pattern camouflage uniform. We'd been away from home for a long time, emotionally as well as physically, and it was strange to see this newcomer among us. He'd been in Washington only a few days before and would be there again just a few days later. He seemed like an ambassador from another world.

And yet he fit right in with us. Instead of a long and politically correct monologue, he stood up after dinner and told a story about a combat deployment of his own, many years before.

"You'll be spending the 226th birthday of the Corps out here. My favorite Marine Corps birthday was also spent in the field — 10 November 1967 as a lieutenant with my rifle platoon in Vietnam. We mushed a bunch of field ration pound cakes together to make a cake, drizzled chocolate on top, and sang 'The Marines' Hymn.' Unfortunately, it was the monsoon, and we couldn't get the candles lit, so we went back to our fighting holes and continued killing Vietcong." The Marines in the room cheered.

Before sitting down, General Jones looked straight at our table of lieutenants. "Mark my words, gentlemen," he said. "Your time is coming."

# 12

STEPPING OFF THE C-130 in Jacobabad reminded me of every description I'd ever read about another generation of Marines arriving in Vietnam. Only five days after the commandant's speech, it was Bravo Company's turn to secure Shabaz Air Base at Jacobabad, in central Pakistan. Even in November, the sun was so hot I watched dark sweat stains spread across the tops of my tan boots. Sandbagged bunkers ringed the tarmac, and fuel trucks, Humvees, and helicopters were crammed onto every square inch of pavement. Adjacent to the runway stood a metal hangar painted in a splotchy brown camouflage motif. Staff Sergeant Marine and I walked toward it.

Inside, government-issue cots filled half the space. Men slept, their eyes shielded from the light by bandannas and T-shirts. Assault rifles lay within easy reach under the cots. Ponchos hanging from parachute cord provided minimal privacy. It looked like a refugee camp. The other half of the hangar was divided into separate briefing areas, with maps, charts, and rows of metal chairs. Our footsteps echoed through the silent hangar, and no one moved as we walked the length of the room to the doorway on the other side.

I squinted in the bright sunlight. Behind the hangar were a dozen low, white stucco buildings. South of them, stone aircraft revetments were built at random. Neat rows would be more vulnerable to aerial attack. But what interested me was to the west, back across the runway from the hangar. The town of Jacobabad stretched from smoggy horizon to smoggy horizon. It sprawled in a vaguely menacing third world way, with boxy water towers and television antennas sticking up from the alleys. The dusty brown construction blended with the smog. Marine and I walked the whole perimeter of the base, filling Alpha's old positions with our Marines and plotting mortar targets in case we had to defend the field.

Tucked behind one of the revetments was a black Chinook helicopter, propped forlornly on a pile of cinderblocks, missing one of its landing gear. I pointed it out to Staff Sergeant Marine. "That's the Sword bird we heard about. Lost a wheel taking off out of Mullah Omar's compound. Looks like it should be sitting in a front yard in West Virginia."

"Or Maryland, sir."

Jacobabad was a spook fest. A different team of scruffy-looking commandos lived in each revetment. "Lockheed and Boeing contractors" — masquerading CIA and Delta Force operators — mingled with Royal Marines, Special Air Service troopers, Air Force pilots, SEALs, and others. A maintenance crew patched bullet holes in a helicopter, while another group played touch football on the taxiway next to them.

One of the MEU's recon teams manned a position atop a hangar, and we climbed up for a look around. The air was hazy, filled with dust and smoke from a thousand burning trash piles and cooking fires. Scrubby trees ringed the runway, but otherwise the ground was bare, baked into cracks and fissures by the relentless sun. Nothing moved. Rudy Reyes and another Marine wore T-shirts caked with white sweat stains. With sunglasses and zinc-covered noses, they could have been lifeguards. Binoculars, a radio, and a sniper rifle lay between them. Recon Marines trained as observers. Sitting atop the hangar in Jacobabad was a perfect observation mission, albeit without the drama of snooping through enemy territory in the dark.

"You guys ever see anything interesting up here?" Marine asked as if he doubted the answer could be affirmative.

"There's an ambulance casing us," Rudy said. He stood and I noticed a drawing in his hand. He was sketching the airfield's perimeter, recording azimuths and distances to landmarks so he could call in mortars or air strikes with precision. "It has a red crescent on the door, and the shades are always drawn. They come by every day, and a guy with a camera snaps pictures from behind the shades. ISI, probably."

The Pakistani Inter-Services Intelligence agency had helped put the Taliban in power. We knew they were no friends of ours, but I was surprised to hear their surveillance was so bold. Officially, no American forces were operating in Pakistan at that time. When pressed, defense officials had acknowledged a small U.S. presence but stated that it was there only to provide logistical support or to launch search-and-rescue missions. We knew there was precious little difference between search-and-rescue and search-and-destroy.

"Do they watch you watching them?" Marine's interest was piqued.

Rudy shook his head. "We try to stay cool about countersurveillance. Only two Marines up here at a time during the day, and we keep a low profile. The real work happens at night. We patrol out near the town, plant motion sensors, that kind of thing." Recon's mystique had grown out of clandestine missions like those.

To daytime observers, like the men in the ambulance, the air base would have looked nearly deserted. Most Americans slept in the cool shade of the hangar, and the Marine positions on the lines were well camouflaged. Members of the Pakistani air force puttered around on scooters, selling cold glass bottles of Coke.

At night, the charade stopped. A full day's work was crammed into the frantic ten hours between sunset and sunrise. Aircraft landed at five-minute intervals, sometimes having flown nonstop all the way from the United States. Most of them were big cargo planes, carrying supplies for the war in Afghanistan. Jet fighters came and went, and so did Predator reconnaissance drones flown by the Air Force and the CIA. I was always unnerved to be walking down a taxiway and have the pilotless Predator roll past, eyeballing me with its movable cameras. Nighttime also brought more activity outside the airfield's walls. Strings of red tracer fire reached into the sky, and explosions rocked the dark town. Pakistani officers invariably claimed that these were wedding celebrations and cars backfiring. But we were under no illusions — Pakistan's support for the United States didn't extend much below President Musharraf. Life at Jacobabad took on the tone of spy versus spy.

A week into our stay, on an otherwise indistinguishable drowsy afternoon, a man wearing a traditional Pakistani *dishdasha* knocked on the door of the building serving as our company headquarters.

"I must speak to the senior American present."

Captain Whitmer was in a meeting, so I identified myself.

"Sir, there is a telephone call in our offices. Please come with me." His speech was exceedingly formal and lightly accented. A slight bow of his head followed the request.

I went with him across the field to a building I had not yet entered.

Whitewashed rocks lined the walkway, and a Pakistani flag was painted on the bed of stones surrounding a small sign announcing this as an operations center of the Pakistani air force. I knew the general story of the United States' relationship with Pakistan's air force. After paying the U.S. for twenty-eight F-16 fighters, it had received none of them following Pakistan's 1998 nuclear tests. But I hadn't realized the intensely personal effect this soured deal still had on Pakistanis.

Entering the dim ready room, I paused to let my eyes adjust from the sunlight outside. A dozen pilots in green flight suits lolled in chairs, smoking. Conversation stopped, and they stared at me. Taped to the walls were dozens of pictures of F-16s: flying, landing, taking off, flames shooting from afterburners. It looked like an eight-year-old boy's bedroom. The hangars at Jacobabad had been built for the expected jets. Now they sat empty. These pilots had been trained and transferred here to fly them. Now they sat idle.

I picked up the phone, overly conscious that I personified my nation's diplomatic bludgeoning. The line was dead. When I told my escort, he shrugged.

"What unit are you from?" This didn't sound like idle curiosity.

"The U.S. Marines."

"Which unit specifically? How many machine guns do you have?"

I pushed past him and back into the sunlight.

After nearly two weeks at Jacobabad, we were all getting restless. The company received warning orders for three different missions, but none of them launched. Everyone had a different euphemism for Afghanistan — "up north" or "over the mountains." We were fixated on it. On the ship, we had wanted to go ashore. But sitting at Jacobabad wasn't enough. We were so close but not doing anything. We felt like the second string and imagined other units doing all sorts of missions across the border. Our generation had been reared on the hundred-hour war, and we feared this one would end without us.

Early one evening, Jim and I sat on the porch of the building we used as our headquarters. It was incongruous, lounging there on wooden chairs in the dusk, looking out across a baked field to a distant line of trees. Except for the pistols strapped to our thighs, we could have been anywhere. A field ration heater gurgled at my feet, warming a ham omelet for dinner. I took a bag of M&M's from the MRE pouch and tore it open, reading a printed advertisement on the inside of the bag.

"I can enter to win tickets to the Olympics."

"Which ones?" Jim had opted to pass on dinner and was drinking coffee instead.

"Summer Games. Barcelona. *1992*. This fucking MRE is ten years old."

"Enjoy that omelet, bro."

Captain Whitmer joined us. He had just come from the nightly commander's meeting, and he was smiling. We were leaving Jacobabad as abruptly as we'd come. The next morning, the Army's 101st Airborne Division would relieve us, and we would fly back to the ship and prepare for a follow-on mission in Afghanistan. The Twenty-sixth MEU, sailing from North Carolina, was cutting through the Suez Canal to join us. Together, the two MEUs would be known as Task Force 58, commanded by Brigadier General James Mattis. I sat upright. Task Force 58 had been the name of my grandfather's unit at the Battle of the Philippine Sea. That night, we packed our gear, excited finally to be going up north, over the mountains.

"Tomorrow is Thanksgiving. Celebrate it on your own time." The *Dubuque's* captain spoke wryly over the ship's intercom, but his message stuck: we're busy out here, and it's no place for the comforts of home, even if they are only in your mind. I sat at the desk in my stateroom, catching up on paperwork. I had made the mistake of not bringing my laptop to Jacobabad, thinking we would be busy with missions. Now I waged war by keyboard, ensuring that Marines were promoted and evaluations written before we jumped off for our next stint ashore.

In spite of all the competing demands on everyone's time, the *Dubuque's* crew prepared a feast for us the following evening. We sat down at a wardroom table decorated with paper turkeys and plastic pumpkins. Turkey, mashed potatoes and gravy, stuffing, cranberry sauce, and apple pie. For a short time, we were able to pretend that life was normal again. We held hands around the table and said a prayer for our families at home, for the thousands of families celebrating their first Thanksgiving with an empty chair at the table, and for our comrades whose vigilance allowed us the simple gift of sharing a meal together. When we finished eating, I returned to my room to pack for the flight to Afghanistan.

Rucksack, flak jacket, ceramic plates to stop AK-47 fire, helmet, M-16 rifle, twelve magazines of 5.56 mm ammunition, M9 pistol with five magazines of 9 mm ammo, ten quarts of water, sleeping bag and Gore-Tex liner, fleece jacket, wool hat and gloves, face paint, first-aid kit, maps, blood chit, grease pencils, compass, GPS (Global Positioning System) receiver, toilet paper, eight-inch dive knife, two pairs of underwear, five pairs of socks, three T-shirts, one rain jacket, Pashto and Dari translation guides, disposable cameras, calculator, plastic transparencies, case of PowerBars, iodine tablets, earplugs, entrenching tool, picture of my family taken the Christmas before, camp stove, signal mirror, *Angle of Repose,* atropine injector, sunglasses, headscarf, toothbrush, electric razor, American flag, and a thousand dollars in twenties, just in case.

While I worked, I listened to a CD sent to me by a cousin in New York. It was a benefit concert held only a month earlier at Madison Square Garden, an outpouring of sorrow, rage, and resilience in response to 9/11. A New York firefighter named Mike Moran started the recording.

"All I can say, on behalf of my brother John and the twelve members of Ladder Three that we've lost, the twenty members of the New York City Fire Department football team that we've lost, and all the people from my neighborhood, my hometown, Rockaway Beach, Queens, New York, our friends, our neighbors, our relatives, they are not gone because they are not forgotten. And I want to say one more thing, in the spirit of the Irish people: Osama bin Laden, you can kiss my royal Irish ass."

A feeling of profound gratitude that I was in a position to get revenge for 9/11 surged through me. Its intensity was startling. It wasn't just a professional interest in finally doing what I'd trained so long to do. It was personal. I wanted to find the people who had planned the attack on America and put their heads on stakes.

Lifting my rucksack, I stepped on the scale and watched the needle spin to 365 pounds. Subtracting my body weight of 190, I was lugging 175 pounds on my back. I remembered a study I'd read at IOC warning that Marines couldn't carry more than 50 pounds and remain effective. Fifty pounds allowed me to carry ammo, or water, or radios, but not all three. It was just another case of theory dying in the face of practice.

After packing, I went down the passageway to TACLOG to listen as Charlie Company seized the desert airstrip in southern Afghanistan which would become known around the world as Camp Rhino. Rhino had been the code name for the field in October when Task Force Sword had parachuted in, and the name had stuck. I banged on the locked door, and a Marine let me in and updated me on the mission.

"They departed the *Peleliu* on time and are airborne right now. Scheduled to hit the deck there at 1700Z," he said.

1700Z was 2100 local, about thirty minutes away. VJ was out there, and I tried to imagine what was going through his mind. He was probably sitting in the back of a CH-53, watching the dark landscape flash past as they flew "nap-of-the-earth," following the contours of the ground to stay below radar coverage. I felt relieved but a little unworthy in the warm, bright room, drinking a mug of coffee. When we heard that the assault waves were safely on the ground, I went to bed. There was, after all, nothing I could do for VJ or anyone with him. They were on their own, as we would be soon.

I lay on my bunk, unable to sleep, thinking about the latest news. Intelligence had reported that the Taliban were negotiating surrender in Kunduz, under pressure from the Afghan Northern Alliance and American Special Forces. Unfortunately, nothing so promising was being said about Kandahar. Kandahar was the spiritual home of the Taliban movement and seemed to be shaping up as their Alamo. Our mission was to force the collapse of the Taliban there. A camp of four hundred hardened fighters was reported to the east of Rhino, and a Navy jet had a SAM launched at it near Lashkar Gah, north of Rhino. At the same time, the Taliban consul general had announced that "the fireworks would begin" in the United States during the last week of Ramadan in mid-December and that Americans would "die like flies." Eventually, I drifted off into an uneasy sleep.

The next afternoon, the company rode ashore on a hovercraft. I watched through a narrow window as we backed out of the well deck, past the edge of the *Dubuque*'s stern, and thought that this adventure would be over by the next time I saw that lip of metal. We dozed to the drone of the engines on the thirty-minute ride to the beach. It was dark when the doors opened, revealing a quiet cove. Three lines of small breakers lapped at the base of gentle dunes. Overhead, a nearly full moon cast shadows on the sand.

We boarded trucks for the eight-mile drive to the Pasni airfield. I sat on my pack with a group of Marines and talked as we rumbled up off the beach across a flat expanse of scrubby trees.

"So, sir, this is a pretty big deal, right? A battalion of Marines going into Afghanistan. People at home will read about this, won't they?" a Marine asked.

I assured him that they would. This was the deepest amphibious strike ever conducted by the Marine Corps — more than 440 miles from the ships to Kandahar. It was like staging from Boston and attacking Baltimore.

Every kilometer or so, we passed dirt intersections where roads branched off from ours and disappeared into the darkness. Two Pakistani sentries stood guard at each junction, looking like World War I doughboys with laced-up leggings and bolt-action rifles. I pulled farther inside my flak jacket, trying to keep warm. Even on the coast, the desert heat dissipated quickly after sunset, leaving only an empty, bone-chilling cold. After half an hour of stop-and-go bumping, we saw the lights of a runway and heard two C-130s on the ground. A small grove of trees resolved itself into light-armored vehicles (LAVs) and Humvees covered in camouflage netting. We had arrived at the Pasni airfield, the last stop before Afghanistan.

Life at Pasni had a peculiar rhythm. Gear and Marines piled up there to be flown to Rhino. Fear of surface-to-air missiles in Afghanistan limited flights to the hours of darkness. In Pakistan, we kept up the illusion that American troops weren't running offensive operations. That meant hiding in the stone hangars during the day, bored and sweltering. Once the sun set, the base burst into a frenzy of continuous movement. C-130s landed, loaded without even shutting off their engines, and disappeared back down the runway. Helicopters shuttled back and forth to the ships. Mountains of equipment moved from pile to aircraft to gone.

The night we arrived, the hangars were already full, so the platoon staked out a spot in a clearing next to one. I couldn't sleep and took a walk to explore. Strands of white lights decorated baked brick buildings, giving the place a strangely festive air. I expected to see tables set with red-and-white-checked tablecloths and people drinking wine beneath the trees. Instead, I saw only forklifts carrying pallets of ammo and sentries standing along the edges of the field, facing outward toward the darkness beyond.

Before sunrise, we woke up and moved inside. We sat in the hangar all day. I repacked my gear for the fifth time. Marines around me played cards, slept, and congregated near the doors to breathe fresh air and talk.

"So the Cobra pumps a rocket into the building, right there in downtown Tirana," one Marine was saying. "Civilians sitting around drinking coffee, reading the newspaper. Big fucking explosion, fucking concrete falling into the streets. And we're in uniform. 'U.S. Marines' right there on my chest. 'Marines' on the side of the helicopter. Can't just be like, 'Sorry, guys, I don't know what fucksticks are in that helicopter.'"

Another guy ratcheted up the intensity. "Mogadishu, brother. You ain't seen shit if you ain't been to the Mog. Skinny little fuckers running all over the place. Stoned outta their fucking heads on that leaf they chew. Khat, they call it. Makes them get crazy and shoot a lot. Stay away from the walls. Bullets travel along the walls."

From a different cluster of Marines came comic relief. "I'm riding down the main street in Pattaya Beach, two beers in my hands, two whores behind me, and we're on the back of an elephant painted pink. What? Yeah, I knew they were women. I grab-checked them. This wasn't my first fucking deployment."

As I eavesdropped, I realized that although they traveled a lot, they rarely saw the places they visited. Marines aren't travelers in the traditional sense. They view foreign countries either from behind a gun sight or through the haze of a night on liberty. Perspective skews to one dimension, as if the Marines are the players and everything else is a prop. The same would hold true in Afghanistan, I suspected.

We knew strikingly little about where we were going. No one had foreseen operating in this part of the world. We had packed for training in Thailand, Australia, and Kenya, liberty in the Seychelles, Hong Kong, and Singapore, and long-shot contingencies like a final solution to the Saddam problem. Afghanistan was literally not on our map.

We had been given hastily made Pashto and Dari "pointie-talkie" cards, which listed English phrases appropriate to our situation, such as "Drop the weapon, or I will shoot," and then gave both their written and phonetic translations. We had only rudimentary maps. Most American maps of Afghanistan dated from the Soviet occupation. Ours were large-scale with little detail and were plotted according to different data. Rhino was situated right at the intersection of four map sheets, which were rendered in three different scales and data. Finding your position on one map sheet was a simple task of plotting your GPS coordinates. Move a bit west onto another map sheet, though, and you had to move 141 meters north and 182 meters east to match the GPS coordinates with the point on the map. Farther north, and the correction was 130 meters south and 217 meters west. I lay in the hangar in Pasni, half-listening to the Marines' stories, committing all this to memory and hoping I wouldn't have to recall it under pressure.

Shortly after dark, Patrick came over and said, "Here's your ticket." He handed me a manifest sheet with the names and blood types of the Marines who would be on the plane. "We're on the nine-thirty shuttle to Kandahar."

# 13

THREE HOURS LATER, in the dim red light of the C-130's cargo bay, I sprawled on top of a huge rubber fuel bladder as we barreled north. Sitting on five hundred gallons of kerosene stoked my already overactive imagination. I tried to remember the maximum altitude of a shoulder-fired antiaircraft missile and wished I knew how high we were flying. Thinking of 1/1's peacetime slogan — "Safety is paramount" — I realized that priorities were changing. The Marines all played it cool. Some pretended to sleep; others read. But there was enough eye contact made and quickly broken to know it was a front.

We knew we were almost there when the airplane plunged and we floated a few inches off the floor. The landing gear slammed down with a thud, and the fuselage rocked back and forth as we slowed. Dust choked the cabin when the pilots dropped the ramp. My platoon suffered its first casualty when a private caught his leg in a piece of cargo webbing and broke his ankle before even touching Afghan soil.

We lugged our gear off into a frigid, barren landscape. The full moon washed the sand in silver all the way to the horizon. It looked like fresh snow. The crystalline air reminded me of the mountains, and I remembered that Rhino was 3,285 feet above sea level. After the C-130 spun around and roared off for Pasni, the runway lanterns blinked out, and we walked in darkness to a walled compound at the southwest corner of the field. One of the great topics of speculation among the Marines in Afghanistan was the origin of this camp. Ninety miles from Kandahar, more desolate than any place I'd ever been, Rhino was a short dirt runway and a complex of buildings enclosed within a white block wall. Guard towers studded the four corners. Inside the wall stood a high-ceilinged warehouse, a water tower, half a dozen smaller buildings, and a mosque. All were impressively constructed, with marble floors, granite countertops, new lighting fixtures, and white plaster walls. Paved roads flanked by brick drainage ditches connected the buildings. Some people swore that the CIA had financed it early in the campaign to capture bin Laden. Others claimed that it was the private falconing camp of an Arab prince.

The whole place had been shot up during the Sword mission a month before. Each guard tower had a single cannon hole in its roof — direct hits from the AC-130 Spectre gunship we had listened to from the *Peleliu*'s TACLOG. Heavy machine gun fire had raked most of the walls, and small arms casings littered the ground. Many of them were from AK-47s, indicating that whoever had been there had fought back.

We slept on the floor of the warehouse that night, waiting until daylight to move out and take our positions on the perimeter. Bravo Company manned the southeastern corner, with Charlie tied in on our left flank and Alpha on our right. My machine guns and assault section were attached to the rifle platoons to put more firepower out on the line, and Staff Sergeant Marine dug in his mortars behind the center of the company's position. Jim and I went in search of a spot with good visibility. Flat desert stretched almost unbroken to the horizon in every direction, but there was one lone hill next to the runway. We decided to climb it and check out the view.

Afghanistan is one of the most heavily mined countries on earth, so we kept one eye to the ground as we walked, even though a land mine inside the compound was almost unimaginable. While looking down at the ground, I spotted a piece of paper plastered against the dried husk of a bush by the incessant desert wind. I peeled it off. It was notepaper, the size of a thank-you card, bearing a photocopy of the famous picture of three firefighters raising the American flag over the rubble of the World Trade Center. Above them, in block letters, were the words FREE-DOM ENDURES. The flip side of the paper had the same photo, and the Pashto translation of the motto. It looked like a calling card left by Task Force Sword. I pocketed it.

The hill was too far from Bravo's lines to be useful to Jim and me, so we settled for setting up in the guard tower at the southeastern corner of the compound. It stood about thirty feet high, intact except for the shell holes in its peaked roof. From the top, we looked across Bravo Company's entire front — a perfect place to control mortars in a fight.

It would also be a perfect place for the enemy to shoot at, but lacking any alternative, we put that out of our minds.

We stood watch in the tower for almost a week. American aircraft continued pounding Taliban positions, and we often saw them high overhead, tiny fighters hanging on to larger tankers. Besides us, the only Americans on the ground were a few Special Forces teams farther north. They were all fighting in and near population centers — Kabul, Mazar-e Sharif, Kunduz. No one lived around Rhino. Our patrols went out every night and saw nothing. We watched from the tower all day and saw nothing. To be of value, we had to go where the bad guys were.

One afternoon in early December, Jim stood watch while I lay on the floor of the tower to write letters to my two younger sisters. A sentence into the first one, I fell asleep. Thudding footsteps on the spiral steel staircase woke me an hour later. Three women and a man, all Navy doctors, poked their heads above the floor. They were anesthesiologists and trauma surgeons, sent to Afghanistan from San Diego's Naval Medical Center with thirty hours' notice. They wore their pistols self-consciously.

"What do you guys do up here?" The woman's glance took in our binoculars, maps, and arsenal of weapons piled in the corner.

"Give you all three or four minutes' early warning before the human wave assault," Jim answered blithely.

She blinked but didn't smile.

"So why all the doctors?" I tried to deflect more questions by asking one of my own.

A man with the carefully gloved hands of a surgeon explained that the nearest trauma facility was in Oman, about four hours away by C-130. With a growing American presence in Afghanistan and correspondingly more casualties, higher command had decided to set up a tented operating room in Rhino's courtyard.

"We can perform three simultaneous lifesaving surgeries," he said.

Jim and I nodded gravely, unsure whether this was meant as reassurance or merely information.

The doctors took a last look from the tower and retreated down the stairs. The surgeon, looking over his shoulder, said, "We hear you're leaving soon. Good luck up north. We'll be here if you need us."

That one was definitely meant as reassurance.

\*    \*    \*

Heading north was news to Jim and me, so we called Staff Sergeant Marine to take our place in the tower and went to visit Captain Whitmer at company headquarters. As we walked across the sand toward the olive-drab tent hidden in the dunes, a figure approached us with an unusual collar insignia glinting in the sun. It didn't look like a bar or an oak leaf.

It was a star. General Mattis had arrived to take command of Task Force 58.

"Good afternoon, sir." Our greeting tried to make up in vigor what it lacked in salutes, since Marines in the field never salute officers for fear of attracting enemy sniper fire. That seemed unlikely here, but it was policy nonetheless. I certainly didn't want to be reamed out by the general for a life-threatening show of respect.

"Good afternoon, young warriors." General Mattis stopped to speak with us. Of slender build and wearing glasses, he carried his pistol in a leather shoulder holster. Without preamble or small talk, he praised our mission in Afghanistan. "You need to know how much you've already accomplished by being here. You prove that the United States has the balls to put troops on the ground in Afghanistan. You've emboldened the Northern Alliance to renew its pressure on the Taliban and al Qaeda in Kandahar. You've reassured Americans at a time when they sorely need it."

He shook our hands in the way that generals do, grasping us each behind the elbow for emphasis. Part of me wanted to be unimpressed, but Jim and I both walked a little taller toward the headquarters tent.

The next afternoon, we climbed the stairs to the task force COC and pushed through the plastic sheet doorway into the warmth and light of the crowded room. The effect was all cheer and goodwill after the cold emptiness of the desert outside. The doctors were right: we were heading north the next day. The plan was mostly set, and platoon commanders were brought in only for the final confirmation brief.

Computer stations filled the back corner, and track lighting overhead bathed laminated maps taped together across the longest wall. Rifles were stacked by the door like umbrellas. Forty infantry officers, helicopter pilots, SEALs, Australian Special Air Service operators, and CIA liaisons crowded around in a whatever-keeps-you-warm assortment of fleece jackets and skullcaps. Most sat on piles of carpets, which outnumbered chairs by two or three to one.

Captain Eric Dill, commander of the recon platoon, held his face six inches from the map, tracing a line with his finger. Dill shaved his head bald and had a reputation for frankness and good analysis. I joined him.

He greeted me with "One vehicle per minute at night."

"What?"

"Surveillance assets report an average of one vehicle each minute on this stretch of road between sunset and sunrise." He pointed to a black line snaking west from Kandahar toward the town of Lashkar Gah.

"Who are they?"

Dill arched an eyebrow. "How many Afghan farmers have you seen tooling around in Toyota pickup trucks?"

I hadn't seen any Afghan farmers. I hadn't seen any Afghans at all. But I knew that the Saudis had sold the Taliban several hundred Toyota pickup trucks. They weren't quite as identifiable as a tank with a Taliban flag painted on the side, but they were close.

The square-headed MEU operations officer called the room to order. We minimized note taking in secret briefs, so I rolled my watch cap above my ears to hear better.

Australians worked in the Helmand River valley to our west. Joint Special Operations Task Force South, made up of SEALs and Special Forces, operated along the Pakistani border to our east. Opposition leader Hamid Karzai continued to pressure Kandahar from the north, and another opposition commander, Gul Agha Shirzai, was moving aggressively toward the city from the eastern town of Spin Boldak. His fighters had captured a bridge only seven kilometers from Kandahar International Airport the previous afternoon. The Taliban and al Qaeda were reported to have nineteen thousand supporters in Kandahar.

An intelligence analyst wearing jeans and a flannel jacket pushed his glasses back on his nose and stepped to the center of the room. But for the pistol on his hip, he could have been in front of a college class. He predicted that Kandahar would collapse within a week, certainly by mid-December. The Taliban were expected to defect and run for home, some to Pakistan, some to Iran, and many to the hills around Kandahar. Al Qaeda, by contrast, would be more ruthless. Many fighters would prefer death to surrender.

"We'll give it to 'em," the operations officer said, then continued briefing the plan. Within an hour, a force of recon Marines would depart Rhino to drive north nearly one hundred miles. By the following morning, they were expected to identify a landing zone and a site for a patrol base near the highway between Kandahar and Lashkar Gah. LAR and CAAT, the light-armored reconnaissance company and combined anti-armor teams, would join them that afternoon. Their LAVs and Humvees would provide the bulk of the force's punch. My platoon and a rifle platoon would follow via helicopter late that night or early the next morning. Together, we would be known as Task Force Sledgehammer. Our mission was to interdict traffic on the highway to prevent the Taliban and al Qaeda from escaping the Northern Alliance onslaught against Kandahar. Despite the task force's name, we would be the anvil to Hamid Karzai's hammer.

Locking eyes with me and the other young commanders in the room, the operations officer finished with a recap of the "Five Bullets" that every Marine in our platoons had to know: mission statement, challenge and password, rules of engagement, lost Marine plan, and escape and recovery plan. It amounted to knowing what we were doing, how not to get killed by our own people, how to ensure that we were killing only bad guys, and what to do in case we got lost.

The brief ended, and the men in the room disappeared into the dark to make their final preparations for the day to come. Eric and I stood by the compound gate. As I pulled gloves from my pocket, I asked him, "What do you think — good aggressiveness or a bridge too far?"

Eric reflexively tugged on the magazine of the M4 rifle slung across his chest. "We're way outnumbered, that's for sure. But with all our airpower, it shouldn't be a problem. I think we have to kick somebody's ass once, and then word gets out."

Later that night, I walked my platoon lines to check on the Marines. After midnight, there was no ambient light within a hundred miles and probably fewer than three dozen internal combustion engines. The air was so clear that the Marines on patrol would report headlights or campfires on the horizon, only to realize that they were watching stars rise.

My first stop was the mortar pit, where I found Staff Sergeant Marine on watch while his Marines slept.

"Evenin', sir," he said.

"Good news. Day after tomorrow, we're flying north. Just third platoon and us, and some other parts of the BLT. I'll have more details tomorrow."

Marine took the news with a quick nod, leaning to spit a stream of tobacco juice into the sand. "Good. The sooner we kill 'em, sooner we go home."

"What happened to all that talk about 'golden memories and no ghosts'?"

"That time is past. We're committed now. No more pray for peace. Now it's shoot to kill. Fight to win."

I shivered and hoped that Marine would attribute it to the wind. I changed the subject. "You reading anything good right now?" Marine was an avid reader, and we often traded books.

"Funny you should ask, sir, funny you should ask." He reached into his pack and pulled out a paperback. In the moonlight, I read "Rudyard Kipling" on the cover. "I'm not much for poetry, but this is almost enough to convert me:

> "When you're wounded and left on Afghanistan's plains
> And the women come out to cut up what remains
> Jest roll to your rifle an' blow out your brains
> An' go to your Gawd like a soldier."

"If I'm wounded, Staff Sergeant, and you fuckers leave me on Afghanistan's plains, I'll put my last bullet between your shoulder blades before I put it in my own head," I replied.

Marine laughed and shot another stream of brown saliva into the sand. "I expect you will, sir." He paused and added, "Even Hadsall might've done that."

I continued down the line to see the rest of the platoon. A white halo surrounded the moon, looking like an iris around a pupil. The moonlight cast my shadow across glowing sand, again reminding me of new snow. Normally, I chafed under the twenty-pound weight of my flak jacket, but now it was the only thing keeping the icy wind off my skin. I imagined the chill air pouring off glaciers high in the Hindu Kush and racing across miles of desert without a tree to slow it down.

One of my machine gun teams was dug in with Patrick's platoon, anchoring the far flank of the company's lines. They were in the middle of Sergeant Espera's squad, the former repo man with whom I'd flown into Pakistan on the Sword mission. For a few hours each night, Espera turned one of his holes into the company's social center, brewing coffee and debating the issues of the day with all comers. I slid into the hole, and Espera caught me up on the night's discussion.

"Sir, we're talking about Lindh. These guys" — he nodded at the other Marines in the hole — "think he's a freedom fighter."

John Walker Lindh, the so-called American Taliban, had been captured the week before at Qala-i-Jangi prison in northern Afghanistan. Now he was imprisoned in a metal container a few hundred yards from Espera's hole.

"And what do you think?" I asked Espera.

"Traitor. And the most vicious kind. He turned his back on the society that raised him, that gave him the freedom and idealism to follow his beliefs."

"But what was his crime?" I goaded Espera, happy to play devil's advocate. "Other than being in the wrong place at the wrong time?"

"Joining the Taliban. Claiming to be a member of al Qaeda. Shit, sir, if that ain't enough for you, his buddies killed a Marine!" Mike Spann, a CIA officer and former Marine captain, had been killed shortly after interrogating Lindh. "If my grandma killed a Marine, she'd be on my shitlist."

Espera turned serious again. "We're young Americans out here doing what our nation's democratically elected leaders told us to do. And he's fighting against us. Why's that so hard to figure out? And already the press is bitching about how he's being treated. He's warm. He's protected. He eats three meals each day and sleeps all night. Do I have that? Do my men have that?"

"Their freedom to voice stupid opinions is part of what we're fighting for," I said. It was well after midnight, and I still had more positions to check on, so I climbed out of the hole as Espera and the other guys resumed their debate.

Farther down the line, in the middle of a gravelly flat near the runway's end, I approached another fighting hole, careful to come from the rear and listen for the verbal challenge. It was an assault rocket team, and there should have been two Marines awake. In the moonlight, I saw three heads silhouetted against the sky. I slid down into the hole with a rustle of cascading dirt. General Mattis leaned against a wall of sandbags, talking with a sergeant and a lance corporal.

This was real leadership. No one would have questioned Mattis if he'd slept eight hours each night in a private room, to be woken each morning by an aide who ironed his uniforms and heated his MREs. But there he was, in the middle of a freezing night, out on the lines with his Marines.

General Mattis asked the assault men if they had any complaints.

"Just one, sir. We haven't been north to kill anything yet."

Mattis patted him on the shoulder. I had heard that he was old school, that he valued raw aggression more than any other quality in his troops.

"You will, young man. You will. The first time these bastards run into United States Marines, I want it to be the most traumatic experience of their miserable lives."

# 14

TURBINES WHINED in the predawn darkness. Pure potential energy, building, storing, promising to go kinetic on the thundering gallop north. Blue static electricity spun off the rotor blades as the platoon ducked aboard. I climbed forward to the space between the pilots' seats and plugged into the intercom. We had met the night before to rehearse the mission, so there wasn't much to say. A platoon commander's only job on a flight like this is to track the pilots' navigation and make sure they drop us in the right spot. It also pays to have some situational awareness outside the helicopter in case the bird is forced down and the Marines have to shoot from the hip.

As always, we lifted off hesitantly. The big Super Stallion rocked back and forth while inching upward. A cloud of dust, the frenzied rotor wash, enveloped us. Suddenly finding its purpose, the helicopter's nose dropped, and we blew through the murk, seeing the horizon again and picking up speed. Two more birds followed close behind.

We flew low, rising and falling with the contour of the hills. Our destination was one hundred miles due north, just outside Kandahar, one hundred miles from the nearest Americans. I had read enough about Afghanistan to know that helicopters had an uninspiring history there. The Soviets had been wearing down the mujahideen until the CIA introduced Stinger missiles and turned the tide of the war. A Stinger is small enough to pack on the back of a donkey and homes in on an aircraft's hot exhaust. In 1986, an Afghan commander named Engineer Ghaffar fired the first Stingers of the war and blew three Soviet Hind helicopters out of the sky near Jalalabad.

Marines call the CH-53 "the Shitter." I'd heard two different explanations for the nickname. One was that mortar fire destroyed a CH-53 on the ground at an airfield in Vietnam; the wreck became a makeshift latrine, and the name stuck. The other story was simply that the big bird poured out so much hot, smoky exhaust. I imagined flocks of Stingers chasing that heat signature and hoped the former explanation was the right one.

My paranoid sightings of Stinger teams behind every hill resolved themselves into trees, shepherds, and at least one camel. We saw remnants of the Soviet occupation — the circular berms of artillery positions and rusting trucks staining the soil red. Roads cut across the desert, many showing tread marks from tracked vehicles, tanks perhaps. The United States had no tracked vehicles in Afghanistan.

Behind me, thirty members of the platoon sat facing one another on two rows of fold-down canvas seats. Their packs were piled between them. Gunners stood in the open doors, crouched behind .50-caliber machine guns, their visored heads stuck out in the slipstream. One clamped an unlit cigar in his jaw. I wondered idly what would happen if they started firing. Bursts of spent shell casings would fly through the cargo bay, whipped along by the wind to burn any skin they touched.

The pilots talked back and forth, monitoring gauges and pointing out potential threats of rising terrain and figures on the ground. I was irrationally reassured by the fact that they were on edge, too. I looked out the side of the Plexiglas windscreen at the other helicopters. They flew impossibly low, throwing plumes of dust into the sky behind them. This made us more visible from a distance, but flying low and fast meant that we would be past a gunner before he had time to see us, aim, and fire. At least I hoped so.

The GPS made it easy to track our progress. Even without it, dark mountains on the horizon announced our emergence from the flat deserts of the south. Their jagged regularity conjured up dragon's teeth and welcomed us to the Afghanistan of myth and legend: Alexander the Great, the Great Game, the Hindu Kush. Looking at the snow, I thought that nature could be as deadly as any terror network. I'd felt this way in New Hampshire's White Mountains, usually in the late fall, racing darkness to the trailhead, aware that being caught on the mountain overnight meant losing fingers, or even worse. Our canvas desert boots weren't designed for tromping through snowdrifts. We had only light jackets and thin gloves. Nights at Rhino had been uncomfortably cold; in the mountains, they would be dangerously so.

"Five minutes!" I extended an open hand to the seated Marines. Goggles down, weapons loaded, packs grabbed by a strap for a quick drag down the ramp. Pocket the map, turn on the radio, last savor of sitting here, last comforting illusion of a short hop to safety.

"Thirty seconds!" Standing now, thanking the aircrew, removing my headset. The blades' pitch changed as we flared to land, the smooth whir becoming a choppy clatter. Nose up, tail down, and the thump of landing gear settling onto the ground. The ramp dropped, and the platoon ran out, fanning to secure a perimeter around the landing zone. The other two birds followed their leader, and two more streams of Marines arced into the circle. I bent my head and closed my eyes as the climbing helicopters blasted us with sand. They turned south and left us in a growing silence.

LAR and the recon teams already manned positions on a rocky rise two kilometers away. Our two infantry platoons completed the package. We shouldered our packs and moved to join them. It was colder here, less than a hundred miles north but much higher in elevation. A sharp wind rustled the carcasses of plants still upright in the ground. Others rolled along like tumbleweeds in an old Western. Afghanistan's rugged, spare beauty reminded me of the deserts of Nevada and Arizona. That beauty can overwhelm a person when its immensity isn't tempered by a lodge or a campfire. Infantrymen feel the immensity. They are part of the landscape, not observers of it. No windshield or cockpit separates them from the mountains and the wind. The sense of space and time is like gazing at the stars.

Staff Sergeant Marine organized the platoon's digging while I joined the other officers for a brief in the tiny tent that served as the battalion's traveling command post.

"Welcome, Bravo Company, to Patrol Base Pentagon." The battalion commander, who went by "Shaka" in honor of the famed Zulu warrior, had been awaiting our arrival. His brief was triaged — most vital information first. Aerial surveillance reported a radar dish to our south and a multiple launch rocket system (MLRS) to our north. An MLRS is a set of rocket tubes on the back of a truck. It can obliterate a square kilometer. First priority for the battalion was to learn more about those threats. The colonel sent Jim along with an LAR patrol to check on the radar and recon to investigate the MLRS.

The next priority was a rough outline of our short-term plan. A few klicks to our north was a river, its banks dotted with villages and farms. The highway from Kandahar to Lashkar Gah paralleled the river on its north side. That night, according to the colonel, our little band of Marines was slated to be General Tommy Franks's main effort. Franks commanded all American forces from the Horn of Africa across the Middle East to central Asia. All eyes would be on us. We would patrol the highway to interdict traffic and send a message to the Taliban.

"Go after them, gentlemen," the colonel said, pointing at the young commanders along the sides of the tent, "until they fear us more than they hate us."

We expected to continue this tactic for the next several nights, probably moving the patrol base each day to make it more difficult for anyone to attack us. When Kandahar fell to the Northern Alliance, a portion of our force would move to secure the airport there in order to replace the runway at Rhino with something larger and more permanent. The colonel couldn't speculate on possible missions more than a few days out. Our enemy would adapt as we adapted, so we couldn't expect to set the agenda. We would initiate as much as we could, but we'd also have to respond to the other guy's moves.

I was still in the tent when the LAR patrol, with Jim in command, reached the reported radar site.

"Shaka, this is Cossack. We've reached the location of that reported radar dish. It's a tree."

"Negative, Cossack. We had good reporting that it was a radar, maybe disguised. Take another look."

I imagined Jim cursing and running his hands over the bark.

"Shaka, Cossack. Roger, we checked again. It's definitely a tree."

Recon found that the MLRS was actually an MLRS, but it was unusable, probably rusting in place since the Soviet withdrawal twelve years before. For the moment, Patrol Base Pentagon was safe.

Jim and I occupied the highest crag on the rock pile the battalion surrounded. We lined up our laser range finders, rifles, binoculars, and scopes for easy use. Then we began to dig. We rotated digging and watching over the valley beneath us. I dug while Jim stood watch, and then we switched. The sand was dry and loose between the rocks, but digging was slow. We didn't have full-size shovels, only collapsible entrenching tools that attached to the outside of our packs. By prying rocks from the ground, we built a parapet in front of our deepening hole and soon had a protected vantage point overlooking the valley.

"People down there are checking us out." Jim pointed out along a rocky ridge that extended below us into the valley. Two figures peeked from behind a boulder. I focused my binoculars on them. Young guys, maybe our age, dressed in traditional *shalwar kameez*. I didn't see any weapons.

"Probably shepherds or villagers from down by the river. Maybe they saw our helicopters."

We watched shadows in the valley lengthen in the dusk. The wind picked up, and the temperature plummeted. My thin gloves had holes in all the fingertips, and I resolved to fix them as soon as I had time. We fantasized about building a fire, but nothing attracts bullets in the dark like a flame. So we sat and shivered and watched. After sunset, the eastern horizon flashed as if with distant lightning.

"Air Force is pounding the piss out of Kandahar," Jim mumbled around a piece of dried grass stuck in his mouth. He reclined on his elbows, perfectly at ease.

I tried to feel some remorse, some sense of the gravity of watching people die by the score. But I couldn't. The explosions' flickering yellow light reflected off the high overcast. Low rumbling followed the biggest flashes.

"Poor fuckers," Jim said. "Most of them have probably never even seen an airplane up close, and now they have JDAMs coming down their chimneys."

Jim was referring to the Joint Direct Attack Munition, a GPS-guided "smart bomb" that could hit targets with pinpoint accuracy. Our conversation was interrupted every few minutes by radio calls from the LAR patrol that had departed at sunset. The patrol was supposed to move down into the valley, where recon was looking for a site to ford the river, and then stop traffic along the highway. So far, the night had been a bust.

We listened in as the recon platoon got a Humvee stuck in the river's silt and spent three hours trying to free it. Meanwhile, Cossack was teaching us all a lesson about the unforeseen complications of real-world operations. In training, LAVs burn diesel fuel. But pulling up to the pump is not so easy in Afghanistan. We relied on aerial resupplies of fuel from the helos based at Rhino. They carried five-hundred-gallon bladders that the LAVs could pump from when they landed. To stream-line our logistical tail, all the vehicles burned JP-8, the same aviation kerosene burned by the helicopters. But JP-8, being cleaner than diesel, burns hotter and faster.

"Shaka, this is Cossack. We're burning fuel at an unbelievable rate. I'm almost at half a tank, and we haven't even crossed the river yet."

Shaka aborted the mission, and the LAVs whined back into Pentagon long before dawn. Our night as the main effort had been a frustrating waste.

Two nights later, I shook Jim awake shortly before midnight.

"Your watch, man."

Our new hole was perched on a sandy ridge, hundreds of feet above the river and the highway. We had moved from Pentagon to reduce the roundtrip time and distance for the patrols. I had gone on the last one, the night before. We had sat near the highway for two hours, unable to find any targets. Another fruitless mission. But this night looked more promising. I had watched throughout the evening as lights winked out in the windows of the houses clustered in trees along the riverbanks. Around dusk, traffic began to move on the highway — trucks mostly, traveling west from Kandahar.

This patrol base, perfectly situated for defense and observation, had one crucial flaw: the high ridge obstructed line-of-sight radio commu-nication between the colonel and the patrol. Jim and I, with our radios and antennas, sat right on the edge of the ridge. We had a clear shot to the patrol on the highway and to the headquarters tent a few hundred meters down the slope behind us. We became the radio link between the two.

After climbing out of his sleeping bag, Jim hopped into the hole, rub-bing his hands together, and I briefed him. "Cossack is moving toward the highway for interdiction. A recon team, Quizmaster, is looking for a ford site on the river. Patrol doesn't want to come back the same way it went out. A Huey-Cobra mixed section should launch from Rhino soon to be on station for a couple of hours while they're stopping traffic. And it's freezing."

Jim took the radio handsets, and I clapped him on the back. I shook out my sleeping bag and shimmied in, zipping it up to my neck. The only sound as I closed my eyes was a subdued chirp each time Jim keyed the handset to relay a message.

Less than an hour later, he woke me with a shake. By the time I sat up, Jim was twenty feet away, dropping back into the hole. "Get dressed, bro. Shit's about to go down."

Climbing out of my bag, I caught my breath, as if I'd jumped into a cold river. I rushed into my jacket and hat, Kevlar vest, and gloves. The temperature was probably only in the twenties, but the cold had a way of seeping inside you and draining your warmth. We'd been living outside day and night for weeks, without fires or showers or roofs and walls to protect us from the weather.

A high overcast had blown in, and a cold wind whipped across the ridge, flapping my jacket as I struggled to zip it. Airpower was our lifeline, and we scrutinized the clouds like aspiring meteorologists. They looked high enough to have little effect on us. From left to right, I scanned the sweep of dark horizon. No lights visible. No sounds. No immediate threats. Jim juggled the radios, briefing me between message relays. The raid force was in place down on the highway. The LAVs sat back off the road, with recon closer to the pavement. They had strung a piece of concertina wire across the highway to stop traffic. A Navy P-3 surveillance plane reported a vehicle approaching the roadblock from the direction of Kandahar.

"Where's that mixed section?" I wanted the comfort of a pair of attack helicopters nearby.

"They crashed, bro."

"*What?*"

"Heard on the radio that at least one of them crashed on takeoff at Rhino. So, yeah, they're not coming."

We watched from the heights, trying to see the LAVs down on the dark plain. Headlights approached from the east and became a Toyota pickup truck. Seeing the wire, the driver slowed, then gunned the engine. He succeeded only in wrapping his axle with wire, and the truck slid to a halt near the Marines. A recon team approached the truck. Their translator told the men to put up their hands.

Instead, two figures in the truck's bed sat up from under blankets and raised AK-47s. The Marines opened fire, killing all the men in the truck. Fuel and ammunition ignited. Rocket-propelled grenades (RPGs), lying in the bed, cooked off, streaking wildly past the LAVs. I watched the tracer fire in the dark, tendrils of red drawn across a black canvas.

With dead bodies sprawled on the pavement and the truck now engulfed in flames, the Marines on the scene hurried to put some distance between themselves and the ambush site. As they scrambled to free an LAV, spinning helplessly in soft sand, the battalion radioed a warning from the P-3: two more vehicles approaching from the east. Down on the highway, the forward air controller set up his laser marking system. A minibus and a dump truck, carrying dozens of armed men, stopped a few hundred meters short of the burning wreckage.

The Marines hunkered down in the shadows, eager to avoid a fair fight. The forward air controller whispered into his radio, talking a Navy jet onto the target. I heard its engine pitch change to a high whine as the pilot dropped the jet's nose, accelerating, putting the trucks in his sights. Two five-hundred-pound bombs dropped off the wings and whistled through the dark sky. I watched the jet's glowing afterburners fade into the overcast. Ducking in anticipation, I instinctively closed my eyes.

I had seen dozens of air strikes in training, dropped thousands of pounds of ordnance in the Nevada and California deserts. But this was real. Three, two, one . . . I counted down to the bombs' impact. The concussion cracked past. Two trucks full of Taliban soldiers disappeared in the flash, leaving only twisted metal and charred lumps of flesh on the highway.

# 15

THE RAID FORCE MADE a triumphal return to Pentagon in the predawn darkness. Weeks later, General Franks would send the MEU a note declaring that its prowess as a "power projection strike force was superbly demonstrated" that night. I laughed when I read the accolade. I hadn't thought of a few buddies with rifles as anything so grand as a "power projection strike force."

Just before sunrise, in the coldest hour of the day, Jim relieved me at the radios, saying, "Don't touch your rifle without gloves on." He opened his fingers to show me a palm missing a quarter-size piece of skin. "Cold stuck me right to it."

Without even taking my boots off, I lay on the gravel and pulled my sleeping bag over me. I had slept only one hour in the past twenty-four. Thirty seconds later, Jim stood above me.

"Don't shoot the messenger, but Shaka wants the platoon commanders at the tent for a brief."

"When?"

"Three minutes ago. Sorry, bro. I must have missed the first call."

The wind cut through my skin and I was nearly blind with exhaustion as I stumbled down the ridge. I remembered a night march at Quantico when I'd fallen asleep in midstride and woken up on the pavement with bloody hands. This was why our training had emphasized fatigue. War pares existence to its core — little food, little sleep, little shelter. The only thing I had in excess was stress.

A dozen people packed the tent. Body heat warmed it, and the generator-powered bulb overhead made the place almost homey, a long way from the dark holes up on the ridge.

"We're closing the ring, gentlemen," Shaka said. He looked tired, too. "Karzai is close to Kandahar. Shirzai is in part of the city. Intel thinks Mullah Omar fled to Pakistan, but Kandahar is still important to us. As you all know, it's the spiritual capital of the Taliban. And we need that airport."

He paused for a moment and turned a page in his green commander's notebook. "I don't normally call everyone in here for operations orders, but I wanted to look at each of you. I've had officers tell me they can't accomplish missions because their troops are too tired. Bullshit. *You* are tired, and those Marines are capable of more than they know. We had a two-hundred-meter gap in the lines last night. It's sloppy, and it's dangerous." He made eye contact with each of us. "Keep your heads in the game."

The battalion operations officer took over at a nod from the colonel and began to brief the day's mission. "At 0130Z 10 December 2001, BLT 1/1 conducts a movement to contact near Kandahar to seize key terrain astride Highway 1 in order to interdict al Qaeda and Taliban forces fleeing from the city."

I scribbled notes as the formal order was translated into plain English. "Gents, we're going to get up on that highway in broad daylight, and you will fuck up anybody who tries to escape until the CIA can sort out who's who. Everyone with a vehicle will drive up there. Bravo Company," he pointed at Captain Whitmer standing next to me, "will set up landing points in the desert here and fly up in two CH-53s."

Catching the major's eye, I asked, "Fire support, sir?" Dill's assessment had been right: outnumbered was fine as long as jets were overhead.

"Cobra escort during your flight, but they have only thirty-five minutes on station. Otherwise, Navy fixed-wing. Two F-14s, call sign Cosby 41. Four F-18s, call sign Noah 55. Six F-18s, call sign Gumby 21. They're on station for two hours."

The operations officer took a last look at his notebook and slammed it shut. "Two more things. Expect tactics of desperation — car bombs, suicide bombers, booby traps, attempted kidnappings. Also, there are known minefields three kilometers east and four kilometers west of where we're going, so don't walk all over the fucking place to take a leak."

After the rest of the force snaked down to the river in a winding convoy, I stood on a flat piece of desert with the platoon, cocking my head to hear distant rotor blades. We saw the Cobras first. They raced to our north, flying low and fast. I knew the Super Stallions would be close behind and turned on my strobe light. It was after sunrise, but a thick overcast blended the morning light and the desert into an indistinguishable gray.

I turned my head as the helicopters roared onto the landing zone we had marked, throwing dust and rocks everywhere. Staff Sergeant Marine and I stood at the tail ramp and counted the Marines aboard. Space was tight because a pallet of fuel cans and ammo was strapped in the center of the cargo bay. I would have to stand on the ramp.

The crew chief, grinning behind his opaque facemask, handed me a nylon strap and scrambled forward, over the laps of the seated Marines, to get behind his door-mounted machine gun. I looped the strap around my waist and clipped into the airframe overhead. With my boots at the ramp's edge, I looked down and watched the desert disappear in a cloud of dust.

We tilted slowly out of the cloud and accelerated, dropping back down to rooftop level. It was a five-minute flight. We passed over the houses I had watched from afar for so many days. The river was a muddy ribbon — sitting, not flowing. Cultivated fields of green, probably poppies, contrasted with the bland rock and sand all around. The sand stretched in an unbroken plain up to the edge of Highway 1. The highway looked like a driveway, no more than a lane and a half wide, the last paved road for two hundred miles to the west and south. A single line of crooked telephone poles stretched next to it as far as I could see in both directions. North of the highway, the ground changed abruptly to a rocky scree field extending a couple of kilometers to the base of the mountains.

We landed in the center of these rocks. Narrow arroyos reached like veins from the foothills down to the road. Beyond it, I saw the trees near the river, and beyond them, the dunes and the ridge where our patrol bases had been. This spot was much more exposed than our previous sites, in plain view of the highway and dominated by the mountains towering above us to the north. I had the unbidden thought of mortars crashing into the rocks, adding jagged flying chips to their explosions of shrapnel.

With the LAVs all around us, the platoon didn't have much of a security mission. I settled them into the deep crevasses, safe from indirect fire, to clean their weapons, eat, and rest while I searched for information about our next move. Commanders are always with the radio antennas, so I looked for the biggest bunch of antennas and walked toward them.

Halfway there, I noticed two Afghan boys walking toward our position, smiling and waving. Remembering the major's warning about suicide bombers, I called for the translator and joined him to intercept them. Lance Corporal Ajmal Achekzai had been working as a cook on the *Peleliu* before 9/11. After the attacks, he let on that he had been born in Kabul and spoke Pashto. Achekzai became the primary translator for the task force.

The boys wore flowing jackets over their baggy trousers. One had leather sandals, and the other walked barefoot on the rocky ground. They had bright, intelligent eyes. The barefoot boy smiled and reached out shyly to touch my hand. In Pashto, he told Achekzai we had been lucky to escape with our lives from the villages along the river.

"They are all Taliban."

I shook my head and laughed. "Those villagers told us they were happy to see Americans and that everyone else in the area was Taliban," I said. Achekzai shrugged. "Don't tell him that," I added. It wasn't a lieutenant's decision to play local politics. "Just thank them for their friendship and tell them we're impressed by the beauty of their country."

The boys smiled at the compliment and waved as they walked back across the gravel toward the highway. I turned to continue my walk toward the headquarters and thought of one more thing. "Achekzai, tell them to keep people away from our positions, especially at night. They could get hurt."

The battalion commander and his staff clustered in the center of three Humvees, sitting on campstools. A map of southern Afghanistan was spread at their feet, and puffs of cigar smoke dissipated in the cold wind. I waited a few feet away until the meeting ended and Captain Whitmer joined me.

"What's the word, sir?"

"We're staying here. Reports of Taliban in a village to the southeast and al Qaeda to the northeast. You know the drill by now. Set up a good integrated defense. Rest half your Marines at a time, and be ready to support any patrols or other missions the battalion decides to run."

"Right. So do nothing, but be prepared to do anything."

Captain Whitmer laughed. "Seems like a pretty good general rule."

\* \* \*

Two hours after sunset, we had just settled into our defense for the night. I was nestled in a narrow wadi, monitoring the radio and trying to clean my rifle by feel in the dark. A terse order crackled through the handset to pack up and prepare to move immediately. I slipped my rifle back together and ran to the colonel's Humvee. Several other Marines were already there. The operations officer updated us.

"Electronic intercepts are picking up Pashto radio chatter nearby. At least two groups of fighters know where we are and are moving into position to ambush us with RPGs."

One of the LAR officers spoke from the darkness. "So what? We're in a good defense. Even if they lob 'em, RPGs won't reach out much more than a klick. We'll just use the thermal sights on the LAVs and hose anyone who closes within a kilometer of us."

All suggestions that we should stay in place were brushed off. "The battalion commander wants to move. We're stepping off in fifteen minutes and going south of the highway, less than ten kilometers from here. Everyone with a vehicle is in it. Bravo Company is on foot."

I raised my hand. "Sir, I'm packing almost two hundred mortars and ten thousand rounds of 7.62. I need to get some of that weight into the vehicles so my platoon can keep up."

He replied that the vehicles were full and that adding more weight risked breaking the axles.

"OK, so we'll put the ammo in them, and some of their Marines can walk." This seemed logical to me.

"Lieutenant Fick, I don't want units all mixed up. Guys in the trucks stay in the trucks. You figure out a way to carry those rounds."

With all our other gear, that meant each of my Marines would be carrying almost two hundred pounds of equipment.

"Sir, that's bullshit." I worked to soften my angry words with a deferential tone. "I'll have Marines breaking ankles on these rocks, and then we're all fucked. Do you expect me to go back and tell my guys we're carrying two hundred pounds apiece while everyone else rides in trucks?"

The operations officer fixed me with his most authoritative glare and lowered his voice an octave. "Lieutenant, you're about to feel the wrath of a field-grade officer."

I stumbled back through the rock field to the platoon, cursing the operations officer, the Marine Corps, Afghanistan, and the fact that a well-armed force of Marines was running away from a few ragtag jihadis with RPGs. After all the talk about aggressiveness and taking the fight to the enemy, we were turning tail instead of going hunting or setting an ambush. I dropped down into the wadi, where Staff Sergeant Marine had taken over for me on the radio. He shook his head when I told him the plan.

"Running like this is a bad idea," I said, stripping off my extra clothes and stuffing them into my pack.

"Sure as Christ made little red apples," Marine replied as he stood to pass the word to the platoon.

The column formed up and began to move south across the highway and away from the mountains. Weapons platoon shuffled along next to the Humvees, struggling under the weight of weapons, flak jackets, packs, helmets, ammunition, water, food, radios, batteries, shovels, and bad attitudes. None of the Marines in the vehicles walked.

Each of my men carried his body weight or more. The ground underfoot was a jumble of head-size rocks, too large to walk over but too small to hop across. It was ankle-rolling hell. Faces gleamed with sweat in the moonlight. We crossed the highway within feet of the burned-out trucks from two nights before. I pulled the "Freedom Endures" picture of the firefighters from my cargo pocket and slid its edge into the metal frame of a truck skeleton, where it waved defiantly.

Near the back of the column, a machine gunner began to crumple beneath the gun resting across his shoulders like the yoke on an ox. I watched as a corporal, already carrying one machine gun, took it from him and threw it across his own shoulders. The two guns together weighed more than fifty pounds. I carried six mortar rounds in my pack, plus the radios and all their batteries. But most of the Marines carried even more. I thought of the operations officer sitting in his Humvee.

I thought, then, of my favorite time at Quantico, those moments in the bunk after we sang "The Marines' Hymn." Now, as I had at OCS, I sensed an outpouring of grit, pride, and raw desire to live up to the traditions we'd inherited. These Marines came from places like Erie and Tuscaloosa and Bedford Falls. The most junior of them earned nine hundred dollars a month. Some had joined the Corps for adventure, others for a steady paycheck or to stay out of jail. Now they all kept walking for one another.

I took one of the guns from the corporal and resolved that I would never again cut a corner in training or accept an excuse when it came to the physical fitness of my men. Captain Whitmer was right: train in bloodless battles to fight bloody exercises. Television commentators could pontificate from their climate-controlled studios about technology and the "revolution in military affairs," but out on the battlefield that night, long history marched unchanged into the twenty-first century. Strong men hauled heavy loads over rough ground. There was nothing relative about it — no second chances and no excuses. It was elemental and dangerous. It was exactly why I'd joined the Marines.

# 16

SHORTLY BEFORE CHRISTMAS, every conversation started with a whisper. Al Qaeda's top leadership, maybe including Osama bin Laden himself, was holed up in a cave complex near Tora Bora. It was rumored that we would be sent to capture him, "dead or alive," as President Bush had put it. Three days after the ambush on Highway 1, Task Force Sledgehammer had returned to Rhino. Kandahar fell, and the Taliban collapsed with it. American attention in Afghanistan turned to al Qaeda.

The Tora Bora mission was supposed to be a secret, but everyone seemed to be talking about it. The name lent itself to the lineage of Marine battles: Iwo Jima, Khe Sanh, Dak To. Tora Bora had the right flavor; it fit. On a night when neither Jim nor I could sleep, we stood in the tower, keeping watch over the desert and thinking about the mission. Tora Bora lay far to our north and east, in the mountains near Jalalabad, ten thousand feet above sea level. In December, the snowdrifts would be waist-deep, and night temperatures would fall below zero. There were no passable roads, and the mountains were too high for most of our helicopters to cross. They, and we, would be confined to the valleys, vulnerable to attack from the ridgelines above.

As I laid out these challenges, Jim was quiet, thinking. Finally, he said, "Do you think we'd get the reward if we caught bin Laden?"

After a week of swirling rumors, I began to suspect the mission was just wishful thinking by commanders who always wanted a bigger role in the game. Then the cold-weather gear arrived. We had shivered through a month of freezing nights, and there was never any talk of supplying us with the coats, socks, boots, and gloves the Marine Corps surely had stored somewhere. Now word spread quickly that a C-130 had landed with pallets of fleece jackets, down parkas, and thick winter gloves. This, too, I dismissed. Then the platoon was lined up and issued the gear. Wearing my new gloves, there was no more denying it. Maybe, I thought, we would go to Tora Bora after all.

On December 22, I woke up covered in frost. A heavy dew and freezing temperatures had coated my sleeping bag overnight, and it cracked as I sat up, sending little avalanches of ice onto the sand next to me. Tora Bora. It was my first conscious thought each morning. I stood up stiffly and hobbled toward the COC, willing the blood back into my legs. Captain Whitmer was there, studying a map.

Our plan had been refined. We would fly to Bagram and then on to Jalalabad. Part of the task force was already up there and had reported that the runway would support a C-130. From the Jalalabad airfield, we would move overland to two valleys near the Pakistani border. There we would set up blocking positions while special operations units called in air strikes on the caves where the fighters were hiding. If they tried to flee, they would run right into us. Captain Whitmer gave me a map of the valleys and told me to memorize it. This mission, once fantastic, was inching from possible toward probable with each passing hour.

I joined Patrick on Christmas Eve at a Mass near the end of the runway. It was nearly dark, and a couple of dozen Marines stood around a makeshift altar — a poncho liner thrown across stacked boxes of machine gun ammo. The chaplain was relaxed and wry, noting the old adage about there being no atheists in a foxhole. "I suspect many of you are more lapsed than my normal crowd, but given the circumstances, this can't hurt, right?"

We sang "Silent Night" and "O Come, All Ye Faithful." I closed my eyes and crossed the ten thousand miles to home, imagining my family doing the same thing. They would go out for Chinese food, an old tradition, and then to a party we'd gone to every Christmas Eve for more than twenty years. The night would end at Midnight Mass, where they would sing these same songs. I hoped they would know I was safe and wished I could tell them that most of my days were a walk in the sun.

Our service was interrupted by a line of airplanes thundering overhead. Each began as a drone far up in the dark sky. Because of the missile threat, planes arrived over Rhino at ten thousand feet. Then, with the safety of Marines below, the pilots flew a steep corkscrew down to their final approach. The C-130s flew in darkness until near the runway threshold, when they flipped a switch and bathed the field in light. Their landing lights stretched from wingtip to wingtip, like ten cars driving abreast. C-17s looked the same, but only through night vision goggles. Their landing lights were infrared, invisible to the naked eye.

Mass was over. Thinking about the night's long-range patrol out beyond Rhino's lines shattered my fragile illusion of peace. I had to get back to the tower to finish planning for it. Patrick and I walked off into the darkness together. We were both so busy with missions and our platoons that we rarely had time to talk.

"How you doing?" His tone invited a longer answer than the question usually did.

"Frustrated, man." I poured out all my bottled-up gripes — sitting in the static defense, running from the RPG teams, the operations officer's callous treatment of my platoon, sleeplessness, concern about the Tora Bora mission. All of it. Patrick stopped walking and turned toward me, cradling his rifle across his chest. He nodded encouragement and listened without interrupting as I continued. After so many weeks of wearing a stoic mask before the platoon and Captain Whitmer, bitching to Patrick was a relief.

"Feeling better now?" he asked with a smile, knowing that I did.

We shook gloved hands and wished each other Merry Christmas before returning to our platoons.

Christmas morning dawned clear and cold. The patrol had been uneventful, and I walked the lines to see the Marines. I thought some of the younger guys might have a hard time that day, but they were festive. A captured tumbleweed stood next to each fighting hole, pruned by hand into the triangular shape of a little pine tree. Candy and mini Tabasco bottles from MREs hung from the branches. There were even gifts. During the past week, Marines had squirreled away packets of cheese or pound cake — MRE delicacies — for their buddies. The mortar section, with great ceremony, presented me with a dog-eared porn magazine. I returned the favor, flipping two cans of Copenhagen into Staff Sergeant Marine's hands.

When I returned to the tower, Jim was standing over a cardboard box, looking disgusted. A Christmas card from the commander of U.S. Naval Forces in the Middle East, based in Bahrain, was taped to the outside. It was addressed to "U.S. Marine Platoon, Camp Rhino, Afghanistan." Inside were two dozen bags of microwave popcorn, an electric fan, and Jackie Collins novels with titles like *Hollywood Husbands* and *The World Is Full of Married Men.*

"Bro," he said as I climbed the stairs, "do you ever get the feeling that no one has a clue what we're doing out here?"

The next morning, I was called to the COC for a brief. Our mission to Tora Bora was canceled. No American forces would take part in the operation. Instead, our Afghan allies would do the job. There were already rumblings about most of the assembled fighters slipping away across the border into the wilds of Pakistan's North-West Frontier Province. Colonel Waldhauser said that fear of casualties had prompted the cancellation at the highest levels of the U.S. government.

Back in the tower, Jim kicked the wall when I told him the news. "Goddamn chickenshit decision. Casualties? What the fuck do they think happened on 9/11? This is our chance to get those bastards."

I agreed with him, and so did Staff Sergeant Marine. He heard us yelling in the tower and came up to see what was happening. "Afghan allies? We don't have any Afghan allies. We got Afghans who'll do what we say *if* it helps them and *if* we pay them to do it. Bin Laden will trade 'em a goat and escape."

With that mission went our dream of laying hands on America's most wanted man. But we felt relief, too. A winter fight in the high mountains against hardened mujahideen would have been ugly. They'd fought the Soviets on that ground for ten years. It was a measure of the mission's significance that the Marines knew all the dangers and still wished we'd gone.

The cold-weather clothing was collected, leaving us again to shiver through the nights on watch. But those nights were few. The Northern Alliance had routed the Taliban. They would probably live to fight another day, but their control of Afghanistan was over. Hamid Karzai was already positioning himself for a role in the replacement government. The Twenty-sixth MEU, the other half of Task Force 58, held Kandahar International Airport. Rhino had outlived its usefulness. The dirt runway required hours of maintenance each day just to withstand another night of landings and takeoffs. And the remote location, once a welcome boon to security, was now merely an inconvenience. We were told to prepare for our return to the ships.

Charlie Company was first out, then Alpha, LAR, and recon. By January 3, 2002, Rhino was almost empty. The entire MEU had either moved up to Kandahar or back to the ships. Bravo Company was alone. The afternoon our plane was scheduled to arrive, most of the company packed its gear and moved out to the runway. Captain Whitmer instructed Jim and me to stay in the tower and to leave the mortars set up until the plane was on the ground. We scanned the horizon in every direction but saw nothing moving. The air was cold and clear beneath a wintry overcast. A few snowflakes drifted down.

"This place is straight-up hell," Jim said as he threw a tiny Tabasco bottle into the sand beyond the tower.

"It'd be great to come back someday and explore, though," I replied. "Like old guys going to Normandy or Monte Cassino."

"Shit, bro, I'll be back when there's a golf course, a Hilton, and direct flights from Nashville. Until then, this place can fucking rot."

When a dark speck in the distance resolved itself into a C-130, Jim and I shouldered our packs, took one last look out across Rhino, and squeezed down the spiral staircase. The courtyard, once full of radio towers, cooking fires, and Humvees, was silent. We walked through the gate and pulled it shut behind us. I dropped the latch into place. Taking a last look inside, I thought I knew what astronauts had felt like leaving the moon. I would never be back.

Jim asked, "How long before the bad guys are back in this compound?"

"They'll be digging up our MRE trash before sunset tomorrow."

The Hercules blasted us with a prop wash of sand, pebbles, and kerosene exhaust. Captain Whitmer waited at the tail ramp, grabbing our shoulders as we climbed aboard. The C-130 rose off the runway at a steep angle, the pilots piping AC/DC's *Hell's Bells* through the plane.

Arriving on the *Dubuque*, we were corralled from the helicopters down into the well deck to be stripped and deloused. I stood with the platoon as a sailor blasted us with a hose, like a herd of cattle. After forty days without bathing, no one complained. I climbed, barefoot, up to my room to take a real shower. While we were ashore, someone in the ship's crew had taped a political cartoon to my stateroom door. It showed the backs of three armed Marines walking across a desert toward distant mountains. Above them was a scroll with the words "Peace on Earth," and below them a caption: "We're working on it."

Hot water melted caked grime from my face, and I had to shave twice to cut through the matted grit. Finally looking in the mirror, I could see the outline of my skull beneath my face. My eyes shone, bluer than normal, but they were sunk to the back of two caves. I had lost seventeen pounds. The fresh camouflage uniform felt impossibly soft. I was accustomed to cammies stiffened with sweat and dirt. Down in the wardroom, I nearly fell asleep while eating my third plate of spaghetti. But once I got into bed, I couldn't sleep at all.

I also found I couldn't stay inside for more than a few hours at a time. After living beneath the sky for six weeks in Afghanistan, the *Dubuque*'s cramped spaces pressed in even more than usual. So it was that I found myself on Monday, January 7, standing at the rail in a scuddy mist, taking in Kuwait City's skyline. The balls and spires had been made famous during the Gulf War, and I could have identified the city without knowing where we were. The *Dubuque* slid slowly up the harbor and into a berth, but our stay was short-lived.

A terrorist threat against U.S. ships in the Persian Gulf forced us offshore after only a few hours at the pier. Out past the harbor entrance, the three ships swung in a row on their anchor chains. Wind-whipped waves crashed against the bow. The view was better from out there anyway, and Patrick and I spent the evening talking over the snapping of flags against a novel backdrop of city lights.

"I'm still trying to figure out if we were in combat," Patrick said. His hair was long, his face chapped by a month of desert wind.

"If we have to ask, that probably means we weren't," I answered.

"Yeah, but where we were and what we were doing . . ." His voice trailed off. "That was some dangerous shit. Bombs and land mines and missiles."

"The official criteria are something like sustained ground combat where there's a grave danger to the individual."

Patrick exhaled. "So does that mean Americans won't be in combat ever again? It'll be JDAMs and Tomahawks and lasers? What about the guys on the ground who make all the high-tech toys work?"

Beneath us, on the dark water, landing craft churned back and forth through the night, loading the MEU's equipment aboard for the trip home. I was ready to leave the Middle East but regretted not having the chance to explore Kuwait City. It was that old Marine dilemma again. Like business travelers, we saw plenty of airports but never got a sense of the places we visited. I was even a little depressed, thinking I might never see this part of the world again.

\*　　\*　　\*

The *Dubuque* started the long trip home with a steel-beach picnic. For a whole day, the flight deck was transformed into a big backyard barbecue. Sailors flipped burgers and grilled chicken breasts. Smoke swirled out of the shelter of the superstructure, to be whipped away into nothing by the wind of the ship's movement. Music pumped over the loudspeakers — Bruce Springsteen, U2, and Johnny Cash. Two teams of Marines turned the stern into a football field, until a long pass sailed over the side and into the Indian Ocean. The best treat of all was two beers for each man, our first since that night in Darwin 127 days before. I held mine, one in each fist, for a few minutes, just savoring the cold sweat on the cans. As I was sitting in the sun, drinking beer with the stereo pumping, the frigid nights near Kandahar seemed far away. Already, the memories were starting to fade.

I was grateful for the *Dubuque*'s old boilers and top speed of under twenty knots. We all needed time to adjust after Afghanistan. We traveled south through the Indian Ocean, past Sri Lanka, and across the equator to the Antipodes. My insomnia subsided, and I began to gain the weight I'd lost. My windburn and chapped lips healed. A week in Perth was all sun, sailing, food, and drink. Sydney was the opera house, runs along the water, shopping, and swimming. In early February, we turned east, across the Pacific, for home.

Eric Dill and I met every afternoon to lift weights. It was in the *Dubuque*'s gym, beneath the American eagle sharpening its talons, that he first made me an offer.

"So, Fick, how'd you like to come over to recon?"

"Who's asking?"

Eric explained that he had spoken with First Recon Battalion's new commander and had recommended me as his own replacement. I was honored but unconvinced.

"Why should I?" I asked. I knew what recon offered but wanted to hear it from Eric.

"Autonomy." Eric widened his eyes as if the answer were self-evident. "You'll have a platoon of smart, mature, well-trained Marines. The best equipment. More training dollars. Freedom to run it the way you think it ought to be run."

"What about missions?"

"That's the best part, Nate," Eric explained. "Lots of guys live for the violence of being Marines. They thrive on it. I've never been that way, nor are you — I can tell." He sat down on a weight bench, swigging from a gallon jug of water. "When a recon team does its job well, it doesn't fire a shot. And the information it uncovers can save a lot of lives. When you do shoot, it's not just spray and pray. This is a thinking man's game. You should consider it."

Eric interrupted his pitch to do a set of curls. After dropping the weights, he added, "Your boss is coming over as the operations officer. Talk to him about it."

Captain Whitmer was reading *Code of the Samurai* when I knocked on his stateroom door. He invited me in to take a seat.

"Sir, Captain Dill says you're going to recon when we get back, and he invited me to take over his platoon."

Whitmer nodded, looking at me expectantly. It was typical of him to keep the news quiet, allowing events to unfold in due time. It seemed as if he'd foreseen this conversation weeks ago.

"Well, sir, why me?" Recon applicants usually had to try out and then pass a grueling indoctrination before even being considered.

Whitmer explained that recon's new commander wanted to bring the battalion back to basics. The recon community had gotten too caught up in "high-speed, low-drag" training such as parachuting and scuba diving. "This country's facing an era when units like recon may get used a lot. And it probably won't be the sexy stuff. It'll be the fundamentals you learned at Quantico — shoot, move, and communicate. We need young officers with hard infantry skills and experience. You're one of them."

Now I was excited. Saying goodbye to the platoon would be tough, but I would have to leave anyway. Officers did only one tour as infantry platoon commanders in order to make room for new guys coming in behind them. My other option was probably to be a company executive officer, the second-in-command, whose primary duties were paperwork and discipline. Going to recon would mean all the good things Dill had said, plus another year or two of command and the chance to deploy again.

"I'd be honored, sir," I said.

When we got home, I was going to recon.

We never returned to the country we'd left. I hadn't been in the United States since a month before the terrorist attacks, so the differences stood out. People seemed kinder, more considerate, and also edgier. I saw in them traces of what I had learned in the previous half year — a new appreciation of life's simple pleasures, of safety and friendship and family.

I made the requisite pilgrimages to Ground Zero and the Pentagon, and went to a ceremony on the South Lawn of the White House commemorating the six-month anniversary of 9/11. I saw mourning and sorrow, but also bluster. Posturing. People vowed not to interrupt their daily routines, not to let "them" destroy our way of life. My time in Afghanistan hadn't been traumatic. I hadn't killed anyone, and no one had come all that close to killing me. But jingoism, however mild, rang hollow. Flag-waving, tough talk, a yellow ribbon on every bumper. I didn't see any real interest in understanding the war on the ground. No one acknowledged that the fight would be long and dirty, and that maybe the enemy had courage and ideals, too. When people learned I had just come from Afghanistan, they grew quiet and deferential. But they seemed disappointed that I didn't share in the general bloodlust.

I was happy to get back to Camp Pendleton in March. I felt more comfortable being around other Marines. Most of 1/1's platoon commanders looked forward to a few months of downtime before moving back into the MEU training cycle. Patrick took over as CO of Bravo Company, and Jim went back to an artillery battery. Sitting on my desk was a stapled set of orders: "You are directed to report no later than 1200, 25 March 2002, to 1st Reconnaissance Battalion for Temporary Assigned Duty for a period of approximately 65 days." Recon, but only provisionally. First I had to survive the training.

# 17

EVERY MARINE THINKS he's the toughest guy in the room. Most will agree, though, that the toughest unit in the Corps is recon. Of 175,000 active-duty Marines, fewer than 3,000 serve in reconnaissance units. Recon lacks the cachet of the Navy SEALs and the Army Special Forces because a bureaucratic decision in the late 1980s kept recon out of the U.S. Special Operations Command. The Corps's leadership vowed that there would be no "special" Marines and chose autonomy over the command's money and missions.

The result is a slight inferiority complex manifested in brutally hard training. Recon selection begins with candidates whose paper qualifications are sterling — expert shots, perfect physical fitness tests, glowing recommendations from previous commanders. These performers are put through the two-week Recon Indoctrination Program, a nonstop battery of swims and runs led by a cadre of current recon Marines. The aptly abbreviated RIP pares the field by half. Survivors continue to the ten-week Basic Reconnaissance Course in Coronado, California. BRC trains the reconnaissance fundamentals of patrolling, observation, and communications. Its rigor cuts the class in half again. I knew a captain who'd been dropped from BRC after breaking his back during the course.

RIP and BRC taught me almost nothing. I had learned most of the tactics and technical information during my earlier training and in Afghanistan. But they imparted something even more valuable: legitimacy. BRC, for enlisted Marines, is the gatekeeper to recon. Graduation changes their MOS to 0321, "Reconnaissance Man." It's a rite of passage. By suffering through the same three months they did, I'd be a known commodity to them. I had been there, too. Earning rank was easy compared to earning spurs.

In June 2002, my BRC class returned to First Recon Battalion on the Friday afternoon of our graduation. As new recon Marines, we would go on to advanced parachute and scuba training, survival school, and specialized courses in foreign weapons, demolition, mountaineering, and others. We had ranked our preferences a few weeks earlier. I put "practical" training at the top of my list: special operations mission planning and a certification course to rig helicopters for inserting and · extracting recon teams with ropes and ladders. Running my finger down a scheduling board in the battalion's admin office, I stopped at the school written next to my name: advanced water survival. It had been my last choice. My one irrational fear was being trapped, powerless, underwater. Drowning. Someone had noticed, and starting at 0400 on Monday morning, that weakness would be beaten out of me.

With the Marines fighting alongside the Army in most recent wars, people tend to forget that the Corps falls within the Department of the Navy. It is fundamentally an amphibious force. The Combat Water Safety Swimmer Course, our instructors told us during the predawn brief, was designed to nurture comfort in the water through exposure to extreme discomfort. "We'll find your soft spot and make it hard." They promised to push our limits so far that exceeding them would probably kill us. "You will be, for all intents and purposes, drown-proofed." Listening to them, I felt sick. This was the course I had hoped to avoid, which was precisely why I was there.

"Hardness," I was learning, was the supreme virtue among recon Marines. The greatest compliment one could pay to another was to say he was hard. Hardness wasn't toughness, nor was it courage, although both were part of it. Hardness was the ability to face an overwhelming situation with aplomb, smile calmly at it, and then triumph through sheer professional pride.

A high white fence surrounds the pool at Pendleton's Camp Las Pulgas, isolating it from the rest of the world. Recon unit insignia cover the boards — skulls, scuba divers, and parachute wings with slogans such as *Celer, Silens, Mortalis*" — the Latin version of First Recon's "Swift, Silent, Deadly." A rickety wooden tower looms over the deep end of the pool. It narrows successively to three platforms — one at ten feet, one at twenty feet, and one at a dizzying thirty feet above the pool.

Across the tower's face in black block letters is the course's motto: IF YOU ARE STILL CONSCIOUS, THEN YOU HAVE QUIT.

We began each morning by swimming a few thousand meters. This was normally a daily workout for me, but here it was only a warm-up. Retrievals came next — sinking into fifteen feet of water to drag rifles, rubber bricks, artillery shell casings, and weights from the poolside gym back to the surface. The stated purpose was to make us "see Elvis on the bottom of the pool." As in every other part of the course, the real purpose was to create calm where once there had been terror.

One morning, I succeeded in getting my hands around a barbell holding two twenty-five-pound plates. I pushed off the bottom and slowly clawed my way toward the shimmering light above. Bubbles raced past as I kicked and grunted, each little exertion bleeding irreplaceable air through my nose and lips. My vision was gray when my head broke the surface. I opened my mouth to gulp and was knocked back under by a jet of water. The staff trained a fire hose on the heads of the surfacing Marines, pushing us back beneath the water. Drop your weight and you fail. I struggled to hold the barbell and kicked back to the surface. Vision shrinking to little gray spots at the end of black tunnels. Fear rising. Again the water knocked me under. No way to get back to the surface now. Sinking. Just as I went limp, a hand pulled me to the side of the pool. I still held the barbell in the crook of my elbows.

More laps followed, and then the legalized hazing called "water aerobics." The class lined up along the pool's edge while instructors commanded from the tower. On a whistle blast, we crossed the pool using whatever mutated stroke they ordered — underwater, no arms, wearing boots, carrying a barbell, wrists tied to ankles. When the last man clutched at the far wall, we recrossed the pool. Whistle. Swim. Whistle. Suffer. Whistle. Hyperventilate. Whistle. Black out. Water aerobics kept me awake at night. I didn't want to fall asleep because I knew I'd wake up only a few hours from the next session.

Twenty Marines started the class; eleven graduated. In its own way, those two weeks were as transformational for me as OCS had been. I faced a fear and beat it. Grabbing my diploma, I was buoyant, ready to return to recon and meet my platoon. But the battalion had other plans. Despite Captain Whitmer's assurance that First Recon wanted to avoid "high-speed, low-drag" training, I was handed an airline ticket and orders to Fort Benning, Georgia, where I would become a paratrooper.

\*      \*      \*

Recon had done exactly three real-world parachute missions in its entire history, and none since Vietnam. My three weeks at the Army Airborne school was time I could have spent working with my new platoon. I was noticing a trend in my career: train to lead a rifle platoon, but get a weapons platoon; train to raid the coastline in rubber boats, but go to war in a landlocked country; train to jump into patrols via parachute, but use boots or Humvees in the real world. It could be maddening, but I chose to see it as a tribute to flexibility. "Improvise, adapt, and overcome" was a Marine Corps mantra for good reason.

Airborne reminded me of OCS. We left our rank at the door. Aspiring SEALs, Special Forces troopers, Army buck privates, ROTC cadets, and recon Marines stood in formation each morning, doing push-ups and being berated by Army instructors in black hats. Their only name was "Sergeant Airborne."

"Give me thirty pushups! Fifty from you jarheads!"

For two weeks, they drilled us in muscle memory. Jumping from wooden boxes into a sandpit. Jumping from something called the "swing landing trainer," hanging five feet above the ground in a mock parachute harness before being dumped unceremoniously into a gravel pile. Jumping from a thirty-four-foot tower and sliding down a zip line to simulate the airplane's slipstream. We were told that the height was carefully chosen for maximum psychological effect: any lower and the jumper thinks he can fall unhurt; any higher and the fall becomes abstract. My knees ached, and my hips were purple with bruises from all the practice landings. Evenings I spent making trips to the hotel ice machine and popping Motrin by the handful.

Skydiving was supposed to be fun. Another trend in my training had been taking a pleasant pastime and turning it into hardship. Hiking, swimming, boating, shooting — all were corruptible. The reason was that we had to perform these commonplace activities under uncommonplace conditions. Airborne's hundreds of practice jumps prepared us to do just that — keep our heads, deploy the chute, and land safely at night, carrying a heavy load, from low altitude, at high speed. During the last week, we did it for real.

Beyond the tips of my boots, a neighborhood slid past twelve hundred feet below, complete with kids waving from backyard swimming pools. When the red light to my left turned green, I would step from the C-130's door and make my first jump. We were "slick" — no packs — and starting in daylight. Behind me, standing in a line with one hand over their reserve chute handles and the other grasping their static lines, was my thirty-man stick. "Mine" because, as a first lieutenant, I was the senior guy in the group. The first one out the door. We couldn't speak above the roar of the four engines, so we smiled reassuringly at one another and pretended to know what we were doing.

Sergeant Airborne stood by the door, ready to kick me in the back. He grinned and shouted, "Don't worry, jarhead. I'll push you, and gravity'll do the rest."

When the light turned green, I jumped. No way would he get the satisfaction of pushing me. A proper exit puts a jumper's feet together, his body bent at the waist, and his hands and elbows tight to the reserve parachute on his stomach. I hit the slipstream with my feet apart and my arms flapping. Head over heels. Sky. Dirt. Sky. Dirt. The shock of the chute deploying stabilized me.

"One thousand, two thousand, three thousand, four thousand. Check canopy and gain canopy control." It was a testament to our training that I remembered exactly what to do, counting aloud as I tumbled through the sky. I checked the risers to make sure they weren't twisted and looked up to see that the chute was round, with no panels blown out. Around me, parachutes filled the sky. Some jumpers were in a hover, caught in thermal updrafts. Hundred-pound ROTC cadets drifted down like fall leaves. My route to the ground was more direct.

During every jump, there's a definite transition point between flying and falling. I learned this as the pleasant floating sensation ebbed away and the ground rushed up. I checked the canopy again, expecting to see panels missing, but it looked unripped. Finally, I grabbed the risers and fixed my eyes on the horizon as I had been taught. Don't anticipate the landing. Back straight. Knees slightly bent.

Impact knocked the air from my lungs. Instead of rolling gently to the side and dissipating the force along the long axis of my body, I went from my feet to the back of my head. There was a flash of blue and then blackness. My chute refused to collapse, and filled by a complicit wind, it dragged my stunned body across the rocky drop zone. I finally pulled the D rings to release it from my harness and lay on my back as the next wave of airplanes passed over, pouring jumpers into the sky. Sergeant Airborne stood above me.

"Four jumps to graduation, jarhead. Only three more landings.

Chute don't even have to open on that last one. We'll send the wings to your mom."

Four landings later, I stood at attention while Sergeant Airborne pounded silver jump wings above my left breast pocket, drawing blood. It was the only time I would wear them. Unlike the other services, which decorate their uniforms with badges and patches, Marines wear no special insignia. I flew back to California with a skill I wouldn't use and wings I couldn't wear. My only memento of Fort Benning was the pair of red dots on my chest where Sergeant Airborne had taken out his frustration on the United States Marine Corps.

A few weeks later, I froze in the darkness as a spotlight washed over me. My heartbeat sounded like a gong in my ears. Surely, it could be heard a hundred yards away. When the light moved on, I pressed my body deeper into the gravel of the dry riverbed, squirming to put another millimeter of earth between me and the light. With the light were dogs. With the dogs were armed men. Capture meant torture, maybe death. I had to escape from the light. Our C-17 crashed somewhere in the Balkans, dumping me and a dozen others into the cold woods. We had to travel by night and hide by day, trying to link up with underground collaborators who would spirit us to safety.

At least that was the story. In the riverbed that night, I almost believed it. The woods were actually near Warner Springs, California, in the high country east of San Diego. I was a student at the Navy's Survival, Evasion, Resistance, and Escape school. SERE trains "high-risk personnel" — mainly pilots, SEALs, and recon Marines — to evade capture behind enemy lines and to resist torture if caught. The school's motto is "Return with honor," a summary of the lessons learned by American prisoners in North Vietnam, the Gulf War, and other conflicts.

SERE's first week was a gentleman's course, half days in a classroom at Coronado's Naval Air Station North Island. On the instructor staff were men who'd spent more time in foreign prisons than I had in the Marine Corps. The purpose of the course, they said, was "to learn to overcome the mind-fuck of captivity." They taught us our rights under the Geneva Convention — food, shelter, medical attention, and mail — with wry smiles. "Don't expect to get any of 'em." They drilled us to memorize the six-article Code of Conduct. The code was written after the Korean War because so much information had been extracted from captured Americans through physical and psychological pressure.

The code begins, "I am an American fighting man. I serve in the forces which guard my country and our way of life. I am prepared to give my life in their defense." It continues through pledges never to surrender, always to resist capture and try to escape, and to accept no special favors from the enemy. The code commits Americans to keep the faith with their fellow prisoners and to give up only name, rank, serial number, and date of birth. All other questions are to be evaded "to the utmost." The code ends, "I will never forget that I am an American fighting man, responsible for my actions, and dedicated to the principles which make my country free. I will trust in my God and in the United States of America." During SERE's second week, we got the chance to live it.

We boarded a bus on the Saturday morning that marked the course's midpoint. As an infantryman, I was accustomed to traveling light. I had survived in the field for weeks with only the contents of my rucksack. That morning, I carried in my left pocket all the gear allowed for SERE's field week: a compass, a toothbrush, and ten feet of parachute cord.

The first few days in Warner Springs were dedicated to hands-on application of skills we had learned in the classroom — navigation, camouflage, signaling, and foraging. Nothing new for a Marine grunt. We slept in piles beneath tiny squares of parachute silk, struggling to keep warm. In six days, I ate one carrot, a few handfuls of wild barley, and a little bit of rabbit. Much of SERE's fearsome reputation was based on this starvation, and it slowly degraded our decision making, putting us in a more vulnerable state of mind.

Toward the middle of the week, our final exam began: the simulated plane crash behind enemy lines, evading the packs of men and dogs pursuing us, and, when captured, resisting interrogation in an isolated prisoner of war camp. No one evades the whole time; everyone goes to the camp. But the one thing the staff can't control is the clock — the course ends when it ends. The trick is to avoid capture for as long as possible, spending time on your own terms in the woods rather than at the mercy of your captors in the camp.

So I crouched in the riverbed until the shouting shadows with the spotlight moved on. Taking a deep breath, I began to crawl, thankful for the silence of the sand. Like any American forces operating within or above enemy territory, we had been briefed on a "designated area of recovery." Mine was a hut where I would link up with collaborators who would help spirit me to safety. It was still several kilometers away. I moved quickly, knowing I had to reach it before dawn or find a place to hide until the following night. Moving in daylight almost guaranteed capture.

Night in the high country around Warner Springs is cold, even in summer. We wore only our summer-weight uniforms, and I disciplined myself to slow down, resisting the urge to run for warmth. I liked being on my own. It was a test of wits, with the gratification of an instant reward. Each second of freedom meant I was winning. Part of SERE's training is to develop a coping strategy. Mine was to turn the exercise into a game, and it kept me going. I reached the hut before dawn and joined five classmates inside. We had been scattered after the crash and had moved independently to the hut. Its owner, a burly Bosnian who was probably a Navy chief in real life, assured us that we were safe and suggested that we sleep for the day, since we would have a long movement that night. I drifted off on the dirt floor.

Barking dogs woke me. There was shouting in a foreign language, and a rifle bolt slammed home. We had been betrayed. The sun was high in the sky, and I knew we were captured. I felt crushed. SERE's realism, and a thought-scattering week without food, made it easy to forget that this was only training. In my mind, on that morning, I was somewhere in the Balkans and had just been condemned to a prison camp.

Rough hands pushed me to the ground from behind. I saw a boot and nothing else. A burlap sack was dropped over my head, and I was half-led, half-dragged down a dirt road and into a clearing. I kept my bearings by looking downward through the sack's opening. My mind raced, trying to remember what I had been taught the week before. This was initial capture, the most dangerous time of all. I could expect a field interrogation, and I had to give up enough information to be kept as a prisoner instead of being killed outright. Know-nothings and hardheads usually ended up with a bullet in the base of the skull.

I felt almost elated being slammed against a metal wall. Field interrogation; I had been right. A swarthy guy with a mustache had me by the collar, bouncing me back and forth against the wall. After two or three bounces, he would ask my name. I said, "American." He slapped me across the face, and the bouncing continued. We went back and forth like this a couple of times before he pulled out a gun. I recognized the danger sign and told him my name. The rule of captivity is to bend, not break. Be the willow, not the oak. Getting killed means you failed the test. We went back and forth on a few more questions, and then I was hurled into the bed of a truck.

The next day and night passed in a blur of beatings and interrogations. I was stripped to my underwear and shoved alone into a cinderblock cell, shorter than I was tall and narrower than I was wide. My legs cramped, and I shifted onto my feet. Then my back cramped, and I repeated the cycle for hours on end. Isolation is brutal, even for a short time. There was nothing to look at, no one to talk to, no way to keep track of time. We were made to feel completely powerless so that we would understand that our fates were in the hands of our captors.

After dark, a scratchy recording echoed through the camp. I recognized it as Rudyard Kipling's "Boots," in a droning British monotone. Over and over, it played a continuous loop: "There's no discharge in the war!"

When dealing with stress, we crave human contact, a connection with others who can empathize with our pain and provide the simple hope of shared hardship. I was cautiously excited when, hours after sunset, the guards dragged me from my cell and led me at gunpoint down a long underground corridor. Even hearing them talk and seeing them move took my focus off myself.

I entered a carpeted room, warm and bright. A man behind a desk greeted me with a gracious smile and, in accented English, asked me to sit. He pushed a candy bar and a steaming mug of coffee across his desk, inviting me to enjoy them. Mind-fucking me. I refused, but not without a long glance at the rising steam. He introduced himself as a representative of the Jamaican embassy. I nodded. He asked about my treatment. I replied that Article 25 of the Geneva Convention required that I be housed in decent accommodations, while Article 26 guaranteed me basic daily food rations. I had received neither. He smiled and said he would see what he could do to help. He put on a concerned look and asked about my physical condition. At his prompting, I moved my head up and down, and back and forth. I bent my arms and legs.

Going through the charade, I knew this was a "soft sell" interrogation. Torture is generally a weapon of the weak. Americans are social creatures and especially susceptible to those who will eviscerate us with a gentle smile and a kind word. By obeying politely but accepting no favors, I had defeated the conniving Jamaican. I was returned to my cell.

Alpha Company, Second Platoon at Marine Officer Candidates School in Quantico, Virginia, in the summer of 1998. Sergeant Olds stands in the front row, at right. I'm on the right in the sixth row. Posing for a platoon photo was a candidate's first hint that he might survive to graduate from OCS. *United States Marine Corps*

Standing on the right, I take the oath of office as a second lieutenant in Dartmouth's Baker Library, June 1999. *Niel Fick*

For the first month of The Basic School, each day started and ended with a three-mile hike to the rifle range, where we learned to shoot an M-16 and an M-9 pistol. Every Marine, regardless of specialty, is a rifleman, and every Marine officer is, first and foremost, an infantry officer.
*Nathaniel Fick*

A Bravo Company Zodiac lands aboard the USS *Dubuque* during workups off the California coast. Boat training was impractical preparation for real-world missions, but suffering together on the cold ocean made our company a cohesive unit.
*Captain J. P. English*

Forward Observer First Lieutenant Jim Beal (left) and Platoon Commander First Lieutenant Patrick English in the North Arabian Sea shortly after 9/11. During this deployment, which took us to Pakistan and Afghanistan, I worked most closely with Jim and Patrick. *Nathaniel Fick*

Patrick English aboard a CH-53, returning to the USS *Peleliu* after recovering a crashed American helicopter along the Pakistan-Afghanistan border. The sign above the ramp reminds exiting passengers to turn left to avoid hitting the tail rotor blades. *Nathaniel Fick*

Bravo Company boards a C-130 in Jacobabad, Pakistan, in November 2001. The venerable Hercules was our lifeline, carrying Marines and supplies to remote airstrips throughout Pakistan and Afghanistan. *Nathaniel Fick*

Marine base Rhino, viewed from the tail ramp of a CH-53 in November 2001. At lower left is the dirt strip that served as the only American runway in southern Afghanistan during the early days of Operation Enduring Freedom. *Author's collection*

Marines in my platoon, each carrying more than a hundred pounds of gear, move out to their positions around Rhino's perimeter. This photo ran in *Newsweek* in December 2001 with the headline "A New Breed of Soldier." *Jim Hollander/Reuters*

The flag flies from a makeshift pole inside Rhino's walled compound. It was removed after only two days for fear of seeming "imperialistic." *Nathaniel Fick*

The view from the tower stretched across Bravo Company's lines.
Cannon fire had punched holes through the roof. *Author's collection*

Staff Sergeant Keith
Marine (his real name)
and I during the Task
Force Sledgehammer
mission to Kandahar
in December 2001.
Marine, more than
anyone, taught me
what it meant to be a
platoon commander.
*Author's collection*

A light-armored vehicle near Kandahar. A year later, Iraqi fedayeen would call LAVs "the great destroyers" for the damage they wrought with their 25 mm cannons. *Author's collection*

Marines emerge from a CH-53 near Highway 1, between Kandahar and Lashkar Gah, in December 2001. We knew that the mujahideen had shot down plenty of Soviet helicopters, but Afghanistan's terrain often made travel by other means impossible. *Jim Hollander/Reuters*

Left to right: Patrick English, Major Rich Whitmer, and I at the Marine Corps Birthday Ball in November 2002, eight months after we returned from Afghanistan. Whitmer had distinguished himself as Bravo's unorthodox, imperturbable company commander and was now operations officer of the recon battalion I had just joined. *Author's collection*

Recon Marines run with fifty-pound packs along Camp Pendleton's mountainous fire breaks. A Friday morning at Recon meant an eight-mile run to the beach, a two-mile swim in the Pacific, and an eight-mile run back. *Author's collection*

After shivering for a few hours, I was again led out, this time blind-folded and bound at the wrists. Inside another room, I was forced into a wooden box. It measured perhaps five feet by two feet and was no more than two feet deep. A lid slammed over me, and I heard a latch slide into place. It was like being buried alive. I struggled to stay calm, to breathe easily, and not to thrash around and let them know they'd gotten to me.

When I was finally let out, the guards pushed me up a flight of stairs and made me kneel on a wooden floor. They tightened the blindfold so I could see nothing. My hands remained tied behind my back. A voice began to fire questions at me — name, rank, service, reason for being in the country, number of Americans on my plane. The floorboards creaked as he walked around me. I didn't know where the blows would come from.

I struggled to use the resistance techniques I had been taught, craft-ing a story that was believable, logical, flexible, and consistent. Alter-nately, I slipped into vagueness and ran down irrelevant tangents. I filled my speech with military acronyms and claimed a faulty memory. Whenever I sensed a fist winding up in the dark, I gave him a piece of information. I verbally bobbed and weaved until my knees were sore. Finally, a rifle barrel prodded me to my feet and planted itself in my rib cage as I limped back to my cell.

Coping strategies. I stared at the cell wall, shivering. I had no idea how many hours remained before sunrise or how many days I'd be in the camp. Then I remembered the tap code. One of the classes in Coronado had been in a Morse code–like tapping of letters to spell words through cell walls. I tapped "hi" on the wall in front of me. H-I H-I H-I.

It surprised me when someone tapped back. I missed his first few taps and scratched at the wall, the signal to start over.

S-F S-F S-F.

Semper fi. Always faithful. I smiled in the tight confines of the cell and sat back to wait for my next mind-fuck.

When SERE ended, the staff carefully debriefed each student on his per-formance. A Navy petty officer sat with me in an empty Coronado classroom.

"So, sir," he said with a smile, "how long do you think you were locked in the box?"

"An hour, maybe two," I replied.

"Eight minutes."

The two times I was led from my cell had, as I guessed, been my soft and hard interrogations. The hard sell had been a total success — I had given up almost no information and had used the resistance techniques so effectively that the interrogator had never resorted to torture. The soft sell had been a different matter. As I sat in silence the petty officer played a videotape. There I sat in the warm room, looking pale and thin. Apparently, there had been a hidden camera I never saw. A voice-over asked questions that were never actually posed to me, and my reactions had been spliced in.

"Do you care that you bomb and kill the little children of our country?"

I shook my head no.

"Do you think America is evil for the war crimes it commits here against our peace-loving people?"

I nodded an emphatic yes.

My neck stretches in response to the Jamaican's health questions had been used against me. Despite the best intentions, I had fallen victim to the soft sell. The petty officer was sympathetic. "Don't worry, sir. Getting mind-fucked once is the best way to make sure it won't happen again."

# 18

THE FOLLOWING Monday morning, I put on my green dress uniform for the second time. It had been nearly two years since I'd checked into 1/1, and I wasn't a boot anymore. I wore a few ribbons from Afghanistan on my chest and all the confidence that went with them.

Recon's headquarters was called Camp Margarita, a collection of single-story offices near Pendleton's airfield. A sign at the entrance bore the insignia I remembered from Colonel Leftwich's statue at TBS: a skull and crossbones surrounded by the words "Swift, Silent, Deadly." The battalion had been formed in 1937, and had fought with distinction in almost every Marine campaign since.

The clerk collected my orders and sent me to the battalion commander's office, saying the commander liked to shake hands with each of his new officers when they checked in. Lieutenant Colonel Stephen Ferrando, trim and fine-featured, was on the telephone when I knocked on his door. He motioned me to a seat. A bout with throat cancer had left him with a raspy voice, and I understood why the battalion, under his command, used the call sign Godfather. After hanging up, Colonel Ferrando didn't waste time on pleasantries.

"Your job is to be the hardest motherfucker in your platoon," he said while pointing at me across the desk. "Do that, and everything else will fall into place."

He added that I was assigned to Bravo Company, call sign Hitman, and wished me luck.

I stood at attention, about-faced, and stepped straight into Major Whitmer. He had been promoted after our return from Afghanistan and was recon's new operations officer. Just back from ten weeks at combatant diver school in Panama City, he looked tan and fit. I was happy to see him.

"Congratulations on getting through the pipeline, Nate."

"Congratulations on your promotion, sir. I hope you didn't get the field-grade lobotomy that goes with it." It was a running joke among lieutenants and captains that field-grade officers traded their common sense for the rank.

"Careful, Lieutenant. You're about to feel the wrath of a field-grade officer." Whitmer smiled, and I laughed, remembering the warning from 1/1's operations officer in Afghanistan.

A genial captain commanded Bravo Company. He was a former all-American football player, an intelligence officer by trade, with virtually no infantry field experience. But unlike the infantry, recon operated at the team and platoon levels. Since the company existed only for administrative reasons, the CO's background didn't bother me. He welcomed me aboard and asked which news I wanted first, bad or worse. I chose bad.

"You have second platoon — Hitman Two — and there are three Marines in it." Dill's full-strength recon platoon had had twenty-three Marines. After returning from Afghanistan, some had left the Corps or moved to different units; others were away at school but would return later, in the summer and fall.

"And worse?"

"We're leaving next week for a month at Bridgeport. I hope you weren't planning to go on vacation after all those schools."

The Marine Corps Mountain Warfare Training Center is in the High Sierra, near Bridgeport, California. It opened in 1951 to train Marines to fight on Korea's snowy peaks. Afghanistan's terrain is similar, and in the summer of 2002, a return to Afghanistan seemed likely. The battalion would spend three and a half weeks rock climbing and running recon patrols through the mountains. Had we known then what we knew a few months later, we would have gone instead to the desert training ranges at Twentynine Palms.

Since my "platoon" was smaller than one full-strength team, I spent most of the time at Bridgeport in the reconnaissance operations center (ROC), learning all the details of planning recon missions. By the end of the first week, I felt like a college student again. Late nights under fluorescent light, surviving on sludgy coffee, getting lots of theory but no practice.

I told my CO that I wanted to go on patrol with a team. His answer surprised me.

"Yeah, it'll make us look good."

Look good? I couldn't care less. I wanted to see a mission from the team's end of the radio. It was like flipping the map around. Generally, recon platoon commanders coordinated planning and logistics from the ROC while team leaders ran the patrols. I didn't want to step on toes, but I needed a feel for a team's abilities so I could better plan operations once my platoon was manned.

One of the battalion's senior officers, later nicknamed "Major Benelli" by the Marines because he insisted on carrying a Benelli shotgun, disagreed. "That's not your job, Lieutenant. Just stay in your lane." Benelli couldn't speak to someone of lower rank without smirking.

But Major Whitmer pulled me aside. "Go out with the team. You'll learn a lot. There'll be plenty of time to rot in the head shed when you're a major."

The mission's scenario had the battalion operating clandestinely inside a hostile country. Army Airborne was planning an invasion the following week with a mass drop of soldiers and equipment. Recon's job was to creep close to the drop zone and report back with details of its suitability for the mission. It was a classic, foot-mobile recon mission — get in, take a look, and get out without being seen.

It was midmorning when our helicopter settled toward the landing zone. I was shadowing a six-man team. The only man I knew was Rudy Reyes, the sergeant who had led workouts on the *Dubuque* and then manned the observation post atop the hangar in Jacobabad. He was serving as the team's radio operator. The team leader was in command; I would just bird-dog them. Through the window, I saw an impossibly small patch of yellow grass bordered by a wire fence. But the pilots were reserve lieutenant colonels, willing to put their bird into any zone an inch wider than the diameter of the rotor blades. The wheels thumped down, and the team filed toward a skirmisher line of scraggly pines. Flashes winked from the shadows. All I heard was the roar of the rotors turning a few feet behind me.

"Contact! Back to the bird," the team leader yelled. Another group of Marines was playing the opposition and shooting at us. The team deployed into a staggered line, with half the Marines firing while the other half moved. They struggled under the weight of eighty-pound packs, aiming from a knee and then turning to lumber toward the helicopter. The team leader and the pilots shot clipped sentences back and forth.

"Under fire. Gotta go."

"Twenty more seconds. Don't leave us."

A door gunner leaned into his machine gun, blazing away at the shadows in the tree line. With the last team member still on the ramp, the helicopter rose from the compromised field. We flew to the team's alternate insert point and made the drop-off. The team leader led his men off the zone and settled them into a tight circle, each man watching and listening as the helicopter clattered away. After the noise and motion of the insert, eyes and ears needed time to adjust to the more subtle rhythms of the woods. I watched pupils darting within bright whites, the Marines' only recognizably human features. Even those would fade with a day's fatigue, as bodies adjusted to dusky equilibrium with the forest around them. The team remained frozen for thirty minutes. Birds resumed their song, and squirrels again scurried through the fallen leaves. Only then did the Marines rise.

Three miles of mountainous terrain separated us from the drop zone. Landing any closer would have been too risky. The team planned to move into position around sunset to observe the objective and take photos to send back to the battalion. Then we would use the safety of darkness to recon the zone up close before moving to our extract landing zone, known as Sparrow, for pickup in the morning.

The patrol moved out with a corporal on point. He placed each heel on the ground, slowly rotating his foot to shift his weight silently to the ball. Behind him walked the team leader, followed by Rudy, moving sprightly even under the weight of the radios. Two junior Marines lugged the bulk of the team's supplies — mainly water and batteries — and also the firepower of the team's one light machine gun. The assistant team leader walked tail-end Charlie, watching for stragglers and ready to take over if something happened to the leader. I shadowed the assistant team leader at the rear of the patrol, watching the team move, charting our time and distance on the map, and trying my best to be invisible.

Just before sunset, the team stopped in the densest, most inhospitable thicket they could find — a perfect patrol base. Three men would remain there while three others went on a leader's recon of the objective area. I opted to move with the leader's recon.

We padded through a piny glen and reentered the sunlight to climb a shallow ridge of exposed rock. Enough shrubbery clung to veins of soil in the stones to conceal our movement, and we climbed quickly to a vantage point almost a thousand feet above the proposed drop zone. As two Marines scanned for threats, the team leader unpacked his equipment and went to work. He spun a telephoto lens the size of a wine bottle onto the camera body and began snapping a panoramic series across the length and breadth of the objective. He took five more shots with a different camera. After stowing the cameras, he unzipped a nylon bag and took out a sketchpad and a handful of colored pencils. In quick, confident strokes, he drew the outline of the drop zone, adding obstacles such as trees and ditches, penciling in estimated heights and dimensions. After cramming the page with data, he zipped the bag and stood. We clambered back down the ridge.

At the patrol base, the other Marines had set up the high-frequency radio while waiting for our group to return. They wanted to transmit their information back to the battalion so that even if the team got captured or killed, the mission would not have been in vain. The team leader furiously typed a report on his tiny laptop while Rudy tried to contact the ROC.

"Godfather, this is Hitman Two." They were using my call sign, the second platoon of Bravo Company, to call the battalion.

Static.

"Godfather, Godfather. Hitman Two. Come in. Over."

Static.

The mountains interfered with a conventional whip antenna, so Rudy shinnied up a nearby tree and wrapped a spool of thin wire around its branches, effectively turning it into a huge, field-expedient antenna.

"Godfather, this is Hitman Two."

"Hitman Two, Godfather. Send your traffic."

The team sent its pictures and text report back to the battalion as an encrypted digital burst transmission. I knew the Marines in the ROC would be clustered around the receiving computer, anxious to see near-real-time imagery sent by a team miles away. Even in training, this was impressive technology. After sending the report, the team packed its gear and waited for dark before moving to the drop zone.

I was learning lessons that would help me make better use of my platoon in the future. Recon teams never have enough time, enough batteries, or enough information. They always have too many questions to answer, too many mandatory radio checks to make with headquarters, and too many mouths to feed.

The point man drifted down the slope like a wisp of blown fog. I dropped night vision goggles in front of my eyes to track the team in the dark. Without them, I had not even crunching footsteps to follow. I was amazed at how good they were.

We split into two groups at the southern edge of the drop zone and zigzagged along the edges of the field, with a kilometer of grass between the team's two halves. A rising moon illuminated each condensed exhalation from my mouth. I labored silently under an eighty-pound pack filled with warm clothes and batteries. No grunting. No cursing. No carelessly snapping a twig underfoot. We threaded single file along the shadow paths cast by pines. Moving in the open under this moon was too conspicuous. Far overhead, airliners slid through the dark, winking red and white. I imagined coffee cups being collected and tray tables placed upright in preparation for landing in San Francisco. Twenty minutes for them; twenty light-years for us.

The teams linked up expertly north of the drop zone. Radio calls, flashes of infrared light, a cautious approach, a whispered password, a hurried reply. Pastry. Tiger. The team leader steered the team halfway to the extract landing zone before settling into a tight circle. There we repeated the earlier drill of composing and sending information to the battalion. The drop zone had been free of obstructions. Let the airborne invasion commence. With dawn an hour away, there wasn't time for sleep or food. Rudy compensated for both by sprinkling instant coffee crystals on his tongue, grinning with all the satisfaction of a content connoisseur.

The eastern sky was still dark when we began the final sprint to Sparrow, balancing stealth with the new need to meet the helicopter. The point man still placed each heel down with care, but his steps fell in quicker succession than before. I looked at the map — just under two kilometers to the zone. A rule of thumb in terrain like this is one kilometer per hour. We had twenty minutes to do nearly twice that. I imagined the pilots flying toward Sparrow, trusting us to be there. Just as we approached the zone, rotor blades echoed through the valley. The team leader contacted the bird.

"Moonlight, this is Hitman Two. We're oscar mike to the zone." (He used the abbreviation for "on the move.")

"Roger, Hitman Two. Give us a buzz saw and a NATO-Y."

The pilot had requested the most favored method for guiding a helicopter into a landing zone in the dark. The NATO-Y, standard throughout the Western militaries, is four chem lights tied to premeasured lengths of parachute cord. When laid on the ground and pulled taut, they form a Y. One of the Marines pulled it out, already tied, and cracked the four chem lights. He laid them across the landing zone, with the base pointing into the wind and the two legs marking touchdown points for the helicopter's main landing gear.

The buzz saw is a single infrared chem light tied to a two-foot strip of parachute cord. The Marine cracked it and began swinging the cord like a lariat. Through night vision goggles, the spinning chem light stood out as a circle of shimmering light, a beacon to guide the aircrew into the little patch of grass where the team squatted in the tree line.

I turned my head as the rotor wash blasted dust and twigs against our bodies. Dull green light spilled from the cargo bay as the ramp dropped. The team leader counted his team aboard, placing his hands on each man. Then he reached into the grass beneath the ramp and yanked the NATO-Y up into the helicopter. Leave no trace. The pilots added power, and we headed toward breakfast. I'd heard recon Marines call themselves "the quiet professionals," and now I understood why. Except for radio calls to the ROC, the team had spoken fewer than ten words in twenty-four hours.

By September 2002, the platoon had filled to full strength: twenty-three Marines divided into three teams of six and a five-man headquarters section. The whole battalion gathered on a Friday afternoon in the adobe mission-style chapel at the base. The topic was Iraq. It was an incongruous setting for a war briefing but the only building that could seat everyone comfortably. I walked in with Gunnery Sergeant Mike Wynn and Sergeant Brad Colbert.

Gunny Wynn was from Texas, wise and wiry. He had served in combat as a sniper in Mogadishu in the early 1990s, and then again while working at the U.S. embassy in El Salvador. When I'd learned he was going to be my platoon sergeant, I had called Eric Dill at his new post in Hawaii. "Get on your knees and thank God," he said. "You got one of the best." Like Staff Sergeant Marine, Wynn wasn't a yeller. He earned the respect of his men by being honest and fair. As a more seasoned lieutenant, I didn't require the same coaching I'd needed two years before, so Wynn and I were partners from the start.

Sergeant Colbert would lead Team One. He was a blond, cerebral San Diegan, known as "the Iceman" for his cool performance as a recon team leader on our raids near Kandahar a year before. We all slid into a wooden pew together and chatted before the start of the brief.

President Bush had recently told the United Nations that its failure to enforce resolutions against Iraq would leave the United States no choice but to act on its own. The senior Marines in the battalion had seen all this before, and the general consensus was still that diplomatic blustering would result in some kind of negotiated solution. No American tank would ever roll into Baghdad. The room grew quiet as the division chief of staff, a colonel, took his place on the altar.

"Worshiping the god of war," Colbert muttered.

The colonel introduced representatives from the division staff, each of whom would brief his own area of expertise. A pimply lance corporal, described by the colonel as "the most knowledgeable person in the division about the Iraqi army, its weapons, and its tactics," climbed the altar to give an intelligence brief. Gunny Wynn leaned toward me. "If that's true, then we're in a world of shit."

I heard only pens scratching on paper as representatives from the division's logistics shop ran through plans to use funnels to conserve water and explained how to test captured fuel for contamination. Suddenly, the colonel interrupted the brief.

"I don't hear any motivation, Recon Battalion. Give me a 'Kill.'"

He wanted us to shout "Kill!" to prove we were motivated by the brief. Looking at Wynn, I asked, "Who is this clown? Does he think he's talking to recruits at Parris Island?"

The battalion chuckled and shifted uncomfortably, offering only a tepid response to the colonel's order.

"Get up, go outside, and come back in here with a little more fire."

I thought he was joking, but he pointed at the door without smiling. We shuffled out to the parking lot, about-faced, and reentered to sit down again. Gone were the professionalism and concentration. I saw and felt surliness and disappointment. We had come for a brief about the war. The colonel had treated us like children and lost us. I hoped our lives would never depend on him.

General Mattis arrived a few minutes later, clearing the atmosphere like a thunderstorm on a humid afternoon. Mattis is kinetic. The troops who knew him from Afghanistan loved him, and everyone else loved him by reputation. Stars on a collar can throw a barrier between leader and led, but Mattis's rank only contributed to his hero status. Here was an officer, a general, who understood the Marines, who, in fact, was one of them. I caught Wynn's eye and leaned toward him to whisper a question: "You know what Mattis's call sign is?" He shook his head. "Chaos. How fucking cool is that?" Wynn nodded admiringly as General Mattis began to speak.

"Good afternoon, Marines. Thank you for your attention so late on a Friday. I know the women of Southern California are waiting for you, so I won't waste your time."

General Mattis didn't talk battle plans and tactics — those would be disseminated through the chain of command beneath him. Instead, he focused on seven general principles. He ordered us to reflect on them, internalize them, and make them real. The division's success in battle, he said, would depend on them.

"Be able to deploy without chaos on eight days' notice." I thought we could probably get out in eight days, but not without chaos. All our routine maintenance and repairs had to be completed. Gear had to be organized and packed for shipping. Desert uniforms issued. Manifests prepared. Anthrax and smallpox vaccinations given. I thought, too, of my personal life. A house to pack up, a car to store, bills to pay, family and friends to see. Deploying for war would be a mess, no matter what.

"Fight at every level as a combined-arms team." Combined arms was another Marine Corps mantra. The idea was to put the enemy in a dilemma in which hiding from one weapon exposed him to another. A lone rifleman and a grenadier could be a combined-arms team, and so could the division and its air wing. We were good at this. Recon teams had more experience with air and artillery than anyone except perhaps former weapons platoon commanders.

"Aggressive NCO leadership is the key to victory." Never a problem in recon. The team leaders, mostly sergeants, were the battalion's backbone. They were well trained, motivated, and experienced. I suspected my challenge would be tempering their aggression, not stoking it.

"Mistakes are forgivable, but a lack of self-discipline will be met with zero tolerance." Light discipline, noise discipline, and fire discipline would be demanded at all times. Mattis knew that victory hung on the details. Sloppiness in the little things led to sloppiness in the big things.

He would quash it at the lowest level he could. Thinking back to the silence of the patrol at Bridgeport, I was confident of recon's discipline.

"Build confidence in your NBC equipment." NBC stood for nuclear, biological, and chemical. The general paused and looked deliberately around the room. "Expect to be slimed with chemicals." This, frankly, terrified me. Marines spent at least one day per year in the gas chamber learning to use and trust their gas masks. But that was with tear gas. I had seen pictures of Saddam's gas attacks on the Kurdish village of Halabja. Green corpses, choked to death by sarin or VX. Gunny Wynn summed it up: "If we get hit with chem, we're fucked."

"Train to survive the first five days in combat." They were the most dangerous. This sounded good, but I wasn't sure how training for the first five days differed from training for the next five days, or the last five days. Besides, drawing on memories of the last war against Iraq, many Marines didn't think the war would last five days.

"Finally, get your family ready to be without you." Mattis never explained whether he meant for the duration of the deployment or forever. Probably both, I concluded. My life insurance policy was current, and I had a will, but I decided to write letters to the important people in my life, just in case.

General Mattis closed with a divisionwide directive: no Marine in the First Marine Division would deploy with more personal gear than was allowed to an infantry lance corporal. No cots, no coffeepots, no Game Boys, CD players, or satellite telephones. No double standards. Every man would sleep on the ground, and every man would shoulder an equal portion of the daily hardship. It was a Spartan concept, quintessentially Mattis, and I liked it.

Throughout the fall, tensions with Iraq grew. In October, Congress authorized a U.S. attack if Iraq failed to give up its weapons of mass destruction. In November, the U.N. Security Council passed Resolution 1441, stating that Iraqi noncompliance with its demands to disarm would be met with "serious consequences." Even so, my daily life remained mostly unchanged. I still lived near the beach with VJ, and we ran together almost every evening, talking about the growing crisis as the sun sank into the Pacific. We still believed it would come to nothing. In mid-November, Patrick English and I and our girlfriends went to the division's Marine Corps birthday ball in Nevada. Officers in their dress blues swirled dates across the dance floor or clustered at the bar telling stories. I felt the eerie sense of looking at a photograph from 1939. It was the division's last quiet month.

Warning signs began to appear at the battalion. We were told that none of the possible military options in Iraq had a role for foot-mobile reconnaissance. The war would move too fast. Instead, we would be equipped with Humvees and heavy machine guns. Such a drastic change in our doctrine was almost inconceivable. I decided to wait and see if the promised equipment actually showed up. By Thanksgiving, it had. Still, I remembered the mission to Tora Bora. All the equipment had shown up for that, but the operation had been scrubbed. By early December, there was no more denying it; we began full-time preparation for a war with Iraq.

The battalion gave each platoon five Humvees, two Mark-19 40 mm automatic grenade launchers, and two .50-caliber heavy machine guns. Most of the modifications needed to make them battle ready were up to us. Much of the gear was old, but the Marines weren't fazed. They just wanted permission to make the changes they needed.

Gunny Wynn and I suspected that the company would deny any unconventional requests to modify the Humvees. "Wouldn't make us look good," I said, mocking my CO's oft-repeated criterion for whether or not we should do something.

So we opted to beg forgiveness rather than ask permission. I knew from Afghanistan that the rules would change when the first shot was fired. By then it would be too late. Using their Afghan experience, Colbert and Sergeant Larry Shawn Patrick opened Second Platoon's chop shop. Patrick, known as "Pappy" because of his grandfatherly thirty years, led Team Two. He was an unflappable North Carolinian, tall and thin, who had started his recon career in Somalia ten years before.

The platoon labored for weeks in the motor pool, often working late into the night. We strung lights so that we could see in the dark, and everyone contributed money, tools, and supplies. Colbert's Humvee had light armor, but the other four were open, like dune buggies. We mottled the beige-colored exteriors with brown and gray to break up the vehicles' outlines and reduce their visibility at dawn and dusk. Camouflage netting, rolled and hung from the roofs, was rigged to release quickly with the pull of a single strap. Each Humvee, when stationary, could be made to look like a bush within seconds.

The heavy machine guns would be mounted atop three-foot-high metal posts in the Humvee beds. Gunners would stand behind them, with the firing handles at chest level. Sergeant Steve Lovell bolted racks over each wheel well to hold extra cans of ammunition near the gunners who would need it. Lovell, leader of Team Three, was new to recon. He had grown up on a Pennsylvania dairy farm and served in the infantry as a sniper.

"One thing I learned as a sniper," he told me while riveting an ammo rack to a Humvee, "is that nothing in the world's as useless as ammo just out of reach."

Corporal Josh Person, another Afghanistan vet now serving as the driver in Colbert's team, mounted civilian CB antennas to the rearview mirrors, running cables inside to the radios. After some trial-and-error tuning, their static-free transmissions became the envy of the other platoons. Colbert bought Garmin GPS antennas at RadioShack, allowing the teams to mount their GPS receivers against the windshield rather than holding them outside open windows to pick up satellites.

By the time we had finished outfitting the Humvees for combat, we had invested hundreds of man-hours and thousands of dollars from our own pockets. The vehicles were concrete examples of the lessons learned on patrols in Afghanistan. The day the teams declared them ready to go, the battalion sergeant major, its senior enlisted Marine, came down to the motor pool to take a look. Sergeant major is a position of great influence when held by the right man. Our sergeant major, though, was distrusted by the Marines because of his fixation, on the eve of war, with trivialities such as proper haircuts and polished boots.

Looking at the Humvees, he sneered, "Y'all are nothing but a bunch of cowboys who don't trust the Marine Corps to provide you with everything you need to win."

Except for the cowboy part, he was right.

# 19

M Y ATTITUDE IN DECEMBER was proof of the human ability to rationalize away pain. Congress had voted for war. The president had stated publicly that he would fight alone if necessary. Recon battalion had received hundreds of thousands of dollars in specialized equipment for a desert fight in Iraq. Troops were being sent to the region. But still I doubted that the war would happen. The very idea of American tanks in Baghdad, of U.S. troops in an Arab capital, was too far removed from any point of reference in my life. That I would be among those troops was simply unthinkable. I could intellectualize my way through how the war would unfold, but I couldn't feel it. It wasn't real.

I spent the holidays at home in Baltimore. Four days before Christmas, the president announced the deployment of troops to the Middle East in response to Saddam Hussein's noncompliance with U.N. resolutions. Recon would surely be among the first to go.

At our traditional Christmas dinner, my grandmother took me aside and said, "Nathaniel, I want you to have this. Now seems like a good time." She handed me a small box.

Opening it, I found an aluminum horseshoe less than two inches wide. I read the inscription. "Sakashima — Kamikaze — June 7, 1945." I remembered seeing it years before.

"Your grandfather had it made from the shrapnel that hit him. He always considered himself lucky. Maybe some of it will rub off on you."

The next morning, I made a necklace out of the horseshoe by stringing parachute cord through it. I put it around my neck and pledged not to take it off until I returned home again.

\* \* \*

On the last day of January, I left the office early and drove home to en-joy what I expected would be my final weekend in San Diego. We had been told to be ready to deploy within a week. After changing, I jogged down the street and headed west for the beach. The tide was low, the air was warm, and the setting sun reddened as it sank toward the ocean. I ran south through Carlsbad to the rock jetty that marked my normal turnaround point. But the evening was so beautiful that I kept going south and stretched the run into a ninety-minute workout. Racing home in the fading light, I felt content and invigorated.

The blinking red light on my answering machine shattered the illu-sion. Four messages. Without even dialing, I knew what it meant. My commanding officer and Gunny Wynn both had the same news: be at the battalion by ten P.M. Our summons had come.

VJ and I went to dinner at Jay's, our favorite Italian restaurant. He was already assigned to an upcoming MEU, so he'd be sitting this war out. Waiting for our food to arrive, the realization slowly formed in my mind: I was being sent to war. It was different from Afghanistan. Then, we were already gone. Now, I was leaving this quiet seaside town, with its pasta, Barbaresco, and palm trees, and going to war. *To war.* There was nothing I could do about it except go to prison if I refused.

I looked around at the other tables. There were people my age on dates, whispering and smiling. Older couples, comfortable and relaxed. Waitresses brushed against tables, steam rose from entrées, and I was going to war. These people looked forward to Saturday, and Sunday, and the coming months and years of their lives. Mine felt as if it had ended. I didn't have a future. Trying to conjure up a mental image of myself after Iraq, I found that I couldn't. Iraq loomed like a black hole into which all the thoughts and acts and hopes and dreams of twenty-five years were being sucked. I couldn't imagine what might come out the other side. We walked out of Jay's, where I had eaten dinner on my first night in California, and I wondered whether I would ever be back.

The battalion was in total disarray. Under floodlights, Marines staged and restaged packs on the parade deck. First by company, then by pla-toon, then by company again. Wives and kids stood by, watching the circus, surely wondering how they could trust this organization to bring their loved ones back safely. It was cold for California, which seemed somehow fitting. Wynn and I counted heads and sat down on our packs to wait for the buses. Orion shone directly overhead. In the coming months, I would often think back to that moment as I gazed up at the constellation on very different nights in very different places.

Midnight passed, the night grew colder, and family members began to leave. Still we waited. Finally, around two A.M., the headlights of the white school buses slowly approached the camp. Marines tossed packs and seabags aboard two tractor-trailers and, with much counting and re-counting, climbed onto the buses like so many third graders. Armed sentries, called "Guardian Angels," were posted on each bus in case Saddam or al Qaeda decided to keep us off their turf by launching an attack along I-15 between San Diego and March Air Reserve Base near Riverside. This precaution proved unnecessary, and we rolled onto the base just before dawn.

We lined up our bags for loading aboard the Air Force C-5 Galaxy cargo plane that would be carrying us to the Middle East, then claimed patches of space on the acres of concrete hangar floor. The Red Cross provided coffee, hamburgers, and a large television tuned to CNN. We watched as NASA lost contact with the space shuttle *Columbia* and, as the morning progressed, smoldering pieces were collected from fields across Texas.

"Fuck," Sergeant Espera said. "We couldn't read a worse omen if we spilled a goat's entrails right here on the floor." Espera had come to recon with Captain Whitmer and me. Now he was Sergeant Colbert's assistant team leader.

In true military fashion, our flight was delayed, and then delayed again. We passed a precious Saturday stewing on the floor, watching cars whiz past on the highway just a few hundred yards away. I pretended to read. There was too much time to think. I watched my Marines talking and sleeping, and thought about their wives, children, and parents. Each of their lives touched so many other lives. Each of those lives relied, at least a little, on my doing my job well. Our generation was often portrayed as one without consequences, without responsibility. Now, I thought, we were making up for it.

I drifted to sleep on the hangar floor with boots on and a rifle by my side, the first of many such nights. At three A.M., I woke to the rustle of Marines rising, stretching, and throwing on gear. Our flight had been called. Out on the tarmac, the slate-gray C-5 was nearly invisible in the darkness. A white light on its tail was so high that it seemed to blend with the starry sky. We shuffled across the ramp, weighed down with flak jackets, helmets, weapons, and packs. Our Humvees had already been loaded — twelve of them in two rows stretching the length of the immense cargo bay. Chained in the glare of the fluorescent lights, they looked like animals in a zoo, out of place and forlorn.

Passengers in a C-5 sit in rows of airline-style seats perched high above the cargo bay. We climbed a spiral ladder to this passenger capsule and wedged ourselves into place among the piles of gear. The flight attendant, a grizzled Air Force technical sergeant, gave a quick brief. Flying time to Morón, Spain, would be twelve hours, with midair refueling over Greenland. In flight meals were MREs, and there wouldn't be a movie. The plane had no windows, so I relied on my imagination as we rumbled down the runway and climbed smoothly to cross the country, above my sleeping family, and out over the Atlantic.

I passed time writing in my journal before being jolted awake as the wheels touched down in Spain. It was midnight, and we hurried to board buses and eat a meal before catching our next flight. Base rules required us to put our weapons in the armory before heading to the chow hall. Why Marines en route to a war couldn't be trusted to carry their unloaded weapons around a military base was a mystery to us. So we stood in line for an hour at the armory, shivering in the cold. Finally, we arrived for what we expected would be our last real meal. I felt the stares of the Spanish employees behind the serving counters. Our desert camouflage gave away our destination.

I sat at a table with the other platoon commanders and platoon sergeants. Talk turned to the last Gulf War and the memories of the Marines who had been there twelve years before.

"I remember the artillery," one Marine recalled. "You'd try to bury yourself in the sand as rounds shrieked in over your head. There was always a second or two between first hearing it and knowing where it was going to hit. That was the worst part — that second or two of not knowing, thinking maybe your number was up."

General reminiscing began. "I remember the fires. The whole damn country was on fire. You couldn't see, couldn't breathe, never knew what was going to pop out at you from a cloud of smoke."

"What about all the POWs? Remember them? Pitiful little fuckers. Walking around holding hands. What a worthless fucking adversary."

"Yeah, but Saddam's got a lot of weapons. Doesn't take a stud to push the button on a Scud, and it'll kill you just as dead."

The battalion commander stood to leave, and the conversation trailed off. We rose to follow him, dumping our trash with a last wistful glance at the dessert case.

We left Morón in darkness, flying east. The big C-5 carried us across Europe and the Mediterranean before dropping quickly into Kuwait City International Airport. As we screamed down to land, I lurched forward, held in place only by a taut seat belt, floating two inches above the seat. My ears popped, and the wind whistled past the fuselage. The combat descent was our first hint that we'd arrived in a different world.

We sat in the plane for an hour, waiting for it to park on the crowded ramp. A long line of aircraft disgorged pallets and people. Another line of planes waited to take off in a cloud of shimmering exhaust. Trucks raced back and forth, honking at disoriented newcomers looking for a sign, a guide, anything. A group of soldiers in a pickup truck finally met us. They scanned our military ID cards with a handheld computer, recording our arrival for Central Command's nightly news briefing about the size of the force opposing Saddam. The soldiers herded us aboard a bus, and we pressed our faces to the windows as we rolled past the terminal toward a gate. Sandbagged bunkers sat at every corner, manned by soldiers with machine guns. Roving patrols of Humvees cruised slowly along the airport's access roads, weaving among the Jersey barriers in front of checkpoints protected by razor wire. Beyond the fence, a gravel plain stretched into the distance, broken by a highway and piles of whitewashed buildings.

Outside the airport, we had to draw the curtains on the bus. Angry Kuwaitis, seeing armed Americans flooding into their country, might have been tempted to spray us with rifle fire. It had already happened twice to other groups. Through cracks in the drapes, I tracked our progress, noting that we picked up armored Humvee escorts that took positions around the bus. We traveled west through the suburb of Jahra before turning north. Our destination was Commando Camp, the temporary headquarters of the First Marine Expeditionary Force. It sat about twenty miles north of Kuwait City, at the base of Mutla Ridge, the only significant topographical feature in Kuwait. Commando had been a Kuwaiti military camp and was now teeming with Americans. Rumors promised showers, hot food, and tents with bunks. Even if these were true, we knew that the pleasures would be short-lived. Commando was home to rear-echelon pogues, support troops whose derisive name came from the acronym for "persons other than grunts." Combat forces were slated to move into Spartan camps in the northern Kuwaiti desert, where we could train, shoot, and flex our muscles along the Iraqi border.

We beat our jet lag at Commando with long runs every afternoon, around and around the inside of the camp's fence. The rules required us to carry gas masks everywhere in case of an Iraqi attack. It was a pointless regulation because without chemical protection suits and gloves, the gas would simply seep through our skin and kill us anyway. But we dutifully ran with the masks chafing against our hips.

On our second, blistering afternoon at Commando, I went out with three of the platoon's hard-core athletes: Sergeant Rudy Reyes, now serving as Sergeant Patrick's assistant team leader in Team Two; Corporal Anthony Jacks, Team Two's heavy machine gunner; and Corporal Mike Stinetorf ("Stine"), Team Three's heavy machine gunner. Because of the military's hierarchy, I spent most of my time with Gunny Wynn and the Marines one step above or below me in the chain of command — my CO and the team leaders. I was glad of this chance to get out and talk with other guys in the platoon.

By our second lap, there wasn't much talking. Reyes was in the lead. Stine, powerfully built, followed close behind. Jacks and I worked to keep up, shoes pounding rhythmically on the pavement. As we turned a corner in the farthest part of the compound, a mechanical whine slowly built to a shriek. The gas attack alarm. Incoming missile. We stopped and pulled our gas masks from their canvas carrying cases. I was still breathing heavily as I slipped it over my head, and the sweat on my face steamed the eyepieces. Under the best circumstances, wearing a gas mask is like breathing through a straw. I felt ready to collapse.

Rudy started off again at a trot. We fell in behind him as a voice over the camp loudspeaker announced that the alarm had been only a test. But wearing the masks had become a test, and we kept them on. By the next day, the whole platoon was running in gas masks. It forced the Marines to get comfortable with them. Iraq's chemical threat was our biggest concern, but those runs convinced us that we could fight through a chemical attack. We could survive. We could, in fact, win.

After dinner on our third night at Commando, Colonel Ferrando gathered the team leaders, platoon sergeants, and platoon commanders for a brief on the Iraqis' order of battle and the First Marine Division's scheme of maneuver. The order of battle was what units and equipment the enemy had and where, and the scheme of maneuver was how we planned to defeat them. It was our first glimpse at the official plan for the war.

The brief was held in the officers' tent. Sentries patrolled outside to keep eavesdroppers away from the thin canvas. The battalion's intelligence officer hung maps from the walls, lit by bare bulbs high in the tent's peak. Marines crowded around, seated on MRE boxes, ammo crates, and campstools. I sat with Gunny Wynn and our team leaders, Sergeants Colbert, Patrick, and Lovell. We shared a Michelin map of Iraq I had bought at Barnes & Noble before leaving San Diego.

The intel officer started with an overview of the forces we would face. Southern Iraq was guarded by the Iraqi army's Third Corps, composed of three divisions: the Fifty-first Mechanized, near Basra; the Sixth Armored, north of Basra; and the Eleventh Infantry, strung along the Euphrates River east of Nasiriyah. Together, this force included more than thirty thousand men and three hundred tanks. It had faced the First Marine Expeditionary Force before, in 1991, and likely remembered its brutal whipping. The morale of Iraq's Third Corps was assessed as low, and an intense psychological campaign was under way to persuade its soldiers not to fight. The message was "Surrender — and live to be part of the new Iraq." The bottom line was that we could expect no serious military resistance before reaching Republican Guard–controlled territory much farther north. "These poor guys don't even have enough food, let alone bullets, trained leaders, or the will to fight," the intel officer concluded.

He offered one huge caveat to this assessment: weapons of mass destruction. Iraq was thought to have chemical and biological weapons, and the means to hit our forces with them. They would be fired in missiles, mainly the notorious Scuds and lesser-known Frog 7s, and in artillery shells. The United States believed that there were "trigger lines" in place for Saddam to use chemical weapons. Unfortunately, no one knew what the triggers were. We saw ourselves as a vise with the White House turning the crank to tighten it. Sending us here was a turn of the screw. Crossing the border would be another. Crossing the Euphrates. Engaging the Republican Guard. Right up to kicking down the door of a presidential palace and cutting Saddam's throat. Each step put mounting pressure on him. When would he make a last stand? Artillery and missiles were the first targeting priority for coalition aircraft. All we could do was trust in our gas masks and chemical suits, move quickly on the ground, and stay unpredictable.

Colonel Ferrando followed the enemy update with an overview of how the Americans planned to start the campaign. Ideally, there would be three fronts: the Army's Fifth Corps from the southwest, the First Marine Expeditionary Force from the southeast, and the Army's Fourth Infantry Division from the north, through Turkey. The Turks were still balking, though, and Ferrando warned that all the forces might have to come through Kuwait. Within the Marines' zone, Regimental Combat Team 7 (RCT-7), built around the Seventh Marine Regiment, would be farthest east. They would isolate Basra and destroy the Fifty-first Mechanized Infantry Division. Just to their west, RCT-5, composed of the Fifth Marine Regiment with reinforcements, would seize the Rumaila oil fields to prevent their destruction by Iraqi forces. This not only would prevent an environmental catastrophe but also would guarantee the economic vitality of postwar Iraq. The First Marine Regiment, known as RCT-1, and Task Force Tarawa, a force of six thousand men built around the Second Marine Regiment from Camp Lejeune, North Carolina, would pass Rumaila to the west and secure bridges across the Euphrates.

Ferrando paused to let the rush of information sink in. A team leader in the back stood up and asked about First Recon's role in all this. The colonel admitted that our mission was still evolving but suggested that it might include forward reconnaissance for the division, screening missions along the flanks of larger units, controlling air strikes to destroy enemy armored formations, and finding alternative crossing points on the Euphrates in case the Iraqis blew up the major highway bridges.

"You'll be killing something, gents," he said. "That's the only thing I know for sure."

# 20

TWO DAYS LATER, we left Commando. Our Humvees had arrived from the airport, so we were spared the caged indignity of the closed-curtain buses. Starting north on Highway 80, we climbed the Mutla Ridge, where, in 1991, the Second Marine Division caught up with the Republican Guard as it fled from Kuwait. This was the infamous "Highway of Death," where American jets had destroyed hundreds of Iraqi vehicles. Columns of power lines marched to the horizon over a modern highway of new asphalt, but I thought only about black acres of smoldering trucks. The CNN images had been seared into my memory in the eighth grade. I was surprised no trace remained.

We joined a procession of other convoys rumbling north. British "Desert Rats," their faces wrapped in cloaks, steered tanks under flapping Union Jacks. They looked surprised to be driving toward the Iraqi border. U.S. Army convoys hauled past in the fast lanes, knowing what was over the next rise. After thirteen years here, this land was practically theirs.

We traveled in the slow lane at a sedate fifty miles per hour. Every few minutes, a cruise ship–size Mercedes with shimmering hubcaps flashed past, giving us a fleeting glimpse of the driver — always male, always robed in white, and always disdainful of more than the difference in speed. Twice our progress slowed to allow camel herds to clear the pavement. Boys with sticks walked behind them, slapping their flanks. We passed a fluorescent green sign that read, GOD BLESS U.S. TROOPS — certainly the only one of its kind in the Arab world.

All along the desert that stretches fifty miles from the Mutla Ridge to the Iraqi border, dirt trails led off the highway. Military convoys peeled east and west on these innocuous-looking tracks, passing behind privacy berms and entering whole cities hidden in the sand. Kuwait's government had declared the northern third of the country a military exclusion zone and relocated the local populace, mainly Bedouin tribes, to grazing land farther south until the end of the hostilities.

We turned left off Highway 80 and passed through a checkpoint rimmed with razor wire. The road snaked two kilometers into the desert before twisting around a rock outcropping and leading straight into the center of a new metropolis: Camp Matilda. The reference was to the Australian song "Waltzing Matilda," which became associated with the First Marine Division when it moved to Australia following the retaking of Guadalcanal in 1943. Despite its charming name, Matilda was a bleak, unfinished camp. Dozens of white tents stood in rows. No electricity, no hot food, and no showers for at least another week. We stood outside the tents, bemoaning our loss of Commando's comforts, when an F-16 fighter jet screamed overhead waggling its wings. The jet was returning from a patrol over Iraq's southern no-fly zone, and the pilot decided to motivate us. It worked. We started carving out a place for ourselves at Matilda and planning our training for the coming weeks.

I woke up early one morning a week later, enjoying the silence in the tent. The platoon lived together in its own tent, while Gunny Wynn lived separately with the other staff NCOs, and I lived with the junior officers. My sleeping bag was in the corner, a coveted spot that gave me a tad more privacy than those in the middle. A slight breeze blew cool air through the tent flap near my feet. I reached over and tuned my shortwave radio to the BBC, hoping to catch the hourly news.

"It's two o'clock GMT and this is the BBC World Service from London. Holes have been reported in the fence on the Iraqi border with Kuwait, and armed men in the DMZ identified themselves as U.S. Marines. More on this story now from Kuwait City."

Forty miles from the border in a camp full of Marines, I got my local news from London. The radio had been a gift from my parents, and it was one of my most prized possessions. I listened for another ten minutes before slipping out of my bag and getting dressed. I ducked through the tent flap with my toothbrush and a bottle of water to scrub and spit on the sand beneath the pink sky. Two tents down, another figure was doing the same thing. After brushing his teeth, he poured water onto his hair and began to slap his face and shake his head. I recognized Gunny Wynn's distinctive morning ritual and called out to him. "Hey, Gunny, want to go to breakfast when you're done primping?"

"Mornin'. Yeah, give me two more minutes." The shaking and scrubbing continued.

As we walked across the camp to the chow tent, Wynn and I returned to the topic that occupied most of our idle planning time — tweaking our roster to maximize efficiency and combat power. We were that rare thing, a fully staffed Marine platoon. Twenty-one Marines, from private first class to gunnery sergeant, one Navy medical corpsman, and one officer. Ordinarily, these twenty-three men would be divided into three recon teams of six men apiece, each led by a sergeant, and a headquarters section of five: platoon commander, platoon sergeant, corpsman, communications specialist, and a designated "special equipment NCO" to care for the parachutes and diving rigs we had not brought to Kuwait.

That arrangement worked well for traditional reconnaissance missions, where foot-mobile teams moved independently and the headquarters stayed mainly out of the fight. Tradition had not been consulted in drafting our role in the upcoming war. After a lot of walks across the camp for morning and evening meals, we settled on a modified plan. Sergeant Colbert's Team One would be divided into Team One Alpha and Team One Bravo, each in its own Humvee. Sergeant Espera would control Team One Bravo, operating effectively as a fourth team within the platoon. Colbert's armored Humvee would carry four Marines. Espera would have five Marines riding in his open Humvee. Sergeant Patrick's team, trimmed by one, would consist of five men in a vehicle. Sergeant Lovell's arrangement was the same. Navy HM2 "Doc" Tim Bryan, our corpsman, was one of Lovell's five. Wynn and I would ride in the only Humvee without a heavy machine gun. For protection, we relied on Corporal Evan Stafford, nominally the platoon communicator, and Private First Class John Christeson, our nineteen-year-old special equipment NCO, who was not an NCO and had no special equipment. They would stand in the back with rifles while Wynn and I focused on the navigation, coordination, and communication that went into running a platoon.

Our goals were redundancy and mutual support. Team One Alpha and Team One Bravo would fight together as a pair, while Teams Two and Three did the same. The weapons mix was supportive as well —

One Alpha's Mark-19 paired with One Bravo's .50-caliber gun, and Two's Mark-19 paired with Three's .50-caliber. The fifties excel at drilling one-ounce bullets into and through nearly anything, but they travel in a straight line and are easy to avoid by hiding behind a solid object. The Mark-19 lacks some of the .50-caliber's raw stopping power, but its grenades can be lobbed. Skilled gunners elevate the gun to drop grenades behind walls and even into fighting holes. Alone, each has a weakness; together, they're a destructive duo, a perfect example of General Mattis's order to fight in combined-arms teams. Most of our movement would be in a column, with Colbert and Espera at the front, Wynn and me in the middle for ease of control, and Patrick and Lovell behind. The team leaders concurred with this arrangement, and we began long days of training, first at Matilda and then out in the desert.

A typical early morning at Matilda found Second Platoon rolling sleeping bags and sweeping the sand that dusted us each night. The twenty-one Marines lived in a section of tent thirty feet by twenty feet. Poncho liners hanging from a piece of parachute cord separated their area from another platoon's space. The tent canvas, white on the outside, was yellow inside, lending an incongruous cheery glow to the cramped, plywood-floored room.

Gunny Wynn and I ducked through the tent flap, pushing past a cardboard sign that read BRAVO COMPANY, SECOND PLATOON beneath a black Recon Jack. This is recon's unofficial symbol, a stylized collage of parachute wings and a scuba diver, with a crossed knife and a paddle behind it. With us were Spool and Mish, the morning's instructors. Spool was a Huey pilot whose real name was Mike, but his squadron-mates had long ago given him the nickname because of his tightly wound enthusiasm. Mish, a Kuwaiti civilian, had volunteered to put his hatred of Iraq to positive use by helping us as a translator. He claimed that the Republican Guard had executed his cousin during the Gulf War and then forced his family to pay for the bullet. Mish always looked as if he wanted to sell me a joint.

The platoon split in two, forming semicircles on opposite sides of the tent. They wore green PT gear, filmy shorts, and too-small T-shirts. The stagnant air reeked of body odor, farts, and yesterday's workout clothes. Spool reviewed close air support procedures with one group, while Mish practiced basic Arabic phrases with the other, and then they switched.

"*aaGuf Lo iR-Meek.* Stop, or I will shoot."

In unison: "*aaGuf Lo iR-Meek.* Stop, or I will shoot."

"*iH-Nah iH-Nah HuT-Ta iNSaa' a-Dek.* We are here to help you."

"*iH-Nah iH-Nah HuT-Ta iNSaa' a-Dek.* We are here to help you."

I expected the Marines to lose interest. These phrases were too alien, too detached from all prior experience, to resonate with them. But the Marines listened, and they learned. In the coming days, I heard Christeson speaking more Arabic than English.

Spool wasted no words: "We're dividing the Garden of Eden into kill boxes." Each kill box measured thirty square kilometers and provided a set of shared reference points for aircraft and ground units. The Third Marine Air Wing would fly in support of the division from two airfields farther south in Kuwait. As we advanced north, they would move forward and fly from captured Iraqi airfields and straight stretches of highway.

He laid a map on the floor and ran through mock air missions with the Marines. "OK, you're driving along, come over a rise, and bam! Iraqi tank in the road. What do you do?"

Colbert recited the air procedures. Run the pilot in from a preplanned point in each kill box. Give him a heading and distance to the target. Describe the target and give him a good grid location. Mark the target — laser is best. At night, illuminate it with an infrared pointer. In either case, be ready to talk the pilot onto the target using landmarks recognizable from fifteen thousand feet up. Warn him about friendlies in the area and then give him instructions for coming off the target to try to keep him over ground held by Americans.

"Fine," Spool said with a nod. "OK, now let's assume the unthinkable. Sergeant Colbert fucked up the grid, didn't kill the tank, and it pumped a main gun round into your Humvee. Fingers and toes are everywhere. Colbert's head's a fucking smashed watermelon." He pointed at the youngest member of Colbert's team, a nineteen-year-old lance corporal named Harold Trombley. "Now you need a casevac bird. How do you call it?"

When the classes ended, I went for a run. High clouds dimmed the sun, and a wall of darker sky rose above the western horizon. Sandstorm. These storms blew in around Matilda like August thunderstorms in Maryland — sudden and ferocious. I hoped to cram in at least a few miles before the blast hit. Exercise was one of my few reprieves from the frustrations of life in the camp. We had early mornings, late nights, no privacy, and no escape from the grind of preparing for war. Talking about war. Thinking about war. War equipment. War maps. War plans. For fifty minutes on the gravel road around Matilda, I was somewhere else. Pushing myself to make each lap faster than the last, I enjoyed the effort, enjoyed the slow release of tension. I stopped my watch after six laps and walked a seventh to cool down and take in the far corners of the camp in more detail.

A long line of Marines stood outside the chow tent. NCOs hovered near the end of the line, turning some people away. I walked over. Apparently, the field kitchens had been spread too thin, and there was food for only about a third of the men in the camp. In Marine Corps fashion, that food would go not to the first Marines to arrive and not to the senior Marines who could pull rank, but to the most junior Marines at Matilda. The NCOs were allowing only privates and lance corporals to get in line for dinner. I remembered a story I'd heard from General Jones, the commandant who'd eaten dinner with us on the *Peleliu*. He'd quoted a former Marine officer who went on to be a Fortune 500 CEO. When asked for his guiding principle, the CEO replied, "Officers eat last." The philosophy is simple, and it goes a long way.

The sand on the Udairi Range stretches to the four horizons like an earthen sea. Navigating there is more like steering a Zodiac on the Pacific than walking a patrol across Camp Pendleton. The platoon went to Udairi for two days in late February to start using the skills we had worked on at Matilda. It was a five-hour drive to the west, out toward the Saudi border. Also, incidentally, toward the Iraqi border. I wanted the teams to feel the realism of training next door to hostile territory. I wanted them to see the fence and maybe even an Iraqi border guard in the light of his tower at night.

We started with contact drills — how we'd respond if we were driving along and someone started shooting at us.

"Contact front! Two hundred meters. Small arms." I made the radio call as we drove in column across the desert. Immediately, Espera pulled next to Colbert, and Lovell slid abreast of Patrick. Four guns could now pour fire ahead of us, instead of the one we had been able to marshal only a few seconds before.

"Assault through!" I gave the order to continue forward. We rushed into the mock ambush and then circled up to debrief.

Winning a firefight requires quick action by leaders. The key is to make decisions about your enemy and act on them faster than he is acting on decisions made about you. In training, I was taught the OODA loop, a four-stage decision-making process described by Air Force fighter pilot Colonel John Boyd: observe, orient, decide, act. That's all we did in the Humvee contact drills — observed the enemy threat, oriented on it, decided what to do, and did it. We practiced enemy contact to the front and rear, left and right, in daylight and darkness. We repeated the drills again and again, so that in a crisis our reactions would be instinctive. When we were exhausted, we did more. The drills were simple, but they taught us how to turn an ambush back on the ambushers, and that skill would save our lives in the coming weeks.

Infantrymen are Luddites by nature, knowing that research labs and testing centers usually can't account for the heat, cold, wet, dust, and bumps of the real world. Infantry Marines live only and forever in the real world. Every war has its innovations — the machine gun in World War I, the jet fighter near the end of World War II, the GPS-guided bomb in Afghanistan. An overweight civilian contractor had looked me in the eye at Matilda and sworn that our innovation would be the Blue Force Tracker.

This was a computer screen tied to a GPS receiver in front of the passenger seat in Colbert's Humvee. It looked like the setup in a state trooper's car. The computer was loaded with maps of Kuwait and Iraq. Our location on the map showed up as a tiny blue icon. What made the Blue Force Tracker so special was its network: every other vehicle equipped with the system also showed up on the map. We could click on their icons and send text messages directly to them. We, and every other user, also could upload reports of enemy locations, which then showed up on the map in red. The result was unprecedented situational awareness for individual Marines across the battlefield. On the drive back to Matilda, I shoved my maps under the seat and let Colbert guide us right to the platoon's tent using only the Tracker.

On a hazy Sunday afternoon in early March, the commanding general of the First Marine Expeditionary Force, Lieutenant General James Conway, visited Matilda to speak with his officers. He had been the one-star commander of Marine officer training at Quantico when I was a student there, and then the two-star commander of the division when I was with 1/1. Although he never knew my name, I felt that he and I shared a little history. Conway looked like a general should: tall, tanned, and white-haired, with a deep voice that was both soothing and authoritative. Whenever he spoke, I thought of the radio announcer Paul Harvey. General Conway commanded instinctive respect.

The general stood on top of an amtrac, backed by the U.S. and Marine Corps flags. His voice boomed through a microphone to the hundred or so men standing beneath him. The theme was rules of engagement, and he wanted to make four points very clear. First, commanders had an inherent obligation — not merely a right, but a legal and ethical obligation — to defend their Marines. Second, when the enemy used human shields or put legitimate targets next to mosques and hospitals, he, not we, endangered those innocents. Third, a commander would be held responsible not for the facts as they emerged from an investigation, but for the facts as they appeared to him in good faith at the time — at night, in a sandstorm, with bullets in the air. His fourth and final point distilled the rules of engagement to their essence. He called it Wilhelm's Law, a tribute to General Charles Wilhelm: if the enemy started the shooting, our concern should be proportionality — responding with adequate, but not excessive, force. If we started the shooting, the concern should be collateral damage.

I took notes as he spoke, thinking that this guidance was pure gold to be passed on to my troops. The rules of engagement harked back to my college classes on Saint Augustine and "just war" theory. I couldn't control the justice of the declaration of war, but I could control the justice of its conduct within my tiny sphere of influence. Doing right, I thought, wasn't only a moral imperative but also the most expedient way to lead the platoon. The rules of engagement would be for the Marines' minds what armor was for their bodies. I made a note to include all this in the formal operations order I would issue a few days later. But I kept the general's last statement to myself: "Officers," he said, "please don't get yourselves killed. It's very bad for unit morale."

# 21

B Y THE MIDDLE OF MARCH, war sounded less likely. The BBC reported that Iraq was destroying its al Samoud missiles — a key step toward compliance with the U.N. resolutions — and chcif wcapons inspector Hans Blix claimed that overall cooperation was accelerating. There were rumors at Matilda that maybe we would pack up and go home. That sounded too extreme. High-ranking officers speculated that we might cross the border in something less than combat mode, perhaps as part of a U.N.-sanctioned multina-tional force to ensure Iraq's compliance. I knew these speculations were bogus when the media showed up.

A bus groaned into Matilda and disgorged two dozen hard-bitten war correspondents. They wore beige vests and cargo pants. Most of them were male and bearded; they looked a lot like us. We had, after all, come of age in the same parts of the world. The press wasn't there to cover anything less than a full-blown attack.

"So who are you guys with?" Gunny Wynn and I stood in line for dinner, still more than a hundred yards from the lit triangle of the chow tent door. I turned in the darkness to look at the speaker. A foot shorter than me, he squinted up at us through thick-rimmed glasses. He held his tape recorder high, like an offering. "C'mon, what unit you with? Hometown? Name? Anything? I'm so excited to be here."

I would have ignored him but for the discomfort of standing to-gether for another twenty minutes.

"First Reconnaissance Battalion," I said.

"Oooh. Recon. You guys are special, right?"

"Only to our mothers."

"So I just got up here from Commando. I'm riding with some wrench-turners. What's your mission?"

Sure enough. Thirty seconds and the guy was pumping us for information we couldn't share. "To support the division in any way we can," Gunny Wynn said slowly, enunciating every syllable.

"C'mon. That's not very exciting."

Wynn and I parried with the reporter until we reached the head of the line. After grabbing our trays, we slid into two empty seats at an otherwise full table and smiled as he looked expectantly for the seat we hadn't saved for him.

After dinner, we picked our way through Porta-Johns and tent stakes back to the battalion. A staff meeting had just broken up, and the company commanders drifted slowly toward their tents, finishing hurried conversations in the dark. My CO saw me and called out.

He briefed me on a few updates for the next couple of days and then pointed to a figure standing in the dark nearby. "This is Evan Wright. He's a reporter from *Rolling Stone*. He'll be embedded with the battalion."

Wright smiled disarmingly. I pegged him with all the traits of my earlier assailant: a clueless opportunist chasing a Pulitzer Prize on the backs of men he wouldn't speak to on the street at home. As a citizen, I supported the Pentagon's much-touted embedded media campaign as a way to give Americans an uncensored look at the war and the warriors. As an officer, I dreaded dealing with the information leaks, distraction to my Marines, and constant moral oversight of people who knew little about our culture and the demands of combat decision making.

The next evening, I ducked into Gunny Wynn's tent at dinnertime, but he was still running. I started out across the camp alone.

"Lieutenant Fick!"

I turned and saw Wright. Filthy khaki trousers hung on his frame. He wore a brown Superfly T-shirt and a chunky gold chain that glimmered in the fading sunlight. Not a Marine. Quietly, even formally, he asked if he could join me. I said yes but felt self-conscious as we passed groups of Marines on our way to the chow tent.

We talked about our backgrounds. Wright had studied medieval history at Vassar, and he was amused to learn I was a former classics major. People like you are supposed to be in the other corps, he said, the Peace Corps. He was soft-spoken and gave the impression of being exceedingly gentle. Having patrolled in Afghanistan with an Army platoon and cruised the Persian Gulf aboard Navy ships, Wright wasn't a complete newcomer to the military. But this was his first time with the Marines. As we picked at our mashed gray chicken, I asked about his first impression of the Corps.

"Well, I live in the tent with the senior officers. They work a lot, and read, and sleep."

Sticking with the officers was a big mistake, I told Wright. To report on the Marines, he had to spend time with Marines, not staff NCOs and certainly not senior officers. Sergeants and below. The young, crazy, honest men who pulled triggers for a living. When we walked back across the camp, I pointed out my platoon's tent and invited him to speak with my men anytime. He wanted to meet them immediately. We pushed through the flap and into the platoon's living area. Colbert was reading. Reyes was doing pushups on his knuckles. Two corporals, Garza and Chaffin, were flicking each other with the tips of their eight-inch dive knives, just enough to draw blood. I walked away, feeling as if I had thrown a rabbit to the greyhounds.

When I issued my operations order to the platoon a few days later, Wright was there. We had reached a basic agreement — I would let him ride along with Sergeant Colbert's team, and he would stay out of the way and not reveal our plans. I had written hundreds of orders in training, and a few real ones in Pakistan and Afghanistan, but this was the longest. We had the luxury of time to plan, and it would have been negligent to have ignored any contingency we could think of. At ten A.M., I walked into the tent and hung my map on the wall. The men gathered close on MRE boxes and rolled sleeping bags, quiet for once.

"Most of this won't be new to you. Gunny Wynn and I, along with Doc and the team leaders, have tried to anticipate problems and questions and to answer them in the text of the order. Take good notes but treat them carefully, since they'll be classified. And get comfortable — this is going to take about two hours."

I started with the big-picture political and strategic decisions that had put us in Kuwait. Slowly, I worked my way down through the layers of Iraqi divisions and American regiments. That took about five minutes. Then I turned to the roles of the twenty-three men in that tent, individually and collectively.

I led the platoon from their seats at Matilda to the border, from the border up into the marshes of south-central Iraq. The Euphrates River flows generally west to east across Iraq, acting as a natural obstacle between our staging area in Kuwait and Baghdad. The First Marine Division had been training to cross the Euphrates for years by holding an exercise each summer on the Colorado River. We assumed that the Iraqi military would blow up the highway bridges in Nasiriyah, and so the division would have to find another place to cross. Each recon platoon was assigned a bridge to investigate and secure. Ours was in a sleepy town called Chibayish.

We talked about calling in air strikes, handing out food, capturing prisoners, and finding fuel as we made our way to Chibayish. We memorized radio frequencies, unit call signs, and sunset tables. We studied the map, passed around photos, and pushed toy cars across the tent's wooden floor, rehearsing formations and what we would do when the enemy attacked. Two hours turned into three and then four. By the time we captured the bridge at Chibayish, we had missed lunch, and I was going hoarse.

That night, I plugged a set of coordinates into the GPS and saw that my sleeping bag was 99.1 miles from the Euphrates River bridge at Chibayish. I fell asleep wondering what those hundred miles would hold.

Our intelligence changed constantly. Nearly every day, I checked with the intel officer for updates. On March 17, the night the U.N. arms inspectors evacuated Iraq and President Bush issued a forty-eight-hour ultimatum to Saddam Hussein and his sons, the intel officer told me that new overhead imagery was available for Chibayish. Gunny Wynn and the team leaders and I walked over to the division's intelligence tent to look at the latest pictures.

Situated in the infield of Matilda's ring road, the tent was surrounded by a field of antennas. We tripped and cursed our way through the guy wires to the tent's entrance. Pulling back one layer of heavy black rubber, we entered a small antechamber and closed the flap behind us before shouldering through the next flap and into the brightly lit room. Coffee was brewing. It was like a suburban office, with everyone working in a hum of cooperation and good humor.

I grabbed an imagery analyst. "We're the recon platoon going to the bridge at Chibayish. Can you get the latest U-2 film?" The pictures had been taken by a U-2 spy plane a couple of days before.

We pulled up two folding chairs and two MRE boxes and waited for the sergeant to return with the pictures. He lent us a ten-power magnifier, and we slid it over the film to get a closer look at our area of operations. The resolution was incredible. Individual people, goats, and bushes were visible. Colbert had a natural eye for reading the film. "OK, here's where we release from the battalion," he said, pointing at the tiny black-and-white rendition of a road intersection we'd been reading about and envisioning for days. "So then we drive up this way," he said, dragging a finger along the spool and turning the crank with his other hand to scroll the picture in the direction of our movement, "and enter our platoon zone by scooting through this gap in the dikes."

We were looking for three things: trafficability, the condition of the Euphrates River bridge, and signs of the enemy. Based on tire tracks and vehicles in the photographs, the whole area looked trafficable. This was the Hawr al Hammar, the Iraqi marshes where people had lived a life apart until Saddam Hussein pumped the water away in retribution for the Shia uprisings of the 1990s. Their tragedy was to our benefit: what would have been incredibly difficult ground to traverse now appeared hard and dry. The bridge itself also looked promising. It was a simple concrete span of two lanes, about a hundred meters long and studded with streetlights. There were no signs of anything amiss. People and cars were seen crossing the river, and fishing skiffs slid under the bridge. No tanks, no guns, no minefields. Nothing at all to suggest that the people of Chibayish knew anything of our interest in their remote town.

We bent over the film late into the night. It was our opportunity to answer questions in the safety of the camp so that we could make better decisions faster in Iraq. By the time we left the tent, we had a solid grasp of what Sergeant Colbert called "the recon mission of a lifetime."

I woke up the next morning to the bellowing of Major Benelli. The division, he said, would be conducting a "mobility rehearsal" that afternoon, and we had to be staged on the gravel road at noon, ready to leave. A tired voice in the corner asked how long the rehearsal would take.

"Six months, maybe a year."

So this was it. The morning we had been waiting for. We spent the next six hours loading all our gear into the Humvees. Fuel, water, food, and ammunition were already portioned out, so it was a simple matter of arranging. But knowing this was for real, we packed and repacked. I agonized over the placement of every item. Everything had to be safe, accessible, and distributed among enough Humvees to keep the destruction of one vehicle from robbing us of a capability or a needed supply. By noon, the battalion's eight platoons and their Humvees were loaded and ready.

Our platoon's vehicles groaned over every bump leaving Matilda. They sagged beneath ten tons of provisions. Even so, I worried that we were forgetting something. When we stopped at the camp's edge for a radio check, Gunny Wynn and I raided an abandoned tent, piling cases of water and MREs into the back of our gorged Humvee. I thought of the patrol at Bridgeport and the lesson that recon teams never have enough food or water.

We passed a series of U.S. Army camps named for the battlefields of 9/11 — New York, Virginia, and Pennsylvania. Bradley fighting vehicles and Army tanker trucks joined the convoys of Marine vehicles snaking north toward the border. Military planners had tried valiantly to build roads that could support a mass mobilization. It surprised me to see slabs of concrete peeking from beneath the drifting sand. But the desert always won. The roads were sand with patches of pavement, not the other way around. Rooster tails of dust rose from each pair of tires. Drivers wore goggles and bandannas. Everyone hacked and cursed and blew wads of sandy snot through open windows.

On that drive north from Matilda to the Iraqi border, I felt no fear, no apprehension. I felt relief. I'd realized that war was inevitable for some time. I had nursed illusions about a diplomatic solution, but I knew we wouldn't be home until a war had been fought and won. We were ready. The platoon was physically and psychologically primed. Being ready and staying ready are, however, two different challenges. Another month of waiting in the desert would dull us. The poor diet, lack of sleep, spotty exercise, stress of separation, and uncertainty would take a measurable toll. We weren't a gun to be cocked and put on the table. More like a slingshot. Load a stone, pull it back, and wait. Wait too long and the elastic goes slack, leaving you standing there with only a rock.

The sun set and the moon rose as we crept along. A full moon, washing the desert with a silvery glow. I winced as I watched Humvees moving many kilometers off our flanks. One of the U.S. military's greatest advantages is its night-fighting ability, and we had hoped to launch our first attack on the Iraqis under only 20 or 30 percent illumination. This was closer to 100 percent. We swallowed our regrets. So be it. If ordered, we would attack under a full moon.

Our dispersal area near the border was recognizable only to the GPS. We circled the battalion on a patch of desert no different from the miles of sand and gravel around it. I had studied the range rings for Iraq's artillery and missiles. We now sat well within a few of them. We received orders to put on our bulky, charcoal-lined chemical protection suits, known as MOPP gear. Until further notice, we would wear the suits twenty-four hours a day and always keep our gas masks and rubber gloves with us. We dug sleeping holes, called "ranger graves," and crawled inside. Sweating in my chemical suit, I stared up at Orion high overhead.

# 22

EIGHT MILES FROM the Iraqi border, I learned about the start of the war from the BBC. Tomahawks and stealth fighters kicked it off a day early in an attempt to kill Saddam Hussein. Around us, the desert was quiet. A breeze blew thin clouds across the sky, birds still flew, and nothing moved all the way to the horizon. We seemed to be alone. I didn't even see another American unit. Somehow I had expected more drama at this moment.

Minutes later, shouts of "Gas, gas, gas! Inbound Scud!" erupted in the camp. I donned and cleared my gas mask, pulled on rubber gloves and boots, grabbed a radio, and trudged over to my shallow hole. Lying on my back with the handset near my ear, I was convinced that the missile would land directly on me. I struggled to calm down, knowing I would probably pass out if I started hyperventilating inside my gas mask.

We repeated this drill three times during the morning of Thursday, March 20. Twice they were false alarms, but once we heard a rocket whoosh over our heads. Finally, in exasperation, Sergeant Colbert said, "We've kicked the hornets' nest, and instead of standing around, we'd goddamn well better start killing hornets."

With the war already under way, we still had no idea whether our movement on the ground would be preceded by aerial bombardment. This had been a subject of debate for the previous month. In the first Gulf War, the air campaign started thirty-eight days before the ground war began. But our desert camps in Kuwait were vulnerable, and planners feared that air strikes would provoke Saddam into attacking us there, possibly with chemical weapons. We heard only three or four jets pass overhead all day. Gunny Wynn and I scrounged around the battalion for information, but everyone was just as lost as we were. The only thing we knew for certain was that once the order to go was received, we would be rolling immediately. It might be weeks before we again had the luxury of speaking with the whole platoon at one time.

I radioed the teams and asked every Marine to come to the headquarters vehicle. Our sister platoons to the left and right agreed to keep watch over our sector for a few minutes. Wynn and I watched the Marines approach through blowing sand, looking like sci-fi space travelers in chemical suits and goggles. When everyone had gathered, I read General Mattis's "Message to All Hands," a single sheet of paper passed down to platoon commanders the day before.

> For decades, Saddam Hussein has tortured, imprisoned, raped and murdered the Iraqi people; invaded neighboring countries without provocation; and threatened the world with weapons of mass destruction. The time has come to end his reign of terror. On your young shoulders rest the hopes of mankind.
>
> When I give you the word, together we will cross the Line of Departure, close with those forces that choose to fight, and destroy them. Our fight is not with the Iraqi people, nor is it with members of the Iraqi army who choose to surrender. While we will move swiftly and aggressively against those who resist, we will treat all others with decency, demonstrating chivalry and soldierly compassion for people who have endured a lifetime under Saddam's oppression.
>
> Chemical attack, treachery, and use of the innocent as human shields can be expected, as can other unethical tactics. Take it all in stride. Be the hunter, not the hunted: never allow your unit to be caught with its guard down. Use good judgment and act in the best interests of our Nation.
>
> You are part of the world's most feared and trusted force. Engage your brain before you engage your weapon. Share your courage with each other as we enter the uncertain terrain north of the Line of Departure. Keep faith in your comrades on your left and right and Marine Air overhead. Fight with a happy heart and strong spirit.
>
> For the mission's sake, our country's sake, and the sake of the men who carried the Division's colors in past battles — who fought for life and never lost their nerve — carry out your mission and keep your honor clean. Demonstrate to the world that there is "No Better Friend, No Worse Enemy" than a U.S. Marine.

From the silence I gathered that the war was beginning to feel real to the platoon. It certainly was to me. There wasn't much else to say, so

Gunny Wynn and I dismissed the men to return to the lines. Hitman Two was ready to go.

We sat there all day cleaning and recleaning weapons, checking and re-checking maps, saying and resaying prayers. At six P.M., as predicted, a rushed radio call warned us to be ready to move in fifteen minutes. We tore down camouflage nets and did final radio checks. Vehicles were started and warmed, rumbling and humming as Marines added oil and cinched hoses with extra zip ties. Every maintenance problem that had been on our "maybe" list for days was fixed in those fifteen minutes.

Sergeant Colbert pulled me aside. "Sir, can you please tell me what our company commander has done to his Humvee?" He nodded to-ward the CO's headquarters vehicle, which had black duct tape covering all the windows except the windshield.

Earlier in the day, I had asked the captain the same question. He said he wanted to be able to read his maps by flashlight at night and not have the light visible outside the vehicle. When I pointed out to him that he wouldn't be able to see outside the Humvee, he shrugged it off, as if situational awareness was what he had recon teams for.

"Sergeant Colbert, you know better than to ask me a question like that."

Colbert smiled. "Roger that."

Behind him, Corporal Person sat in the driver's seat of Colbert's Humvee. He drummed his fingers on the armor door, singing a Tupac song about dying in a gunfight. Person caught me watching him and explained, "Moto music, sir. Brings out my inner psycho."

The last thing I did was tie down a pink air panel on the hood and mount a firefly high on the Humvee's whip antenna. During daylight, the air panels would identify us as Americans to pilots overhead. Fire-flies were small, flashing infrared lights that ran on a nine-volt battery. They were invisible to the naked eye but showed up like so many real fireflies when viewed through night vision goggles. In Iraq, they would be our primary means of recognizing friendly vehicles in the dark. Looking around through my goggles, I saw little lights winking reassur-ingly from each team's Humvee.

The battalion stretched into a line and slowly started out across the desert. As the sky darkened, I saw columns of winking lights on every horizon, all converging on the same two points. Marine engineers would blow two breaches in the fence and berms along the Iraqi border.

Our orders sent us to the western breach. Farther to the west, I knew the Army's Third Infantry Division was flowing toward its own breach near the border with Saudi Arabia. To our east, I saw flashes as Marine artillery pounded Safwan Hill, the only high ground along the border. Another Marine platoon would soon drop onto Safwan to kill any survivors at the Iraqi observation post there.

I passed radio reports on to the teams: change of plans — we would use the eastern breach; change again — back to the western breach; Iraqi tanks and armored personnel carriers spotted near the border; Iraqi soldiers near the border laying mines; trenches of oil ignited to decrease our visibility. We drove this way for five hours. Stop and go, fifty trucks and Humvees bumping through the dark across an uneven desert, our only reference points the infrared flashes on the vehicles we followed. I was disoriented, trusting the map and GPS but unable to get a good intuitive feel for what they told me. I knew the lieutenant whose platoon was in the lead. He would be on point for the battalion all the way up to the bridges. I had watched him labor over the route for weeks at Camp Matilda. While other officers had watched movies and written letters, he had huddled over his maps and laptop, plotting and replotting, memorizing every turn and landmark on the route. I trusted him and relaxed a bit.

We approached the breach around midnight and stopped to wait our turn in the flow through the narrow channel. To our right, an artillery battery blasted volley after volley northward. The howitzers belched huge fireballs into the night, illuminating the faces around me as if we were sitting by a campfire. In the distance, across the Iraqi border, a fire burned. We cocked our heads, listening for jets overhead — our surest salvation — but heard nothing. Some Marines took advantage of the pause to stretch out on the ground and sleep for a few minutes. I wandered among the platoon, trying to read the Marines and looking for vehicle problems.

Major Whitmer ran past me, on his way to the rear of the column. He stopped to say there were reports of Iraqi tanks moving just ahead of us. Laughing, he said he hoped my platoon's AT4s were within easy reach. I laughed also, and felt for a few seconds the irrational excitement of heading into battle. We hugged each other awkwardly, slapping backs and clanking weapons together. The good cheer faded when Major Whitmer disappeared into the darkness. Tanks.

I sat down on the hood of my Humvee. Artillery still rattled my teeth every couple of minutes, but between shots the night was quiet. That feeling I'd had during my last dinner at Jay's was back. I stood at the brink of something unknown and unknowable. Throughout my life, I'd always had some sense of what was coming next. People build continuity into their lives — places, friends, goals. We go to work on Monday with plans for Friday night, enroll as freshmen intending to be seniors, and save money for retirement. We try to control what comes next and shape it to meet our will. This was too big for me to shape. I was absolved of responsibility for my future. It was replaced with responsibility for twenty-two other futures. Nothing in my history seemed to matter beyond that line on the map. I didn't know what to expect, could not even imagine what might come next. Strangely, I tried to conjure up images of what I might see and how I might react, but all was blank. I hoped this was only the effect of standing at the crease. I told myself that once we crossed the border, I would again be able to guess at my future.

As dawn approached, we linked up with a light-armored reconnaissance company and moved toward the breach. The LAVs would escort us through the berm before breaking off to do their own mission. Their extra firepower was especially welcome here, at the one point where the Iraqis knew we would be. Gunny Wynn drove as we spun toward the breach through deep sand. We had driven along the border at night during previous weeks, but I had never seen it up close. On the Kuwaiti side, a chainlink fence ran to the eastern and western horizons. Bulldozers or tanks had punched a gap in it a hundred yards wide. The next obstruction was a tall sand berm, followed by a ditch, then a road on which the United Nations had patrolled, followed by another fence, another berm, and a final ditch. When we climbed up out of the second ditch, we were in Iraq. It was five o'clock in the morning, Friday, March 21. H-hour. D-day.

According to my compass, we advanced due north. After twisting through scrubby plants and past rusting tanks, reminders of the war twelve years before, we started across a flat, sandy plain. I deployed the platoon in a wedge formation, with Colbert and Espera at the front and Lovell and Patrick at either flank. This maximized our firepower to the front by allowing each team to shoot forward, rather than being masked behind one another. I was struck by the sight of Sergeant Lovell's team racing through the desert a few hundred meters to my left, their Humvee throwing a tail of dust into the sky behind it. It was a scene of pure aggression.

We passed desolate homes, where families eked out a living with goats and emaciated cattle. Our first Iraqis. We trained binoculars and machine guns on them, but they only waved. We waved back, thankful for their welcome, and continued pushing north at forty miles per hour. According to our intelligence, this was Iraq's empty quarter, a vast and sparsely populated desert. By noon, we'd seen more people than I had seen in all my time in Afghanistan. It was our first clue that the civilian population of Iraq would be a major factor in the war.

With vehicles shimmering in the midday sun, we drove across a gravel sea. Some high power lines allowed me to pinpoint our location on the map. It showed a cluster of buildings to our front. As I strained to see them, antennas rose on the horizon, and we stopped a few kilometers south of a walled compound. Through my scope, I saw black human dots at the gate. The battalion called for Cobra attack helicopters, which clattered up from the south a few minutes later. They flew low over the buildings, dropping their noses menacingly at the men loafing outside. Under cover of the Cobras' cannons, we sent a translator toward the compound. The Iraqis told him that they had been ordered to guard this communications site against the Americans, but all they wanted to do was go home. We bypassed them as the guards smiled and waved.

Minutes later, Marines in the lead Humvee spotted three land mines poking up from the rocky soil. Either they were old and had been exposed by the constant wind, or they had been lazily buried. While Colbert marked them on the Blue Force Tracker, we shifted our formation to single file, and each driver steered carefully to stay in the tracks of the Humvee in front. I was sweating in the tenth vehicle and could only sympathize with the guys up front. Soon we climbed up onto a paved road and raced along it for several miles before turning north across a trackless waste of gravelly desert.

As sunset approached, we slowed. Highway 8 cut across our path a few kilometers ahead. It was a modern highway — six lanes with guardrails and a wide median — running from Basra to Nasiriyah and then on to Baghdad. No American forces had yet crossed north of it. In recon terms, a road like this was a linear danger area — an obstacle to be dealt with most carefully. We would be exposed while crossing the highway and couldn't know whether Iraqi tanks lurked nearby. American airpower was superb, but with so many ground units moving, we couldn't expect complete coverage all the time. I knew only what I could see.

We crept up to the highway, planning to send vehicles down it to the east and west to guard the flanks of the crossing point. Just as we left the comparative safety of the desert and committed ourselves to crossing, two trucks came up over a rise to the east, traveling quickly toward us on the pavement. I raised my binoculars. They looked like Toyota Land Cruisers, painted desert brown and filled with people. Classic Iraqi military. A few days later, those trucks would have disappeared in a fireball anywhere within a mile of us, but this was the first day of the war. Killing and destroying had not yet become routine. Reconnaissance units train to collect information and report it back to combat commanders, who generally oversee most of the destruction. So when the trucks drove over the hill, the teams fell back on their training: instead of firing, they reported what they saw. I listened to meticulous descriptions of the trucks on the radio and wondered why no one at the front was shooting.

By the time we processed that the Iraqi military was "declared hostile" and could be engaged without provocation, the trucks had stopped, and uniformed men stood next to them with their hands in the air. Half of the battalion was already across the highway, so each passing Humvee simply trained its guns on the bewildered Iraqis and continued north into the desert beyond the road. After all the tough talk, all the doubt, fear, and wonder, our first encounter with Saddam's army ended with us pretending we hadn't seen them. I was grateful that we had scraped by without anyone on either side being dumb enough to fire.

We saw plumes of smoke to the east and turned to our best source of information to find out what they were. The BBC suggested that the Army was already nearing Nasiriyah, in the desert to our west, that Marines were working to secure the port city of Umm Qasr to our south, and that a few oil fires were burning in the Rumaila oil fields — the probable source of the smoke around us. They also reported Central Command's claim that a thousand Tomahawk missiles and a thousand air sorties had been launched the night before. Wynn and I looked at each other and smiled. The more the jets destroyed, the less there would be to oppose us. We continued driving as the desert turned pink and the long shadows cast by our Humvees faded into gray.

Nightfall found us parked along the raised tracks of the Baghdad–Basra railroad. Gunny Wynn and I refueled the teams from our spare fuel cans and then drove a few kilometers back to battalion headquarters to refuel ourselves from a tanker truck. By the time we dug our ranger graves and began a radio watch rotation, rain was falling. It rained through the night, turning the dirt beneath my head into sticky clay. I steamed inside my MOPP suit as my body heated the moisture. When it dried, I wrapped myself with a crinkling space blanket in a futile attempt to keep warm. By morning, I was stiff, tired, and caked with reddish mud. It was H+24, one full day since the start of the invasion.

# 23

O UR MISSION KEPT CHANGING. Eventually, I expected to move north through the marshes to recon the bridge at Chibayish, but for now our only guidance was to "screen the flank of RCT-1." The Regimental Combat Team was moving toward Nasiriyah on Highway 8, so presumably we were there to give early warning of a massed Iraqi assault on their northern flank. The only Iraqis we saw, though, were in no shape to attack anything.

Sunrise revealed bands of men moving in the distance. They walked toward us along the elevated railroad tracks, streaming slowly from east to west. Through binoculars, I saw they wore a motley assortment of army uniforms, Western clothes, and traditional robes. Some carried AK-47s. Others lugged duffel bags and what looked like antifreeze bottles full of drinking water. Most limped, and none moved quickly.

The sight of Iraqis, especially soldiers, was still novel, and we moved forward to intercept them. The men in the lead saw us and dropped their weapons. Behind them, the gesture trickled down the line until soon the ground was littered to the horizon with discarded weapons and stripped uniforms. Grown men stood in their underwear, waving and crying. Through Mish, we learned that they were from the Fifty-first Mechanized Infantry Division, based around Basra. Their unit had surrendered and collapsed almost without firing a shot, and now they were walking to their home villages along the Euphrates near Nasiriyah, another hundred kilometers or more across barren desert. They were nearly out of water. One man cried and clutched at me, telling through his sobs of regime-controlled death squads of fedayeen executing soldiers for surrendering or abandoning their posts.

The last thing I wanted to do was get bogged down processing prisoners. Recon was the eyes and ears of the invasion force. We were in a constant race for relevance. If we fell behind the main body of the division, we fell out of the fight. Searching surrendering Iraqis was a job for the military police or another rear-echelon unit; our job was to attack north and keep attacking all the way to Baghdad. In the absence of orders, however, we had to stay there, and we couldn't stay without at least taking a cursory interest in the hundreds of armed men flooding our position.

"Toss him a humrat," I said.

"Humrat" was Marine slang for a humanitarian ration, a yellow plastic bag of food about the size of a small-town telephone book. In Afghanistan, the Air Force had dropped hundreds of thousands of humrats across the country, but the infantry had never gotten any. So we'd passed out regular MREs to curry favor and make deals. The hungry Afghans had torn into the meals with little regard for the contents and felt duped after eating non-halal entrées such as pork chow mein. Some people had even eaten the water-triggered chemical heaters, with predictably ugly results. In Iraq, then, each vehicle carried a case of humanitarian rations. They contained crackers, jelly, and simple dishes such as red beans and rice — no pork and no heaters.

The Iraqi soldier crouched on his haunches and watched with wide eyes as Reyes sliced open the yellow bag and held it out to him. It seemed logical that the humrats were a bright and recognizable color so that people could spot them more easily. Unfortunately, certain bombs also were painted yellow — to warn innocent people to stay away from them. Iraqis later told us stories of children confusing the two. But the soldier happily munched a Tootsie Roll, oblivious to the history and controversy surrounding his meal.

Until midafternoon, we repeated the same ritual dozens of times. Approaching Iraqis saw us and got scared. They altered course and tried to move around us. Since we wanted to prevent masses of armed men from converging on the RCT near Nasiriyah, we dispatched Humvees all over the desert, herding the Iraqi soldiers as sheepdogs do sheep. Many men waved American propaganda leaflets above their heads, as if those were guarantees of safe passage. They said that aircraft had dropped millions of leaflets all over their barracks and bases outside Basra. The leaflets promised that American forces would bypass any Iraqi who surrendered but would kill any who chose to fight. Enough of the soldiers remembered the first Gulf War to take the threat seriously. By late afternoon, we had spoken with members of three Iraqi divisions — the Fifty-first Mechanized, Sixth Armored, and Eleventh Infantry — and all told the same story. The psychological campaign in southern Iraq appeared to have been a success.

When we had a large group cornered, we would disarm them, search for anything of intelligence value, pass out humanitarian rations, and refill their water. Many men sobbed when they realized we were feeding them instead of shooting them. A young boy, dressed in military trousers and a T-shirt from the Janesville, Wisconsin, YMCA, laughed and smiled, shouting, "I make love George Bush."

Many of the men carried gas masks. After trekking across the desert, they had discarded all they could do without, but they clung to their rifles, their water, and their gas masks. I noticed one man standing quietly to the side. He was clean-shaven and wore a dress shirt. His head turned to follow conversations as if he understood English. I introduced myself, and we shook hands. He was a battalion commander, a colonel, and most of these were his men. He thanked me for our kindness, and I replied that we, as soldiers, had more in common with each other than we did with many people in our own societies. I asked about the gas masks and whether he thought the Americans were going to use chemical weapons against Iraq.

"No," he replied. "We think Saddam will use them against you and we will be caught in the middle."

By midafternoon, we had searched dozens of Iraqis, and hundreds more were visible in the distance. They were mainly enlisted conscripts from the regular army. Most were Shia, and none would shed a tear at the death of the Hussein regime. This wasn't our enemy. The Marines were getting impatient. Finally, around three o'clock, we got the order to move. Our instructions were to drive west and resume our reconnaissance to the north into the marshes toward Chibayish.

We hurtled across the desert at over sixty miles per hour. I bounced all over my seat and watched artillery pieces being hauled by trucks on the highway south of us. A race for relevance. We were already too far to the rear. Soon we curved to the right, and the highway fell out of sight. We were alone again. In the dusk, we wended our way through a ravine of sandstone bluffs. A narrow gravel road clung to the hillside, which fell off below to a canal. The dappled water flowed slowly and reflected what little light remained in the sky. I squinted at my map to find the waterway's name: the Mother of All Battles Canal.

Ahead of us, I watched the lead Humvee bump uncertainly up onto the Ar Ratawi railroad bridge and creep out over the canal. The driver seemed to lose his nerve midspan, because the Humvee accelerated suddenly and dropped off on the far side to set up security for those of us behind. When Gunny Wynn pulled us out onto the bridge, with our wheels straddling the train tracks, I leaned sideways from my seat and looked straight down to the water below. Perhaps six inches of bridge extended on either side of our tires.

Reassuring darkness enveloped us on the other side as we stopped along the banks of the Saddam Canal and set up for the night. Our mission was simply to look north across the canal and give early warning of any Iraqi movement against RCT-1 to our south and west. After looking with satisfaction at the winking fireflies up and down the riverbank, I swung my entrenching tool to dig a ranger grave in the soft ground. Sitting with Sergeant Reyes by the radios, we watched bursts of antiaircraft fire climb into the dark sky north of us. Nearly every string of bobbing tracers was followed by a flash as the jet overhead responded with a bomb. Our heads moved left and right to follow the fire, and we cheered in hushed voices as if it were a tennis match. The night passed quietly on the canal, and when the sun rose, I dumped all our captured AK-47s into the water and watched them bubble down out of sight.

Our mission changed completely on March 23. During planning in Kuwait, and during the first few days of the war, we repeatedly made the same mistake: assuming that the Iraqi military would do what we would have done in their situation. If a foreign army were attacking Washington from the south, any American officer in any hypothetical war game would recommend blowing the bridges over the Potomac, thus turning the river into a natural obstacle between the enemy and his objective. We thought the Iraqis would do the same with the Euphrates. This expectation that the major highway bridges in Nasiriyah would be blown up is what launched First Recon on its mission through the marshes to investigate other, smaller bridges at more remote points on the river. On that Sunday morning, we learned that the bridges in Nasiriyah were intact. We backtracked to the south, happy at our good fortune and never suspecting, at least at my level, that the Iraqis might actually *want* us to use the bridges in Nasiriyah.

At dawn, we recrossed the Mother of All Battles Canal and merged into the westward-flowing stream of war machines on Highway 8. Marine tanks and amtracs mixed with boxy British trucks and the Polish army's Soviet-made armored vehicles. The Poles always startled us because the Iraqi army used the same equipment. The traffic jam rolled along at thirty or forty miles per hour, making Highway 8 look something like the Santa Monica Freeway at Armageddon. Gunny Wynn and I were amused to see traveler rest areas every few miles — picnic tables with multicolored umbrellas and big plastic highway maps of Iraq. Farmers and their families lined the pavement, sometimes waving but mostly begging for food. Piles of MREs bespoke the generosity of those who had passed before us. Twice, children darted into the road to retrieve poorly thrown pieces of candy and were nearly smashed beneath the wheels of our Humvees. I passed an order over the radio forbidding any more handouts. Besides, we might need that food ourselves in the days to come.

Three hours later, the whole column slowed to a halt about thirty kilometers south of Nasiriyah. Stopped traffic stretched ahead and behind as far as I could see. We sat in the yard of a few small huts, with no idea how long we would be stopped. For the first hour, the Marines stayed in their seats, ready to move again. Slowly, they migrated into clumps near the vehicles, then sat on the roadside, and finally formed a defensive perimeter with coffeepots boiling and weapons torn apart for cleaning. I heard firing to our front. Artillery. Sitting on a roadside, heading toward the sound of guns, reminded me of stories about World War I. I recalled that those stories usually turned ugly once the narrator reached the source of the firing.

Throughout the afternoon, helicopters ferried overhead. Marine CH-46s and Army Black Hawks flew north and then disappeared back to the south before flying north again. Back and forth. Back and forth. Through the afternoon, dusk, and darkness, the helicopters never stopped. We knew what they were doing. The Marine helicopters were painted an anonymous slate gray, but each Black Hawk bore large red crosses on its nose and sides. Casevac. They were casualty evacuation aircraft, flying dead and wounded Marines from the battlefield back to aid stations in the rear. Marines just like me were on those helicopters, and I was moving inexorably toward the place that put them there, just another cog in the machine. It was a helpless feeling, a powerless feeling, but not a self-pitying feeling. Just the opposite. I began to see a quiet resolve in the Marines around me, and I felt it myself. The platoon recleaned weapons and rechecked maps. Each passing helicopter bled energy into the Marines beneath it. We prided ourselves on being professionals, on thinking clearly with the world evaporating before our eyes. We could turn the violence on and off. But emotion began to creep in. I was angry. I wanted revenge. For the first time, my blood was up.

We spent the night there on the roadside, under the stars and the crisscrossing helicopters. The intel officer passed out aerial photographs of Nasiriyah for each platoon, paper blankets four feet wide that showed each alley and house in clear detail. The town sprawled about five kilometers square, bounded on the south by the Euphrates River and on the north by a canal. Highway 7 stretched northward on the western side of town, and Highway 8 paralleled it to the east. South of the Euphrates, Nasiriyah's outskirts gave way gradually to palm groves and farmland — our current location. The Marines had decided to use Highway 8, calling it Route Moe, but already it was known simply as "Ambush Alley."

I gathered the team leaders under my Humvee's tarp, and together we studied the picture. The battalion's mission on Monday would be to drive into Nasiriyah and join Second Battalion, Eighth Marines on the south side of the eastern bridge over the Euphrates, the southern end of Ambush Alley. We knew little about what had already happened in Nasiriyah. The BBC reported dozens of American casualties but offered few details. We heard vague reports that an Army maintenance unit had mistakenly entered the town on Sunday and been ambushed by fedayeen. Task Force Tarawa entered the town to rescue survivors and open the bridges for RCT-1 to pass over on its blitz to Baghdad. Now it looked as though the Marines were stopped and engaged in heavy fighting. We were about to join them.

We started north slowly on Monday, March 24, driving through fields next to the road in order to bypass all the supply trucks waiting for Nasiriyah to be secured. The cascvac helicopters continued their morbid rounds. We passed the head of the traffic jam and continued alone. I jumped in my seat as a well-camouflaged Marine artillery battery fired a salvo from its howitzers just as we drew abreast of them. Fields gave way to concrete block buildings and metal warehouses. Men stood along the sides of the road, some jeering, some watching impassively, all menacing. To our right, an oil storage tank burned, throwing flames and a black plume high into the sky. We crossed a bridge over railroad tracks and looked down on the burned hulks of Iraqi tanks still sitting in their revetments.

Over the past four days, we had seen dozens of wrecked Iraqi vehicles. Tanks hit by American jets, trucks and antiaircraft guns blown up on the roadsides. Now we saw more wreckage in the southbound lanes. But something was different. I stared.

"Holy shit, Gunny. Those are Humvees."

Bloody hands had pawed at the doors, leaving plaintive prints. Bullet holes frosted the windshields. Congealed blood, more blood than I thought a human body could hold, pooled around the flattened front tires. These were the sad remnants of the Army's 507th Maintenance Company, which had blundered into Nasiriyah after making a wrong turn and was all but wiped out by fedayeen militiamen. At least nine soldiers had been killed and six captured, including Private First Class Jessica Lynch. All we knew that afternoon, though, was that Americans had been in those Humvees, and it looked like those Americans had died.

We were only three kilometers south of the bridge. Every tree, every wall, and every building looked hostile. I was afraid for the first time in Iraq. Against the white noise of the blood rushing through my head, I heard my feet tapping involuntarily on the Humvee floor. My knees stitched up and down like a sewing machine. My mouth felt dry and gummy. Everything seemed to pass in a blur. I thought of war stories that talked about hyperclarity in combat, seeing every blade of grass and feeling colors more intensely than ever before. But for me, whole city blocks faded into a gray fuzz. I feared I was processing information too slowly, seeing only one of every ten things I should. I felt shortchanged. I wanted hyperclarity, too.

# 24

MACHINE GUNS RATTLED somewhere to our front. Mortar rounds thumped into fields off the sides of the road, leaving brown columns of dust hanging in the air. Wreckage blocked half the highway. We sped up, careening over the curbed median to drive north in the southbound lanes.

"How'd we go from quiet fields to this in half an hour?" Wynn asked, steering with his left hand while aiming a rifle out the open door with his right.

I'd been asking myself the same question. "Southernmost city on the way to Baghdad. We're right where they want us."

Radio reports of gunshots and suspicious activity stopped as we entered a maelstrom of shooting and moving. There was too much to call in. Forward of the artillery batteries and support troops, but still behind the infantry units up at the bridges, we took small-arms fire from palm groves along the road, which meant the grunts ahead were surrounded. Finally, we passed Marine vehicles herringboned on the highway and saw infantrymen strung out in the fields in shallow holes. At the southern end of the bridge leading to Ambush Alley, we swung to the left and pulled into the defilade of a small dirt lot surrounded by palm trees.

My first reaction was to laugh. We had stumbled onto the set of a Vietnam War movie. Dense green palms encircled us, and a fence of dried fronds lined the side of the clearing. Gunfire echoed everywhere, and Marines darted back and forth, hunched low. Cobras thumped overhead, launching rockets into buildings along the far side of the river. I half-expected the notes of "Fortunate Son" to come drifting through the trees.

An artillery round crashed into the field across the road. It sliced through power lines, which sprung back and whipped through the air like angry snakes, spitting sparks. Wounded Marines fell, and calls of "Corpsman!" rose above the fire.

Alpha and Charlie companies moved forward to the riverbank, and we listened to a deafening roar of outgoing fire as they lit into enemy positions on the far banks. Bravo Company remained in the lot, waiting for instructions. I jogged over to the palm frond fence and slipped through it to talk with Marines dug in on the far side. They were facing south and west, guarding our flanks. A water buffalo rotted on its side in front of them, a victim of the crossfire. I found their platoon commander hunkered down in a hole with a rifle and a radio. He said the platoon was from Fox Company 2/8. They had been under fire all day, and he warned me about walking around like I was.

"They're in the trees, man. They're fucking everywhere, and the fuckers can shoot, too."

Vietnam.

I went back to the lot and got orders to strip all nonessential equipment from my Humvees. When Task Force Tarawa attacked across the bridge into Nasiriyah, my platoon would race in after them to evacuate casualties. There were too many RPGs in the air for helicopters to fly over the city, so all casevac would be on the ground. It was morbid, planning to evacuate Marines who were now walking around, talking with their buddies, and preparing for the attack. While we worked to dump excess fuel and add extra stretchers and medical supplies to the Humvees, mortars exploded into the dirt across the road, showering the pavement with clods of clay and clattering pebbles. I stood talking with Sergeant Patrick when a metal object sailed over the guardrail and clanged into the back of his Humvee, bouncing through the bed.

"Grenade!" The call went out, and we dove to the ground, waiting for the blast. Waiting and waiting. Finally, Patrick and I stood and peeked into the back of the vehicle. A jagged piece of shrapnel sat inside, not quite harmless, but no grenade either. We laughed. Combat slides emotions so far up the scale that amusing events become hilarious. Sometimes, in mid-firefight, I would see Marines laughing maniacally.

Helicopters continued strafing the city blocks across the river. Marines cheered as a Huey did a slow pass, raking the riverfront with its door-mounted Gatling gun. Chunks of masonry fell from buildings. Cobras swooped in fast, rockets streaking from their pods, before pulling off at crazy angles and rushing back toward ground held by the Marines. An F/A-18 Hornet thundered low over the river, all intimidation. I saw the pilot's head in the cockpit as the gray dart slashed past. He pulled up in a rolling turn, followed by smoke puffs and strings of tracers. So much for intimidation.

Dusk settled over Nasiriyah. For us, that meant only that the tracers were easier to see. The promised attack across the bridge hadn't happened, and we prepared to spend the night there at the bridgehead. I divided the platoon in half to provide security and dig fighting holes. No sooner had we begun to dig than word trickled down to drive three kilometers south and join RCT-1 for a nighttime mad dash through Ambush Alley.

We drove back the way we had come. Smoldering fires along the road lit our windshield with flickering light. South. I couldn't believe we were giving up ground, even if only to regroup and rush north again. We had been told for months that most Iraqis wouldn't fight, that any resistance this far south would be sporadic and ineffective. But we heard reports that the Saddam Fedayeen, Saddam's "Men of Sacrifice," were assembling for a fight in Nasiriyah. Before the war, the fedayeen had specialized in torture and executions. It looked as if they had two Marine regiments stopped in their tracks.

Hundreds of vehicles were stacked along both sides of the road. Tanks, amtracs, Humvees, and support trucks idled in the darkness. We found our place in line — right atop the railroad bridge, where we were fully backlit by an oil tank burning in a field east of the road. Any twelve-year-old with a hunting rifle could have hit the silhouettes we made in the fiery glow. I jogged up the road to the company commander's Humvee and asked to move a hundred meters forward or backward to a better position.

"I can't give you permission," he replied, "without checking with the battalion."

"So check with the battalion."

"Bothering the battalion about something this minor will make us look bad." He said it with exaggerated patience. "Besides, we'll be moving soon."

Six hours later, after alternately dozing under the Humvee, listening to radio chatter, and counting the artillery salvos sailing north into Nasiriyah, we still hadn't moved.

I passed some of the time pacing in the road and ran into a classmate from Quantico. He looked exhausted, with dark eyes sunken in a face glowing white in the reflected firelight. I asked how he was doing.

"Hell of a day. We had some Iraqis surrendering earlier. Marines walked up to them, and the hajis dropped their white flag and pulled AKs out from under their robes. Ten minutes later, some fucker was shooting at us with a rifle in one hand and a little girl in the other. My guys are trying to do the right thing, but I don't want to get them fucking killed in the process. There's a bunch of dead Marines on the road in town. You'll see 'em when we roll through."

"What happened?"

"Depends who you ask. RPG ambush. Friendly fire from an A-10. Hell if I know."

We had spent the day making veterans. Most of the Marine Corps had gone ten years without a real fight. I hoped we were up the steep part of the learning curve already. General Mattis had told us to survive the first five days in combat, the most dangerous days. That left four more. Just a day before, Marines talked about this being a repeat of the hundred-hour war. The greatest fear was that it might end without us firing a shot. Surrounded by fires, I sat on the hood of the Humvee and watched the horizon flash as artillery shells crashed into Nasiriyah. Near dawn, we started the engines.

By the time we reached the southern bridge, we had opened gaps between vehicles for maneuvering room. Gas pedals were on the floor. I watched Corporal Garza standing at the machine gun in Espera's Humvee. He was swaying, holding on with both hands to keep from falling into the street. According to the map, there were three and a half kilometers between Nasiriyah's southern and northern bridges. Less than four minutes. We passed the bridgehead where we'd stopped the day before and began to climb the span across the Euphrates. I felt the anticipation of ratcheting up a roller coaster. We crested it and looked up the length of Ambush Alley. It was the pause at the top of the hill, just before the plunge. We hurtled down into town, speeding past cinderblock buildings and wrecked cars. Whole blocks were in rubble, and stray dogs yelped as we passed.

An infantry battalion manned a picket line in the city, lining Route Moe with amtracs and dismounted infantrymen. I didn't envy their job, sitting in a hostile city with thousands of nervous, trigger-happy

Marines rolling past. Small-arms fire chirped to our front and rear, but I saw nothing to shoot at. Long cross streets stretched into the distance, lined with telephone poles. I expected to see figures darting between alleys, shooting from the hip, but the streets were empty. Fighting holes pocked the ground, and I waited for a scarf-wrapped head to pop up and shoulder an RPG. None did.

What we saw was the detritus of earlier combat. An amtrac sat in the road with its roof peeled back like a sardine can. Packs and sleeping bags littered the ground, and I saw lumps covered with ponchos. Dead Marines. It must have been bad for the dead to be lying where they fell the day before. I drove past knowing that each Marine in my platoon was seeing his fallen comrades. We saw Iraqis, too. A truck full of anti-aircraft guns sat in the southbound lanes, with the driver's bullet-riddled corpse hanging from the cab by his feet. His head nearly touched the ground. Another man lay in the street, where dozens of tracked vehicles had smashed him nearly flat. His torso spread across the pavement in a red smear. The Marines referred to him afterward as "tomato crate man."

At the northern end of Ambush Alley, we crossed another bridge and turned left at an intersection. LAVs lurched through the fields next to the road, blasting away at assailants unseen. I was grateful for their covering fire and kept our speed up. A right turn put us on Highway 7, which we would follow all the way north to Al Kut, on the Tigris River.

The two-hundred-kilometer stretch of highway between Nasiriyah and Al Kut would take us ten days to travel. While the Third Infantry Division, RCT-5, and RCT-7 swung wide to the west through open desert, RCT-1 and First Recon battled through every town on Highway 7 in the ancient "land between the two rivers." Our mission was to engage Iraqi units and keep them from falling back to defend Baghdad. The Army and the other RCTs would pay their dues farther north when they led the charge into the capital, but for the next ten days, much of the fighting would take place along this highway.

We started north from Nasiriyah trying to figure out if we were the lead American unit on the highway. Two battalions had crossed the Euphrates bridge ahead of us, but they were garrisoned along Ambush Alley and at the intersection. That put us at the front. Our conclusion was confirmed by reports of an Iraqi BM-21 rocket launcher in the road just ahead. We stopped while a jet rolled in and blew it up.

I knelt next to the Humvee while we halted. Stopped vehicles are magnets for RPGs, and I, like every infantryman, always felt better with my boots in the dirt. Looking around, I saw an industrial slum of junk-yards, machine shops, and trash piles. Green and black flags drooped from buildings in the morning heat, and yellow-eyed dogs stared at the invaders. We scanned the alleys and windows for human movement but saw nothing. Stopping like this invited trouble. I didn't yet appreciate the awesome firepower of a Marine platoon in a tight circle.

Shadowy human forms danced in my peripheral vision. I never turned in time to see them fully. A man in a window. Another dodging from one building to the next. A third peeking over a distant berm. After Nasiriyah, I kept an earplug in my right ear, my shooting ear. It amplified the sound of the blood whooshing through my head. I wanted to blaze away with the machine guns and level everything around us. Clear fields of fire would make us safe. But we couldn't do that. We could only sit and wait and watch with flickering eyes.

The highway passed into a flat and featureless countryside. It was ele-vated a few feet above the surrounding fields. Dikes and ditches criss-crossed them, but there wasn't any cultivation. The wind blew across barren squares of brown mud. Walled houses lined the road at broad intervals. The image of harmless, depressed farm country broke down when we began to pass fighting holes, blown-up trucks, and bodies. Marine aircraft had swept the road clear ahead of our advance, and the remains burned along both shoulders. Piles of RPGs, pickup truck "technicals" with antiaircraft guns mounted in the back, tanks black-ened and flipped on their sides. We didn't see a single live soldier.

After three hours of driving, the battalion pulled off the highway in a herringbone formation so we could shoot to our flanks and cover one another. Marines climbed down and walked in front of their vehicles for security. I waded into neck-high scrub, silencing each step as I looked left and right over my rifle barrel. Branches screeched along my trousers, and each broken twig sounded like a rifle shot. I climbed slowly over a small berm and stopped. Below me was a fighting hole. Blankets lined it, and a kettle still hung over a fire. Untouched food was neatly dished onto two plates. Footprints in the dust disappeared into the brush.

"Christeson, Stafford, get over here."

The two Marines came running and began walking a double helix along the footprints, cutting back and forth like dogs on a scent. But the hole's occupants were gone. I imagined two guys, probably my age, told to sit in their hole and shoot at the Americans when they came. They would be protecting their village, their mothers and sisters, from the infidels. Even if they died, they would enter heaven as martyrs to live in eternity with their ninety-nine virgins. It probably sounded like a pretty good plan until they saw a column of Marines stop in front of them.

We had halted so the commanders could plan our next move. I was called forward to receive an operations order for the rest of the day. Spreading my map on a Humvee hood, I listened and scribbled notes. RCT-1 would be advancing on Highway 7, and First Recon would move east of the highway to patrol through the farmland five to ten kilometers from the road. Our mission was to screen the RCT's flank and provide early warning of attacks from that direction. With a blue marker, I traced our proposed route along dirt roads and irrigation dikes. Bravo Company would lead the battalion, with my platoon leading Bravo.

Screening was a good reconnaissance mission, and this task was simple, with a clear purpose. Best of all, as Sergeant Lovell pointed out, "We'll be in the countryside, where we can fight, instead of in the towns, where we just have to bend over and take it."

We started driving again, with Sergeant Colbert's Humvee on point. Sergeant Espera followed him, then Gunny and me, and behind us Patrick and Lovell. We left the pavement near a small village called Jahar and bumped slowly east on a narrow, dusty track. A body sprawled in a ditch at the turn, torn apart, it seemed, by helicopter fire.

The road twisted through fields broken by dry ditches. We wound between palms and stands of reeds, farther and farther from the highway and into greener and greener country. Mud huts lined the irrigation canals, lush and cool in the shade of the sheltering trees. The roads were built for donkey carts and foot traffic, not for three-ton Humvees. Dirt slid from under the tires into the ditches, the sides threatening to collapse and throw us down into the stagnant water. We inched across a narrow bridge and found ourselves in a yard without exit. I stopped and called a warning back to the company. Our sister platoon, Hitman Three, turned away from the bridge and took the lead for the battalion. We watched as the rest of the column inched past, then we fell in at the rear. Now we were the last vehicles in the battalion column. Patrick and Lovell swung their machine guns around to cover our backs.

Word of mouth outpaced our tortuous progress, and soon people lined the trail as we approached. Most were friendly, smiling and cheering, but it registered that they knew where we would be before we arrived. There was only one passable route through the canals. The road turned gradually north, paralleling Highway 7 beyond sight to our left. I enjoyed the shade and the greenery, the water and crops and glimpse of survival in the fabled southern marshes. This Shia way of life was vanishing, and I wished we could enjoy it without the taint of war.

Two little girls came sprinting from a house, yellow dresses flapping. They skidded down a steep ditch between us and their home, then hopped daintily across the water, causing two basking turtles to duck under. The girls clawed and clambered up the near side of the canal and ran into the road directly in front of my Humvee, smiling and waving to the Marines in Espera's team. The Humvee stopped. Garza elevated the machine gun away from the girls and leaned down with two humrats in his gloved hand. Tenderly, he placed them in the girls' outstretched arms. I fumbled for my camera but missed the moment. The girls, shrieking in glee, tumbled back down across the ditch and ran home, where their father took the rations and waved solemnly to us.

Slowly but perceptibly, the atmosphere changed. Our path angled slightly back toward the highway, toward a small town we planned to approach before veering east again on another trail to continue our screen. I never acquired a sixth sense in combat, but my original five became more finely tuned. We began to notice danger signs. People watched impassively as we passed. I made eye contact with a man my father's age. He drew his finger slowly across his throat. Farther on, women with wrapped bundles on their backs walked south, opposite the direction we drove. They clutched their children and stole glances at us. One man chugged along in a tractor dragging a trailer filled with kids and household goods. This couldn't be normal. They were fleeing from something.

"Hitman Two, we're about to get hit. Lots of civilians around. Shoot only discrete targets."

My warning was unnecessary. The Marines could read the signs as well as I could. They knew our contact drills and rules of engagement. But it made me feel better. I had formally cocked the pistol. Now we just pointed it around and waited for someone to make us pull the trigger.

As if on cue, gunfire cracked to the front, and the column halted. Instinctively, we knelt in the dirt next to the vehicles, hating to be caged inside.

"Alpha Company's in contact. Stand by." Alpha was leading the formation.

Just as we stopped, the wind picked up. Swirling dust cut our visibility to a few hundred yards. It stung my eyes, forcing me to drop goggles across my face, further blocking my sight. These *shamals*, or sandstorms, blew in without warning. They filled everything with sand — Humvee air filters, machine gun chambers, mouths and eyes. We sat in a small depression, which gave us a little protection from the wind and enemy fire. On the radio, I learned that Alpha was calling in artillery to break up whatever resistance they had run into. We heard the occasional staccato of small arms, punctuated by the deeper roar of a machine gun. With the distance and the wind, I couldn't tell whether the fire was ours or theirs.

We waited tensely for fifteen minutes. The Marines scanned the fields and trees around us, looking for anything to shoot at. All we saw were villagers continuing their frightened exodus. Gunny Wynn and I lay on our stomachs on the side of a berm. He scanned a tree line through the scope of his sniper rifle while I kept my ear to the radio.

"It's that town up ahead," he said. "Every time we get near a town, they'll hit us. Luckily, it looks like we're just skirting this one, and then we'll be back out in open country. At least we're learning."

I agreed with him. The last thing I wanted to do was repeat Nasiriyah, and I suspected our commanders felt the same way. Then the radio beeped.

"Hitman Two, stand by to move. The screening mission is over. We'll be proceeding west to the highway through the center of this town."

# 25

COLBERT ACCELERATED AHEAD of me, turning hard to the left at the entrance to the town. Espera, faithful teammate, followed close behind him. The teams' gunners stood in their turrets, fully exposed. Wynn floored the gas pedal, and I clung to the windshield strut to keep from being thrown sideways out the door as we made the turn. To the right, a row of three-story buildings fronted the street. The dark recesses of doors and windows hid behind wrought iron balconies and cracked shutters. Sparkling muzzle flashes blinked in each black rectangle.

Sensory overload paralyzed me. I saw mud buildings set many meters back from the road. Beyond the turn, the buildings were concrete and seemed to tower above the road on both sides, trapping us in an urban canyon. Flashes of incoming fire surrounded us, but I didn't hear it, and I couldn't tell whether my platoon was shooting back. There was no fear, but no bravado either. I felt nothing. I was a passive observer watching this ambush unfold on a movie screen.

When Gunny Wynn yanked the wheel straight, I snapped back to the present. My hearing returned all at once: roaring machine guns, Humvee engine shrieking. I saw the street, the fedayeen positions, and my platoon in a fight. Fire poured from the buildings on both sides. Wisps of smoke swirled in the wake of each bullet. We drag-raced down the street, but it felt like a crawl. I lifted off my seat as we crashed through potholes and over missing slabs of pavement. Colbert darted left around a wrecked car smoking in the middle of the road. Wynn followed, and we jumped the median, swerved past a light pole, and picked up speed. Muddy water and sewage sprayed in rooster tails from the Humvees' tires.

"This is Hitman Two, in contact. Taking small arms, left and right. We're engaging." I couldn't even see the rest of the battalion ahead of us.

"Roger, Two," headquarters replied. "We took some on our way through, too. Just keep pushing."

Survival and command tugged me in different directions. A normal human survival reaction would be to curl up on the Humvee floorboards and close my eyes. This is precisely the reaction Marine Corps training is designed to overcome. And it worked. After the initial shock of the ambush, I felt calm and completely self-possessed. The Marines looked the same. They were aiming their shots, calling out targets, and moving as one.

For a platoon commander, the job was simple. Haul balls through town, shoot enough to keep the bad guys from aiming, and hope to get everybody out the other side. My biggest fear was that a driver would be shot or a Humvee blown up and we'd have to stop to pick up survivors. Stopping meant dying, and I stayed on the radio with Team Three at the back of our column, just to make sure they were still there.

"Two-Three, how you doin' back there?"

"Two-Three's up. Runnin' and gunnin'."

My best concession to the survival instinct, at this point, was to shoot. The first lesson every young infantry officer learns at Quantico is that your job when being shot at is to shoot back. "Gain and maintain fire superiority" is how the Marine Corps describes it. There were only twenty-three of us, so every gun counted. There was no artillery to call, no updates to give my commander. I was just another shooter. I leaned into my M-16 and began firing into windows and doors. The rifle's sharp reports were deafening inside the Humvee. With the radio handset pressed to my left ear, my right ear rang from the gunshots. I realized my earplug had fallen out, and I irrationally reached down to find it. I needed both hands on the rifle, though, in the bouncing Humvee.

My magazine held all tracer rounds to mark targets for the platoon, and I could see that I wasn't hitting anything. All the jarring made it hard to aim. My rifle had an M203 grenade launcher slung beneath the barrel. Close is good enough with grenades, so I reached into a bag of 203 rounds hanging from the roof of the cab. Pumping the breach of the grenade launcher, I fired as fast as I could reload.

Aside from insects and plants, I'd killed one living thing in my life. While mowing my parents' lawn as a teenager, I'd accidentally wounded a chipmunk with the mower blade. Gritting my teeth, I'd cut off its head with a shovel. Even this mercy killing had bothered me. I'd never been hunting and had no desire to go. Now, shooting grenades at strangers in an unnamed town, I was kind of enjoying myself.

The long-sought hyperclarity had kicked in. I saw a young man crouching in an alley. He wore dark trousers and a blue shirt. His silver belt buckle gleamed. He bent forward on one knee, bracing his upper body against the wall of a building. He held an AK-47 and sighted down its barrel as he fired at us. The rifle jumped in his hands, and little spurts of flame flashed from the muzzle. He seemed very small to me, although he could not have been more than thirty meters away. I lobbed a grenade at him and the round exploded against the wall just above his head. I watched him fall over the rifle. We flashed past the alley, and I reloaded, firing more grenades into windows and open doors.

My chest slammed against the dashboard as Wynn stood on the brakes. Ahead of us, the Iraqis dropped an overhead power line onto Colbert's vehicle, knocking Corporal Walt Hasser from the turret. He sprawled backward across the roof. I watched a pair of hands reach up and pull him upright. For an eternity of two or three seconds, we sat almost motionless. In the lull, I heard a Mark-19 roaring behind me as Corporal Jacks tore a building in half. He was bellowing as he fired, yelling at us not to stop moving. When enemy fire erupted from a mud-brick building to our left, Jacks stitched it with dozens of grenades, collapsing three stories into two and silencing the fedayeen guns. When Hasser sat up, we jumped forward again.

Colbert's team made a forty-five-degree turn at high speed, and I saw the Humvee's outer wheels unweight themselves and threaten to leave the road. Corporal Person corrected, and they kept barreling east. Espera and Wynn followed through the turn, and I was briefly aware of a turquoise-domed mosque surrounded by a masonry wall. Shots rained down from the minaret. I thought, absurdly, that this was against the rules. We were in the home stretch now, approaching the edge of town. On the radio, Team Three assured me they were behind us, following Team Two. I still couldn't see anyone else from the battalion ahead.

Finally, we flashed through a walled gate. We hit the T intersection with Highway 7 still doing over fifty miles per hour. To the south, herringboned off the road, sat the tanks of RCT-1. Rows of dismounted Marines crouched behind berms, watching in disbelief as our Humvees rocketed out of the town. Colbert was moving too fast to make the turn onto the highway and rumbled down an embankment on the far side. With bullets still whizzing from behind us, we all followed, trying to put some dirt between us and the town.

Colbert turned south on the hard-baked dirt at the bottom of the embankment. There was a hazy tree line a mile away across the open field. Tactically, this was still pretty easy — shoot, move, communicate. Team Three halted behind us, in partial defilade behind the berm so their machine gun could fire back into the town to take some pressure off us. Stinetorf hunched forward with dark goggles over his eyes, blazing away. We had escaped. Then everything went to hell.

With a sickening crunch, Colbert's heavy-armored Humvee cracked through the field's dirt crust and sank to its frame in tar. The field was *sobka* — a huge crème brûlée, baked hard on top but deep and soft underneath. We'd all been briefed on Iraq's sobka fields but had yet to see one. Now we were mired in one and still under fire.

Colbert's team piled out as we set up a hasty defensive perimeter. Team Three continued to cover our rear, and I sent Espera ahead to give us some visibility across the berm to our front. At that point, my worst nightmare was a wave of angry fedayeen seeing us helpless and streaming across the road to finish the fight. The wind had picked up, and blowing sand turned the sky orange and cut our visibility to a few hundred meters. Patrick crept forward to the edge of the sobka and hooked a winch to the rear of Colbert's Humvee. Rudy threw the vehicle into reverse, whining, straining, not moving an inch. It was futile. We needed something with more torque and more horsepower.

I called the battalion on the radio and requested Goodwrench, the mechanical support team. The motor transport guys are not recon Marines, and the younger team operators sometimes deride them as pogues. I never heard these disparagements from the older Marines in the platoon. That afternoon, I learned why.

Five minutes after my call for help, Staff Sergeant Brinks came chugging up the highway in his hand-me-down five-ton Army truck, oblivious to the bullets snapping past. He eased down the embankment, where Stinetorf continued to unleash bursts on our assailants. Hopping down from the cab with a grin, Brinks said, "Howdy, sir. What's up?" I was so strung-out on adrenaline I could hardly speak, and I wasn't sure if his cheeriness was heroism or folly. In time I would learn it's simply the best way to get the job done.

Brinks sized up the Humvee with a professional eye and barked some orders to his Marines in the truck. They piled out and quickly attached a chain. With a tug and a pop, Colbert's Humvee jumped from the sobka, and we were ready to move. We trained our guns on the town to cover Goodwrench's departure and then followed him in single file. Colbert's Humvee crabbed along on bent rims, clumps of tar seeming to double the width of its frame. After half a kilometer, we climbed back up onto the highway and accelerated past RCT-1's dozens of armored vehicles. Why had we, in little more than dune buggies, just charged through a hostile town while tanks and LAVs sat here with their crews dozing in the dirt?

We saw the battalion circled in a field off the highway, and I led the platoon into our place along the perimeter. When halted in open terrain, the three companies formed a big circle, with each one taking a third of the clock — ten o'clock to two o'clock, two to six, and six to ten, with twelve being north. Bravo Company had six to ten, so we faced west across a mile of open field to a distant line of palm trees. Squeezing into a gap in the lines, the whole platoon covered only a hundred meters of frontage. After we pulled to a stop and Gunny Wynn shut off the engine, neither of us got out. For a few minutes, we sat quietly before turning toward each other. Wynn cracked a smile, and we both began to laugh. The laughs were forced, and I noticed he looked pale, the skin of his face drawn tighter than usual across his skull.

When he spoke, Wynn sounded hoarse. "Holy shit, huh? That was crazy."

"We almost got hosed." I looked at the map. "Al Gharraf. The name of the town is Al Gharraf."

I left the platoon to set up our defense and went in search of company headquarters. Stumbling across the uneven field under the weight of my gear and MOPP suit, I saw a cluster of Marines around a figure on the ground. I walked up and heard bits of a story, surely being retold now for the tenth time.

"So Darnold's driving through that fucking town, rounds zinging in from everywhere, and all of a sudden his arm slams sideways off the steering wheel. He says, 'I'm hit!' and Sergeant Kocher leans over to look. Sure enough, Darnold's bleeding from a hole in his forearm. Well, Kocher, real cool, wraps a tourniquet around it and says, 'You're fine. Keep driving.' Darnold shut up and drove, and we ended up here with everyone else. Goddamn."

I stared for a moment at First Recon Battalion's first combat casualty.

Darnold looked fine. There was a small red hole in his forearm where the bullet had entered and lodged.

At company headquarters, the captain had no further instructions for me — just settle in for the night and be ready to move in the morning — so I returned to the platoon. By now, the Marines had hacked sleeping holes from the soft dirt and had begun the daily routine of security, cleaning weapons, eating, cleaning feet, and sleeping.

And storytelling. Every fight is refought afterward. Sometimes quietly, sometimes boisterously; sometimes with laughs, sometimes with tears. The telling and retelling are important. Platoons have institutional memory. They learn, and they change. Most of that learning happens after a firefight. Some officers squelched the stories, considering them unprofessional and distracting. I encouraged them, as psychological unburdening and as improvised classrooms where we sharpened our blades for the next fight.

But something about the retelling unnerved me, too. Faith in our senses is what anchors us to sanity. Once, in college, I went cross-country skiing during a snowstorm. As I crossed an open meadow, the blanket of snow on the ground merged with the snow falling from the sky. With no horizon and no depth perception, I got vertigo. A twig poking through the snow near my feet looked the same as another skier hundreds of yards away. My head spun, and I had to sit down.

Combat is a form of vertigo. I was trained to thrive on chaos, but nothing prepared me for the fear of doubting my own senses. Frequently, I found that my memory of a firefight was just that — mine. Afterward, five Marines told five different stories. I remembered turning left off the dirt road onto a paved street running west through Al Gharraf. I saw fire coming from buildings to the right and remembered a drag race of four or five kilometers out to the highway. That was my memory, my accepted truth of what had happened.

But the map showed the distance was only about fifteen hundred meters, less than half of what I'd estimated. Some in the platoon remembered armed men standing to our left as we made the turn; I never saw them. The domed mosque was burned into my memory, but only Colbert and Wright could remember seeing it as I described it. Person was adamant that we had driven across a bridge during our sprint to the highway. Not one other person in the platoon remembered a bridge, but there it was on the map.

\*　　\*　　\*

Marines manned three of the four machine guns in the late afternoon. They searched the horizon with binoculars, calling out points of interest to one another. The fourth gun lay in pieces across a Humvee hood. Over it, Corporal Jacks labored intently. I watched his big dirty hands cleaning each small part with tenderness, even love. He reassembled the gun and then began to wipe down each individual grenade in the linked belts of Mark-19 ammunition. Watching Jacks clean his gun before eating, sleeping, or cleaning himself, I saw a bit of the essence of the Marine Corps, the spirit that has sustained young Marines in bad places for more than two hundred years. This was no idle patriotic reverie on my part, though. It was the kernel of a growing unwillingness to watch these Marines mistreated or wrongly employed by those with more power than experience. I cautioned myself not to pass judgment too quickly. As a platoon commander, I saw only a tiny piece of the puzzle. But every tactical fiber in my body said driving through Al Gharraf had been a mistake. We had gotten lucky, and it would be dangerous if someone mistook that luck for skill.

The sandstorm shrouded what was left of the daylight, and I hurried to finish preparing for a night on the line. I squinted through my compass to give left and right lateral limits to each machine gunner. The gunners marked these limits on their guns' traversing bars so that in case we were attacked in the dark, the guns' sectors would all overlap but wouldn't include any other friendly positions. This was routine procedure, essentially unchanged since World War I. Battlefield success came from timely creativity atop a firm foundation of grunt work. Recon's reputation was built on creativity and individual improvisation, but woe to the young lieutenant who failed to heed the unglamorous basics. Upon them, all else rested.

And so I went down the line, sighting, calculating, and drawing lines on my map. As I worked, Gunny Wynn also visited each team, looking for injuries and equipment damage and checking our ammunition. Through the whole engagement, the platoon had fired only about a thousand rounds, and we carried enough extra ammo in the back of my Humvee to top everyone off. At the end of the line, members of Lovell's team were counting bullet holes in their Humvee and marveling at holes in the rest of their gear. Stinetorf showed me a long gash through the canvas of his North Face backpack where an AK-47 round had carved its path only inches from where he'd been standing.

"I'm guessing their warranty won't cover this," he said, fingering the rip.

Colbert's Humvee had also been shot up. There were twenty-two bullet holes in it, including six in the door next to Evan Wright's seat. When I walked up, he was studying them with a kind of awe.

"How you feeling, Evan?" I half-expected him to say he had enough information for his story and wanted to leave on the next resupply helicopter.

"Embedded," he replied. "More embedded than I ever thought I'd be."

Espera put an arm around his shoulders. "But he's staying with us. Dude's got balls."

Gusts of wind swept across the field, blowing dust through little knots of Marines still reliving the day's drive. I dropped my pack on the downwind side of the Humvee and stripped out of my flak jacket and helmet, feeling light and free under the breezy overcast. I swung a pickax into the earth, carving out my bed. Far from a chore, I found digging therapeutic as the day's tension flowed from my arms through the handle to dissipate in the ground. While I dug, I thought about the relativity of safety. My friends and family at home were surely worried about me at that very moment. For them, Iraq was a dangerous place. For me, some towns were dangerous, and some were safe. Within the dangerous towns, some blocks were dangerous and some safe. On a dangerous block, one side of the street could be dangerous and the other safe. I finished digging the hole before I could work out whether that meant I was always safe or always in danger.

Darkness fell, and the wind picked up. Thunder mixed with the rumbling of distant explosions, and lightning blended with the flash of artillery rounds shooting overhead. Gunny Wynn and I sought refuge in the cab, where we monitored the radio and tore into our first MRE of the day. I realized that I was ravenous. Wynn gnawed on a Tootsie Roll as I watched his face reflected in the windshield by the dim green radio lights.

"What's on your mind?" I asked.

"After Nasiriyah and this last place, it's pretty clear to me what the Iraqi strategy is. They won't touch us out here in open country because we'll blast the shit out of them. They'll wait till we're in the towns, and then they'll attrit us. When we fight back and wound civilians, they'll get paraded all over TV and make us look like thugs."

I looked at the map, tracing my finger up Highway 7 from Nasiriyah to Al Gharraf. Then I continued tracing north along our proposed route. An Nasr, Ash Shatrah, Ar Rifa, Qalat Sukkar, Al Hayy, Al Kut — a string of towns stretching all the way to the Tigris. And north of the Tigris lay Baghdad, the biggest town of all.

"Well, it doesn't look like it'll get better anytime soon," I said.

We traded radio watch back and forth for the rest of the night. Sometime before dawn, as I lay in my hole, it started to rain.

# 26

THE MORNING OF MARCH 26 cleared, as if the rain had washed all the dirt from the air. Sunrise revealed Marines caked in a muddy crust, stretching sore limbs and beginning the daily ritual of brewing coffee. Austere living intensified our appreciation of life's simple pleasures. At the top of that list was a hot mug of coffee, the thicker the better. Next to each Humvee, battered canteen cups perched atop flaming pieces of C-4 plastic explosive. Brews were passed around and shared communally; to drink an entire cup yourself was poor form.

Having slept in my MOPP gear and boots, all I had to do after waking was stand up. I rolled up my sleeping bag and stuffed the wet, misshapen lump in the back of the Humvee. Despite the discomfort, this lifestyle hummed with efficiency. No shaving, showering, or ironing clothes. No blow dryers, breakfast, newspaper, or e-mail. Just wake up and live.

A radio call summoned me to company headquarters, where the same morning routine was under way. The captain briefed the day's plan: get on the highway in thirty minutes and attack north. No Americans were currently farther north than Al Gharraf, and we'd be leapfrogging up the highway with other elements of the RCT. Changes would be briefed on the fly, he said, so be sure to keep the radios up and running. Oh, yeah, and watch out for RPG ambushes and car bombs.

Gunny Wynn and the team leaders waited around the hood of our Humvee. I grabbed my map and joined them.

"Everybody's favorite mission: movement to contact," I said. "We're driving north on Highway 7, and we're attached to RCT-1." The team leaders took notes, studying their own maps. "We'll be leapfrogging and strong-pointing as we go. All friendlies are on the road, so if anything off to the flanks worries you, it's probably enemy. Cobras will be on and off. Any questions?"

"Sir, do you think Hooters girls would look better in white shorts than orange?" I grinned, and the others laughed. These guys were blessed with perfect timing.

We continued through a few serious concerns and contingencies before breaking up for the team leaders to brief their men. Gunny Wynn and I cleaned our rifles, rubbed pencil erasers on all the radio connections to scour off corrosion from the night's rain, and started the engine. Ten minutes later, in fits and starts, the battalion snaked out of the field and up onto the single ribbon of Highway 7.

Like many bad days, this one started out well. We hummed north, passing the massed combat power of RCT-1 spread out along the highway. They were still stopped near the road intersection where we'd shot through Al Gharraf and landed in the sobka field. The town sat three hundred meters east of the highway, shuttered and menacing. As the sky continued to clear, sunlight dappled rich fields and green trees. Cooking fires smoked in chimneys. Young shepherds waved as we passed, while their sisters, dressed in robes of red and deep purple, peeked shyly from behind gates.

We halted at the southern end of An Nasr, pulling off the pavement in a herringbone. I walked to each vehicle, checking on the Marines and telling them we'd be holding for a few minutes while part of the RCT passed us to enter the town. The three snipers uncased their rifles and scanned our flanks, watching for Iraqi shooters.

In many cases, the Iraqis seemed almost completely indifferent to violence. We could be locked in a raging gunfight, with mortars exploding and jets screaming overhead, only to see three women saunter past with buckets on their heads, strolling to the town well. This made our obligation to spare civilians even harder. Snipers are the ultimate smart weapon because they hit only what they mean to kill.

As we talked, a company of tanks rumbled past. Some were painted green and some desert tan. All had names such as "Peacemaker" and "Avenger" stenciled on their barrels. The crews stood in their hatches, looking robotic beneath goggles, armor, and helmets. I noticed that once they'd passed us, they closed the hatches and proceeded toward An

Nasr buttoned up tight. A company of LAVs followed them, also buttoned up, with their turrets alternating to the left and right. The highway rose south of An Nasr on a graceful, modern span of concrete, crossing low green fields and a small river before dropping back to disappear into the cluster of buildings. The tanks clanked over the bridge and out of sight. Overhead, four Cobra gunships raced north, splitting into two pairs and turning low circles over the center of town. Finally, it seemed, we were entering a town properly.

The word came to move out, and we began to climb the bridge. An Nasr's streets were deserted, gates closed and shutters latched. Nothing moved. Tanks sat at all the cross streets, turrets leveled along the roads to discourage anyone from approaching. We passed block after block, and I started to relax. Maybe the fedayeen weren't here, or maybe our firepower had intimidated them. As my shoulders loosened and my breathing slowed, a long burst of automatic-weapons fire roared over my right shoulder.

Incoming.

Tight shoulders, shallow breaths. "Hitman Two, taking fire from the east." I tried to keep my voice steady and measured as I passed the warning.

The Humvee wove back and forth as Wynn fumbled with his rifle and the steering wheel. "Goddamn it. I don't see anything."

Another burst of fire ripped overhead with a series of sonic cracks.

"Where are the shooters?" I swiveled my head, looking for the source of the fire. We couldn't shoot back indiscriminately, but I didn't want our attackers to think they had us running scared. Our mission was clear: get to Baghdad. We choked down our rage and continued north, never firing back because we saw nothing to shoot at. Within minutes, we passed once more into open fields and groves of trees.

Bravo Company led the battalion, and Second Platoon led Bravo. Ahead of us was only LAR, and it sounded as if they were in a fight. I heard the hammering of chain guns and the whooshing of 25 mm cannons. Smoke curled into the sky ahead, and I saw flaming trucks through my binoculars. We pressed forward. I found that instinct took over in firefights, and fear was replaced by the countless small tasks of living, leading, and fighting. The anticipation was worse. As we drove toward the guns, I unconsciously pulled my arms and legs inward, trying to tuck inside my body armor. My doorless Humvee, which south of An Nasr had satisfied me as a pleasant way to enjoy the beautiful countryside, now felt ridiculously exposed. In my mind, every tree, rooftop, and berm hid a fighter with an RPG, and that RPG was surely going to hit me square in the chest. At first, I stayed off the radio for fear that my voice would sound funny. But when I made a call, I was surprised to hear it steady and calm.

LAR left the fedayeen few options but to flee, surrender, or die. We passed a minibus that had recently exploded. Its occupants were charred lumps, some hanging from the shattered windows. Only the driver was alive, and he waved feebly, still seated behind the steering wheel and burned nearly black. On the sides of the road, dead gunmen sprawled from fighting holes. We drove gingerly past one still clutching his RPG launcher. Rocket-propelled grenades littered the ground around his corpse.

Four pickup trucks burned along the shoulder. Each had been mounted with an antiaircraft machine gun and parked facing north, so the guns could be fired south as we advanced up the highway. Now the guns were blackened and bent, and their skeletal crews smoldered in the dust. Container trucks and tankers burned farther off the road, sending clouds of greasy smoke into the sky. I turned to focus on a flash of color in my peripheral vision and saw a dead girl in a blue dress sprawled in the road. She looked to be about six years old. Next to her, crouched on his haunches with his hands atop his head in surrender, a uniformed soldier hissed at us as we passed. Reaching back to four years in a Jesuit high school, I found myself mouthing the Twenty-third Psalm: "Though I walk through the valley of the shadow of death . . ."

We sprinted through the town of Ash Shatrah with every available gun hanging out our windows. We didn't know it at the time, but Ash Shatrah would later take on symbolic importance in the war. A supply convoy would be ambushed on this same road, and a Marine sergeant would be captured and mutilated, some said crucified. (Our battalion's Alpha Company was sent to work with the CIA and the Free Iraqi Forces to recover the Marine's body and teach the people of Ash Shatrah a lesson about desecrating Marines. Just before the operation, however, the Marines realized that most of their Iraqi allies had fled in the night.)

The next town on the map was Ar Rifa. Battalion headquarters called to say that we would reverse the An Nasr plan — recon would enter the town first and strong-point it for the RCT to move through. My platoon would lead the battalion into Ar Rifa, peeling off the road at the first major intersection to set up a strongpoint. The rest of Bravo Company would continue a kilometer farther north and do the same. Then Alpha and Charlie would pass by us to establish their strongpoints in the central and northern parts of town. Once we were all in place, RCT-1 would thunder through to continue the push north. By the time we entered the town, it was early afternoon, but we expected the whole process to take less than an hour.

Ar Rifa stank. The town sprawled west of the highway, stopping at a wall just fifty meters from the road. Sewage flowed through drainage ditches, and trash piles dotted the roadside. An electrical substation stood just east of the highway. It was on fire; the bluish white blaze smelled like fried wiring. Three hundred meters past it were a smattering of mud huts, a row of palm trees, and a few berms. South of the power station, a small road joined the highway from the east. This is where I led the platoon to set up our strongpoint.

We parked our five Humvees in the shallow defilade of a drainage ditch and posted security in all directions. The snipers peered through their scopes at walls, gates, and rooftops. Machine gunners trained their guns on likely targets, one north, one south, one east, and one west. Gunny Wynn and I studied the map and plotted targets for on-call artillery to speed up the response time in case we needed help fast. As we worked, the rest of the battalion roared past, smiling and waving, clearly happy not to be stopping at our sorry excuse for a strongpoint.

"I've got armed men moving in the trees!" Christeson shouted, then pointed as three or four men darted through the tree line, carrying RPGs and looking our way.

I talked Wynn onto them, and he rested his M40 sniper rifle on the hood of the Humvee. Patiently, he stared through the scope, ignoring the noise and confusion swirling around him. His finger tightened on the trigger, then slackened again, waiting for the perfect shot. I was turning to answer the radio when his rifle cracked.

"Don't know if I hit 'em, but that'll make 'em think twice."

Two of the men ran out from behind a berm. Christeson opened up with a light machine gun, spitting 5.56 mm rounds at them in bursts of eight or ten. I saw through my binoculars that he was aiming high. Tracers arced over their heads as they ran.

"Lower, Christeson. You're shooting too high." My voice sounded calm, almost like a coach on the rifle range. Again, this surprised me. I was learning that leadership under fire is part theater. There must be competence to back it up, but appearances go a long way toward setting the tone for the whole platoon. Christeson dropped his rounds, and the men fell. "Keep an eye out, Christeson, and kill anyone else who comes at us from that direction."

Only a football field away in the other direction were the walls of Ar Rifa. Like most Iraqi towns, this one blended the East African and Soviet brands of despair. The houses were some combination of mud, cinderblocks, and unfinished wood. Water cisterns perched on flat roofs, and makeshift television antennas crawled from upper-story windows like steel ivy. Dark windows, many without glass, broke the thick walls. The buildings sat close together, separated only by narrow alleys closed off with wrought iron gates. Government buildings, generally made of stone or poured concrete, stood out among the houses. Their spare, symmetrical forms oozed authoritarianism. Often their only ornamentation was an Iraqi crest over the door, and sometimes a tattered green-and-black flag flying in front. In my military judgment, Ar Rifa was a densely concentrated natural fortress of thick walls and tall gates, and we sat far too close to it.

Our sporadic gunfire died out, and no one moved in the fields around us. The Marines settled into a tense wait, eyeing their watches and damning RCT-1 for being so slow. I stood next to Christeson as he scanned the tree line. As far as I knew, the earlier shooting had been his first at close human targets, and I wanted to feel him out a bit.

"That was good shooting, Christeson."

He looked surprised that I was addressing him. "Thanks, sir." Christeson was the youngest member of the platoon. Normally, in a recon unit full of senior Marines, a private first class would be fresh meat. But Christeson could hold his own. He had received an appointment to the U.S. Naval Academy to become an officer but had turned it down after 9/11 to enlist as a Marine grunt. I respected him for that.

From the south, artillery boomed. They were shots, not impacts, and Wynn glanced at me with a raised eyebrow. I shook my head. Don't know. The rounds rustled overhead and exploded into the northern end of Ar Rifa. Someone was controlling the fire mission, and the only Americans up there were recon's other companies. I got on the radio. Alpha Company was shooting at the Ba'ath Party headquarters. We wondered about the wisdom of dropping high-explosive artillery shells into a crowded town, regardless of the target's legitimacy. More questionable news followed: our company commander was on his way to our position to work up a mission to deter those gunmen moving in the trees to our east.

I met the captain when his Humvee pulled into our small circle. "Sir, we took some shots at them, and they seem to have gotten the idea," I said. "We're glassing the area but haven't seen anyone moving."

"Yeah, but Alpha Company's up there calling for fire, and I want to call a mission, too."

I couldn't believe it. We were going to fire artillery to keep up with Alpha Company. "Sir, I'd rather go on doing what we're doing. We've got things under control."

"You just keep tabs on your platoon, Lieutenant Fick, and let me work up the mission." Three minutes later, I listened as he made a botched call for fire to the battalion. I sat on my hands until he called in a target location only two hundred meters from where we stood. Anything inside six hundred meters was considered "danger close" — requiring special care due to its proximity to friendly troops. In this open ground, we'd be showered with shrapnel from our own rounds. I started to intervene.

"Sir, that's way inside danger close. Cancel the mission," Gunny Wynn said with growing alarm.

"We're shooting it. Keep quiet," he replied.

"It's an empty field!" I shouted. "We're watching it. You're going to hit us with the rounds, and probably RCT-1, too, since we don't know when they'll be coming up the road. Cancel the fucking mission." I reached to take the radio handset from him.

I later found out that Major Whitmer was on the other end of the radio, and he was even angrier than I was. He threw the handset down in disgust, screaming about "that fucking idiot," whom the battalion staff secretly called "Shitman." His candor earned him a disapproving look from Colonel Ferrando, since the division chief of staff was within earshot. But he rejected the mission and put a limit on the damage wrought by the captain's ineptitude. The CO drove off after threatening me for challenging his authority.

In keeping with our tradition of a crisis a minute, Sergeant Espera ran up, crouching low behind the Humvees to thwart any snipers watching us. "Sir, I've got a flat tire. We need to change it now so we're ready to move."

I considered this, using the framework my Quantico instructors referred to as "turning the map around" — looking at the options from the enemy's perspective. What would I do, as a fedayeen commander, if I saw a Marine Humvee up on a jack with men frantically changing a flat tire? I'd capitalize on their weakness and attack. At worst, I'd catch them immobile and inflict casualties. At best, I'd force them to withdraw, leaving the Humvee for me to burn as a trophy of American impotence.

"Espera, I can't let you do that here," I said. "You have to take your team and drive up to Goodwrench's position. They have more people and can help you change the tire faster. Sorry. Get your boys together and go now. We could be moving any minute."

He shot me a glance, half-trusting and half-doubting. Another second's consideration and Espera nodded, seeing the logic. "Roger that, sir. I'll call you when we're en route back here."

Espera's open-back Humvee crept out from the drainage ditch and raced up the highway, bumping unevenly on its rim. Watching them go, I felt another pang of responsibility, and of respect.

Three hours after stopping, we still hadn't seen a single Marine from RCT-1. Watching the sun slide down the sky, I was more and more uncomfortable about sitting in one place. Tactical catastrophes are rarely the outcome of a single poor decision. Small compromises incrementally close off options until a commander is forced into actions he would never choose freely. I didn't want to become the subject of a case study taught at Quantico, and I certainly didn't want to be pictured in Dr. Death's killology slide show.

Although Ar Rifa's gates and shutters had been closed when we arrived, curious townspeople gradually began to venture outside the walls, peering at us. Some waved, while others drew their fingers across their throats. Up the road, dozens of Iraqis scoured the pavement, scavenging spent brass bullet casings from the earlier shooting. I called battalion headquarters to request a translator. Ten minutes later, a Humvee roared down the road and deposited Mish in the mud next to me.

Mish, a Kuwaiti, despised the Iraqis, who had overrun his country only a decade before. He weighed more than 250 pounds, and he kept his long hair coiled in a pile beneath an American-issue helmet. Even after the Marine Corps concluded that weapons of mass destruction were no longer a threat and allowed us to remove our MOPP suits, Mish could never be found without his chemical suit, gloves, and cumbersome rubber boots. Now he eyed the growing crowd with distaste before ambling across the road to talk.

I watched as the residents shook their fists and spat in Arabic at Mish. He shrugged and listened with heavy-lidded eyes. Three men from Ar Rifa pointed at us, their voices raised and their feet stamping angrily. I told Lovell's Marines to keep an eye on me and walked out to join Mish.

"What are they saying?"

Mish paused, savoring his importance. "They say they are happy the Marines are here, and they're grateful to be liberated."

"Goddammit, Mish, cut the bullshit."

"They wonder why you are sitting here and are afraid you will attack the town and kill them. They say the fedayeen are at the other end of town, in the old headquarters of the Ba'ath Party. They want to help us kill the bad guys."

Now we were making progress. "OK, ask them if they can do something for us." I handed Mish a fistful of infrared chem lights. "Tell them to wait until after dark, then crack these chem lights and put them on the roofs of the buildings where the fedayeen are holed up. American helicopters will be able to see the lights and may destroy the buildings."

This was a plan we'd been briefed on earlier. I had my doubts about it, given what I'd already seen of Iraqi tribalism. Most of these lights, I expected, would end up on the roofs of people to whom these men owed money. Still, it might work if we could corroborate the identity of the buildings with another source. The men thanked me profusely for the lights as Mish extorted cigarettes from them. Dusk had deepened over Ar Rifa, and we jogged back across no man's land to the relative safety of the Humvees.

The battalion repeated instructions to stand by and wait for RCT-1, so we settled in for an uneasy night. The Marines attached batteries to our fireflies, and soon the little infrared lights winked comfortingly from each Humvee when viewed through night vision goggles. A few Marines dozed on the ground while their teammates scanned the fields and town for movement. I checked our perimeter security again and stopped at Colbert's Humvee to use the AN/PAS-13. This black plastic sight was about the size of a tissue box and enabled us to see heat. Traditional night optics amplify ambient light, hence the nickname "starlight scopes." Thermal optics like the AN/PAS-13 see heat differentials and paint any heat source, such as a human being, as a bright white blob moving against a dark background. Satisfied that we were alone, I walked back to my Humvee to monitor the radio and choke down a cold MRE. A call from headquarters interrupted me.

"Be advised we have a friendly logistics convoy approaching from the south."

I raised the handset to reply as machine gun fire shattered the night. Red tracers streamed east and west from the highway as trucks rumbled closer. I looked in vain for incoming fire.

"Get down! Everybody down!"

The platoon was already diving from turrets and hoods onto the dirt. I dropped behind the engine block with the side of my head pressed into the mud. Yelling "Cease fire" into the handset, I watched the convoy of trucks racing toward us, still pumping rounds into the trees and buildings along the highway. Not a single tracer round traveled toward them from the darkness. For a moment, I fixed on the irony of waiting to be shot by fellow Marines. Rage followed cynicism as I thought indignantly of how we had spent the entire day sitting in this dangerous spot, making it safe for their passage, and now these pogues were blasting through at fifty miles per hour, shooting everything in sight. My neural tangent circled back to how good it would feel to return fire, knowing we could waste the careless bastards. By then, though, the trucks were nearly abreast of us, and I pushed deeper into the dirt, watching beneath the Humvee as seven-ton trucks and tractor-trailers roared past, spewing tracers in wild streams far above our heads. Thank God they couldn't aim. I called a warning north to the other platoons before sitting up and leaning back against the tire. Mud caked the side of my face.

Colbert shouted from the darkness, "Fuckers thought our fireflies were muzzle flashes." Another voice volunteered that support troops should carry clubs instead of guns.

Near midnight, the battalion called to tell us we'd be linking up as a battalion on the north side of Ar Rifa before beginning a long drive north to an airfield near Qalat Sukkar. Gunny Wynn and I huddled beneath a poncho, shining a red-lens flashlight on our maps and trying to figure out how to get there. Qalat Sukkar was the next town north on

Highway 7, about twenty miles away. The airfield, though, was east of the town on a road labeled Highway 17. It looked like forty or fifty miles of nighttime driving, without headlights, through enemy territory far forward of any American positions.

Wynn turned to me with a resigned look and said, "Being in this battalion is like winning the lottery every fucking day."

# 27

NORTH OF AR RIFA, we spotted the battalion's fireflies flashing in a field east of the highway and silently rolled into the perimeter. While the platoon prepared for the long drive to Qalat Sukkar, Gunny Wynn and I sat in on a brief of the night's mission. I was reaching a numbed equilibrium where nothing fazed me. In the past twelve hours, I had been shot at by other Marines, overseen the killing of a group of men intent on killing us, watched artillery pour into a crowded town, nearly been killed by my own CO, and now was about to be launched on a long-range mission into enemy territory.

The colonel pulled his officers and staff NCOs into a tight circle and rasped through the plan. The British Parachute Regiment would assault the Iraqi military airfield at Qalat Sukkar the next morning in order to use it as a staging base for the push to Baghdad. We would do reconnaissance on the field before the attack. There were reports of tanks and antiaircraft guns there that posed a significant threat to the British force. No more details were given. We'd be racing sunrise and had to leave immediately to be of any use to the assault force. A platoon commander in the back asked the colonel if he had ever seen a movie called *They Were Expendable*.

I drove the first leg of the trip, allowing Wynn to catch a bit of much-needed rest. Night vision goggles restricted my sight to two narrow fields of grainy green. Ahead of me, Espera's Humvee wove up the highway, its driver clearly struggling as I was. Colbert and Lovell carried the thermal sights at the front and rear of the platoon. Routine banter crackled back and forth on the radio as possible targets were identified and then dismissed as sheep, goats, or early-rising farmers. We were exhausted. I remembered Shaka's scolding in Afghanistan about officers transferring their own fatigue onto troops who were capable of more than they knew. He was right. But you could only push so hard before something broke.

We left Highway 7 south of Qalat Sukkar to circumvent the town on empty country roads. For two hours, we crept through the darkness. I was taking limited cues — a glimpse of a house or the condition of the road — and building a story around them: population density, terrain, the likelihood of the Iraqi army being nearby. It occurred to me that my impressions could be completely wrong, that I could drive that route in daylight and make entirely different assumptions. Our assumptions governed our responses — whether to attack or withdraw if we got hit, whether to respond with massive force or precision fire, whether to call for reinforcements. I figured I was getting half my assumptions right. The thought was chilling. Fatigue, darkness, stress, and a vague mission conspired to envelop us in a fog. Emotionally, I felt as if we were driving a hundred miles an hour down a highway in a blinding snowstorm.

Each roadside ditch and clump of trees was a potential ambush point, and I caught glimpses of alert Marines in the dim glow of GPS receivers and radio lights. The terrain opened up as we neared the airfield, and the clouds dissipated, unveiling a sky of shining stars. Just before dawn, in the coldest part of the night, we stopped and draped camouflage netting over our vehicles. Everyone but those pulling security collapsed into sleep, and I went in search of company headquarters to ask about our next move. The captain said that two foot patrols would be sent out to look at the airfield, but we were not included. I expected that the patrols would observe the field, confirm or deny the reports of significant defenses, and then pull back as we watched the British attack at first light. There was nothing more for me to do, so I returned to the platoon, inspected the lines, and stretched out in the tall grass to sleep.

Christeson woke me twenty minutes later. "Sir, we're getting ready to move." The eastern sky was already turning pink. Dew had soaked my poncho liner. I threw it in the back of the Humvee. My mouth was dry, and my eyes burned with the irritation of too many hours awake. I felt clumsy and disoriented as I joined the captain for an update.

The patrols were still not in position to see the field, but the division wouldn't authorize the British attack without some idea of Qalat Sukkar's defenses. I had visions of burning British helicopters falling from the sky and nodded in agreement. It would have been easy, I thought, to delay the attack and use the daylight to do a thorough reconnaissance of the airfield. The morning was clear. We could stack aircraft overhead to obliterate anything that threatened us. But the commanders ordered that we, in our light-skinned Humvees and with no preparation time, would attack the airfield immediately. Reconnaissance in force.

I had first felt fear in Iraq on the initial drive into Nasiriyah. The next three days of gunfights had hardly affected me. Hearing that we were about to seize the airfield, I was afraid for the second time. The fear this time was not of Iraqi defenders and my own violent death. Instead, it came from realizing that my commanders also felt the effects of fatigue and stress. Fear filled the little cracks and growing voids in the trust I had placed in them. Remembering General Mattis's insistence that we train to survive the first five days in combat, I thought how ironic it would be to die on this morning of the sixth day.

Coupled with the fear were resignation and helplessness. I was a Marine. I would salute and follow orders. Without knowing the big picture, we had to trust that they made sense. My Marines and I were willing to give our lives, but we preferred not to do so cheaply. The fear was a realization that my exchange rate wasn't the only one being consulted.

Engines were already cranking as I briefed the platoon. My operations order took thirty seconds. We'd rush down the airfield's main access road and crash through the front gate. Once inside, we'd do a starburst, with Bravo Company continuing straight ahead, Third Platoon on the left, and Second on the right. Alpha and Charlie would break off in different directions. We'd advance across the field and engage any Iraqi forces we found. Consolidation would be on the main runway once we overwhelmed any resistance. Air Force aircraft would be overhead, but their call signs and contact frequencies were unknown. Part of me expected open revolt, but the team leaders nodded, loaded their teams, and formed up to move.

Backlit by the rising sun, we raced down the airfield access road. I looked to my right and saw one of the night's foot patrols facing us with crossed arms raised, our signal for "friendly — don't shoot me." The road was several kilometers long, lined with brush and small trees. It looked as though we were alone.

Gunny Wynn drove, and I juggled my rifle and two radios in the passenger seat. Just seconds before we reached the chainlink fence surrounding the airfield, a warning from company headquarters went out to all vehicles. "All personnel on the airfield are declared hostile. I say again, all personnel on the airfield are declared hostile."

We normally operated within certain constraints. We could respond proportionally in self-defense — "fire if fired upon" — or we could shoot first at obvious military targets. Both categories depended on the target being a clear and present danger. "Declared hostile" meant there were no rules of engagement. It meant shoot first and ask questions later. At Quantico, we had learned about Vietnam's free-fire zones. They had been, it was acknowledged, immoral and counterproductive. Qalat Sukkar was being declared a free-fire zone.

I clicked the transmit button on my radio handset to countermand the order. I wanted to tell the platoon to hold fast to our normal rules of engagement. But I stopped. I thought that maybe the battalion or the company had access to other information they had no time to share. I trusted that making the "declared hostile" call would save my Marines' lives when they ran into that unknown threat by shaving crucial nanoseconds from their response time. I let the order stand and shouldered my rifle, pointing it at the landscape flashing past.

A machine gun in front of us fired a short burst. I caught a blurred glimpse of people, cars, and camels running through the brush. Men carried long sticks, maybe rifles. A garbled radio transmission warned of "muzzle flashes . . . men with rifles." Something near the people flashed, but we were already beyond them, sprinting for the runway. We crossed a tarmac inside the fence line and saw guard towers lining the field's perimeter. Gunny Wynn and I broke to the right, leading the platoon across our side of the airfield. We surged over berms and irrigation ditches, straining to reach the runway and its promise of fast driving. An Air Force A-10 Thunderbolt attack jet stood on a wingtip, its pilot looking down at us. He flashed over so low I could smell his exhaust. I hoped he saw the bright pink air panel on our hood.

We reached the runway and deployed in a semicircle to protect the battalion's flank as other platoons pressed forward to investigate the airfield's buildings. Reports of tanks and guns in the trees flooded the radio. We saw nothing.

As the sun rose higher, I took stock of our new conquest. A single cratered runway bisected the field. Grass grew forlornly from cracks in the pavement. A few hangars and other buildings lined the fence on the far side of the field, but there wasn't a single sign of human activity. The A-10 made one final pass before departing to the south. In the quiet that followed, I was conscious of birds pecking in the grass and the breeze rustling trees, their leaves speckling the ground with shadows. Once again, the war staggered me with its disjointed shifts between violent action and peaceful repose. I felt like an intruder on this beautiful morning.

Qalat Sukkar airfield was deserted. It looked as if it hadn't been used in years. High command canceled the British assault since First Recon had already seized the field. The battalion moved to a large pasture north of the airfield and halted. My platoon was assigned five hundred meters along the L bend of an irrigation canal. We parked the Humvees at hundred-meter intervals and began digging in. I didn't know whether we would be here for an hour or a week.

The numbness returned. We had been lucky — again. Disaster was averted not by our own skill, but by Iraqi ineptitude. One well-camouflaged tank on that airfield could have blown up our whole platoon before the A-10 got it. I swung my pickax into the cracked earth. The Marines knew the airfield mission could have been disastrous. There had already been open talk about their welfare being ignored. I had disagreed. The best way to get everyone home alive would be to win quickly and decisively. My thoughts were jumbled as I continued to dig. Ideas and connections were coming together, but below the level of conscious thought.

The Marines thought that Colonel Ferrando was cavalier, that he sent them on missions with more regard for his career than for his men. Again, I disagreed. Command is a mask. A leader can agonize behind it, should agonize behind it. I knew I did. I suspected the colonel did, too, but he couldn't show it.

Movement in the distance caught my attention, and I stood up straight, leaning on the pick and craning my head to see. In front of Lovell's team, five people shuffled toward us. Two Marines advanced on them, weapons ready. I slid into my body armor and followed. As I got closer, I could see that two women were dragging an object wrapped in blankets. Behind them, three men pulled another bundle. All through Iraq, villagers approached us seeking medicine for their ailments, but this seemed different. I quickened my pace and saw Doc Bryan, with a medical kit slung over his shoulder, jogging toward the Iraqis, still a football field away from me. I began to run.

By the time I reached them, Bryan had unwrapped the bundles, revealing two young boys, both in their teens. Brothers. The older one had a bullet wound in his leg. Coagulated blood crusted his calf and ankle. I saw the younger boy's face before I saw his wound. He looked like the body I had seen at D.C. General Hospital. Pale green wax. The color revealed how much life had already seeped from the four holes in his abdomen. The boys' mother and grandmother hovered over them. A few steps away stood the boys' father. They betrayed no emotion.

Bryan inspected the wounds for a few seconds and announced they were from 5.56 mm rounds. The only such rounds in Iraq were American, and the only Americans there were us. In horror, I thought back to our assault on the airfield a few hours before. The pieces fell into place. Those weren't rifles we had seen but shepherds' canes, not muzzle flashes but the sun reflecting on a windshield. The running camels belonged to these boys. We'd shot two children.

The platoon jumped into action. Two teams took over security, while Doc Bryan went to work on the boys. He triaged them and turned to the gut shots first. Tearing open his med kit, he grabbed IVs and saline bags, blankets, scissors, and gauze. I reached down to help, recoiling unconsciously as blood seeped into my gloves, turning the green to black. The urge to help was overwhelming. This couldn't happen. I had to make it right. Bryan was gentle in reminding me that I could be more useful in other ways.

"Sir, we have this under control. Can you get Dr. Aubin over here and try to get an aerial casevac? Tell 'em we have an 'urgent surgical.'"

I expected everyone else to feel the same urgency we felt, but I was wrong. I ran into company headquarters, breathless, and explained what had happened. The captain simply said that a decision to help the kids was above his head. There was no time to fight with him. I moved on. Major Benelli sat in the shade of the battalion headquarters tent, digging at an MRE.

"Sir, I have two wounded children in my lines. We shot them during the assault this morning. My corpsman's doing what he can, but one of them's urgent surgical."

He shrugged. "So?"

I explained again that we had led the attack just after the call that all personnel on the field were declared hostile. We had seen people, flashes, maybe rifles, and had fired. But they weren't soldiers. We had shot two kids, and now at least one of them was bleeding to death in front of my platoon.

"The colonel's asleep. Just tell them to go back to their house. We can't help them." He went back to his food, dismissing me.

My vision narrowed to a tunnel. There was no clean, clinical explanation for what I felt and what I wanted to do. I wanted to tell the major that we were Americans, that Americans don't shoot kids and let them die, that the men in my platoon had to be able to look themselves in the mirror for the rest of their lives. I wanted him to get out there and put his hands in the kid's chest to stop the blood that flowed in rhythmic spurts from the holes. I wanted to cradle the major's head between my arms and twist.

But there wasn't time. I was still conditioned to accept senior officers' decisions, regardless of their stupidity, criminality, or inhumanity. So I walked away and found the battalion medical officer, Navy Lieutenant Alex Aubin. I briefed him quickly. Aubin's eyes were wide. He grabbed his equipment and went to join Doc Bryan while I returned to battalion headquarters. We still needed permission to evacuate the boys, and I couldn't do that on my own. Benelli smirked when I approached.

"The colonel's still asleep, Lieutenant. I'm not waking him, and I'm not endangering Americans to evacuate those casualties. Deal with it."

Those cracks in my trust were getting wider, growing into chasms, filling with fear and rage, sorrow and regret. I felt impotent, but I wasn't powerless. I had an assault rifle in my hands. I could shoot the motherfucker. I could hold him hostage until he called in that helicopter. There was just enough cool self-awareness left in my mind to stop me. This was one of those times I'd been told I'd face. After all that training, all the ego-inflating and power-tripping that went with being a Marine, this was it. My very own leadership challenge. I drove back to the platoon.

Our values were being inverted, and it threatened to destroy us. Good Marines were sent on a stupid mission governed by harebrained rules of engagement, and now they were being abandoned to suffer the consequences of other people's poor decisions. I thought of the untold innocent civilians who must have been killed by artillery and air strikes over the past week. The only difference was that we hadn't stuck around to see the effects those wrought. Our actions were being thrust in our faces, and the chain of command was passing the buck to the youngest, and most vulnerable, of the troops.

I hadn't been seized by a sudden burst of conscience. Pro-war. Anti-war. War for freedom. War for oil. Philosophical disputes were a luxury I could not enjoy. War was what I had. We didn't vote for it, authorize it, or declare it. We just had to fight it. And fighting it, for me, meant two things: winning and getting my men home alive. Alive, though, set the bar too low. I had to get them home physically and psychologically intact. They had to know that, whether or not they supported the larger war, they had fought their little piece of it with honor and had retained their humanity. If they got killed or went insane, I had to be able to look at their mothers and explain that they hadn't been victims of their own comrades' mistakes. Those Iraqi boys could die, but I couldn't let them die in our hands.

Doc Bryan looked up expectantly as I approached. He and Dr. Aubin had stabilized the boys but made it clear that the younger one would die without immediate surgery. The older child would probably linger on for a few days before infection killed him. Colbert stood there, with tears in his eyes.

I pulled Aubin aside. "Sir, the battalion says these kids can get fucked. They want us to let them die. What're the rules if you take control of a casualty?"

There was our escape. Once the battalion medical officer had control of wounded civilians, we were legally and ethically required to give them all available care. We gathered eight stretcher-bearers and struck out, on foot, across the field to battalion headquarters.

"Here you go, sir. You want to let them die, they can die right here in front of your tent." Doc Bryan gingerly lowered the stretcher in front of Major Benelli, who, for once, had nothing to say. Faced with a small-scale mutiny and the growing realization that posterity would frown on Marine officers who sat by while children died of Marine-inflicted gunshot wounds, he slipped around the back of the tent to wake the colonel.

Ferrando ordered the boys' immediate evacuation to RCT-1's field hospital, where they would be treated by a shock-trauma platoon. Doc Bryan rode along with them to maintain continuity of care until they were turned over to the surgeons. I walked back to the platoon, trying to think of what I could tell them.

Gunny Wynn and I spent the afternoon cleaning our weapons. I sat in the sunlight next to the Humvee and took off my boots for the first time in two days. My feet were white and shriveled. They smelled like something between cheese and roadkill. I spread a dirty rag in my lap and pulled my M-16 apart. First I wiped down the receiver with oil and set it aside. Then I popped off the plastic hand guards and cleaned the barrel with the rag. I punched a cotton swab down through the chamber; it emerged black with carbon. Tapping the bullets from each magazine, I wiped the dust and grit from every round and then stretched and cleaned the magazine springs. Staff Sergeant Marine had taught me that most weapon failures were due to problems with the magazines. After reassembling the rifle, I pulled my Beretta from its holster and unloaded it. Racking the slide to the rear, I took it apart, laying the pieces in my lap. One by one, I cleaned them, turning them over in my hands and watching the sun glint off the dull blue steel. There was comfort in doing this; it gave me time to think without appearing to daydream.

When Doc Bryan returned, I called the Marines together. Platoons are families. In the worst platoons, the Marines love one another. But in the best, they also like one another. We had one of the best. I couldn't bear to see it destroyed. Conflict and disagreement had to be aired, or they would fester, simmering below the surface and corroding the relationships on which our combat effectiveness was built. We had to talk about what had happened. I had to be psychiatrist, coach, and father, without anyone suspecting I was anything but platoon commander.

"Fellas, today was fucked-up, completely insane. But we can't control the missions we get, only how we execute them," I said. I explained that the battalion had an obligation to General Mattis, an obligation to provide him with options instead of excuses. We were at war, and a different set of rules applied. There was no way to eliminate all the risks, either to ourselves or to the people around us.

"I failed you this morning by allowing that 'declared hostile' call to stand. My failure put you in an impossible position." Tragic as it was, shooting the two boys had been entirely within the rules of engagement as they had been given to us. There would be no command investigation into what had happened. Investigations exist in a narrow sense to assign blame, but they also serve to propagate lessons learned. I tried to draw out those lessons for the platoon.

"First, we made a mistake this morning," I said. Technical details aside, we were U.S. Marines, and Marines are professional warriors fighting for the greatest democracy in the world. We don't shoot kids. When we do, we acknowledge the tragedy and learn from it. Unfortunately, I didn't think it was the last time we'd have to make those kinds of decisions.

"Second, I need you to compartmentalize today." I told the guys to tuck the experience away in their brains, way back there with their wives and their girlfriends and their dogs. It wouldn't help them survive tomorrow. I needed every one of them to learn from it and put it away.

"Third, no second-guessing and armchair-quarterbacking." We made fast decisions all the time. Sometimes we were right, and sometimes we were wrong. We couldn't hesitate tomorrow because of a mistake today. That could get us killed. Come what may, we were a team, and we'd stay a team.

When the Marines went back to their places on the line, they walked in groups of two or three. They would stand watch together, eat together, and joke together. But I was alone. I sat in the cab of the Humvee and watched them go. In Afghanistan, I had had Jim and Patrick, my fellow lieutenants. Recon was different, more independent, and combat forged bonds within platoons, not across them. Gunny Wynn and I had passed the stage of purely professional teamwork and become friends. I confided in him my doubts about the war, the company, and members of the platoon. But never about myself. The events of the day overcame me all at once, and I struggled to breathe without crying.

As darkness fell over Qalat Sukkar, I sat alone in the dim green light of the radios. I felt sick for the shepherd boys, for the girl in the blue dress, and for all the innocent people who surely lived in Nasiriyah, Ar Rifa, and the other towns this war would consume. I hurt for my Marines, goodhearted American guys who'd bear these burdens for the rest of their lives. And I mourned for myself. Not in self-pity, but for the kid who'd come to Iraq. He was gone. I did all this in the dark, away from the platoon, because combat command is the loneliest job in the world.

# 28

A FLASH OF LIGHT burned through my closed eyelids and snapped me from my first deep sleep in days. I poked my head from the sleeping bag and squinted as columns of sparks rolled into the dark sky. Concussions shook me as more blasts rocked the ground beneath my back. Purple and orange flames lit the platoon, now a mass of supine sleeping bags scooting like inchworms behind and under Humvees. Incoming artillery rounds hit so quickly that I thought they must be from an MLRS. No conventional Iraqi cannons could mass firepower so well. March 30 was our eleventh night in Iraq and the first night we had not dug ranger graves to sleep in. I rolled under the Humvee, cursing the predictability of my impending death: if the surest way to get rained on is to forget your umbrella, the surest way to come under artillery barrage is to neglect to dig holes.

We had departed Qalat Sukkar that morning after a three-day stay. While welcoming the break as a chance to rest and resupply, we were concerned by the need for it. Rumors spread of the Army requesting a thirty-day pause for the Third Infantry Division to consolidate its supply lines. Even to tired Marines starved for real news, this sounded unlikely. Waking up more than once in the same place was real enough, though, and fueled the rumors. I tried to think of each day at Qalat Sukkar as another day of American airpower pounding Iraqi forces, and I was content to use the time to rest and prepare for the inevitable call ordering us forward once more. When that order finally came, it sent us only a few miles west to the intersection of Highways 7 and 17, where we joined the headquarters of RCT-1. The morning was bright and cool, and I was excited to be on the move again.

After so much time alone, the regimental command post looked like a metropolis. Hundreds of tanks, amtracs, trucks, and Humvees stretched down both sides of the highway. Cobra and Huey helicopters squatted in the dust next to their fuel tankers. Thousands of Marines wandered past tents and antenna fields. We drove into this makeshift city and parked in the defilade of a tall sand berm, feeling content within the outer security cordon of infantry Marines and satisfied that holes were unnecessary that night.

An hour later, I ducked into the battalion headquarters tent for a brief on the next morning's mission. Colonel Ferrando stood at the center, with his staff and officers arrayed around him on MRE boxes, ammo crates, and the ground. Before turning to the mission, he spoke briefly about combat and our execution over the past ten days.

"Gents, a bad attitude spreads like a yeast infection. I need you to set the tone. You are the ones who set the example, who lead by your example. We just had a short reprieve, but we'll be moving again tomorrow, and there *will* be more fights. Luck is not a method, and neither is hope. Hard work is."

The mission called for First Recon to attack north up the highway before crossing a small bridge over the Al Gharraf River and screening to the west of the road as the RCT advanced. We'd be on our own, moving through the countryside and small villages, protecting the flank of the larger force. Our goal was to reach the town of Al Hayy by nightfall, a distance of about fifty kilometers. We would have no tanks and only limited airpower. In military jargon, it was a "movement to contact." When I returned to brief the platoon, their interpretation was more direct: "So, sir, we're gonna drive until we get shot at."

Shortly after midnight, the artillery hit. We had finished the brief and looked forward to a full night's sleep before stepping off. In a show of true combat jadedness, heads came up to watch the explosions, but not a single Marine chose to leave the warmth of his sleeping bag. After all, we couldn't fight against a distant missile launcher. The artillery battery next to us used its radar to locate the source of the enemy barrage and lobbed volley upon volley of counterbattery fire. I slipped back to sleep beneath a comfortable blanket of outgoing death and destruction.

Our march north started uneventfully. The battalion attacked up the highway and crossed the bridge as planned. We entered a bucolic world of farms, rivers, and trees. Farmers drove their cattle, and kids waved as we passed. "Go America! Go George Bush! Give me money!" I fought the temptation to see the day as too beautiful to be dangerous. We moved slowly along dirt roads, keeping Highway 7 in sight across the river to our east. Trees lined the riverbank, and freshly dug fighting positions were hidden beneath them, providing clear shots at the American forces moving on the highway. All the new bunkers and holes made us wonder what had happened to their occupants.

"Mish, go talk to those guys and see what you can learn," I said, sending the translator to a group of Iraqi men on the roadside. He grumbled and grunted at them while they shifted from foot to foot. They began to speak, but Mish ignored them and returned to my Humvee.

"They say they're farmers, but they're lying." I already knew that. Iraqi farmers wear sandals and traditional robes. These guys wore leather shoes and were dressed in natty Western-style shirts and trousers. Their hands were soft and uncallused.

"Regular army or fedayeen?"

"Regular army, I think. Local guys — like your National Guard — who saw us coming and took off their uniforms. They don't have that radical militant look."

Ahead of us, Third Platoon's commander made a radio call. "We have eyes on a dozen men throwing bags in the river. They're running from us. Moving forward to investigate."

We accelerated into the dust clouds thrown up by Third Platoon's vehicles. They could probably handle this on their own, but we fell back on the golden rule of the infantry: guns are good, and more are better.

The Iraqis stopped and stared sullenly at the machine guns surrounding them. I joined the Marines fishing burlap sacks out of the river. Cutting them open, we found bales of Iraqi currency, dinars bearing Saddam Hussein's portrait.

"Well, goddamn. Look at this." A Marine held up a green military uniform, its underarms still wet with sweat. "National Guard, my ass. These fuckers are Republican Guard." He pointed to a red triangular patch on the shoulder, the symbol of Saddam's elite force.

"Cuff them. They're coming with us." The Republican Guard wasn't supposed to be this far south. According to all our intelligence reports, they were in defensive positions north of the Tigris. The Iraqis wore Saddam mustaches and stood with hands thrust into their pockets. One sat on the ground with his legs crossed, fingering prayer beads and sipping from a Pepsi bottle. Third Platoon bound their hands behind their backs and lifted them into the bed of a truck.

Across the river, the infantry advance caught up with us while we were stopped with the prisoners. Two Humvees, armed with antitank missiles in their turrets, prowled side by side up Highway 7. We watched as Iraqi pickup trucks screeched to a halt in the southbound lane ahead of the Marines, then turned around and raced back north. Because of the turns and rises in the road, the Marines across the river couldn't see them. Each time they spun around, the pickups flashed their headlights. They were signaling to fedayeen along the highway. I radioed this assessment to the battalion, and they passed it over to the infantry. The next pickup to spin around and flash its headlights disappeared in a fireball when one of the Humvees launched a missile into its cab. The Humvees rolled slowly past the wreckage, which sent plumes of greasy smoke into the sky.

Small-arms fire erupted on our flank, and a squad of Marines jumped from their amtrac to move into an enclosed courtyard. More firing followed.

"Frag out!" a Marine yelled, then pitched a hand grenade through a door. Smoke and dust poured from the building's windows. Two Marines emerged on the roof seconds later, flashing a thumbs-up to their comrades on the highway and yelling, "Clear!"

The advance continued for the rest of the morning and into the early afternoon. We moved forward and to the flank of the RCT, protecting it from attacks launched from our side of the river. The heavy armor and infantry moved methodically up the highway, clearing resistance as they went and marching ever closer to Baghdad.

Around one P.M., my platoon took over point for the battalion and immediately ran into a village straddling the road. It hugged the riverbank, just a small collection of mud-brick homes and a few abandoned cars. Laundry drying on lines provided the only color. We had learned our lesson about rolling through such obvious ambush points, so half the platoon moved into the village on foot while the other half supported them with the heavy machine guns on the Humvees. The surest way to protect vehicles in a town is to put troops around them. Gunny Wynn controlled the vehicular force. I joined the Marines on foot, passing quick instructions over my headset radio.

"Vehicles, move just forward of the foot squad and be prepared to suppress so we can maneuver or break contact," I ordered. "Foot mobiles, clear each building, collect all weapons and paperwork. Be alert for booby traps. We'll link up on the north side and continue. Let's go."

Jogging across the field in a cautious crouch, I tucked my rifle into the crook of my shoulder. I felt safe there, on my feet, in the dirt. I never got used to sitting in a Humvee on the highway, waiting to be ambushed. On foot, I was in my element: man, boots, rifle.

Marines clambered over irrigation ditches and moved stealthily into the collection of mud huts. Chickens scattered, squawking, as we stacked against walls and burst into rooms. Most of the village was deserted. The squad collected two AK-47s and an RPG launcher, along with a pile of military uniforms bearing the Republican Guard's red triangle. I walked one over to Major Whitmer, who was surrounded by maps and radios in the back of the battalion operations Humvee.

"Here you go, sir. A little souvenir of Saddam's finest."

He laughed and said, "I bet you thought you were coming to recon to get away from clearing villages on foot."

At the northern end of the village, a group of women and children huddled together in a one-room school. They had seen us coming and retreated there in fear. We reassured them that we meant no harm and asked why no men were in the village. They answered through Mish.

"We are poor farmers. The men work all day in the fields."

"Where are the Ba'ath Party, the fedayeen?"

"There are no fedayeen here. We are happy to see the Americans come."

"Where did these Republican Guard uniforms come from?" The women had no answer and stared silently at the packed-dirt floor.

Satisfied that the village posed no threat to RCT-1's advance, we kept driving north, snaking through groves of palm trees filled with colorful birds, singing as we passed. The shade provided refuge from the sun, and I enjoyed the cool interludes between stretches of barren fields. Clearing the village had been hard work in the midday heat. The Marines looked pale, with red-rimmed eyes. My sleeves were encrusted with white salt stains, and I gulped warm water from the plastic canteens fastened to my flak jacket. It tasted like water from a swimming pool.

Alpha Company took over on point, and I rotated the platoon to the back of the battalion formation. Somehow, we always ended up at

*Top:* The youngest member of the platoon, nineteen-year-old Private First Class John Christeson, prepares to launch a surveillance drone during a training mission in Kuwait. Christeson turned down a place at Annapolis to enlist in the Marines after 9/11. *Nathaniel Fick*

*Center:* Recon Team Leader Sergeant Shawn Patrick briefs his team at Camp Matilda shortly before the Iraq invasion. From left: Corporal Anthony Jacks, Patrick, Sergeant Rudy Reyes, and Sergeant Michael Brunmeier. *Evan Wright*

*Bottom:* Mike Wynn, platoon sergeant of Hitman Two, talks with Sergeant Tony Espera. Both men brought combat experience to Iraq: Wynn from Somalia and El Salvador, Espera from his years as a Los Angeles repo man. *Evan Wright*

*Top:* Recon's Humvees in Iraq were more dune buggies than armored vehicles. Using unarmored Humvees allowed us to move faster and carry more supplies; they were the right choice before roadside bombs became endemic in Iraq. *Eric M. Kocher*

*Center:* Hitman Two's camouflaged Humvees in the dispersal area along the Iraqi border on March 19, 2003. From one hundred meters they looked like Humvees under camouflage nets; from one thousand meters they disappeared into the sand. *Nathaniel Fick*

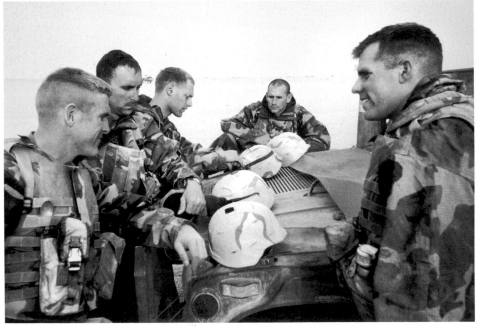

I brief the platoon just before crossing the Iraqi border. From left are the team leaders Sergeant Steve Lovell, Sergeant Shawn Patrick, and Sergeant Brad Colbert, and Platoon Sergeant Gunny Wynn. We wear heavy, charcoal-lined MOPP suits to protect us from chemical weapons. *Evan Wright*

A captured soldier from Iraq's Eleventh Infantry Division eats a "humrat," an American humanitarian ration. We took dozens of prisoners during the first days of the war. Farther north, though, few surrendered. *Eric M. Kocher*

*Above:* Hitman Two digs in for the night after being ambushed in Al Gharraf. The Humvee in the foreground is armed with a Mark-19 grenade launcher; the one in the background carries a .50-caliber machine gun. *Nathaniel Fick*

*Left:* Four Marines get precious sleep while a fifth stands guard behind the machine gun. Round-the-clock operations required Marines to stay awake for days at a time. *Evan Wright*

*Left:* Gunny Wynn, surounded by radios, night vision goggles, binoculars, and boxes of grenades, in the Humvee we shared. He and I spent countless hours together in this cramped cab and formed a friendship that transcended the boundaries of rank. *Nathaniel Fick*

*Below:* Multitasking. While speeding north from Al Hayy, I direct an artillery strike against a fedayeen convoy. *Evan Wright*

Sergeant Colbert's Humvee passes a truck destroyed by the platoon at a roadblock north of Al Hayy. We knew its occupants were enemy fighters when, the next morning, local Iraqis danced and cheered around the unburied bodies. *Evan Wright*

The bridge in Muwaffiqiya on the morning of April 1, 2003, only hours after we were ambushed while trying to cross it. The platoon killed a dozen Syrian jihadists hiding in the trees to the right. An enemy machine gun, fired from near the spot where the photo was taken, wounded Sergeant Patrick and Corporal Evan Stafford.   *Inset:* The sacred geometry of chance. Sergeant Reyes holds the AK-47 bullet that wounded Sergeant Patrick in Muwaffiqiya. He wears camouflage paint in preparation for a clandestine recon patrol. *Nathaniel Fick*

*Top:* Mish, our Kuwaiti interpreter, extorts a pack of cigarettes from an Iraqi driver. Mish told us that he'd volunteered to help the Marines because Saddam Hussein's forces had executed his cousin, then made his family pay for the bullet. *Evan Wright*

*Center:* In Ba'quba, Mish smiles after interrogating an Iraqi prisoner of war. The man, seated in the Humvee, said he fought against us because the Ba'ath Party was holding his five daughters hostage and threatened to kill them if he surrendered. *Evan Wright*

*Bottom:* The platoon relaxes between patrols at a power plant north of Baghdad in mid-April 2003. Visible from left are Gunny Wynn, Sergeant Reyes, Sergeant Lovell (back to camera), me, Sergeant Espera, Sergeant Colbert (kneeling), Corporal Gabriel Garza (standing), Corporal Michael Stinetorf, and Corporal Teren Holsey. *Evan Wright*

*Top:* From the roof of the Iraqi State Tobacco Company, I watched fires burn around the Saddam City neighborhood in northern Baghdad. Sergeant Lovell and I had nearly been shot by an enemy sniper at the base of the building a few hours earlier. *Author's collection*

*Center:* The amusement park on the Tigris River investigated by Hitman Two in April 2003. We found a fedayeen headquarters there, filled with Russian night vision goggles and maps of American positions in Baghdad. *Nathaniel Fick*

*Bottom:* Sergeant Colbert treats a wounded Iraqi girl near the bridge to the amusement park. Aiding civilians, though often at odds with our assigned mission, became crucial to the platoon's psychological health. *Evan Wright*

Hitman Two poses with a statue of Saddam before leaving Baghdad. Seated in front, left to right: Evan Wright, Corporal Gabriel Garza, Sergeant Steve Lovell. Second row: First Lieutenant Nathaniel Fick (standing), Sergeant Brad Colbert, Sergeant Tony Espera, Corporal Josh Person, Sergeant Leandro Baptista (standing). Third row: PFC John Christeson, Sergeant Michael Brunmeier, Sergeant Rudy Reyes, Corporal Jason Lilley, Corporal Michael Stinetorf. Fourth row: Corporal Walt Hasser, Lance Corporal Nathan Christopher, Corporal James Chaffin, Lance Corporal Harold Trombley, Corporal Teren Holsey. Top row: "Doc" Tim Bryan, Corporal Hector Leon, Corporal Evan Stafford, Corporal Anthony Jacks, Gunnery Sergeant Mike Wynn. Missing is Sergeant Shawn Patrick, evacuated to the United States after being wounded at Muwaffiqiya. *Evan Wright*

*Inset:* The insignia of the First Reconnaissance Battalion. The stars represent the Southern Cross as it appeared over Guadalcanal during the epic battle that marked a watershed for the battalion and the Corps. *United States Marine Corps*

the front or the back, never in the comfortable middle. Patrick's and Lovell's teams swung their guns behind us, serving as tail-end Charlie. We continued rumbling north at a walking pace, poking through villages and watching the people at work in the fields for clues about what lay around the next bend or over the next rise. The column halted. I climbed down and took a knee in the dirt next to the Humvee, stretching the radio cord to keep the handset to my ear. Wynn did the same on his side of the vehicle.

"Good day so far," Wynn said, sounding unusually upbeat. "At least we're doing something useful. Could you believe those fighting holes along the river? The Iraqis could have hosed the RCT and then melted away before they even knew where the fire came from."

I didn't share his enthusiasm. "I'm a little wigged-out by all the Republican Guard uniforms," I said. "What else don't we know?"

A radio call interrupted us. All platoon commanders to the front for a meeting. I shook my head at the battalion's order. It figured that we'd just taken our place at the far rear of the formation. Laughing at Wynn's gently mocking smile, I slung my rifle across my chest, handed him my portable radio, and started walking past the long line of stopped vehicles. The battalion sat in single file along a narrow dirt road that curved to the right and disappeared into a thicket along the riverbank. Far ahead, I saw a mosque's turquoise dome sticking up above the palm fronds. To our left, an irrigation ditch paralleled the road, and beyond it a planted field stretched for more than a mile across flat ground. The river flowed a few feet to my right, at the bottom of a steep bank. Across it, dense palm forests bordered a field of waist-high crops. I saw a white sedan parked in the field.

As I walked, a wooden rowboat approached, drifting with the current while two Iraqi men halfheartedly paddled. They flashed me a smirk, which caught my attention. Only kids smiled. Men their age stared or avoided eye contact. I called up to a Marine high in a machine gun turret. "Can you see anything in the bottom of that boat — weapons, packages, anything?"

"Nothing, sir."

Damn. I would have welcomed the excuse to sink it. Something about those two was aggravating me. As combat heightened and honed my senses, I saw details and made connections that would otherwise have passed unnoticed. Instinct began to take over, and I learned to trust my instincts. They told me to shoot the guys in the boat.

No sooner had they disappeared around the bend to our rear than an unearthly whooshing noise made me drop face-first in the dirt. Any sound that loud and strange had to be dangerous. I caught the barest glimpse of an orange fireball as it streaked over my head. I lay pressed into the ground, thinking, *Return fire*. But I couldn't see the fireball's source. Facing the river, I saw my platoon to the right, stretched along the banks in a conspicuous line. A string of flaming pumpkins floated across the field and ricocheted off the riverbank, passing within feet of their Humvees. Marines abandoned turrets and fell from open doors into the road, diving for cover. Another string arced toward me and passed overhead with the sound of bowling balls hurled through the air. I dragged myself into the irrigation ditch, joining the Marines already there.

"That's goddamn triple-A!" The Iraqis were shooting a large-caliber antiaircraft gun at us from somewhere in the far-off palm trees. I aborted my walk to the commanders' meeting, consumed by the need to get back to the platoon. Because of the way the river curved, it looked as if my guys were the most exposed to the gun. It also looked as if they might be the only ones who could see it and return fire against it. I stood up to run and dropped again as another flaming bowling ball whined past. The berm wasn't even going to slow one of those things down. I couldn't believe they hadn't hit one of our trucks yet. Nearly the whole battalion crouched in the muddy water at the bottom of the ditch. My rifle felt like a popgun. We needed air support. My radio was back with Gunny Wynn. I hoped someone was calling for Cobras.

I again stood to run, then fell to avoid another burst of fire. I thought of a quote I'd once read, something about war being a thousand private acts of cowardice. Ducking behind the dirt berm, knowing my men were exposed to the fire, I was ashamed. This wasn't leadership. This wasn't what I'd been taught at Quantico. Marine training is essentially a psychological battle against the instinct for self-preservation. Every impulse screamed for me to curl up behind the berm and wait for someone else to make the Iraqi gun go away. All the rituals derided as brainwashing, the instant obedience, the infusion of the Corps's history and traditions, existed for moments like this one.

I took a breath and began to run. Another burst of fireballs burned past, overshooting again and landing with puffs of dust far out in the field to our west. A Mark-19 roared in response, and I saw a gunner in Colbert's Humvee pumping rounds toward the source of the AAA fire.

As I got closer to the platoon, my confidence returned. I was back in command.

Trombley crouched near the Humvee, leaning into a huge pair of binoculars. Hasser stood in the turret behind the Mark-19, looking down at Trombley.

"See where the tree line ends on the right?" Trombley said. "About two fingers left of that, set back in the trees. I think that's where the gun is."

Hasser loosed a burst, walking the exploding grenades in on the spot described by Trombley. It looked like the AAA gun was near the Mark-19's maximum range, maybe even out of range. They could shoot us, but we couldn't shoot them.

In the driver's seat of Colbert's Humvee, Person was singing.

"One, two, three, four, what the fuck are we fighting for?"

"You have to answer that for yourself," I said as I crouched against the fender, scanning with my binoculars.

"Well, sir," Person said, turning in the seat to face me, oblivious to the fight all around him, "I guess I'm fighting for cheap gas and a world without ragheads blowing up our fucking buildings."

"Good to know you're such an idealist."

"That world sounds pretty ideal to me right about now."

Two Cobra attack helicopters swooped in low. The lead Cobra jerked sideways to avoid a stream of orange fire reaching up at it from the trees. The Cobras rolled in to attack, firing guns and rockets into the tree line. Dirt and dust hung in the air, and another burst of AAA fire floated up toward the helicopters. The white car we'd seen in the field was driving in tight circles, flashing its headlights. We'd witnessed this act too many times and directed the Cobras in on the car. A burst of cannon fire stopped its circling, and the driver slumped as smoke rose from beneath the hood. The AAA gun continued to fire. It must have been jamming, or maybe its operators were poorly trained, because it would let a few rounds rip before falling silent for seconds or minutes before firing again. Better aim and quicker fire could have torn us up.

With our attention focused east across the river, I turned in surprise at an explosion behind me. A plume of dust rose from the field beyond the irrigation ditch. As I watched, another rose next to it, followed by a rattling thump. Mortars.

"Snipers! Start scanning. Find that mortar observer," I shouted. Mortar fire is ineffective unless it's controlled by someone who can see the intended target and send corrections to the gun crew, allowing them to walk their rounds in on whatever they're trying to hit. In this case, we were the intended target, and we began a deadly race to kill the observer before he succeeded in walking the mortar rounds in on our position.

Gunny Wynn put his eye to the sniper rifle's scope, bracing himself on the Humvee hood to steady his view.

I alternated between two radios and the binoculars around my neck. "How many crises can we handle at once?" I asked the question idly, almost rhetorically, expecting a grunt from Wynn.

Instead, he paused and looked up from the scope, suddenly thoughtful. Mortar rounds continued falling. I wanted to retract the question and tell him to keep scanning.

"Always one fewer than we have."

Shawn Patrick and Rudy Reyes also searched. They climbed onto a berm, lying shoulder to shoulder and interlocking their legs for stability. Reyes peered through the spotting scope as Patrick adjusted his rifle for a long shot. Marine snipers have a mythical reputation, and for good reason. Scout-sniper school at Quantico weeds out seven of every ten Marines who begin the course. The graduates can hit human targets a mile away with their modified Remington hunting rifles.

"Sir, check out that gray car." Reyes rose from his belly to point at a vehicle barely visible beyond an irrigation ditch far out in the field. "I range it at one thousand fifty yards. There's a guy inside looking at us and talking into a radio or a cell phone."

I raised binoculars to my eyes and confirmed Reyes's report. The car sat all alone in the middle of the field. A dark figure inside was clearly looking our way, periodically raising something to his head and moving his mouth as if talking into it. I briefly wondered if this were evidence enough to kill a man. Immediate self-defense is easy; this was something colder and more calculating. Another mortar round crashed into the field, closer this time, with almost no gap between the explosion's flash and its bang. Slowly, inexorably, they were walking the rounds in on top of us.

"Take the shot." Snipers don't shoot to warn or dissuade. Patrick would try for a lethal first-round hit in the head or torso. I watched him regulate his breathing as Rudy called the wind.

While the Cobras raced the AAA gun, and Patrick and Reyes raced the mortar observer, I worried about distractions. The military calls this a combined-arms ambush. The Iraqis had us on the horns of a dilemma — get up to move away from the mortars and risk catching a high-explosive antiaircraft round, or hunker down to hide from the AAA and wait for the mortars to rain hot steel down on us. Fortunately, they were doing a bad job of it, shooting from long range and with less-than-overwhelming firepower. My instincts told me that they also would try to hit us from behind. The whole battalion stretched to our north, and we had the protective river to our east. To the west lay an open field, where any threat would be exposed. I was worried about our rear — the dirt road that led south toward the villages we'd just passed through.

"Jacks! Stinetorf! They may try to hit us from behind. Remember positive ID. Lots of civilians are running around out here." Jacks and Stine trained their machine guns down the road, flashing me a thumbs-up.

Sergeant Patrick's rifle cracked. Rudy, staring through the spotting scope, watched the bullet's vapor trail as it streaked toward the target. "Low." He saw the round enter the center of the driver's door. Patrick racked the rifle and prepared for another shot before the target could move. He fired again. "On target." Rudy saw the round break the glass of the driver's window. The man in the car crumpled out of sight.

"Good shooting, Sergeant Patrick. Nice call, Rudy. Let's hope the mortars stop," I said.

"Vehicle from the rear!" Someone sounded a warning as an orange-and-white taxi raced around the corner from our south. Seeing the barrels of two machine guns, the driver stopped, and three men bailed out of the cab.

"Hold your fire! Hold your fire!" I shouted at Jacks and Stinetorf. An officer's job isn't only to inspire his men to action but also to rein them in when fear and adrenaline threaten to carry them away. Unless the Iraqis were armed or came running at us, we'd try to avoid shooting them. Wisely, they ran back to the south, abandoning their car. Less than a minute later, a second cab sped around the corner, and we repeated the drill. Two more men jumped out and ran back to the south.

Something wasn't right. Mortars exploding, helicopters shooting, and these guys were driving right up into our convoy? Not once but twice, and the second cab must have passed right by the first group of men running south. I walked down to the cabs and slashed their tires with my knife. That would prevent them from following us and perhaps attacking us up the road.

By then, the Cobras had destroyed the AAA gun and were sweeping in front of us, searching for targets. No more mortar rounds fell. We had gotten the right man. The battalion, eager to cover ground before the helicopters needed fuel, called for us to move out.

# 29

WE STAYED AT THE BACK of the formation, passing the turquoise mosque and entering the grove where the AAA gun had been. It was dark and smoky beneath the trees' canopy. Brushfires burned under palm trees split in two, their fronds black and crackling. We saw empty fighting holes and a pile of discarded RPG rounds. Once again, the Iraqis' impatience and tactical incompetence had saved us. It chilled me to think that they could have waited to unleash the antiaircraft shells on us at close range. A few shots rang out from the front of the column as Marines reported men moving in the trees. Our speed picked up. We raced down a sunken dirt road between two thick stands of bamboo. I couldn't see more than five feet into the underbrush. Clicking my rifle safety off, I braced my foot on the doorjamb to steady my aim. I expected a burst of fire to rip into us at any moment.

We broke out from the trees and turned right onto a masonry bridge across the small river we'd been paralleling. On the other side sprawled the largest town we'd seen since Nasiriyah. Al Hayy stretched as far as I could see to the south. No one walked in the streets, and the windows were closed and shuttered. A dead city. The sky hung dark and dusky over the rooftops, even though sunset was still two hours away. All through Iraq, the weather seemed to move in lockstep with our tactical situation. The sun shone in safe places, while it was dark, misty, and dusty in ominous ones. A Mark-19 roared ahead of us, and Alpha Company reported sporadic incoming fire. Grenades exploded with rhythmic flashes across the face of a concrete building next to the road. I tried to duck inside my Kevlar helmet and braced for the gauntlet we were about to run. Someone up ahead had a hot mike, his radio transmit button stuck open. "Get some, motherfucker! Get some!" Explosions thumped behind the voice.

We paralleled Al Hayy, continuing north along the river. At the edge of town, we turned east and raced across an empty lot. Trash piles and abandoned cars dotted the ground. Still, no one moved. I waited for a volley of RPGs to streak from behind the walls, but none came. Al Hayy was way too quiet.

Our objective was Highway 7, along which RCT-1 still advanced to our south. First Recon was the northernmost Marine unit in Iraq, with a city of forty or fifty thousand people between us and the other Americans. To our north lay Al Kut and Baghdad, with their Republican Guard armored divisions of tanks and artillery. Even surrounded by three hundred armed Marines, I had rarely felt so alone. Our mission, as passed over the radio, was to set up a blocking position on the highway. In the morning, RCT-1 would attack into Al Hayy from the south, and we would stop the flood of fedayeen escaping north to fortify the next town along our path to Baghdad. We'd successfully flanked the city and were deep in the fedayeen's rear. I felt aggressive, almost euphoric, and saw the same feeling on the Marines' faces. For a week, we had plodded predictably up the same highway, getting ambushed and getting lucky. That afternoon outside Al Hayy, for the first time in the war, we had the initiative. We would do the ambushing. We were the hunters.

After climbing up an embankment onto the highway, the battalion sped off to the north to find a position for the night. My platoon was left behind to set up a hasty roadblock to protect the battalion while it searched. We stopped at the northern end of a modern bridge that swept up from Al Hayy and spanned the dirt lot we'd driven through. I put three Humvees abreast across the highway, with their guns pointed south. Anyone choosing to attack us would have to cross the bridge and face the massed firepower of our machine guns when they were up on the span with nowhere to hide. We had a good position, exposed atop the elevated roadway but also easily defended and identifiable to pilots overhead in case we needed air support.

"Espera, put a strand of wire two hundred meters down the highway and tie some red chem lights to it," I said. I wanted to avoid a close-quarters firefight all alone there on the darkening highway at the city's edge. Drivers would see the lights on the wire, and I hoped they would turn around.

"Roger that, sir." He and two Marines jogged down the road, dragging a coil of concertina wire that Gunny Wynn and I had carried strapped to the hood of our Humvee. They tied three red chem lights to it and turned to run back to the platoon. Over the sound of our idling engines, I heard a vehicle motor droning closer. Two dim headlights popped over the crest of the bridge. Twenty rifles and machine guns zeroed in on them as Espera and his guys slipped back into our lines.

Wynn took control, saying, "Relax, gents. Wait till he gets to the wire and give him a chance to stop. If he comes through the wire, waste him." Gunny Wynn was always at his best when our situation was at its worst. He exerted a natural calming influence on the platoon.

I slid the charging handle of my rifle back to check that I had a round in the chamber, then banged the forward assist to be sure it would fire when I pulled the trigger. One of my secret terrors was that I'd try to shoot in a firefight and hear only the hollow click of a firing pin striking empty air. I joined the rest of the platoon and watched the headlights growing larger.

Suddenly, it seemed as if the wire wasn't nearly far enough away, and I chided myself for not putting it three hundred meters down the highway. If a car hit that wire doing sixty miles per hour, we'd have six seconds to react. On the radio, I learned that we had no air support and that the battalion was still searching for a place to set up for the night. Our instructions remained to stop any traffic approaching from the south.

I exhaled as brakes groaned and the headlights slowed. The beams swung around and were replaced by two red taillights receding back down the bridge. Wire and chem lights had been a good idea. The Iraqi driver had seen them, heeded them, and saved his life. The Marines stood up and stepped out from behind guardrails and armored doors. Smiles, jokes, and backslapping all around. A fight averted is second in exhilaration only to a fight won.

"Lieutenant, check out all that traffic to the west," Sergeant Lovell said, pointing back toward the bridge we'd crossed earlier. A stream of headlights bobbed north along the river.

"Goddammit, they're flanking us," I said. I called the battalion and told them what we saw. It seemed as if our presence on the highway was well known and the fedayeen were either escaping to regroup somewhere to the north or were moving along our flank to attack us from another direction. Major Whitmer requested clarification of the vehicles' exact location and number.

We peered hard through the dusk. Location was no problem — there was only one road over there, and they were clearly on it. We could see six or eight pairs of headlights at any given time, but they continuously came into view and then disappeared again behind the trees. Clearly, there were dozens of vehicles in all. They looked like open-bed trucks full of men — figures clustered together in the back, standing shoulder to shoulder. This was consistent with what we'd seen the fedayeen doing in other towns. Confident that we had a legitimate target, Major Whitmer called an artillery fire mission to the batteries south of Al Hayy, and we watched as rounds began flashing along the distant road. It would be great to kill some fedayeen, but pinpointing artillery onto individual moving trucks was nearly impossible, so we settled for making that escape route less attractive and perhaps keeping some of the bad guys bottled up in town for the next morning's battle.

Our attention snapped back from the distant road to another pair of headlights rushing toward us on the bridge. Unlike the previous pair, these were high off the ground — a truck. I heard mashing gears as it accelerated over the crest of the bridge. It was moving fast, with no sign of slowing down. Maybe the driver couldn't see us.

"Headlights." We'd kept our lights off to avoid being easy targets, but if the truck didn't see the red chem lights, surely he'd see three sets of headlights stretched across the width of the highway facing him. The Marines pulled their knobs, and bright white light illuminated the pavement all the way out past the barbed wire. The truck barreled on, getting louder. It was a yellow tractor-trailer, ten feet high and fifty feet long. *Come on, come on, come on,* I thought, willing the driver to stop and turn around.

The truck's size and speed could carry it into us even after we opened fire. I remembered General Conway's instruction back in Kuwait: "Your first obligation as an officer is the defense of your men." This truck could be full of wounded children, but if I allowed it to crash into our position, we'd surely lose at least three vehicles and their heavy machine guns, along with most of our ammunition, food, medical supplies, fuel, and water. We'd also lose Marines. I knew these guys — they'd die shooting rather than jump to safety to save themselves. The truck raced toward the wire, so close that the driver was either in a panic or intent on killing us.

"Light him up!" The last word was still on my lips when every gun in the platoon opened fire. In slow motion, I watched .50-caliber tracers and Mark-19 rounds arcing over the truck. It closed the gap on the gunners faster than they could lower their guns. For a second, I thought he'd run right into us. The gunners corrected, and grenades exploded against the grille and windshield as armor-piercing incendiary machine gun rounds ripped the cab apart. Only every fifth round was a tracer, but a steady stream of red streaks poured into the cab.

Still the truck rushed closer. Headlights bounced toward us, carving light through the smoke. I dropped the radio handset. It was usually my most lethal weapon, but worthless as the truck closed the last hundred meters toward the platoon. Around me, the Marines were on knees or braced against doors, aiming, firing, changing magazines. I jammed the rifle stock into my shoulder and flipped the selector lever to "burst." The M-16 shoots either semiautomatic single shots or three-round bursts. Bursts are usually a waste of ammo since the muzzle rises after the first shot and the next two pass over the target. But this was a truck, a close truck. It was the proverbial broad side of a barn. I aimed low, at the middle of the grille, knowing the shots would float upward toward the windshield. The rifle stuttered, three little kicks at a time.

The truck drifted right before jackknifing hard left. It skidded to a halt thirty feet from us as the platoon's guns fell silent. There was a pause while everyone waited to see what would happen next. Almost unbelievably, two men jumped out of the cab and ran for the embankment on the side of the highway. If only they'd raised their hands in surrender, they could have survived. Instead, Sergeant Espera took aim with his M4 and dropped them with well-placed shots to the chest. Both men crumpled to the ground and lay still in the full glow of our headlights.

"Hitman Two, proceed north and rejoin Godfather," the radio squawked. Without a glance back at the carnage we'd inflicted, we loaded the Humvees and drove north. I chose to leave the wire in the road, hoping that it, a wrecked truck, and a pair of bullet-riddled corpses would warn other drivers that the highway north of Al Hayy was closed for the night.

We spent the night in ranger graves carved from slick clay. Bravo Company faced south, Charlie faced north, and Alpha guarded the flanks in between. Throughout the night, bursts of tracer fire arced from Charlie's position toward approaching vehicles. The firing always followed the same pattern: a short warning burst aimed high, followed by a longer and more insistent warning burst aimed closer, and finally a frantic drilling rattle as the gunners abandoned persuasion for force. The road north of their position looked like a used-car lot of shattered windshields and blood pooled on the pavement. No cars came toward us from the south, and I was silently grateful for the deterrent value of the bullet-stitched truck. Killing once had saved us from killing repeatedly.

In the dark hours of the early morning, I walked the lines to check our defenses and visit with Sergeant Espera and his Marines. They had done most of the shooting at the roadblock, and I wanted to see how they were handling it. It was easy, on a night like this, for things to look bleak. We had been eating only one MRE a day because the truck carrying our extra food had been blown up by fedayeen near Qalat Sukkar and our resupply priorities were fuel, water, and ammo. I was too hungry to sleep. Low, scudding clouds spat cold rain, turning the clay of our holes into glue. With no moon or stars visible, the night was dark. I slipped and slid through the mud to Espera's position next to the highway. He had ordered his team to dig deep in case another truck tried to blow through our lines. Four Marines huddled together in a chest-deep fighting hole as I approached. I saw the outlines of their helmeted heads and the dim green glow of their night vision goggles as they scanned the highway. They had removed the .50-caliber machine gun from their Humvee and placed it on a tripod in front of the hole, pointed south toward Al Hayy.

"Halt. Who goes there?" they said, challenging my approach.

I froze, thinking of the trip my TBS class had taken to the battlefield at Chancellorsville, where Stonewall Jackson had been mistakenly shot and killed in the dark by his own men. "Lieutenant Fick, looking for Sergeant Espera."

"Howdy, sir. How you doin' this evening?" Espera said.

"Never better. Tired, cold, wet, hungry. I feel like a Marine."

I slid into the hole with the team so we could whisper together and share body heat. Espera smiled. "Last time I saw you in a cold hole, LT, was in Afghanistan. Makes me feel like an old campaigner."

"Regular warhorse, Espera. Just wait. Next year it'll be Syria, then North Korea, and who knows where after that. We'll never have to train again. Just war, war, war."

Before I could bring up the real reason for my visit, Sergeant Espera beat me to it. "Sir, what do you think was in that truck we lit up earlier tonight?"

I had a canned answer ready for him, but it sounded hollow even as it left my lips. "I don't know. What I do know is that each of us has an obligation to protect our men. You had a team to look out for. I gave the order to shoot that truck. The responsibility is mine. If you hadn't fired, it would have destroyed most of our gear and maybe killed Marines. You did the right thing."

"Yeah." Espera nodded, looking unconvinced. I ached for him. No one knows the costs of war better than the grunts. I guessed the television news that night was full of reports of collateral damage and civilian casualties. I wished people could see how much we agonized over our decisions and prayed they were the right ones. These choices didn't always translate into hesitation on the trigger or racking self-doubt, but sometimes it was enough to sit awake in the cold rain just thinking about them.

Shortly after sunrise, the captain called me to his Humvee. "Nate, we're heading back toward Al Hayy in a few hours to support the attack. I want you to take your platoon down there right now and observe this intersection." He jabbed his finger at a point on the map near where we'd shot up the truck the previous evening. "Send back any useful information. Don't get decisively engaged. If you get into trouble, call for help or fall back to us here."

I nodded, happy to be getting out on my own for a while. The platoon eyed me as I walked back to where they filled holes and oiled machine guns. "We're heading down south to recon an intersection. Stay awake — we're all alone. Weapons tight — let's not start something we can't finish."

I saw in the platoon a glimmer of something I was starting to feel in myself: excitement. The adrenaline rush of combat and the heady thrill of being the law were addicting us. This was becoming a game. I was starting to look forward to missions and firefights in the way I might savor pickup football or playing baseball. There was excitement, teamwork, common purpose, and the chance to demonstrate skill. I didn't have the luxury of much time for reflection, but I was aware enough to be concerned that I was starting to enjoy it.

Our five vehicles rolled south on a clear, sunny morning. I sat in the passenger seat while Gunny Wynn drove, munching a granola bar and watching A-10 attack jets loop and wheel over Al Hayy. White phosphorous artillery rounds burst in the air above the city, raining their burning explosives into the streets below. All sound was carried away on the wind as we watched the silent movie of destruction.

"Hitman Two, this is Two-Two," Sergeant Patrick's team called on the radio. "We've got eyes on armed men in the field to our left. Looks like two guys with AKs, watching us and running behind that berm."

"Roger, Two-Two. Cleared hot." I turned from the air show over Al Hayy and watched Jacks lob a string of grenades over the berm next to the road. Two robed figures with rifles ran at a stoop. The grenades exploded with a sequence of thumps muffled by the mud, and the men disappeared. I finished my granola bar as we neared the intersection.

We pulled off into a field where irrigation dikes provided some natural cover, then set up in a square we could defend in all directions. Beyond us, a field of waist-high green grass waved in the morning breeze. The sky overhead shone blue, and sunlight glimmered on the river in the distance. It was the most beautiful spot I'd seen in Iraq. Marines not on security lounged in the grass, smelling the sweet, wet summery heat. The spot seemed quintessentially American. I expected two boys in overalls to come strolling down the road with fishing rods over their shoulders and a golden retriever trailing behind.

The yellow truck was the bucolic picture's only blemish. It had been pushed down the embankment to clear the road. Bloody handprints covered the doors to the cab. Two bodies lay at unnatural angles on the ground, flies buzzing around them. The warm sun, which felt so good on our arms and faces, drew out their stench.

When the battalion joined us, we packed up our scopes, radios, drying boots, and half-eaten lunches to drive north again along the river. We were told that the Al Hayy attack had been canceled because the fedayeen had fled. I took a turn at the wheel, while Gunny Wynn rode shotgun, alternately fingering his grenade launcher and looking at the map. There was no radio chatter.

"Gunny, where's this road taking us?"

"There's a town on the river about ten klicks up called Muwaffiqiya. Captain just said we'll be swinging around it to the east. Looks like open farmland."

Third Platoon raced past us to recon a route around the town. I concentrated on driving while Wynn kept track of the map and radio. Driving in Iraq, even on a pretty day as part of a large American force, demanded full concentration. Berms collapsed, rolling Humvees onto their sides. Roadside bombs were not yet endemic, as they would become later in the occupation, but we worried about land mines and booby traps. I studied the tires of the Humvee ahead of me and tried to stay right in its tracks.

We slowly climbed away from the river, passing through planted fields lined with stone walls. Far in the distance, I saw the smudgy outline of Muwaffiqiya, a collection of buildings and a towering water tank on the banks of the Al Gharraf River. Wynn looked content. "We're finally learning to go around the towns," he said.

# 30

I LEANED AGAINST the Humvee door in the fading light, spooning applesauce from a field ration pouch and watching two ants fight for a dropped grain of rice. It had been days since I'd seen a mirror, but my blackened hands looked no better than those of the gaunt and sunken-eyed Marines around me.

The evening was quiet. We were parked in a field just off a narrow country road, hemmed in by stone walls and hedgerows that looked more like Connecticut than central Iraq. I had double-checked the placement of the platoon's machine guns and hacked a sleeping hole from the soft earth before sitting down to eat dinner and breathe. I dared to hope we'd spend the night in one place, and the field seemed indulgently comfortable.

"Sir, the captain wants all commanders at his truck," Christeson called from the cab of the Humvee, where he was monitoring the radio and cleaning his rifle. I pocketed my dinner and set off to see what bad news was about to shatter our evening.

When the captain finished his brief, I called the team leaders on the radio. "Hitman Two-One, Two-Two, and Two-Three, actuals to my vehicle. Naptime's over."

Walking back across the field, I saw Sergeants Colbert, Patrick, and Lovell converging on the platoon headquarters Humvee. They carried map boards and rifles and looked as if they already knew what I was about to tell them. A Humvee hood doubles as a decent map table, so we held platoon briefings around its ten square feet of dusty fiberglass. They joined Gunny Wynn, chatting together as I walked up.

Colbert grinned and said, "Sir, I don't like that look in your eye."

"Yeah, well, we're saddling up and rolling out of here at 2200 local to move through that town to our west and set up ambushes on the other side to interdict the fedayeen moving toward Highway 7." After a week of being sniped at, shot at, and mortared, we were going to set the agenda. As the Marine Corps puts it, we were going to take the fight to the enemy.

"Ambushes?" Sergeant Patrick snorted. Clearly, this plan did not excite him. Only ten days before, I had listened as Patrick had cautioned his team with one of his countless southern aphorisms: "Never pet a burning dog."

"Yeah. We'll roll through the town as a battalion, then split off as platoons and move to our sectors to set up and watch for fedayeen traffic. At dawn, we'll pull out and move north to link up with everyone else. We have the chance to hunt here rather than be hunted."

"I understand that, sir, but moving into our ambush site in unfamiliar territory in the dark is bad business." Patrick spoke slowly for emphasis. "And then, how are we supposed to identify who's fedayeen and who's not? We can't just walk up to them and ask. Not out there all alone as a platoon."

Patrick was right about the mission. But contrary to what the platoon sometimes seemed to think, I wasn't the ultimate decision maker. That was the mission we were given, and that was the mission we would execute. Our job was to figure out the best way to do it, and we had only two hours.

Gunny Wynn's priority as platoon sergeant, first and always, was the safety of his men. Mine, as platoon commander, was accomplishing our mission. True, each of us cared about both responsibilities, but when the bullets were flying, one goal had to take precedence. Leadership instructors who said naively that the two could coexist had never been in a gunfight. Each of us, on his own, would probably have fallen victim to his natural impulses. Together, though, we had a symbiosis that combined my aggressiveness with his wisdom. And so the debate began.

Around the hood of the Humvee that evening, we ran through different options for executing the mission within the framework of our commander's intent. He could tell us what to do, but we would decide how to do it. Gunny Wynn and the team leaders systematically strengthened the plan, pointing out weaknesses and suggesting improvements. It is a simple fact of human nature that people will more willingly go into danger when they have a say in crafting their fate. In the end, we agreed that our first and greatest problem would be passing through the town of Muwaffiqiya. It would prove a prescient analysis.

Muwaffiqiya was a medium-size collection of three- and four-story concrete buildings on the west bank of the Al Gharraf River. A platoon of Marine LAVs had approached the bridge earlier in the afternoon. We heard a few bursts of gunfire and watched as an LAV raced past with a wounded Marine in the back. While we gathered around the map plotting our next move, Marine artillery boomed from the south, and the western horizon flickered and flashed as 155 mm high-explosive rounds exploded into Muwaffiqiya. So much for peaceful evenings. After cobbling together a plan we could all live with, the team leaders returned to their positions to brief their men while I cleaned my rifle and tried to sleep for an hour.

Artillery explosions, gunfire, and low-flying jets roared in the dark, but I was too tired to care. Curled up on the ground beneath a poncho liner, I woke at 2130 to Christeson shaking my shoulder. I stood to shrug on my gear before doing radio checks with the teams and lining up the Humvees. We would be on point for the battalion, with Sergeant Colbert first, followed by Sergeant Espera, Gunny Wynn and me in the middle, and Sergeants Patrick and Lovell behind.

We rolled slowly into the darkness, the night warm and silent and blowing through our open doors. The plan called for us to move to the near side of the bridge into town and set up a support-by-fire position on the north side of the road. Third Platoon would follow behind and set up a similar position on the road's south side. Once both platoons were set to cover the battalion, it would cross the bridge into Muwaffiqiya, and we would fall in behind. It was a classic example of overwatch, a tactic practiced by Marines in the woods and fields of Quantico, Parris Island, Camp Pendleton, and Camp Lejeune.

There had been murmurs about why we hadn't pushed teams out on foot to recon the bridge earlier in the evening. It was an obvious chokepoint, a logical place for an ambush. Apparently, there just hadn't been time. Countering these fears were a pair of Cobras sweeping in front of us no more than a hundred feet above the road. The pilots reported heat signatures that might be people and fired a couple of rockets at suspected bunkers on the far side of the river. I held a radio handset to each ear but instinctively reached down and pulled back the charging handle on my rifle to make sure a round was chambered. We kept driving.

"OK, we're set." Colbert radioed that he was in place on the north side of the approach to the bridge.

"Negative. I still can't see the bridge. Keep moving." Our mission was to secure the bridge for the battalion's crossing, and I still couldn't even see it. I saw only a thin stand of trees on the left and a few mud-brick buildings on the right, fifty meters from the road. The Cobras orbited behind us, and the night was again quiet. Everything glowed green and grainy in my night vision goggles.

"Roger," Colbert said, and we crept forward again.

Colbert's nickname was the Iceman because he never lost his cool. That's why I had him on point for the platoon on a night when the platoon was on point for the battalion and the battalion was on point for almost the whole Marine Corps. The next thing I heard through my headset radio was his warning: "There's an obstacle on the bridge." Colbert's voice was measured but taut, the way an airline pilot would tell his passengers about an engine fire. Then I saw it, too — what looked like a Dumpster full of scrap metal pulled out into the road. Large-diameter pipes lay scattered on both sides of it. There was only one explanation.

"Back up, back up, back the fuck up." The fear was palpable. You could hear it and feel it and even taste it, like a penny under your tongue. But the Marines stayed calm. We were jammed together with trees to our left, buildings to our right, an obstacle in front of us, and the rest of the battalion pressing in from behind.

We had driven into an ambush. I knew it and wondered, for a fleeting second, when the shooting would start. I ducked my head and tried to pull my arms into my bulletproof vest while still holding the radios and my rifle. Marines call it "turtling."

I gave the order to turn around and got a terse, "Roger, wilco," from Colbert. As his Humvee began its turn to the left, toward the trees, Colbert radioed, "There are men in the trees," and opened fire.

The staccato chatter of his M4 sounded distant and tinny, but then the Mark-19 began to roar, spitting grenades into the trees in quick bursts. The other teams opened up with rifles, the second Mark-19, and the two .50-caliber machine guns. Our volume of outgoing fire was immense. Tracers burned across the sky, and muzzle flashes washed out my goggles, replacing green definition with indistinguishable white blobs. I flipped them up on my helmet and tried to figure out what was going on.

Fear passes quickly. Once the shooting started, I was busy directing the platoon, talking on the radio, and shooting back. It wasn't courage so much as task saturation. Streams of incoming tracers skipped and ricocheted down the road from across the bridge. Passing bullets buzzed and whined, just as they do in cartoons. The enemy machine gunner was shooting low, and his rounds sparked as they caromed off the pavement into our vehicles. Impacts jolted my Humvee.

More enemy fire chattered from the trees. Small arms. Single shots and short bursts. I watched an RPG flash from the right, from somewhere back in the maze of mud buildings. When it blew up in front of me, a shower of sparks burned into my vision and lingered there after the blast faded.

Enemy to our left, right, and straight ahead. This assessment process took only seconds, and I was on the radio requesting air support. I made a conscious effort to be calm and speak slowly, but my request was a shouted, garbled mess all the same. The Cobras roared back, cleared hot to attack anything on the far side of the river or more than twenty-five meters off the road. They poured machine gun fire over our heads, and the whoosh of their rockets blotted out the distant voices in my ear asking for updates.

We had to get the platoon out of the kill zone. Gunfire and shouting rendered our radios almost useless, so dropping my rifle and drawing my pistol, I told Gunny Wynn to turn the truck around while I went out to guide the teams.

"*What?*"

"Turn the Humvee around, break contact to the rear, and I'll be right back." Rarely did I do anything against his advice, but this would be one of those times.

Ducking meaninglessly, since the enemy machine gun fire was at knee level, I ran forward to where Colbert was still frozen in the middle of his turn. My immediate concern was being shot by my own men. They were intent on their firing and couldn't see me running up from their periphery. Each M4 was equipped with a laser, visible only through night vision goggles. Put the red dot on your target and you'll hit it every time. Laser dots converged together on shadowy figures in the trees, wavered as the Marines shook and rattled in the moving

Humvees, and then disappeared as the figure dropped and they moved to settle on the next target. It was an oddly beautiful and well-choreographed dance.

Time was expanding and compressing like a Slinky. I crouched behind the rear bumper of Colbert's Humvee, aware of each rivet in the tan armor. But I had no recollection of getting there. Above me, Corporal Hasser fired the Mark-19. Tongues of flame shot from the muzzle, but the deafening weapon seemed silent to me. I was shouting instructions to the two lead drivers and trying to avoid being shot or run over when a calm voice on the radio cut through the gunfire.

"Team Two has a man down."

Then Gunny Wynn's voice. "Headquarters has a man down."

This was every commander's nightmare. Ambushed and taking casualties. Ironically, I remembered Colonel Ferrando's words from a briefing the day before: "You can't volunteer to go to war and then bitch about getting shot at."

The Marine Recon Mission Essential Task List, that group of skills deemed vital to the job, fills a book. Patrolling, navigation, calling in air strikes, communications, parachuting, diving, shooting, swimming, driving boats, hand-to-hand combat, and so on, seemingly without end. Medical training tended to fall through the cracks, with mock casualties fairy-dusted back to life before they seriously impeded other objectives on any training exercise. I was lucky to have a corpsman who refused to accept that. Doc Bryan was a Special Amphibious Reconnaissance Corpsman, or SARC, one of the most highly trained field medics in the U.S. military.

After joining the platoon a few months before deploying to the Middle East, he'd drilled each man on basic trauma care. In Kuwait, he'd put together blowout kits for the whole platoon. The kits contained the essentials to keep a wounded Marine alive — saline IV bag, battle dressings, and QuikClot, a chemical compound to cauterize arterial bleeds. He'd also led the platoon in making tourniquets, to be worn loosely around the neck for easy access, and threatened to pummel any man caught without his. Doc's final contribution was not material but tactical. He stressed that the job of any Marine wounded in a firefight was to keep shooting until his team or the platoon was out of danger. Wounded men don't have the luxury of giving up the fight. Doc Bryan's gifts became real on the road outside Muwaffiqiya.

When the shooting started, Sergeant Patrick felt his vehicle shudder and his foot slam sideways. He looked down to see blood gushing from his boot, and Doc's training took over. He cinched a tourniquet around his leg; told his team, "I'm hit in the foot — I'm OK, though"; and resumed firing. Perched on the back of the headquarters Humvee, Corporal Stafford, the platoon radioman, had a similar experience. A bullet fragment from one of the ricocheting machine gun rounds tore into his calf, knocking him down. He, too, tied off his tourniquet and got back in the fight.

The firing had slackened. Lovell's team was the last to turn around. They lingered in the kill zone to spray the trees with machine gun fire while the rest of the platoon retreated back into the darkness. On the battalion's order, Rudy raced off with a bullet-riddled windshield and two shredded tires to evacuate Sergeant Patrick to the field we had started from. No one outside the platoon had even fired a shot.

I pulled the rest of the Marines back about two kilometers from the bridge, and we herringboned off the road to check on damage, injuries, and ammo counts. The mood was somber. A few gunmen had just stopped a Marine battalion, and we knew it. I also knew I'd lost one of my best Marines to the tactical error of not reconning the bridge. Finally, I feared the order from the battalion would be to move forward and try again to enter Muwaffiqiya. Tanks and LAVs idled a few miles up the road while we tried to enter this town in open Humvees. From an armchair in Iowa, it would have seemed foolish. From a dark roadside in Iraq, its lunacy ate away at our confidence. The mission had become, in grunt parlance, a goat-fuck.

My CO called with an update: "We're waiting here for thirty mikes while the helos refuel. Then we'll bring up tanks and LAVs and move forward again."

Finally. "Two copies all."

Third Platoon would be on point for the next push to the bridge, with company headquarters in its two Humvees behind them and my platoon in the rear. Team Two still wasn't back from evacuating Sergeant Patrick, so we were too small to lead the movement. Frankly, that was fine with me.

I moved from vehicle to vehicle, checking damage and talking with the guys. Doc Bryan wrapped a bandage around Stafford's leg. Stafford was adamant about staying with the platoon, and Bryan gave his tentative approval. I consented. We'd need every gun we had. The Marines were cleaning and reloading the heavy machine guns, changing night vision goggle batteries, and eating. They were silent. There was none of the euphoric banter that typically followed a firefight. No joking, no stories, no tall tales. This one had been too close, and it wasn't over yet. The focus was still on the mission.

From behind came the distinctive clanking of treads on pavement, and we moved our Humvees off the road to allow the seventy-ton behemoths to pass. Two M1A1 Abram tanks were followed by eight LAV-25s, each armed with a 25 mm Bushmaster cannon. For a grunt, working with tanks is like having jets overhead or being in the bottom of a deep fighting hole. It just feels good. In an embarrassment of riches, two Cobras reappeared from the east, thumping overhead without lights: lethal, menacing, utterly reassuring.

The lead platoon commander radioed that he was moving. A kilometer ahead, the tanks and LAVs fanned off the road, forming a line along the riverbank, pointing their guns toward the town. With a flash of light and a deafening roar, they fired their first salvo. Then another, and another, and another. When a tank fires its main gun in the dark, a tongue of flame shoots ahead, and the flash and bang of the shot is quickly followed by the flash and bang of the impact. The LAVs pumped chain gun rounds in burst after burst. They sounded like paper being torn, or a long guttural belch. From overhead, the Cobras fired Zuni rockets and Hellfire missiles. Each impact sent up a column of liquid fire. We drove forward into this storm, with smoke swirling through the doors and cordite filling our nostrils. As we drew abreast of the tanks, they ceased fire, and we moved forward to the bridge alone.

I planned to put my platoon on the north side to cover Third Platoon as they crossed into Muwaffiqiya. Once across, they would sit in place on the far side of the bridge and cover our crossing. The tanks and LAVs were too heavy to cross with us. I watched through my goggles as Third Platoon's five vehicles crept around the Dumpster and across the narrow concrete span onto the riverfront street. Company headquarters followed behind them. Suddenly, the command vehicle, towing a trailer filled with supplies, lurched and settled, as if about to plunge into the river.

"We're stuck on the bridge," the captain reported. Considering his situation, he sounded calm. Two Cobras hovered over the river, firing rockets into the alleyways on the far side. The Marines in company headquarters were out of their Humvee, trying to rock the trailer from a hole in the deck of the bridge. As much as any firefight we were in, this one typified the strange distance of combat. Third Platoon was trapped in the hostile town, alone, with no way to be reinforced or to fall back. Company headquarters struggled at the center of the bridge, as if spotlighted on a stage. Only fifty meters from them, we could do nothing. I held the platoon in place on the near side of the bridge, as much for moral support as anything else. In the darkness and smoke, we couldn't safely fire close to the other Marines. We pushed out security to the flanks and rear and watched the drama unfold.

An hour later, with dawn approaching, headquarters managed to free the trailer. They reversed across the bridge and halted in front of our position. In the gray light, I watched Third Platoon's Humvees rumble out of the demolished town, one by one, and cross to safety. As they drove past, the Marines looked like caricatures, pale with dark, sunken eyes. Throughout the night, the rest of the battalion had remained behind us, out of the fight. Now a few headquarters officers rushed forward and, as my Marines manned security positions in the fields along the road, eagerly clustered around the men we'd killed. I watched in disbelief as camera flashes popped in the dim light and senior officers laughed and strutted around.

I had kept my cool through almost seven hours of nonstop combat, through killing men so close I could hear them breathe, through evacuating my wounded brothers, through thinking I wouldn't live to see the sunrise. Finally, I lost control. Running up the road, I was in a rage.

"What the hell are you doing?" I shouted. "You stupid motherfuckers. Taking pictures? You make me sick."

A headquarters captain grabbed my shoulder and told me to calm down. I shook free. Major Benelli looked at me with disdain, as if it were in poor taste for me to ruin the victory celebration.

Headquarters began to trickle away; my explosion had not been entirely without effect. I looked at the dead bodies sprawled in the trees. Six or seven of them, young men like us, clean-shaven and dressed meticulously in pleated trousers, button-down shirts, and brown loafers. Their silver belt buckles gleamed. They looked more like computer programmers than Islamic fighters. AK-47s surrounded the bodies, along with RPG launchers and piles of grenades.

Clutched in the death grip of one of the men were two hand grenades, seconds from being thrown. Another corpse stood almost up-right, stapled to a tree trunk by .50-caliber machine gun rounds. A third fighter looked as if he'd died the clichéd death by a thousand cuts. One of the Cobra's fléchette rockets had hit next to him, sending thousands of tiny metal slivers into every inch of his body. There was no blood, only razor-thin cuts. We started picking through their pockets for infor-mation.

"Holy shit, these guys are Syrians!" Each man carried a Syrian pass-port, complete with official Iraqi entry visas. The visas were stamped in red ink with blank lines for the date, place, and reason of entry to be written in by hand. Each of the dead men had entered Iraq during the first week of the war at a crossing point on the Syrian border. Their written reasons were all the same: jihad.

I found no joy in looking at the men we'd killed, no satisfaction, no sense of victory or accomplishment. But I wasn't disturbed either. I fell back on an almost clinical detachment. The men were adults who chose to be here. I was an adult who chose to be here. They shot at us and missed. We shot at them and didn't miss. The fight was fair. All the same, I was happy my platoon wasn't here to see what they'd wrought. Sometimes it's better not knowing.

As I walked away, I heard a shout behind me. "We got a live one over here!"

Far behind the trees, a groaning man lay in the grass, one of his legs nearly severed by machine gun fire. The grass around him was slick with blood. For a second, the Marines looked at me, eyes flashing be-tween my face and my pistol. I think they thought I'd walk up and shoot him in the head, like a lame horse or a shark on a fishing charter. Colonel Ferrando elected to treat and evacuate the wounded man. I felt relieved. Two Marines slid him onto a stretcher and into the back of a Humvee, and he was whisked down the road to our staging area from the night before.

I collected the platoon, and we withdrew back down the highway, the last ones out just as we'd been the first ones in. The teams took their places in the defensive perimeter while Gunny Wynn and I searched for Sergeant Patrick. On our way across the field, neither of us said any-thing. We were preoccupied with the loss of one of our team leaders for the rest of the war, wondering at the stupidity of the mission that had nearly cost us our lives, and just plain exhausted from massive adrenaline overload. The sun had cleared the horizon, and it was a gorgeous morning. Dew on the grass sparkled in the light and reminded me of early-morning practice on the playing fields in high school.

We found the battalion's sergeant major aggressively watching our approach, hands on his hips.

"Morning, Sergeant Major. Where's Sergeant Patrick?"

"How the hell should I know?"

"Well, he was evacuated back here a few hours ago after he got hit. What happened to him?" It was clear from the sergeant major's confusion that he didn't know of Patrick's wound. He hadn't been on the mission the previous evening and was so far out of the loop that he still didn't know what was going on. We bypassed him and kept looking.

On a gentle hillside, we saw a supine form under a poncho liner. Patrick's foot was bandaged, and an IV hung from his arm. "How you doing, Shawn?" I asked.

"Good, sir. What's up, Gunny? How's the platoon?"

"Fine. Stafford took some frag in the leg, but he's OK. Glad to see you talking."

"They couldn't get a bird in last night, so I'm just waiting here. A truck's supposed to take me to the field hospital."

I told Sergeant Patrick about the wounded Syrian. "He'll probably be riding out with you. You good with that?"

"Long as he don't try nuthin'."

"I don't think he's in any shape to try anything."

Sergeant Patrick's assistant team leader walked up. Rudy had evacuated Patrick the night before and then returned to lead his team during our second attempt to cross the bridge. "Damn, brother, you're looking rough," Rudy said with a grin. "The battalion commander always said you looked like a bum, and this morning I'd say he's right."

The four of us were laughing and joking, relieved to be alive and grateful to see Patrick, when the sergeant major ambled over.

"Hey, jokers, get the hell outta here and give Sergeant Patrick his space."

I thought he was kidding and looked over at him. He was serious. "Get lost, Sergeant Major. You didn't even know he was here," I said.

"Now, Lieutenant, that ain't right . . ." His voice trailed off. Walking away, he looked crestfallen — left out of the mission and then not even able to assert some authority in its wake.

We gathered Patrick's gear and put together a small bag of things he might need in the hospital. The platoon rotated over in shifts to wish him well and joke about free rides home, million-dollar wounds, and the rest. Despite their humor, I knew that they were rattled. It was hard to see a man so respected get hit, and even harder to say goodbye. The bluster and jokes were a front for Sergeant Patrick's benefit, but inside we hurt. Gingerly, we lifted his stretcher aboard an open truck and settled him comfortably, one last act of faith for a friend. We loaded the Syrian next and climbed down. Wynn and I waved as the truck pulled away, then we walked back down to the platoon.

The Marines were on autopilot, minds elsewhere as bodies busily cleaned weapons, changed tires, and reloaded ammunition. Gunny Wynn and I took stock of our vehicle. A bullet had torn a ragged gash in the door frame just below his seat, and another had punched a hole behind my headrest that was large enough to fit my fist through. Holes peppered our canvas tarp, one of them surely left by the shrapnel now deep in Stafford's leg. I followed the paths of the other bullets to make sure they hadn't done any hidden damage to our equipment that would become apparent at some inopportune time. One round had passed through the tarp, then clear through a box of MREs, before piercing the plastic of a sniper rifle case and lodging against the buttstock of the rifle. I picked up the misshapen lump of lead and dropped it into my breast pocket. Maybe after a few more towns I'd have enough to make my own horseshoe.

I walked among the platoon, from vehicle to vehicle, visiting each team to listen to stories, take requests, and answer questions. Work continued while we talked, and everyone seemed to take renewed interest in the simple pleasures of eating a bag of pretzels or slipping out of his MOPP jacket to feel the warmth of the sun on his shoulders. Evan Wright was sprawled in the grass next to Colbert's Humvee, laughing with the Marines who stood around him scrubbing their M4s.

"I'm surprised you're still with us," I said.

"Because I should have left or could have been shot?"

I laughed. "Both."

Beneath the banter, the mood was morose. After earlier firefights, I had seen a quiet confidence in the younger Marines, the realization that they had faced the beast and won. That was gone now. The beast had fought back, and although no one was dead, we had paid a blood price. The more experienced Marines were vocal.

"Sir, what the fuck were the commanders thinking, sending us in there with no armor to clear a fucking town? We could have all been killed, and for what? We're sitting in the same goddamn field we were in last night, as if nothing had happened, except we got the shit shot out of us and lost a great team leader."

I walked a fine line. As an officer, I couldn't badmouth decisions the way a lance corporal could. Even as a lowly first lieutenant, I simply had too much rank, too much authority and influence. It would be disloyal and insubordinate, a transgression both moral and legal. At the same time, though, to smile in the face of stupidity and say something about liberating the Iraqi people or living up to the example of Iwo Jima and Hue City would neuter me in the eyes of my men. Men shrink in combat to little circles of trust: us versus them. A platoon that puts its commander in the "them" category is a dangerous place to be. Every young officer quickly learns the difference between legal authority and moral authority. Legal authority is worn on the collar — the gold and silver rank insignia that garner salutes and the title "sir." It doesn't win firefights. Moral authority is the legitimacy granted to a leader who knows his job and cares about his men. In combat, I learned to rely on moral authority much more than on legal authority.

So I conceded part of the Marine's statement. "That was bullshit, bad tactics. After all the artillery prep and with the air escort, no one expected that ambush to happen. We were all wrong. I can't speak for the battalion, but I can tell you that will never happen again in this platoon." I paused and locked eyes with the Marine to be sure he knew I wasn't just talking. "I'm sorry about Pappy. I don't know if we'll be fighting for another three days, three weeks, or three months, but I can tell you one thing. We have to learn from what we do right and what we do wrong, then move on. There were twenty-three of us, back to back. Now there are twenty-two. We have to get each other home in one piece."

The Marine nodded, accepting this line of reasoning. Strong combat leadership is never by committee. Platoon commanders must command, and command in battle isn't based on consensus. It's based on consent. Any leader wields only as much authority and influence as is conferred by the consent of those he leads. The Marines allowed me to be their commander, and they could revoke their permission at any time.

I stopped at Sergeant Reyes's vehicle, where half the team was replacing a tire shredded by machine gun fire while the other half brewed coffee and relived the night's adventure. Behind them, their Humvee's windshield displayed a hole exactly 7.62 millimeters wide where an AK-47 round had passed within inches of Sergeant Reyes's head. Now Rudy himself was serving as barista, carefully bringing water to a boil through coffee grounds, then pouring it with a delicate flourish that topped each cup with white *crema*. He spoke as he worked.

"So I'm driving along when Shawn says, 'Hey, Rudy, turn around.'" He imitated Sergeant Patrick's North Carolina drawl. "I start turning to the left, and *ack ack ack ack,* shooting everywhere. Humvee's rocking. Tracers over, under, past my head. Madness, brother, just madness. Then I see Shawn jump in his seat and yell. Well, I'm busy turning around in this firefight, trying not to run into anything or get us stuck, and I hear him say, real calm, 'I'm hit in the foot — I'm OK, though.' Then that crazy mother ties a tourniquet around his leg, real cool, picks up his M4, and starts shooting again!" Rudy folded at the waist, slapping his knee, struggling to breathe. "Brother, that guy is awesome. Awesome."

I was nursing the coffee Rudy had poured for me when Christeson's voice crackled through the radio. "Sir, the CO needs you at his truck." Looking toward company headquarters, I could see people packing up, getting ready to move.

"Roger, I'm on my way."

I thanked the guys for the coffee, shouldered my rifle, and walked away.

# 31

OW'S YOUR PLATOON, Nate?" The captain's eyes were red. He asked the question with reservation, as if he already knew the answer.

"Licking its wounds, sir. Two Marines shot. Thirty holes in my trucks. And that's just what I can see. The Marines are starting to wonder who's calling the shots here. Hell, I'm starting to wonder who's calling the shots." Keeping a stoic face for the platoon sometimes meant unloading on my commander. "That attack was fucking kindergarten tactics. We all knew it, and no one said a goddamn thing about it. And how am I supposed to keep my Marines on their game when officers are pulling stunts like that photo op this morning?"

The captain cut me off. "All right. We're all sorry about what happened to Sergeant Patrick. This is a war. Direct your frustration at the people who deserve it — the Iraqis." With that phase of the discussion over, he moved on to the day's plan while I seethed. Now I had to focus on getting from myself what I always expected from my troops: attention to the task at hand. What's past is past, but the present and future will kill you.

The plan called for us to move south to Al Hayy, recross the bridge we had crossed two days before, and attack into Muwaffiqiya with the Third Battalion, First Marines. In training, the order for a multibattalion attack into an occupied town would have taken half a day. Here, it was a sentence.

Gunny Wynn, Colbert, Lovell, and Reyes stood around the Humvee hood. The team leaders were laughing, and tried to quiet down as I approached. I spread my map on the hood and began to lay out the day's plan, but the guys couldn't let go of the joke I'd interrupted. When

Reyes and Lovell kept chuckling, I paused. *Goddammit.* Didn't they know how serious this was? Didn't they remember we'd lost Sergeant Patrick only a few hours earlier? Couldn't they see that I carried their lives on my shoulders? I started to speak and stopped myself. I'd nearly repeated what Captain Whitmer had told us in the *Peleliu* hangar bay eighteen months before: "If any of you get a Marine killed today, I'll shoot you myself."

I finally understood why Whitmer had threatened us that night. Commanders always bear the heaviest responsibility. When you're tired and under stress, your efforts to convey that gravitas can come out all wrong. The Marines must have seen my frustration, because they shut up and let me finish running through the plan. When I was done, they nodded and went off to brief their teams. They knew this wasn't the time for questions or arguments, and I was grateful for that.

Our lives were in free fall, spinning so completely out of our control that all we could do was hang on and try to keep up. That was when mistakes happened. Without time to plan or process or recover, we were at the mercy of fate — or worse, of other people. As a commander, taking full responsibility for my own decisions was one thing; taking it for other people's decisions was something else. The weight pressed down on me. I sat in my Humvee, studying the map, until Christeson fired up the engine.

We swung south to Al Hayy and into a world transformed. Of course, the weather had changed. Gloomy, dusty skies gave way to brilliant blue. All along the road, people waved and cheered. Girls in purple and yellow dresses smiled shyly while their brothers sprinted along the road's edge, slapping high-fives and giving the thumbs-up. Shutters and gates, once closed, were thrown open, and laundry fluttered in the breeze on lines above the streets. Traffic darted back and forth through the city, but despite our best attempts at watchfulness, we could see none of it as a threat. The desolate lot we'd raced through two days before was half soccer field, half open-air market. All foreboding had vanished. The only thing missing as we crawled through crowds of cheering Iraqis were streams of ticker tape from above. For the first time, we saw the meaning of liberation and felt the release of pure joy from ordinary lives. It was the best fifteen minutes of our week.

After crossing the bridge, we turned north and followed the river on the road we'd been watching two nights before. Craters pocked the roadside, and telephone poles were canted at odd angles, their wires severed and snaking along the ground — results of the artillery we'd dropped on escaping fedayeen. We stopped just south of Muwaffiqiya. Third Battalion, First Marines was halted ahead of us, waiting while its psychological operations teams blared surrender messages from loudspeakers into the town. I punched two-man observation teams out to our flanks and had the snipers begin scanning through their scopes. This area had been nothing but trouble for us.

As the teams rotated through security, maintenance, and rest, Gunny Wynn and I walked around to check the platoon's pulse. I wanted to see how Team Two was doing without Sergeant Patrick. Every man in the team had stepped up a level — Reyes to team leader and the other guys to a greater share of the collective responsibility now that they were down a man. Reyes knelt on his hands and knees next to his Humvee, scrubbing, while Jacks stood post behind the Mark-19.

"What are you doing, Rudy?"

"Hey, sir. I'm scrubbing Pappy's blood off our vehicle. Bad for our chi."

"Your what?"

"Chi — spiritual energy. It's the life force that influences everything we do. The old man bled a lot before we got him out of the truck, and I'm just trying to clean up a bit while we have the time."

I knelt next to Rudy and ran my finger across the jagged hole where the AK-47 bullet had pierced the Humvee's frame. The bullet had been traveling upward when it hit. I remembered those machine gun rounds sparking as they ricocheted off the road. It was reassuring to know that my snap judgment at the bridge had been right. "Did you find the bullet?"

Rudy smiled and reached into a pouch in his vest. "I'm saving it for Pappy." He held up a shiny 7.62 mm rifle bullet. It was hardly deformed at all. Thankfully. Had it tumbled or mushroomed after hitting the Humvee, it would have torn a ragged chunk from Sergeant Patrick rather than passing cleanly through. I took it in my hand — it was heavy — then gave it back.

"The sacred geometry of chance, sir."

"I like that."

"Espera and I talked about it earlier. We can do a lot to influence the outcome, but sometimes it's out of our hands," Rudy said, then mimed firing a rifle. "A running man shoots a burst into a moving Humvee. Why do some miss? Why do some hit? Why a flesh wound and not a femoral artery? Aim and skill have nothing to do with it. The difference between life and death out here is seconds and millimeters — the sacred geometry of chance." He looked down at the AK bullet in his hand. "Pappy's time came. He was in Somalia and Afghanistan before this. You can only dodge for so long."

"How are you and the team, Rudy? Let Gunny Wynn and I know what you need, and we'll shuffle things around to support you."

"We'll be fine, sir. They're all good guys, and Pappy trained 'em right — they can go on without him. I just can't believe he's not here. I miss him already."

"Me too." I stood to leave, then stuck out my hand. Rudy took it. "You're the team leader now, Sergeant Reyes. I know you're up to it."

The infantry battalion pushed through Muwaffiqiya without resistance. Any foreign fighters and fedayeen in the town had simply melted away. We followed behind the grunts, crawling along a road paralleling the river. Ornate masonry walls surrounded waterfront parks, and wide sidewalks swept along the roadside. Shuttered storefronts lined the stone buildings, clearly a holdover from some earlier, more prosperous era in that part of Iraq. A dedicated afternoon of trash collecting and whitewashing could have vaulted the place into respectability, but that afternoon had never happened.

"Jesus, Gunny, look over there," I said. To our right, across the river, stood a clump of trees by the side of a small bridge — the site of our ambush the night before. The trees, buildings, and bridge were just as I remembered them. We could even see the pile of debris dragged into the road by the Syrians. It was eerie, seeing the scene from the enemy's perspective.

"That machine gun must have been set up right here." I looked around for a telltale pile of brass shell casings but saw nothing. The buildings along the river had been on the receiving end of our heaviest fire — artillery, Cobras, and tanks. Rubble spilled into the street. Whole city blocks had been replaced with piles of shattered bricks. Explosions had cleaved some rooms in half, leaving their intact remnants visible where walls once stood. Furniture still filled the rooms, and pictures hung on the walls. I caught fleeting glimpses of people peeking at us from the ruins. Sympathy was tempered by the knowledge that a handful of foreign fighters could not have remained there to ambush us without the approval, or at least the indifference, of the villagers. And yet children surely lived there, and we had blown their homes to pieces.

"Cars are driving next to us a few blocks that way." Wynn pointed to our left, deeper into Muwaffiqiya. "Creeping along like they're casing us."

I looked and saw a blue sedan, its passengers staring at me as I was at them. A block later, it passed another cross street, still keeping pace with us.

"Hitman Two, halt in place while Alpha moves forward to investigate an arms cache." The CO interrupted our observation with the order to stop, while Alpha Company pushed ahead.

Except for the drivers and turret gunners, we all moved away from the Humvees — juicy targets in the close confines of a city street. I took my rifle and radio and knelt in the alcove doorway of a store, scanning the rooftops and windows across the street. Up and down the road, the platoon melted into shadows. Teams alternated sides of the street, so each could see the windows and roofs above the other. Watching Marines crouched in the rubble reminded me of pictures of the battle for Hue City during the Tet offensive. If Vietnam still grips the nation's consciousness, its memory is doubly strong in the Marine Corps. When officers and staff NCOs in Iraq turned their backs, Marines were apt to slip an ace of spades into their helmet bands or write slogans on their flak jackets. "Born to Kill." "George Bush's Hired Gun." I heard Iraqis referred to as "gooks" or "Charlie," only half jokingly. Vietnam Marines are still the archetypal Marines.

"Hitman Two, be advised that radio intercepts indicate fedayeen regrouping in the city and preparing to launch suicide car bomb attacks against us. No further information."

This announcement from company headquarters was big news. We had never received a warning about a specific threat in a specific place from the signals intelligence team riding with the battalion. Their Arabic linguists scanned local Iraqi radio traffic, so I took the threat seriously and passed it on to the teams. The Marines calmly acknowledged the news, but their hands tightened on pistol grips, and their eyes darted more quickly up alleys and roads. I thought back to the car that had seemed to be shadowing us. Instantly, the sunny afternoon turned tense. I felt a charge in the air like that before a thunderstorm. Even my memory of those moments is in black and white, the very recollection thrown into shadowy high relief.

Moving forward, we drove slowly, looking for the rear of Alpha Company. Near the northern edge of Muwaffiqiya, we linked up. Their lead vehicles turned left at a grassy park and drove away from the river. It seemed odd that we'd be driving deeper into the town instead of continuing north into the open fields I could barely see through thinning buildings. As my platoon reached the turn, Major Whitmer jumped from his Humvee, which was parked at the side of the road.

"Nate, keep going straight. Alpha made a wrong turn. You're on battalion point now. Pull forward a few hundred meters and halt so we can get this unfucked."

Colbert and Espera pulled their vehicles abreast and set up a rolling roadblock to keep any oncoming traffic from running into the battalion as it untwisted itself. We snaked around the park and began to roll slowly past a row of low-slung industrial buildings.

"Vehicle from the front. Blue sedan. Three or four passengers." Colbert's report was terse, spoken in the clipped tones of a guy juggling rifle, binoculars, and a radio handset while reporting to his commander, giving orders to his subordinates, and planning his next move. If anyone could manage this balancing act, it was Brad Colbert. He'd been named the battalion's Team Leader of the Year, and I had boundless confidence in him.

"Roger. Escalation of force. Don't let him pass," I said. But I thought, *Blue sedan? Fuck, I knew it. Fuck, fuck, fuck. Just as we move to the front of the battalion, too. All right, Brad, you were Team Leader of the Year. Do the right thing, my man.*

Since Colbert's first radio call, perhaps five seconds had elapsed. I heard the single pop of an M203 grenade launcher and knew a warning round of colored smoke had been fired at the car. Then I saw it, moving very fast. The two Humvees stopped in the road and their goggled turret gunners aimed in.

A short, zapping burst of fire rattled down the street, echoing off buildings. I was so expecting a heavy machine gun's roar that I first thought this lighter chatter was incoming fire. Seeing the blue car veer off the road to the left, I realized the shooting was ours. Two men jumped from the sedan and disappeared in a blur of billowing robes and flapping sandals. The car's drift to a halt, its opening doors, and the occupants' sprint down the street seemed to unfold in one fluid sequence. I was briefly jubilant that the platoon had stopped it with minimum force, protecting the battalion without hurting anyone. Then I trained my binoculars on the car.

A still figure sat behind the steering wheel with his head thrown back against the seat. A red stain spread down the front of his white robe.

"What's that firing? What are you shooting at?" Some disembodied voice on the radio, surely with more rank on his collar than me, started lobbing questions from farther back in the battalion column.

"Hitman Two just engaged a car that wouldn't stop. We're moving up to investigate. Stand by." Still afraid of a trunk packed with TNT, we inched toward the car. Just as we got close, an order came over the radio to pass it by. We were told to advance half a kilometer up the road and set up another roadblock while the battalion continued to extricate itself from Muwaffiqiya.

I stared at the driver of the car as we passed. He breathed in rough, wheezy gasps. At least one bullet had punched through his face and exited through the top of his skull. *God help us,* I thought, *and God help him.*

A couple of hours before sunset, long shadows fell across fields of crops that stretched for miles in every direction. Up until then, we had seen only the small plots of subsistence farmers. This landscape looked more like the American Midwest. An occasional silo or irrigation pipe completed the effect. I relaxed outside the towns. There we could see, and any threat would have to expose itself to our superior firepower. I fiddled with my shortwave radio and propped it on the dashboard, where the voice of the BBC news anchor could compete with the Humvee's engine and the wind rushing past. From London, she told Gunny Wynn and me what we were doing. The Army's Third Infantry Division was closing in on Baghdad, with reports of fighting near Saddam International Airport. Marines were reported to hold a bridge over the Tigris at An Numaniyah, preparing to assault Baghdad from the southeast.

"That must be RCT-5 and RCT-7," Wynn yelled over the engine. "So how'd we go from being in the lead to being way behind?"

"They swung west through open desert while we shot our way through every shitty little town in central Iraq," I said. "You complaining that someone else is up there to beat on the Republican Guard for us?"

He smiled. "Nope. Just wondering how we got so lucky. Every time we get lucky, something bad happens to even the score."

By piecing together news reports, official intelligence, and what we saw with our own eyes, we could usually figure out where we fit in the bigger picture. The Army and Marines would launch a two-pronged attack on Baghdad in the coming days. While the rest of the division crossed the Tigris at An Numaniyah, we would attack into Al Kut to fix in place a Republican Guard armored division garrisoned there, keeping it from hitting the flank or rear of the force near Baghdad. Al Kut was one of the largest cities in Iraq. I found it hard to believe we'd actually attack into a city that big but had learned in the past couple of weeks to reframe how I thought about risk. Yes, it would be completely insane, and yes, we may well do it.

The countryside was so bucolic and the evening so beautiful that the war faded a bit, and I began to fantasize about a warm meal and a clean bed waiting at our destination. I knew, though, that there would be only a muddy field and a cold MRE. Around dusk, the horizon ahead of us flickered with explosions. They only increased my feeling of normalcy, as if they were summer thunderstorms over Kansas, not jets pounding Republican Guard positions around Al Kut. We drove on through the first hour of darkness. As we got closer, we saw the explosions beneath the flashes. Their low rumble rolled across the fields, audible even over the roaring diesels.

We pulled off the road, and the Humvees strained through deep mud, their tires flinging clay over everything. I slipped and slid from vehicle to vehicle, emplacing the heavy machine guns in my little piece of the battalion perimeter. The night was so dark I had to use my night vision goggles just to see the next truck as I walked the lines. The Marines were exhausted, and we planned to leave at first light, so I considered giving the order to skip digging holes. This mud would absorb mortar shrapnel like a huge, leaden sponge. Remembering the terror of our bombardment near Qalat Sukkar, I thought better of it, and we spent the next forty-five minutes carving ranger graves in the wet clay. Colonel Ferrando was right: combat is unforgiving, and hard work trumps hope and luck combined.

My exhaustion had become insomnia, and I volunteered for radio watch while the other guys slept. Snores rose from sleeping bags as I sat in the passenger seat, staring into the darkness, thinking of home. What was my family doing? It was early afternoon on the East Coast, Wednesday, April 2, 2003. My sisters were in class. My parents were at work. Were they worrying about me? I hoped not. At any given time, I knew how much danger I was in. Usually, it didn't seem like much. They had to assume the worst, and imaginations run wild without hard information. I wished I could tell them I was fine and put them at ease.

Through the Humvee's dusty windshield, I watched flares popping in the distance, not knowing whether they were ours or the enemy's. Each one burned brightly for thirty seconds, swinging in its parachute and silhouetting buildings and palm trees. The radio warned of Iraqi tanks in the area, and a machine gun fired somewhere in the dark. Night radio watch always made me philosophical, and I debated whether the war was more dangerous than I thought. Maybe my family's concerns were justified. Maybe my sense of safety had become skewed. A massive explosion nearby seemed to confirm the thought. I turned away to preserve my night vision from the sudden light and waited for the flames to die down. After a few hours of listening to the radio's soothing hiss, I woke Gunny Wynn and slept fitfully till dawn.

"Balls out. Damn, they're really lighting into them," Sergeant Colbert said. Half the platoon clustered around his Blue Force Tracker, watching a battle unfold a few kilometers to our north. Marine vehicle icons clustered on the bridge into Al Kut, and we could hear them shooting. LAVs, mainly, pumping 25 mm shells and ripping their chain guns. Interspersed with the lighter fire were the occasional explosions of a tank's main gun. Suddenly, just as we expected the Marines to move into the city, they backed off the bridge and raced south down the highway, passing us without a glance. When the vehicles faded from sight, we continued to watch their icons falling off our map screen to the south at a steady clip.

"Hitman Two, stand by to move in ten mikes." The captain interrupted our voyeurism, and we began to throw gear into the Humvees, top off oil, wash windshields, and lube machine guns. The CO came over to fill us in.

"That was RCT-1 in Al Kut. They got right up on the bridge and put on a show. RCT-5 and RCT-7 are north of the Tigris and moving on Baghdad. We're heading south right now, back the way we came, and then eventually we'll swing around and cross the Tigris in An Numaniyah."

I couldn't believe it. "You mean this whole thing was a feint? Everything we've done since leaving Qalat Sukkar was to put on a show in Al Kut?"

The captain nodded. "Looks that way."

It's not that I felt cheated. I knew that every main effort needs supporting efforts, and we'd been the main effort for long enough. It just seemed funny that in the twenty-first century, a feint still meant getting right up on the bridge and pretending to attack a town. I thought of my buddies with RCT-5 and hoped they appreciated our efforts on their behalf.

We spun through the mud and up onto the highway. Driving south felt like an anticlimax. Each previous mile had been closer to Baghdad, closer to victory, the end of the war, and home. Driving south was depressing. I worked hard to stay vigilant. It takes only minutes to set up an ambush, and the fact that we'd driven past the day before meant nothing outside our own minds.

Refugees filled the road. Thousands of them. Young couples with children, old women in black, men our age watching us self-consciously. They trudged south carrying water bottles, bundles of clothes, bags of bread, and one another. We drove past them for two hours. I was hungry but embarrassed to eat in front of people whose lives had been reduced to what they could carry in plastic shopping bags. We had barely enough food for ourselves. Marines who had eaten only one meal each day for the past week gave their MREs to the fleeing Iraqis. I couldn't bring myself to stop them. The worst were the children. Babies could be carried, and adults can fend for themselves, but five- and six-year-olds walked next to their parents. Some limped and some cried, but all kept walking south. Away from the bombing. Away from the coming fight.

We stopped on the side of the highway to await our orders. At four in the afternoon, they came: leave immediately and drive to the Tigris River bridge at An Numaniyah. Be there by morning. Gunny Wynn and I spread maps on the hood. Sheet after sheet after sheet. I whistled.

"Christ, that's almost two hundred miles. We have to go south through Al Hayy to Qalat Sukkar, then swing west through Afak and north again all the way to the Tigris. What do you think?"

"I think we'd better stop dicking around and drive."

Sometimes I felt like a long-distance trucker, living my life in the cab of the Humvee, talking on the radio, and eating meals on the road. At my feet sat a two-liter water bottle to which I'd added six packets of

MRE instant coffee, six creamers, a packet of cocoa powder, and two crushed No-Doz tablets. I had to be careful to sip the brew slowly to avoid peaking and crashing before midnight.

By sunset, we'd passed through Al Hayy and by the intersection where Iraqi artillery had nearly hit us three nights and several lifetimes earlier. We turned west on Highway 17 and accelerated into the fading twilight on a narrow macadam road. Our speed stayed high as we crested a series of small hills, passing farmhouses set back from the highway. Lights shone in some of them, and again I was struck by the peaceful countryside. A video filmed from my seat that evening would have looked like any one of a thousand hardscrabble farming towns in the American Southwest.

We raced through Afak without incident and turned north on Highway 1. Its six lanes of pavement had been in our dreams since south of Nasiriyah, when we'd last traveled them before cutting north on Highway 7 with RCT-1. The Army and the other RCTs had remained on Highway 1, swinging west of Iraq's population centers to speed toward Baghdad. Now we joined the pell-mell rush. Traffic on the highway was thick and eclectic — Humvees, Patriot missile batteries, tanks on trucks, tanks clanking along on their own, hundreds of contracted tankers carrying fuel for the invaders. In the southbound lanes, empty trucks roared toward Kuwait for another load. I watched the massive logistical orchestra and thought of all those nights we'd felt so alone, a few teeth far away from this immense tail. We merged into the flow and relaxed, feeling the false safety of numbers.

Tracking our progress on the maps folded in my lap, I led the platoon off an exit ramp to Highway 27 for the final few miles to An Numaniyah. We arrived in the dead hours between midnight and dawn, joining a queue of Marines assembling to cross the bridge in the morning. I thought a tank might crush me if I slept next to the Humvee, so I crawled beneath it. My eyes closed, but sleep would not come.

At home, I would have gone downstairs and watched TV. Under the Humvee, all I could do was stare at the oil pan a few inches above my nose. I saw my father leaning against the kitchen counter as I told him of my decision to join the Corps. My girlfriend, sobbing beneath a blanket as I said goodbye in a hotel room in Coronado. Shattered windshields. Blood-spattered pavement. And that relentless voice on the scratchy recording: *There's no discharge in the war.*

\* \* \*

After sunrise, we continued our relentless push and crossed the second of Mesopotamia's great rivers. Below the bridge, the Tigris sparkled in the morning sun. Fishermen poled skiffs through the shallows, and crowds gathered along the banks to bathe and draw water. A group of children waved from atop a burned-out Soviet tank. Others clambered onto an artillery cannon and sat, cheering, astride the barrel as if it were a hobbyhorse. Military equipment was everywhere. For the next hundred miles, all the way to the gates of Baghdad, every palm grove hid Iraqi armor, every field an artillery battery, and every alley an antiaircraft gun or surface-to-air missile launcher. But we never fired a shot. We saw the full effect of American airpower: every one of these fearsome weapons was a blackened hulk.

The division had fought its way through there the day before, and evidence of the battle was everywhere. We passed a Humvee, its windshield frosted with bullet holes. American sleeping bags and packs lay in the road. I wondered what had happened to their owners. Frequently, the pavement itself bore the starburst crater and radiating shrapnel scars of a mortar strike. All along the highway, buildings and underbrush smoldered. Smoke was thick in the air, burning diesel mixing sometimes with sweeter burning flesh. Wynn and I stared at a blackened and abandoned Abrams tank.

"I thought those things were indestructible," I said. "How the hell did they manage to bag a fucking Abrams?"

He shook his head. "I don't know, but let's hope whoever did it is already dead."

"Watch out." I pointed at an object in the road, thinking it was a piece of unexploded ordnance. Then I saw it was a human head, slightly charred and staring placidly at the sky. A short distance away, dogs tore at the body.

Wynn and I were momentarily chastened but then had to laugh. "Can you believe this place?" he said. "Heads in the road. Dogs eating bodies. People at home bitch about cigarette butts on the beach."

We drove through dusk and into the night before stopping along the edge of the road. The GPS told me where we were, but that was less important than what was out there. Nothing could tell me what was in the fields and palm groves just beyond our little circle. We had moved so quickly that there was no front anymore. Good guys and bad guys were all mixed up. I had slept three hours in three days.

"Gunny, I can't think straight. I need a couple of hours in the bag," I said. At that point, sleep wasn't pleasant, just a mechanical necessity, like putting gas in a car.

To our left, a five-story factory burned in the dark. Flames leaped high into the sky. The fire didn't crackle; it roared, sucking oxygen from the air around it. I wrapped myself in a poncho and lay on the gravel near the front tire to shield myself from the flickering light.

It was the sleep of the damned. I floated in a netherworld of dreams, memories, and sudden starts. Briefing the platoon. Fireballs. Ragged breathing. Take the shot. Blue cars. Tanks nearby. And the fire, burning, roaring, casting shadows across the palms.

Christeson shook me awake. "It's been three hours, sir. The patrol's on its way back in."

I sat up and rubbed my head, shaking gravel from my hair. "What patrol?"

"Team Three, sir. They went to check out that tank."

"What the fuck are you talking about?"

Down the road, near the platoon's last Humvee, Sergeant Lovell and Doc Bryan were swearing softly in the darkness. Around them, the team sat on the pavement, stripping out of soaked, muddy boots and trousers. They looked as if they'd been wading in waist-deep water.

Stinetorf glanced up at me. "That fucking thing has probably been there ten years, sir. Couldn't drive it out through that swamp if they wanted to."

Slowly, I understood. Some of my dreams had not been dreams. The company operations chief, a senior enlisted man outside the platoon, had come to me and asked to send Lovell's team out to investigate an Iraqi tank that had been spotted in a nearby palm grove. I pulled Sergeant Lovell aside and asked him what had happened.

"Ops chief came and told us to go look at some fucking tank out there in the grove. I told him half the fucking division rolled past it already and I only take orders from you and Gunny Wynn."

I nodded, seeing where this was going.

"So he left and came back a couple minutes later. Said he talked to you and you OK'ed it. We mounted up and went out."

I had given the order without even realizing it. "Sergeant Lovell, he came to me, but I was delirious and thought I was dreaming. I'm sorry."

Gunny Wynn was sitting by the radio when I returned to the Humvee. "I'm losing my mind, Mike. Losing my fucking mind."

# 32

THE CHAPLAIN'S VOICE DRONED, but I paid no attention. I was focused on the dusty pair of combat boots flanking an M4 stuck muzzle-first in the dirt. Horsehead was dead. We'd heard rumors earlier in the day of Fifth Marines getting in a firefight. Horsehead had been wounded, badly wounded, or evacuated, with no further details. But he couldn't have been killed. First sergeants don't die in combat; that's for corporals and lieutenants to do. Besides, Smith was a common last name. There must have been hundreds of Smiths in the Marine Corps, probably even a bunch of First Sergeant Smiths. But no. First Sergeant Edward Smith, Horsehead, a recon legend doing a tour in the grunts before retiring, was dead.

I joined many other recon Marines at a dusk memorial service in a field on the southeastern outskirts of Baghdad. Around us, the entire First Marine Division was massing its combat power. Marines sprawled everywhere, sleeping. Others turned wrenches on Humvees, cleaned weapons, or huddled over huge map sheets with their corners held down by bricks. We hadn't all been together since leaving Kuwait. After almost three weeks moving across Iraq like individual rivulets of water, the division was pooling, preparing to flood the enemy capital. It was a pause, not a stop. In the distance, Baghdad's minarets rose above the palms.

We took turns saying what a great Marine Horsehead had been, what a great husband, father, and man. We bowed our heads in silence and sang a song I cannot remember. I was staring at the boots. When a man wakes up in the morning, he puts on his boots. He laces them up and ties them. He expects to take them off again that evening. Horsehead went through the day without knowing he'd put on his boots for the last time. Maybe I'd already put on my boots for the last time, too. When the service ended, I walked slowly back to the platoon, grateful for my time alone in the dark. Faint strings of tracers climbed into the sky, too far off to hear.

Colonel Ferrando summoned his officers to battalion headquarters the following afternoon, April 8, for a mission brief. We'd spent the morning listening to the BBC and watching columns of smoke rise from Baghdad. The Army had launched an audacious "thunder run" from Saddam International Airport into the heart of the city, and resistance was lighter than feared. The Marines were preparing to unleash their own offensive across the Diyala River and into the city from the southeast. The news reports had an unreal quality to them. Part of me thought we'd never reach that point. American tanks would never roll into one of the great cities of the Middle East. I had laughed in Kuwait when General Mattis talked about using recon as dismounted shock troops during the final urban assault. *Hyperbole for the lance corporals,* I'd thought then. *Never gonna happen.* Well, it was happening. I leaned closer to learn our role in the war's climax.

"Gentlemen, as most of you know, the assault on Baghdad has begun," Ferrando said. As he elaborated on the American seizure of Iraq's capital, I marveled at his uniform. It looked pressed. His clean-shaven face shone in the sunlight, and his hair was neatly combed. I, in comparison, looked as if I had come to the meeting straight from my cardboard box beneath an overpass. Days of sweat and grime stiffened my uniform. My fingernails were black, and I could feel my toes squishing in my socks. I slept at night with my head out of the sleeping bag because I couldn't bear the stench of my own body.

The colonel confirmed that the division would attack across the Diyala River into the city. General Mattis had one overriding concern. The forty-first Armored Brigade of the Al Nida Republican Guard Division was headquartered in Ba'quba, only fifty kilometers northeast of Baghdad. Its tanks could hit the First Marine Division's flank less than an hour after leaving their base. And that's where we came in.

Major Whitmer read the mission statement: "At fourteen hundred Zulu, First Recon Battalion will attack north to Ba'quba, locating and identifying enemy forces in order to help the division develop its situation. Be prepared to engage targets of opportunity. We'll link up with LAR at the zero-zero northing and then continue up to the three-zero northing."

While Colonel Ferrando and Major Whitmer continued the briefing, directed mainly at the company commanders, I studied my maps. The 00 northing was a line on the map about twenty-five kilometers to our north. That meant fifteen miles of unescorted driving up to the LAR company, whose call sign was War Pig. They straddled the road at the northernmost limit of the American advance, which happened to be right at the 00 northing. We would link up with them and attack north for another thirty kilometers into the town of Ba'quba. The map showed a highway split south of town. The left fork swung around to the west and paralleled a river on the western side of Ba'quba. The right fork continued straight north on the eastern side of the city. In the months to come, this town would be a corner of the area called "the Sunni Triangle," with connotations of RPG-toting insurgents and blown-up American Humvees. On April 8, 2003, it was still just Ba'quba, a small town north of Baghdad, whose Republican Guard outpost had yet to feel the brunt of American ground power. First Recon was going to change that.

Fourteen hundred Zulu translated to five o'clock local time, a few hours before sunset. I lined the platoon up an hour early on the dirt road that led out of the division's headquarters compound. Our ritualistic "combat prep" time was important to any successful mission, and I didn't want to rush it. Besides, I had come to enjoy the anticipatory tingle I got whenever we prepared to step outside the wire. Gunny Wynn and I walked up and down the line of vehicles. Doc Bryan was mixing a strong coffee to sustain him through the evening, while Stinetorf racked his .50-caliber's charging handles to clean the moving parts for later. Many of the Marines wore calf-length digital-pattern desert cloaks, leftovers from the first Gulf War which provided great protection from the dust, with an added benefit of being almost impossible to see through night vision goggles. I walked up to Colbert's Humvee and leaned down to talk through his open window.

"OK, point man, back-brief our route to me."

"Sir, we'll leave the compound here and drive north on the paved road that parallels Route 5. We're not the lead element for that portion, so I just follow in trace. At the zero-zero northing, we link up with LAR, and they'll take the lead. I'll be recon's first vehicle behind them. We'll continue north and see what happens."

"Good. It'll be nice having some real firepower with us for a change." I turned and walked back to my Humvee without saying what I knew we were both thinking: *Why did we have this firepower with us for a change?*

Across the road, the Marines in division headquarters sat in little clumps, eating their MREs. They watched as we prepared to leave, envy and relief mixing on their faces. I was sure my platoon pitied them, knowing that they would be safe and warm here in their sleeping bags.

I folded the night's maps and tucked them in my Plexiglas map case. It measured about two feet square and allowed me to see thirty or forty kilometers of road at a time without having maps flapping all over the place in the wind. A bandolier of grenades hung from the visor above my head, ready for quick loading in the M203. On the center console sat two GPS receivers, carefully checked to make sure they read the same, and a pile of rifle magazines loaded with all tracers. Stuck to the inside of the windshield in front of my seat were two laminated cards outlining the request procedures for artillery and air support. Stress has a way of banishing even the simplest things from one's mind, so I was reassured to have the cheat sheets in my hour of need. A red-lens flashlight, hand grenades, night vision goggles, smoke grenades, colored flares, IV bags, humrats, a sniper rifle, and four radios completed the ensemble. For all its size, that Humvee would be a tight fit for us this evening.

Exactly on time, we started the engines and crept slowly from the camp. Out on the road, we entered a different world. Crowds of Iraqis thronged the streets. Most of them paid us little attention; they were preoccupied stealing every movable object in sight. Children drove donkeys towing pieces of scrap metal. A man on a bicycle staggered past with a wooden table balanced precariously on his fender. Behind him, an old woman dragged a plastic jug with one hand and a huge spool of copper wire with the other. We threaded through the crowd, guns elevated in deference to the people but eyes scanning for the signs of trouble we'd learned to look for over the past few weeks: anyone coolly appraising us, cars reappearing, people on radios or cell phones. Soon we escaped into the farmland beyond Baghdad's suburbs, increasing our speed as the shadows lengthened and the sky turned gray.

We passed dozens of blown-up Iraqi tanks and armored personnel carriers. Some of them sat in revetments off the road; others were parked on the shoulder. Fire had blackened their desert tan paint jobs, and overpressure had blown their hatches open. I hoped the record of destruction would continue as we got farther north.

Approaching the 00 northing, we contacted War Pig on the radio. Their hulking LAVs sat in a defensive coil on the west side of the road. A coil is the twenty-first-century version of a wagon train circling up for the night. The LAVs were parked back to back, with their guns pointed outward in a full circle. We pulled to the side of the road and waited as they unlooped themselves and whined slowly up onto the pavement, taking their place at the head of the formation. The dozen LAVs traveled in a staggered column, their guns alternating left and right. Colbert followed behind the last LAV, with the rest of the platoon close at his heels. Behind us, First Recon stretched to the south in a long line. With the confidence of firepower, we accelerated into the darkness, the first Americans to enter that part of Iraq.

I used an alcohol pen to mark our progress on the map. The 05 northing passed without incident, and then the 10. We had traveled ten kilometers into uncharted territory with no trouble. Twenty kilometers of dark farmland lay between us and Ba'quba. As I inked a little check mark next to the 14 northing on the map, a chain gun sounded its tearing rattle.

A general warning went out to all vehicles: "War Pig's in contact. Armed dismounts on both sides of the road."

The road before us curved to the right, and the whole column of LAVs stretched around the gentle bend. Red tracers reached out from the road. Bushmaster cannons thumped, deeper and slower than the chain gun. Still, the only fire was outgoing, nothing coming in. I dropped the night vision goggles in front of my eyes and started scanning the platoon's flanks. Open fields stretched to our left, but a cluster of three or four small buildings stood a hundred meters directly to the right. Everything was still.

I called the teams, thinking they might see something I couldn't. "All Hitman Two stations, I have no targets. What do you see?"

"Two-One's looking. No joy."

"Two-Two. We got nothing."

"Two-Three. Nada."

Ahead of us, strings of tracers arced toward the road from the fields.

They wobbled and wove, like a light show. Harmless-looking, almost pretty. LAR wasn't shooting at shadows: people were out there, and they wanted to fight.

Radio reports were coming in fast. At least two enemy platoons armed with AKs and RPGs hid in the ditches alongside the road. War Pig was tearing them up through thermal sights. A man can hide his body under a blanket in a ditch, but he can't hide his body heat.

Lasers danced along the buildings next to us as Marines aimed at windows and doors, waiting for movement. No one fired. To our front, the shooting increased in intensity, with the crisscrossing tracers sometimes bright enough to wash out my goggles. Behind us, a .50-caliber gun opened up with a roar, followed by the *thunk-boom, thunk-boom* of a Mark-19. We couldn't see what the Marines were firing at, so we kept watching our sector. Still no targets.

The gunfire was so loud that Gunny Wynn and I had to shout at each other across the Humvee cab.

"They're probing for weak points," I yelled.

He nodded in agreement, and added, "We *are* the weak point."

The firing began to take on a pattern. An enemy gunner would let loose a burst, and then Marines responded by pouring hundreds of rounds at him. At each crescendo, the shots were so loud and so frequent that they blended from individual popping and cracking into one indistinguishable roar. We still saw no targets nearby, so there was nothing to do but watch and wait. With thousands of bullets being fired all around us, we sat as if in the eye of a storm.

In the grainy green fields of my night vision goggles, a flash resolved into a blooming cloud of smoke and dust. Mortar. It fell on the west side of the road, to our left. I looked at Gunny Wynn.

"You see that?"

"Yeah. Big one. Eighty-two millimeter at least." Wynn's voice was detached, his assessment almost clinical.

"Let's see where the next one lands," I shouted over the gunfire still popping all around us. "Might be time to get this train moving again."

The next one landed on the right side of the road. Then left again, but closer. They had us bracketed and were walking the rounds in on us. So much for idiotic tactics — this was a combined-arms ambush. They'd stopped us with the infantry and now hoped to hammer an easy target.

Sitting on the road, we made an easy target. But the false security of the night vision goggles protected me. I watched the mortars fall through glass lenses that divided things into two worlds. We lived in the world of color, which then was dark. The mortars fell in a world of green, which then was light. Even the tooth-rattling *crump* of the rounds couldn't shake the impression that a barrier stood between these worlds, protecting us. So it seemed only vaguely threatening when we were ordered forward to help LAR break contact from the ambush.

"Hitman Two, move up on the west side of the road and provide suppressive fire for War Pig to peel back to the south."

I had to smile at the insanity of it. "Hey, Gunny, the CO wants our tin-pot Humvees to go up there and shoot so the LAVs can disengage."

War Pig was already doing an Australian peel, where the lead vehicle turns around as the second in line continues firing straight ahead to protect the turning vehicle. The drill is repeated down the line until the last vehicle turns. I moved the platoon forward, and we fired off into the darkness, hopefully keeping a few Iraqi heads down as the last LAV turned and roared back down the highway. Far to the north, headlights flashed and spun in the dark fields. Mortars continued to fall, including one that hit the pavement nearby, throwing sparks into the sky. When our turn came, each Humvee swung around to the south, and we accelerated behind War Pig, passing the rest of the battalion as it sat facing north.

The night was moonless, with a low overcast threatening rain. Helicopters could not fly under the weather, and jets above it couldn't provide accurate close air support. Facing a coordinated defense-in-depth, with little idea of what lay to the north, the colonel decided to pull back two kilometers and set up a hasty defense on the roadside. With a little distance between us and the enemy positions, we could call in jets and wait for daylight.

I lined the platoon up along a berm a few hundred meters off the road. War Pig had done most of the shooting, so the Marines weren't too amped-up. We started watch rotations, and I crawled under the Humvee to enjoy an hour's insomnia. When the rain started, trickles of water crept across the baked earth and pooled under my back.

Before dawn on April 9, I squirted grape jelly from its plastic pouch onto an MRE cracker. Wynn and I had been sitting together by the radio for an hour, waiting for the sky to lighten. Throughout the night, jets had screamed overhead, above the clouds, and we had felt the *whump* of bombs being dropped near the highway. They could have been JDAMs hitting GPS coordinates provided by the battalion, or other bombs targeted by the pilots using Litening pods, special sensors that could see through darkness and clouds. I was too tired to go and find out, and it didn't matter anyway. Bombs were bombs. They all killed the same way.

I finished my breakfast and walked over to the company headquarters Humvee, parked a short distance away in the center of our perimeter. The Marines would soon be clamoring for news, and I wanted to have something for them.

"Good morning, sir. What's the plan for the day?"

"Shit on Ba'quba," the captain replied, scouring his pistol with a toothbrush.

"We're not just gonna drive up the highway, are we?"

"No," he replied. "LAR and the Humvees will stay on the highway. Each platoon will punch a foot-mobile patrol out to the east or west, and we'll sweep north in a long line."

"Christ, sir, it's damn near fifteen miles to Ba'quba."

He looked at me blankly and said, "Yeah, well, hydrate. It'll be a long day. That's the plan."

I briefed the platoon over the map board on the hood, and shortly after sunrise we retraced our steps toward the ambush of the night before. Gunny Wynn and I decided that he would control the machine guns, while I went with the other half of the platoon on foot. The clouds had cleared, and the sun was already hot. I gulped a canteen of water and slipped a PowerBar into my cargo pocket. This promised to be a slog.

At the 14 northing, I and eleven other Marines from the platoon moved off the western side of the road. We formed a wedge three hundred meters across and started walking north. Sergeant Espera walked point. I walked in the center of the wedge so I could control the formation most easily. Doc Bryan walked next to me so he could move quickly to any wounded man. Gunny Wynn kept the lead Humvee just in front of Sergeant Espera. All the guns were trained our way, ready to support us if we made contact.

Each furrow in the field was a potential ambush site. We found blankets and tin trays, evidence of positions quickly abandoned. I was happy to see that Iraqis had recently been here; it meant there probably wouldn't be land mines. We moved that way for more than an hour, covering a kilometer of ground.

We crossed a dirt path running perpendicular to the highway and saw a truck hidden in a thicket. The squad approached it with weapons ready, but it was abandoned. Its doors bore the distinctive red triangle of the Republican Guard. I could think of no excuse to bring it with us and no way to ensure it would go to good use carrying a farmer's crops to market, so we blew it up with a charge of plastic explosive on the engine block. North of the dirt road, there were a few mud-brick buildings farther west of the highway. Calling back to the battalion, I asked for Mish and for permission to go speak with the people there.

Mish huffed and puffed his way across the field, clearly dismayed not to be napping and eating Skittles in the back seat of a Humvee. I split the squad in half as we approached the buildings. One group would appear to relax, lower its rifles, and stroll over to a meeting with the villagers. The other half would stay two hundred meters back, weapons up, scanning the crowd and the buildings for any signs of trouble. This tactic let the first group be friendly ambassadors without exposing itself to too much danger. I went with the ambassadors.

A group of women and children huddled together outside the largest building. Nearby, several men lolled in the dirt, smoking. The oldest man, bearded and wearing a white robe, approached us with his hands raised, as if in a benediction. He smiled, baring yellow teeth, and crinkled his eyes in evident joy.

Mish maintained a running dialogue between the man and me as I handed him two humrats. We mean no harm and offer you this food in thanks for allowing us to travel through your fields. My doctor is happy to look at any children who are ill. Where are the Ba'ath Party and fedayeen? I tried to be open and respectful, but my eyes kept darting to the man's hands, to the crowd, and to the dark windows behind them. I could feel the Marines' rifle sights boring past me.

The man launched into a long speech, punctuated with pointing and gestures. His hand swept past the children, and he wiped his eyes. Mish nodded, unusually solemn, and turned to me. "He says these people are his distant family. They came here from Baghdad to avoid the bombing. There are Ba'ath ambushes farther north, maybe five miles, at a crossroads. They use pickup trucks to come down and attack the Americans. He is happy we are here but nervous if we stay too close to his home."

"Tell him we'll be gone in a minute, but first I want his help." I pulled a map from inside my flak jacket and unfolded it on the ground. "Ask him to show me where the crossroads is."

Mish relayed the question, and the man squatted next to me, peering at the map. He squinted and cocked his head, then stood up. The man couldn't read a map, but he made up for it by speaking to Mish again.

"He says the road forks about five miles north of here. There are reeds and tall grass at the fork. The Ba'ath have set up in the grass. They are waiting for us."

On the map, I saw a fork in the highway about eight kilometers north of the village. I thanked the man by placing my hand over my heart. He, in turn, reached across the cultural gulf and shook it. With a wave to the little girls, who hid their smiles behind cupped hands, we started off.

We had moved only two hundred meters when the first mortars hit. Plumes of smoke and dust rose from the field with each sharp crack. They had to be Soviet-era 82 mm rounds, the same as the night before. To men caught in an open field with nowhere to hide, they felt as big as artillery.

"Move two hundred meters east and stay dispersed," I ordered. I wanted to get the platoon away from the village so the people firing the mortars would have no excuse to walk them in on the people there. Looking over my shoulder, I saw the family, already displaced from their home in Baghdad, running to hide. It sickened me to think that we had brought this violence to their peaceful farm.

The mortars were still too inaccurate to cause much concern, but they crept closer by the minute. I radioed the ambush location to the battalion. They confirmed that the same information had come in from another source and ordered me to break contact to the south, away from the mortars. The Marines pumped fists in the air as two Cobras thwacked overhead, prowling up the highway in search of prey. Again I found myself in the position of wishing violent death on other human beings. Burn 'em up with those rockets, and don't make it clean. Make it hurt.

After the Cobras destroyed a mortar firing position farther up the highway, we climbed into the Humvees again. My platoon was ordered to drive west on the dirt path where we'd blown up the Republican Guard truck. Our mission was to conduct reconnaissance and screen the battalion's flank as it advanced.

Flies buzzed in the sun, which had burned off all the clouds and now beat down on us relentlessly. I was too hot to eat but drank some Gatorade just to keep from shutting down. The battalion needed a few more minutes to coordinate air support before moving out, so we cleaned weapons and topped off radiator coolant. As I leaned under the Humvee's hood, an F/A-18 roared down the highway, not much higher than the telephone poles. The pilot racked his jet into a climbing right turn and made another low pass, firing his cannon. I imagined the stream of 20 mm Vulcan rounds tearing up the pavement, cars, and fedayeen positions. Even if he hit nothing, the psychological effect on us was noticeable. The Marines were up and moving, ready to go.

The dirt road twisted through small hills and disappeared over a rise. We followed it at a halting pace. I split the platoon into two elements, with Colbert, Espera, and I moving as one unit and Reyes and Lovell moving as another. One group advanced while the other stopped to cover them.

"Tank! Tank direct front! Back up, back up!" Colbert's voice on the radio was frantic. His Humvee wheeled around, with Espera close behind. I jumped from my seat to get a better view. Ahead of us, the dirt road ended at an intersection. Beyond the intersection ran a dirt berm. Pointing over it and directly at us was a beige barrel with a yawning black opening. I expected it to turn Colbert's Humvee to cinders at any second. Over the radio, I asked for backup from an LAV armed with antitank missiles.

From behind us, in the overwatch position, Sergeant Lovell's laconic voice cut through our fear.

"Hey, fellas, is the tank to the left or right of that irrigation pipe?"

Irrigation pipe? I looked again. Our "tank barrel" was a farmer's water pipe. Time froze for a second. Humvees stopped spinning around. Marines abandoned their mad scrambles for AT4 missiles. We stared at the pipe, then looked at each other. I collapsed in the seat and closed my eyes. Would I have made this mistake three weeks ago? Was it heat, dehydration, fatigue, or frayed nerves? The only reason we hadn't blown that pipe away was that we didn't have any weapons that wouldn't bounce right off a tank. What if there had been kids around, or innocent villagers? Not shooting hadn't been discipline; it had been unpreparedness. I looked at Gunny Wynn.

"Hey, don't worry about it. No harm done," he said. I needed the boost.

After self-consciously telling the battalion that the antitank missiles weren't needed, I set the platoon up in a checkpoint at the intersection. The road we had come in on dead-ended there, and the other dirt path ran roughly north-south, paralleling the highway the battalion was on. A white sedan drove up, and the passengers looked startled to see our armed Humvees. Mish and I stood by the driver's window. Before we could say anything, a man in the back seat began speaking rapidly. I waited for Mish to translate.

"He says you are the first Americans they have seen here. Ba'ath people are waiting for you at an intersection up this road. He says about five miles, where this road meets the highway."

"That sounds like what the other guy told us."

"He also says there is a dam near Ba'quba. Many soldiers are at the dam, and they have buried chemical bombs in the ground there."

"No shit? He said 'chemical bombs'? You think he could show it to me on the map?"

"These guys don't read maps."

While I reported the information about the dam to the battalion, Mish continued talking with the men in the car. They kept glancing between him and me. Finally, one of them forked over three packs of cigarettes, and they drove off, looking back at us through the rear window.

"What the hell, Mish? We should be giving *them* smokes as thanks for helping us."

"Yeah, but I'm out. I told them to hand over some cigarettes, or you'd kill them."

"Mish, you can't do that. Pretty soon we'll be fighting the whole goddamn country."

# 33

WE CAUGHT UP with the battalion just south of the intersection where we'd been told to expect an ambush. Aircraft had pounded it. A brushfire crackled in the tall grass, revealing a mortar pit and a twisted machine gun. RPG launchers and unfired rounds carpeted the pavement. We weaved carefully to avoid hitting them. Across the road, a car had suffered a direct hit from an aerial bomb. Its metal frame crinkled in the heat the way a piece of cellophane does over a match. The driver had escaped, but not far. He lay in the dirt, frozen in a lunge with his arms stretched out before him. His whole body was toasted to a deep almond brown, except for one hand. That hand wasn't burned at all. Its white palm was open, waving at us.

The Marines heaped abuse on the dead Iraqi as we passed.

"Hey, check it out. Beef jerky man."

"Shoulda worn sunscreen, motherfucker."

Immense concrete pipes were stacked along the sides of the road. It looked like the town road crew had planned to install a new sewer system before the war changed everyone's priorities. Fighters had been living in the pipes. Their blankets, water jugs, and piles of food were stashed inside. We sat at the intersection while another platoon rummaged through the wreckage and the fighting holes looking for anything of intelligence value. At the crossroads stood an enormous stop sign, more than three feet across. It was the customary red octagon, but the word STOP was written in Arabic. I thought it would be perfect for our roadblocks; it might even keep us from killing someone.

"Christeson, cut that stop sign down and put it in the back of the truck." He looked at me in disbelief. An officer had never before ordered him to commit vandalism.

Alpha and Charlie companies took the right fork in the road, while Bravo and LAR went left. The two roads diverged and then ran roughly parallel about a kilometer apart. By attacking on two axes, we could throw Ba'quba's defenders off balance but still support each other. We spent the next four hours in constant contact with the enemy.

The running firefight started badly. A large concrete building stood in a field between the two roads on which the battalion was moving. LAR halted three hundred meters south of the building to observe it before moving forward. Sporadic rifle shots cracked toward us. As we sat there, engines idling, the captain called me over. "Nate, I want your platoon to dismount and move through this field to clear that building," he said.

I looked at him for a long moment, trying to gauge his reasoning. "Sir, are you nuts? You want me to leave my firepower behind and move across three football fields of open ground toward a fortified position, when we can just drive right up to it with all this armor? I'll be halfway there, and the rest of the battalion will be five miles farther north."

"This isn't the time for debate," he said. I could see his resolve wavering. His orders were experiments to see which ones would stick.

"Sir, is this your idea or a battalion order?" I had so completely lost faith in my commander that I couldn't follow his orders. If the plan had come from Major Whitmer or Colonel Ferrando, however, I would execute it without hesitation.

"I see what needs to be done here. Don't worry — I'll have the LAVs line up behind you to provide overhead machine gun fire." My anger was starting to boil over. Typically, when an infantry attack is supported by machine guns, the guns are displaced ninety degrees from the objective so they can shoot in front of the advancing attackers. He planned to put the machine guns directly behind us to shoot over our heads at the buildings as we moved toward them. We would block the LAVs from firing. These basic tactics are taught during the first few weeks of an infantry officer's training. The captain commanding the LAVs looked at me sympathetically and rolled his eyes.

Command relationships are built on trust. My CO was right about one thing: this wasn't the time for debate. It was the time for my trust in him to override my questions and concerns. It was the time for that trust to translate into instant obedience to orders. But I had no trust, not in him. His poor decision making since before the start of the war had sapped every bit of the natural trust Marines are taught to have in their chain of command. He was a nice, hard-working guy but tactically incompetent, and that's all that mattered.

"Sir, that's a fucked plan, and I can't do it. I'm not worried about getting hosed. If the fedayeen were in that building, they would have opened up on us by now. I'm worried that we'll get way out there in the field for no reason, and then the whole battalion's attack will lose momentum and bog down. Look over there." I pointed through a far-off tree line where Alpha's and Charlie's Humvees continued the attack to the north. "They're moving. We have to be moving."

He shot me a glance without saying anything, and I walked back to my Humvee. I was upset that some of my Marines had been within earshot of the argument. It was unprofessional to discredit the captain in front of them, but circumstance hadn't allowed me many options. Besides, feelings and regulations came in a distant second to winning battles and keeping Marines alive. We started moving forward, passing the concrete building without seeing anything amiss.

On the radio, Alpha Company directed jets in on an Iraqi infantry fighting vehicle, called a BMP, that was shooting at them. The jets' engines screamed as they dove at the target, but I couldn't see anything through the smoke and haze. Cobras hammered targets to our front, and the LAVs poured fire into buildings and palm groves along the road. The platoon had found its rhythm now — talking, moving, and shooting as one organism.

We did our best to hit discrete targets, but the battlefield is an empty place. With smoke, explosions, and rifle shots all around, it feels as if the whole world is a target. But that feeling evaporates when you look through the gun sight. Threats are everywhere, but targets are nowhere. You cannot just shoot at a tree, or a parked car, or a propane tank, or the air. You need a target. Like it or not, targets are usually human beings. But targets are hard to find, because they hide. Many times, the result was that we drove through an inferno but fired very few rounds. That wasn't the case in Ba'quba.

Approaching another crossroads, we passed a field of brilliantly green grass. Two men firing AK-47s popped up from a hole in the field, and a machine gun knocked them right back down. One of the men wore a green shirt and khaki trousers. A .50-caliber bullet, almost as big around as a dime and moving at supersonic speed, blew off the back of his skull. The round hit him so hard that it drove his body backward through the air. It neatly removed a piece of bone bigger than my hand, and as the man fell, his brain spilled onto the dirt. He crumpled five feet from the pool of blood that marked his place of death. I felt the elation you feel at the fair after winning a stuffed animal for popping a balloon with a pellet gun.

A mortar round fell from the sky, seemingly from nowhere. We hadn't heard it launched, and no others fell with it. It struck the ground next to Espera's Humvee, spraying his team with dirt and, I thought, shrapnel. When the dust cleared, I was amazed to see the team still frozen in their seats. Mortars are nerve-racking because they're so random. All you can do is sit there and think about the next one, the one that might be coming for you.

Ordered to stay in place, we looked around. To our right stood a whitewashed building in the center of a dirt parking lot. Red graffiti covered the walls, and I asked Mish to read it.

"Well, the little sign above the door says SCHOOL. The spray-painted stuff says DEATH TO AMERICA, LONG LIVE SADDAM, and WE WILL DIE FOR YOU, O GREAT SADDAM. Lots of others, too, but you get the idea."

"Lovell, take your team and search that building," I ordered. We had time, and the fedayeen had a record of using schools.

Leaving one man on the machine gun, Team Three took its bolt cutters and burst through the door. I waited for rifle shots, but none came. A few seconds later, Sergeant Lovell called from the window, "Sir, you ought to come in here."

I entered a dingy room filled with desks. Children's drawings covered the walls. The team guarded the doors while Lovell and Doc Bryan picked through an open safe.

"Maps, military IDs, documents, a burlap bag of AK bayonets, and a bolt-action Enfield rifle. But who really cares about that shit? Check this out," Lovell said. He held up a plastic trash bag. Inside were dozens of pairs of black boot socks. They were new, still attached at the calf by cardboard tags proclaiming them "Made in Jordan." "Funny how everything in Iraq was made in Jordan, China, and France."

"Yeah, but I'm not a spiteful consumer," I replied. I wanted the documents for the intelligence analysts and the socks for the platoon. We gathered what we could and hurried back outside, concerned that the battle would move forward without us. Two Marines from Third Platoon stood over an Iraqi man lying spread-eagle on the ground.

"Sir, this gomer popped out of a fighting hole in the field. His buddy is the one whose brains are sprayed all over the place back there. Can we cuff him and throw him in the back of your Humvee?"

I agreed, because I had more empty space than anyone else. There was no time to deal with him. The lead vehicles were moving again.

One bridge stood between us and the outskirts of Ba'quba. The countryside was bleak — dusty fields, dusty homes, dusty cars. Dust even coated the palm trees. We started to climb the bridge, but the lead Humvee stopped. I heard a zinging sound and saw strange ripples in the air. The sky above our heads shimmered, miragelike. Large-caliber rounds. Not ours. Incoming. It was another Iraqi armored vehicle.

"BMP on the road, direct front. And he's firing!" I tried not to yell into the radio.

We backed off the bridge in a hurry and vectored an Air Force F-15 in on the BMP. I never saw the jet, or even heard it. Its bomb materialized from the blue sky. For most Iraqi soldiers, death came without warning. We again climbed the bridge and met no resistance. On the other side, the BMP was little more than a greasy black stain on the pavement and a few scattered pieces of smoking metal.

Again the road forked, and again we went left while the rest of the battalion went right. Fields gave way to dense groves of palm trees filled with homes. The Cobras had launched volleys of rockets into the palms, and everything was on fire. I hated being in the close confines of buildings and trees. Drainage ditches lined the road. Dense thickets grew right up to their edges, cutting our visibility down to only yards. Every muscle in my body tightened. I think the exhaustion following combat is partly chemical — coming down off a massive dose of adrenaline — and partly a physical release after hours in this tightened posture. Wiping sweat from my eyes, I worked to breathe slowly, think clearly, and run through my mental checklists in case we made contact. After three weeks of war, I could tell I'd gotten better at this. Calm had become my natural state. It took something truly extraordinary even to raise my heart rate.

A radio call warned that our helicopter escort, our eyes and big fists, was leaving in five minutes to get more fuel. They'd be gone for at least an hour, leaving us alone on the road, where we couldn't see, with a Republican Guard armored brigade lurking nearby. The muscles got tighter. "When the aircraft leave, you are instructed to return to the last intersection and proceed north on the eastern fork. How copy?"

We stopped on the roadside to wait for the LAVs to make their lumbering ten-point turns on the narrow road. I took advantage of the stop to talk with the team leaders. They were doing a great job, and I wanted to let them know that. As I stood near Colbert's window, two Marines raised their rifles, aiming past me and clicking the safeties off. I spun around. Two men walked out from behind a berm less than twenty meters away. A little girl, perhaps five years old, stumbled along between them, holding hands with each. The men forced smiles and waved, but I was focused on the little girl.

Her eyes stared vacantly, looking at nothing even as she picked her way across the uneven ground. She was filthy. Dirt caked her face, and her sweatpants, once pink, were a sickly shade of gray. I knelt down to touch her shoulder, and she shrank back, terrified.

"Food and water — now," I called over my shoulder to the platoon. "Doc, check her out." For some reason, I felt a sense of urgency and responsibility for this girl that I hadn't felt before. Part of it was her small size. Mostly, though, I think I was touched by the contrast between her apparent physical health and her psychological pain. She was far too young to be so afraid. I thought of the Cobras rocketing the palm groves and lighting homes on fire. I remembered the jets dropping bombs and the roar of our own machine guns. Even for armed and trained Marines, there was a lot to be afraid of in Ba'quba. I tried to imagine what the afternoon must have looked like through the eyes of a child.

"Sir, she seems fine physically, just a little dehydrated," Doc reported. "It's like she's shell-shocked." He handed her a bottle of water. The two men, overjoyed that we recognized their plight, laughed and hugged us.

Through Mish, the older of the two men began to speak. He stood with his hands clasped behind his back, looking dignified and relaxed.

"He says tanks and soldiers are at a dam on the river. He says they are keeping people away from the place because chemical bombs are hidden there, maybe buried in the ground."

Two independent reports of chemical weapons nearby. In addition to all our daily missions, we had general tasks that were continuous on every mission. One of the most important was safeguarding any evidence of Iraqi weapons of mass destruction. I picked up the radio and asked for Godfather, the battalion commander himself. Colonel

Ferrando answered with understandable annoyance over a mere platoon commander interrupting him in the middle of a fight. I hurried to exonerate myself by explaining the two reports of chemical weapons at the dam.

"Copy all, Hitman Two. I'll pass it up to division myself," he said.

Our report became a national collection priority, but no chemical weapons were found.

I regretted leaving the little girl to her uncertain fate, but the helicopters were gone, the LAVs out of sight, and I had orders to turn back. We passed the last intersection and looped north on the eastern fork of the highway. Our mission was to set up a blocking position while Alpha Company did the same on other highways and Charlie entered Ba'quba to investigate the Republican Guard headquarters building.

Scanning the mud-brick houses to our right, I saw something that made me stop. Most of the battalion had already traveled past this point, but an Iraqi military truck was parked behind one of the buildings.

"Gunny, stop the Humvee," I said. Half the platoon advanced slowly on the house. The Marines communicated by hand signals, splitting into teams to come at the building from three directions. Just as that pre-firefight tension swelled to the point of bursting, the front door opened and a swarm of children ran out.

"America! America! Good! Good! Good!"

Rifles dropped.

A middle-aged Iraqi man, dressed in Western clothes and dutifully sporting a Saddam mustache, followed the children into the yard.

"Hi, guys, I'm Hassan." He spoke with almost no accent. As if to answer our unspoken question, he explained that he had been an English professor at Baghdad University. The twelve girls and boys, running circles around the Marines and trading funny faces with them, were his children.

He said the Republican Guard had visited his house the night before. Eight antiaircraft guns were piled in the back of the Russian-made ZIL cargo truck. Hassan was terrified that the Americans would bomb it and destroy his home in the process. With a mental bow and flourish, I told him we would be happy to remove the cause of his concern.

The prospect of doing something good for regular Iraqi citizens (and the chance to blow up a truck) galvanized the Marines to action. We hitched the truck to a Humvee and dragged it a safe distance from the house. There Colbert and others built a charge from C-4 and detonation cord. They wrapped the guns and the truck's engine, being sure to include the fuel tanks to help amplify the blast. We gathered the kids and explained what was about to happen. Then we all crouched down together and watched the truck disappear in a fireball. Hassan invited us to stay for dinner and looked a little relieved when I declined, telling him we had unfinished business in Ba'quba.

I picked an open stretch of highway for our blocking position, with good fields of fire in all directions. Flat, open highway would give Iraqi drivers the best chance to see and avoid us. It gave us the best chance of not having to kill anyone. We placed our looted Iraqi stop sign three hundred meters down the highway, along with a large piece of a cardboard MRE box on which Mish had written "Turn around" in Arabic. We all hoped we were learning fast enough to avoid repeating earlier mistakes.

Pausing for the first time all day, I remembered the prisoner in the back of the Humvee. He sprawled face-down on the truck bed with his hands tightly zip-cuffed behind him. Christeson stood over him with a rifle.

"Cut him free and give him some food and water," I said. Christeson looked at me as if I'd suggested letting the lions run amok in the San Diego Zoo, but he cut the cuffs off. The man sat up slowly, rubbing his wrists and whimpering. He looked at me mournfully, his long mustache twitching, and I handed him a bottle of water.

"Thank you."

"You speak English?" I was surprised. Judging from his dumpy appearance, I guessed he was a low-level conscript.

"A little, yes. My heart hurts." He put his hand to his chest, and the mustache twitched again.

"What's your name?"

"Ahmed al-Khirzgee. I am good man."

"What unit are you from?"

"I am not a soldier," he said with a face like a basset hound's.

"Then why are you wearing a military uniform, and why were you shooting at us with a military rifle?"

"I am only a very low soldier from Al Quds militia. I do not want to shoot at you."

"But you did shoot at us. We almost killed you."

"I have five daughters. Ba'ath Party took them from me and told me to fight the Americans, or my daughters would be killed. What would you do?"

I didn't know whether to believe him, but he had struck a nerve. Al-Khirzgee was about my father's age. His clothes were filthy and torn. He looked as exhausted as we were. I remembered my field interrogation at SERE school and thought that, for al-Khirzgee, this was real. He was afraid we would kill him. "Ahmed, I'd probably do exactly what you did," I said. He stared at his lap before meeting my eyes again. "Drink this water and eat some food. Do what we say, and you won't be harmed. If you fight or try to get away, this Marine will shoot you." I turned to wink at Christeson and mouthed "Don't shoot him." Christeson nodded and fixed his sternest guard face on our prisoner.

Across the highway, Sergeant Lovell led his team on a foot patrol into a palm grove. It was too close to our position to leave unchecked. When they returned, Lovell made a beeline for me.

"Sir, I need to show you something," he said. "Just cross the road here, and you'll be able to see."

Two long trailers sat in a clearing. They were painted desert tan, with air-conditioning units on their roofs. They were windowless, and padlocks secured the doors. Everything we had seen in Iraq was filthy, ruined by dust and years of neglect. The trailers gleamed. I knew what Lovell was thinking: mobile biological weapons labs. We had both listened to Secretary of State Colin Powell's testimony before the U.N. and to countless classified briefs on Iraq's weapons program. The trailers matched the descriptions perfectly.

"Take your bolt cutters and MOPP gear," I said. "I'll report it up the chain after you get back to me with details on what's inside."

Team Three headed off at a trot as I got a radio update on the battalion's progress. Charlie Company was in the city. Alpha had blown up at least one Iraqi T-72 tank with an AT4 missile — no small feat. We could hear muffled explosions and the occasional chatter of machine guns.

Gunny Wynn had the shortwave tuned to the BBC. We listened as the anchor described Saddam's statue in Firdos Square being pulled down by Marines in front of cheering crowds. The war, she said, was over.

"Damn," Wynn said, slapping his knee. "I wish they knew that up here." M4s barked in the distance, trading shots with throatier AKs.

"What about the prisoner?" Wynn nodded toward the Humvee,

where al-Khirzgee happily ate MRE pound cake while Christeson stood over him.

"It's a Geneva violation to leave him here," I said. "We have to take him with us. Seems sort of dumb. It'd be easier for everyone, him included, to give him some food and let him walk home. But those are the rules we have to play by."

Lovell's team recrossed the highway. They had cut the lock on the first trailer and carefully climbed through the door. Stainless steel equipment and digital displays lined the walls. Most of the writing was in Cyrillic. They thought we'd struck a jackpot until they began opening the cabinets and drawers. Baking trays, mixing bowls, and measuring spoons fell out. Our mobile weapons lab was a field kitchen for the Iraqi army. We laughed about it, but there was an underlying lesson. The illusions of "dual-use" technology are deceptive, and sometimes a satellite is no substitute for a team of Marines with bolt cutters.

Just before sunset, Charlie Company roared past, waving the captured standard of the Republican Guard armored brigade from the window of their lead Humvee. We cheered as if the whole day of combat had been a game of capture the flag. War Pig led the drive south, and I settled in for the two-hour ride. Gunny Wynn asked the question I was thinking.

"You think they'll hit us again as we drive by?"

"No way. You heard the BBC. The war's over."

Two minutes later came the radio call: "War Pig in contact five kilometers ahead."

We had five thousand meters to think about the fire we were heading into, to watch the tracers swishing through the darkness. I squirmed to put as many vital organs as possible behind the bulletproof ceramic plates in my flak jacket. Wynn floored the accelerator when the vehicles in front of us sped up. Shots rang past the Humvee as we flashed by. I thought of al-Khirzgee and the ironic terror of being shot at by comrades. It made me smile. As we passed back into dark and quiet fields, the illuminated face of the GPS showed that we were crossing the 14 northing. Baghdad glowed on the horizon. For the first time in a month, it lit the sky with electric light instead of firelight.

# 34

DOWNTOWN. After three weeks with the city in our sights, we drove into Baghdad early the next morning, April 10. The platoon had returned to division headquarters from Ba'quba around midnight. While we waited in line for gas until nearly sunrise, al-Khirzgee slept in the back of the Humvee. I gently shook him awake and said it was time to go.

A warehouse near the gas pumps was being used by the military police to hold Iraqi prisoners. A sergeant sat behind a desk inside the door. His belt held a pistol, handcuffs, a club, and a bottle of pepper spray.

"Lieutenant Fick. First Recon. We picked this guy up near Ba'quba a few hours ago. His name's Ahmed al-Khirzgee."

The sergeant jumped up. "Jesus, sir, that's a prisoner? I thought he was your translator or something." His hand went to the pistol.

"Relax. He's been with me all night."

Two Marines stepped from the shadows and grabbed al-Khirzgee by the upper arms. As they led him down a dark hallway into the warehouse, he looked back at me.

"*Salaam alaikum*, Ahmed. I hope you find your daughters."

Baghdad was smoldering when we crossed a pontoon bridge over the Diyala River. The mud-colored Diyala runs lazily between banks often thirty or forty feet high. No bridge large enough for our vehicles had survived the fighting, so Army reservists threw out the mobile bridge, and we crossed slowly, one at a time.

Oily smoke poured from a refinery near the river, and other black pillars rose from all across the city. We drove through a hodgepodge of war and peace. Mark-19s thumped in the distance, while a herd of water buffalo wallowed in the muddy riverbank under the watchful eyes of a boy. He waved as we passed. Near him, on the road, three corpses in green Iraqi army uniforms rotted in the sun. Women carried water from the river in plastic jugs atop their heads. One of them stopped to rest, placing her jug on the hull of an abandoned T-72 tank.

A dirt dike angled away from the river. It separated a canal from a field piled with household trash and wrecked cars. We drove on it to avoid the pools of sewage on either side. Slummy housing blocks alternated with palm groves, giving the place a suburban feel, although Baghdad's concrete high-rises were only a mile away. The architecture was Stalinist in its brute simplicity and uniformity, but instead of gray, everything was brown.

People watched as we passed. Most waved and cheered. Others went about the daily tasks of their hardscrabble lives, as if the Marines in the neighborhood were just another show of force by just another power beyond their control. Four boys perched high on a donkey cart passed us, going in the opposite direction along the dike. They sat atop a pile of looted goods — furniture, televisions, car tires, and buckets of brass shell casings. Down an alleyway, a boy led a donkey dragging a Jet Ski through the dust.

By the time we dropped off the dike onto a paved thoroughfare leading deeper into the city, the platoon had relaxed. Baghdad was not another Stalingrad, not even a bigger An Nasiriyah. It looked like the shooting war was really over. Gunfire echoed in the distance, and helicopter gunships flew low over the rooftops, but life around us plodded along as normal. Produce sellers hawked food from open stalls. Men in kaffiyehs sat at open-air cafés, drinking tea from tiny glasses. Other men smoked and fingered prayer beads, holding our gaze as we passed. We glided along with the traffic, swinging through roundabouts and stopping for traffic signals, jostling for space with trucks, buses, and taxis. A day before, I would have been apoplectic with so many people so close. But in another tribute to the human mind's quest for equilibrium, frustration with traffic replaced fear of an ambush.

Our destination was Saddam City, a sprawling Shia slum in the northern part of Baghdad. We had been briefed that the de facto mayor of the neighborhood was a cleric named Moqtada al-Sadr. We hadn't heard of him and didn't much care. After all, the Shia were supposed to be our friends. I first questioned that assumption on the drive into Baghdad. Walls, adorned a week before with likenesses of Saddam

Hussein, had been defaced. As in the Roman practice of *damnatio memoriae* (condemnation of one's memory), every trace of the former dictator was destroyed. Posters were torn, murals painted over, and statues toppled. Most of Iraq seemed to wait expectantly for whatever symbols would represent a new regime.

But power knew no vacuum in Saddam City. Less than one day after the old regime's collapse, images of bearded, turbaned clerics covered nearly every vertical surface along the sides of the road. U.S.-sanctioned *damnatio memoriae* had begun immediately and contributed to the change. The Americans trumpeted the renaming of Saddam International Airport as Baghdad International Airport and the redesignation of Saddam City as Sadr City. The wisdom of the latter change eluded us.

"That guy's gonna come back and fuck us, sir," Espera told me. "We just gave the fucker the golden key. Compare his shit-hole neighborhood to the rest of Baghdad. Anyone who doesn't think the Shia want revenge needs to spend some time outside his air-conditioned office."

We rejoiced in our new home. Painted in English on the side of the building was a sign: IRAQI STATE TOBACCO COMPANY. The factory grounds included a tall office tower and four warehouses. Fire raged through all but one of the warehouses, releasing clouds of sickly sweet smoke as thousands of bales of tobacco and millions of cigarettes burned. After three weeks of stress-induced smoking and dipping, the Marines rummaged through the one remaining warehouse, gleefully piling cartons of cigarettes in the back of the Humvees.

A concrete wall topped with concertina wire surrounded the compound. Inside the wall grew trees and a small garden. The parking lots were newly paved, and a triple-tiered concrete fountain decorated the lawn in front of the office building. Saddam's sons had run the tobacco company, accounting for its prosperous feel in a sea of third world desperation. Inside the wall were hundreds of Marines in an orderly camp. Outside the wall were five million Iraqis in an anarchic city. The only human interaction across the barrier was provided by Navy SEAL snipers on the roof of the office building. They had orders to shoot any Iraqi with a weapon. They fired every few minutes throughout the afternoon and into the night.

We were supposed to begin patrolling Sadr City the next day. In the cavernous room where the battalion set up its operations center, I unfolded my new map of Baghdad on the concrete floor. The city sprawled across four hundred square kilometers, with a population of more than five million. It was bigger than Chicago, Boston, Atlanta, or Dallas. I carefully outlined the battalion's zone in blue marker. The area covered twenty blocks square on the north side of the Tigris. It was the most densely populated part of the city. Other units' zones abutted ours, so it looked as if all of Baghdad had been carved into manageable chunks.

With most of the Marine Corps and Army converging on Baghdad, there would be a lot of U.S. power in the city. If each small unit took control of a neighborhood and maintained a continuous presence in it, we could accomplish a lot. I envisioned meeting with a town council, maybe sharing tea with the elders, and having the autonomy to address their most pressing needs. Judging by what we'd already seen, I suspected that money, fresh water, and medical supplies would go a long way toward creating goodwill. The key, though, would be continuity. We had to develop personal relationships and deliver on our promises. We had to be in the same places day after day, learning the routines, learning names and faces, and learning to sense when something was amiss. When I finally refolded the map and left the operations center, I felt a new confidence and sense of purpose. The night was warm. As I crawled into my sleeping bag on the pavement, a firefight raged outside the wall. Tracers arced through the dark sky, and I wondered where all the bullets would land.

The next morning, our patrol was canceled. We would be leaving the cigarette factory the following day for another part of the city. First Recon's zone had already changed. My faith in the postwar planning cracked just a bit. I rationalized that it was a mammoth operation and there would be a short adjustment period as all the units settled into place. But two days after the end of the shooting war, looters and criminals owned the city. U.S. patrols kept an uneasy peace during the day, but the Marines were ordered back inside their bases by sunset. At night, a tide of revenge killings ebbed and flowed across Baghdad as running gun battles consumed whole neighborhoods. We were forbidden to intervene. The consensus among many Marine commanders was that revenge would settle into a natural equilibrium. Instead, it seemed to beget more revenge. A finite supply of goodwill toward the Americans evaporated with the passing of each anarchic day. I briefed the platoon on our impending departure from the cigarette factory and already saw the doubt in their eyes.

We drove north from Baghdad to our new headquarters in a children's hospital a few kilometers outside the city. Traffic gridlocked the highway's southbound lanes. Mobs of jubilant people partied their way home after having fled Baghdad weeks earlier to avoid the bombing. Iraqis waved from the beds of dump trucks and the roofs of cars. Marines returned the honks and waves. I marveled at the sheer size of the city, the number of people.

"Can you imagine what it would have been like if these people had actually decided to fight us?" I asked.

"Just wait a few months till we don't live up to their expectations and they do decide to fight," Gunny Wynn said, looking grim.

We pulled into the children's hospital a few minutes after noon. Like most facilities in Iraq, regardless of their intended purpose, it had an air of military order. A gated guardhouse opened to a long, tree-lined road leading to half a dozen whitewashed buildings. Guard towers dotted a sand berm bulldozed up around the compound. Each company moved into its own building of patient rooms, with battalion headquarters settling into what were once the hospital's administrative offices. The entire place had been looted. Smashed bottles, syringes, and piles of paper covered the floor of each room. No furniture remained; even the light fixtures and switch plates had been ripped from the walls. I sat down to eat lunch with the platoon.

"So, sir, what do you think is going to happen?" Jacks asked the question, but he spoke for the others, and all eyes settled on me. Sitting around and talking with the platoon was my favorite pastime in Iraq. Sometimes I'd come up with new topics just because I didn't want the conversations to end.

"It's too soon to say, but I'll tell you what I hope will happen," I said. "I hope we'll stop moving around and be assigned a sector. I hope we'll patrol in that sector day after day. These people don't give a fuck about democracy right now. They need clean water. They need to know they won't get shot in the middle of the night. People put their money on the horse that looks like a winner. We need to convince them that we're the winner."

"But what are the odds of that happening, sir?" Corporal Chaffin asked, as he scrubbed a rifle balanced on his knees. "I bet we keep moving around, making promises we can't keep, and then the normal people will start to see us as occupiers instead of liberators." Chaffin was fair-skinned with reddish hair. His complexion darkened as he spoke. "Pretty soon, no one will want us here, and then the fucking liberals at home will start to bitch, and pretty soon we'll be back in Vietnam. Only instead of reading about it in a book, we'll be living it."

"I guess I'm more optimistic than that," I answered. "This isn't Vietnam — the guys we're fighting have no superpower support, no sanctuary next door."

"Sir, I'm gonna pull your punk card," Espera interrupted. "With all due respect, I think you're wrong." He leaned close and pointed his thin cigar. "Guerrilla wars aren't fought from sanctuaries with support from sugar mama countries. That's political scientist bullshit. They're fought from the mind." He tapped his temple with the cigar. "If these people don't want for themselves what we want for them, then this *will* be Vietnam. We'll get our pride and our credibility involved, and then we'll keep throwing money and men down the pit long after everybody else knows we're fucked. We'll leave, and Iraq will be even worse than the shit hole it was a month ago when we kicked down the door."

"Who'll give us the most trouble?" I asked.

"Guys our age," Espera said. "They hate us. They want to kill us. I can see it in their eyes."

I agreed with him. During the first week of the war, there were definite trends in the welcome we received. Everyone under eighteen was happy to see us. The women all cheered for us. The older men, over fifty-five or so, flashed the thumbs-up. But the young men, the guys in their twenties and thirties, stared silently.

"Why is that, Espera?" I asked. For evaluating motivations on the street, my sixteen years of school weren't worth two weeks as a repo man in L.A., and I knew it.

"Shit, sir, we emasculated them. Cut off their balls and held 'em up for their wives and kids to see. We did for them what they know they should have done for themselves."

"But they had twelve years to do it."

"Don't go getting all academic on me, sir. I'm explaining why they feel that way. I'm not saying they're right."

Colbert cut in. He lay on his back on the concrete floor, scrubbing

M203 grenades with a toothbrush. "What about the fact that the young guys have the most to lose with the old regime coming down? They had the power, and now they're going to lose it."

"That's what the eggheads on TV will say, sure. But they're wrong," Espera said, jabbing his cigar with each word. "You think all the mass graves are full of little kids and old men? These young guys got hosed by the regime just as much as everyone else. Saddam was an equal opportunity murderer. Kids, old guys, women. He killed his own daughters' husbands."

The Marines fell silent. The only sound was Colbert's toothbrush swishing back and forth across a grenade.

The next morning, we made our third move in four days, traveling north and west to the Menin al Quds power plant near the Tigris. Its transformers and warehouses sat in cultivated fields a couple of miles off a main highway north of Baghdad. Just past the entrance gate stood a bronze statue of Saddam Hussein, dressed in a tie and fedora and holding a rifle above him. Some previous visitor had left a pile of feces on his head. Our mission there was twofold: we would provide security for the power plant while workers labored to undo years of neglect, and we would use it as a staging base to patrol the northeastern quadrant of Baghdad. Having heard similar plans twice in as many days, I kept my doubts to myself.

Bravo Company moved into a warehouse at the compound's edge. Gunfire had ruptured an oil tank, and a film of sticky petroleum covered the ground outside. It stuck to our tires and the soles of our boots. The smell made me lightheaded. Inside the warehouse was a cargo bay, and upstairs a hall of offices we turned into sleeping spaces. The bleak building's best feature was a gravity-fed pump of frigid water that allowed us to shower for the first time in more than a month. We wore flip-flops because broken glass covered the ground, and the water pressure almost tore the horseshoe from my neck. But the shower was worth it. As darkness fell and tracers again rose from the city, the Marines of Bravo Company shrieked and shouted beneath the welcome deluge of cold, fresh water.

After showering, I put my filthy cammies back on and walked over to the recon operations center for another of the seemingly infinite briefs and planning cells for upcoming missions, both real and imagined. The

Marine Corps has an institutional culture of doing more with less, and that includes not only less money and less equipment but also less time, less certainty, less guidance, and less supervision. What makes it all possible is more planning and more preparation. While the Marines took advantage of a much-deserved rest, the battalion's officers and staff NCOs debriefed past missions, tracked current missions, and planned future missions. Those who needed rest the most, the decision makers, frequently got the least. I was nearly stumbling with fatigue as I passed a roaring generator and entered the ROC.

The generator powered a row of overhead lights illuminating maps spread across two walls. Little flags marked the last updated position of each of the battalion's patrols. A third wall held a status board, showing the composition, call sign, location, and activity of each team or platoon on patrol. Three Marines manned a bank of radios, whose wires snaked across the floor and out an open window to a small forest of antennas on the roof. Amid the squawks and static, they kept open the vital lifeline linking patrols in the field to aircraft, artillery, and all other forms of salvation. I always entered the ROC with some trepidation. Seeing competent Marines doing their jobs well made me feel more confident when I was the one on the other end of the radio. But I always had a nagging fear that I'd find the radio operators asleep, the map positions hours out of date, and the staff playing cards while a platoon was chewed apart. I knew that the fear was irrational, but I felt it every time.

That night, the ROC thrummed like the generators outside. Marines spoke on the radio in clipped tones, shuttled back and forth with messages from the platoons in the field, and constantly updated the status board and the maps. Major Whitmer sat in the corner, reading reports. He wasn't in my chain of command, but we'd known each other for almost four years, and I trusted him.

"Good evening, sir. May I join you for a minute?"

"Please, Nate. Pull up a chair."

"Sir, you're looking pretty tired. I thought field-grades got eight hours each night."

He laughed, indulging my jab. "You look pretty rough, too."

"Yeah, well, I better get over it. I'm taking the platoon out in the morning for forty-eight hours. We're supposed to patrol south of here along the Tigris. Wanted to see if you could add any insight or special advice." I laid out the patrol plan for him on the map behind us.

"Remember, Nate, we were still fighting less than a week ago. That means three things. People's lives are a wreck, and they'll expect a lot from you — don't overcommit us. Also expect to see some revenge killing — don't get sucked into a fight not of your choosing. Third, the bad guys melted away last week instead of dying in the fight — they may or may not still be bad, but they're out there, so be careful."

# 35

GODFATHER, THIS IS HITMAN TWO, requesting permission to depart friendly lines with five Humvees, one Marine officer, twenty Marine enlisted, one Navy enlisted, and two civilians. Patrol route is as briefed; ETR forty-eight hours from now."

With this call, the power plant gate swung open, and the platoon, with Mish and Evan Wright riding along, rumbled down the dirt road toward Baghdad. Fedayeen had been operating in the area, and intelligence indicated they were working from an amusement park near the Tigris. Our mission was to spread goodwill to the local populace while also collecting information on the fedayeen and inflicting whatever damage we could on them. For the next two days, my platoon would be the only American presence in a sixty-square-kilometer swath north of Baghdad. On the map, it was a mix of palm groves, farms, villages, and some of the city's northern sprawl. We were about to find out how the map stacked up against reality.

The platoon hummed. We were on our own, free to make decisions, to run missions the way we saw fit. For the next two days, the buck stopped with me and Gunny Wynn. Everyone was rested after sleeping in the relative comfort of the power plant, and mail had arrived the night before. We'd gorged ourselves on homemade cookies, beef jerky, trail mix, and all the other delicacies we had lived without for a month. Three days without missions had left us all with a sense of withdrawal. I craved action. We believed that we could bring order to our little slice of Iraq, that we could be examples of freedom and tolerance and generosity. And if anyone opposed us, at least a firefight was more exciting than lying around on a warehouse floor. I needed a fix.

Our first stop looked like a nice American subdevelopment. According to the map, its name was Qalat Abd al Jasadi. It was a small neighborhood, only three blocks square. Large, well-kept houses peeked from behind walls of manicured shrubbery. Children played ball in the street while adults did lawn work and tinkered with cars. The orderly homes had caught my attention from the highway. I reasoned that only Ba'ath Party members or supporters would have lived in such comfort under the Hussein regime. If our mission was to stabilize the city and root out unsavory elements, a Ba'ath stronghold seemed as good a place as any to start. And so I made the natural choice for a Marine platoon commander desensitized by three weeks of war and invigorated by three days of rest: I decided to provoke them.

We drove into the quiet neighborhood, snorting diesel fumes and brandishing weapons. Instead of icy stares, we found open arms. Kids ran to us, and adults gathered around to ask questions in halting English.

"Finally, America come! Iraq a nice country, yes?"

An older man elbowed through the crowd. Hard eyes bored from his deeply tanned and lined face. His white robe glared in the midday sun. I sensed that he was the neighborhood elder, the man who would speak with us on behalf of the others. He looked angry. As I climbed from the Humvee, Mish came to my side. I glanced at Wynn to make sure he was picking up the same vibe I was. He cradled a rifle in his lap, face placid, body tense. Then the older Iraqi broke into a smile and grasped my hand.

"Hallo, hallo. Thank you. Welcome." He explained that most of the neighborhood's residents were physicians and engineers, respected professionals even under Saddam Hussein. "But we are glad Saddam is gone." He complained that unexploded bombs and rockets littered the streets and fields, leftovers from the battles of the week before. The community maintained a neighborhood watch to guard against looters and any fedayeen who might bring American reprisals down on them. With ample electricity and fresh water, their only concern was the unexploded ordnance.

In my triage of worries, ordnance ranked a distant third, behind security and basic services such as water and power. I urged him to keep children away from the explosives and promised that we would return the next day, but I was anxious to see as much of our zone as possible before dark. We drove away to the cheers and shouts of the townspeople. "Tomorrow, America, tomorrow!"

I wanted to see the amusement park in daylight so we could better put it under surveillance after sunset. Doing so would be a lot easier and more effective if we knew the ground. We drove west along a raised irrigation dike, hoping to follow it all the way to the Tigris, where we could drive up a paved road to the gates of the park. No plan survives its first brush with reality. The dike dropped precipitously into a ditch, too deep and steep even for Humvees. Corporal Person was willing to buckle his seat belt and give it a try, but I couldn't afford to roll a vehicle. We backed up and plunged off the side of the berm into a forest of palms.

The grove reminded me of an old-growth pine forest. The trees, spaced widely apart, blotted out the sun. There was no underbrush. We wove between the trunks, sometimes following a dirt track and sometimes allowing the GPS to lead us more directly toward the amusement park. Birds flitted through the fronds high above, and white flowers bloomed in the sunny meadows.

Colbert keyed his handset and whistled. "We just found the Garden of Eden."

Weaving through the trees cut us to a walking pace, and visibility was frequently under a hundred yards. It should have alarmed me. We couldn't see, couldn't maneuver, and couldn't communicate because the trees distorted our radio reception. But there was no malice in the air. Combat had honed our powers of observation — we knew a threat when we saw it. There was no threat in those palms, and we enjoyed the incongruous beauty of our detour.

It was nearly dark when we emerged from the trees onto a paved road paralleling the Tigris. Three men with rifles stood in the road. A concrete barrier and stacked tires stood next to them, preventing traffic from passing. Instinctively, the platoon swung into tactical formation. Espera drew abreast of Colbert to put more firepower to the front. Reyes and Lovell took up positions to the flanks and rear. I rolled one radio over to the battalion's frequency, ready to report that we were in contact.

Colbert and Espera stopped less than fifty meters from the men. They still stood in the road, rifles at their sides. Any advantage the men had was gone. The platoon was cocked, ready to fight, and waiting only for a shot or an order to engage. The standoff seemed to last for minutes, but it could only have been a few seconds before one of the men shouted to us in Arabic.

Mish shouted back, and then yelled over his shoulder, "It's a neighborhood watch. They just want to stop looters."

The men said looters had been ranging through the countryside each
night and stealing anything they could move. Hand-painted banners
hung from the windows of homes along the road. Mish translated them
as THE TOWN OF SALIH HASAN WILL NOT TOLERATE THIEVES.
YOU WILL BE KILLED. The men begged us to stay with them to protect
the hamlet.

Seeing their husbands and fathers with the Americans, women and
kids poured from the gates of Salih Hasan. The children were jubilant,
dancing and skipping along the road in the dusk. The women were
more restrained. They drifted to the sides of their men, hiding behind
veils.

I wanted to help them. Leaving the neighborhood earlier had
smacked of abandonment. It had eaten at me during the drive along the
dike and through the palms. We were out there to do more than sight-
see and wave the flag. I wanted to make good on my own assertion that
Americans had to give concrete gifts to the Iraqi people. An action then,
in the first week of the occupation, was worth a thousand speeches
about the virtues of democracy or the evil of the fallen regime. The
citizens of Salih Hasan believed that their livelihoods, if not their
lives, were under attack. For them, our lone Marine platoon was American power personified. We could make everything right. Leaving them
would be a symbolic desertion they weren't likely to forget.

And yet we had a mission. We had been tasked with planting our feet
in each of the zone's four corners and with reporting back on what was
happening in all of it. Spending the night in one small village seemed, at
the time, like a misallocation of our scarce resources. I reasoned that
looters, seeing Salih Hasan protected, would simply move down the
road to the next town. We couldn't ambush them. Since the end of open
hostilities, force was permitted only in self-defense or to save a life. Thi-
every, from the skewed perspective of the occupiers, was regrettable but
legal. When I told the men that we couldn't stay with them, they didn't
protest. Stoicism is a common quality among Iraqis. No wailing, complaining, or arguing. Just a nod of resignation. They are a people accustomed to neglect. I promised we would return the next day and second-
guessed myself all the way up the road.

As it turned out, we didn't get very far. Delays in the palm grove and
at the neighborhood checkpoint kept us from reaching the amusement

park in daylight. We drove south as darkness deepened, trying to gain a little more situational awareness before settling into a patrol base for the night. In my mind, the plan was changing. It was apparent that neighborhood watches were functioning in almost every community. Armed Iraqis guarding their homes and armed Marines moving in the dark would be a volatile combination. I decided to find a safe place to harbor the platoon for the night and punch out a team on a foot patrol to do some snooping. We found a perfect spot along the canal where we had earlier detoured around the ditch. Instead of driving right up to it, we passed by and watched it for a few minutes before moving back under the cover of darkness.

Perched high above the surrounding fields sat the remnants of an Iraqi antiaircraft artillery position. The gun emplacements were abandoned, but their sandbags and commanding views made the place easily defendable. We pulled the Humvees into a rough circle on the concrete pad and set out concertina wire. A .50-caliber machine gun pointed down each section of the dike we'd driven in on, while the Mark-19s aimed out over the fields, ready to drop grenades down below. We towered thirty feet above everything around us, protected by concrete walls. The place was a natural fortress. I laid out my infrared strobe light and an infrared buzz saw. If we were attacked, I would simply mark our position and let aircraft obliterate anything beyond. The Marines began a watch rotation, while I radioed a situation report, or SITREP, to the battalion.

"Godfather, this is Hitman Two. Stand by to copy SITREP."

"Hitman Two, this is Godfather. We have you loud and clear. Standing by to copy."

"Patrol base location Mike Bravo 4153 9920." I read our exact position from the map in case we needed artillery support during the night, then went on to outline some of what we'd learned that day. As the battalion radio operator read the map coordinates back to me, I thought of the warm room at the power plant, hot coffee, and the Marines updating the status board. I hoped Major Whitmer heard our call and knew where we were.

"Godfather, we plan to remain in place for the night. One foot patrol, call sign Hitman Two-Two, will investigate PIRs as briefed. How copy?" PIRs were priority information requirements — all the little details the division tasked recon with learning. Ours included the locations of schools and hospitals, the trafficability of roads, and anything we could learn about the amusement park.

When the battalion had agreed to the plan, I joined Gunny Wynn and Sergeant Reyes to plot the foot patrol. The missions I couldn't go on were always the worst. It was easy to order the platoon into danger when I was riding with them. That was our job. There was a gung-ho camaraderie in it, a glee in scoffing at the safety-conscious, risk-averse, seat-belt-and-safety-goggle culture that had raised us. After all, I would be right there at the front, in as much danger as anyone, sometimes more. An instructor at Quantico had told me that officers got paid to be gophers: when all the sane people were burrowing in the dirt, it was an officer's job to poke his head up and see what was happening.

But when I sent my men out without me, the mission's rationale had to be ironclad. My litmus test was simple: If someone was killed, would I be able to visit his parents after the war and explain to them honestly why their son had died while working for me? People die in war. Every one of us in the all-volunteer military accepted that. But the death better not be senseless, the mission not unnecessary, the planning not shoddy, the equipment not inadequate. So I felt a little guilty briefing Reyes while knowing I would not be joining him out there in the palms.

The moonlight was eerily bright, casting our shadows across the ground. We spread the map on the Humvee's hood and read it easily without a flashlight. As we discussed the patrol, gunfire erupted from the field to our east. Streams of tracers crisscrossed back and forth through the trees. Evan Wright, tucked comfortably in his sleeping bag, levitated three feet off the ground before rolling across the hood of Colbert's Humvee and into the shelter of the front tire. Red strings reached high overhead, fading into the dark sky. West of us, near the Tigris, more gunfire echoed through the trees. In only a few seconds, raging gunfights grew to surround us on three sides. We ducked instinctively, though no rounds seemed to be coming into our position.

"Christ almighty, what started this?" Gunny Wynn spoke for us all.

We figured it was a combination of revenge killings, citizens defending against looters, and probably some delinquents who just liked shooting in a lawless town. The gunfire continued unabated for almost an hour. Sometimes it chattered for minutes on end before settling into a testy silence as the gunmen presumably reloaded or looked for more targets. Then, inevitably, it roared louder than before, with many weapons firing at once. One of the urban legends of American military training is that our tracers are red but our enemy's are green. I never saw a green tracer. They were all red, and they were everywhere.

Decision time again. I suspected that most of the fire was from people who were nominally our "allies" — Shia killing Sunni Ba'ath Party remnants and homeowners defending against criminals. I also knew they would shoot my Marines without hesitation if the team was seen moving suspiciously through the darkness. The Marines, in turn, would shoot anyone who threatened them. It was their obligation. Major Whitmer's advice came back to me: Don't get sucked into a fight not of your choosing. Don't be in a hurry to get your Marines killed. The odds were slim of anything in this bedlam being of our choosing. Guaranteed risks outweighed long-shot returns.

After Rudy left to brief his team, I looked at Wynn and said, "I think we should cancel the patrol and keep everyone here until sunrise. This isn't aggressive — it's foolish."

"Damn right. Not worth killing Marines to keep someone's TV from being stolen."

The battalion acknowledged our change in plans, and I settled in for radio watch while AK-47s cracked all around us. A warm wind blew cordite across the hill. In the distance, headlights traveled up and down the highway north of Baghdad.

My CO called just after midnight. He updated our taskings for the next day. We were to mark any weapons caches or unexploded ordnance for EOD to destroy. Also, the battalion had received reports of a possible regime palace in our zone. I copied the target's coordinates and saw that they placed it squarely in the center of the amusement park. We were to determine whether it was in use. Twice I asked him to repeat sentences drowned out by the gunfire behind me. After updating our mission, he turned to his second point. "Request full explanation why you canceled tonight's foot patrol. This makes us look very bad." In response, I held the handset up to the gunfire and pushed the button to transmit.

We started our day before dawn. The nearest weapons cache was right below our feet. Concrete bunkers stood just down the hill from the antiaircraft position, and in them we counted more than twelve thousand rounds of large-caliber ammunition. Two surface-to-air missiles lay in the field outside the building. While I examined the missiles for identifying marks, an old man in gray robes approached from a nearby house.

I put my hand to my chest and greeted him. *"Salaam alaikum."*

*"Alaikum es salaam."* He launched into a tirade, spitting and kicking one of the missiles. His Arabic rose and fell in a harsh, guttural staccato. I looked expectantly at Mish.

"He says he is happy you are here and he is grateful to be liberated." I expected Mish's stock answer and kept staring at him, waiting for more. "He also says the Iraqis had a gun here to shoot down American airplanes. They abandoned it about a week ago. He is angry at Saddam for hurting the people but also angry at the army for having no pride. He is embarrassed that they gave up without a fight."

"Tell him there's no honor in getting slaughtered. And ask about weapons and fedayeen in the area." Mish relayed my request, and the man began speaking intently while pointing at a distant tree line. Behind him, the Marines began to get into the Humvees.

"He says there is a house with many missiles in that village in the trees. Large missiles and small missiles together — about twenty of them. Also, he says there is a place up the road where the fedayeen are living. There's a tall tower there. Near a lake."

The village with the missiles was beyond the border of our zone, so we wouldn't be able to follow up on the lead. But the place with a tower by the lake sounded like the amusement park.

On our way up to the park, we passed through Qalat Abd al Jasadi, the neighborhood of professionals from the previous afternoon. Again the residents welcomed us warmly. Without making promises to remove any ordnance, we asked to see everything that worried them. At the very least, I figured I could collect grid coordinates and send an EOD team as soon as possible. A small group, headed by a man who introduced himself as Ibrahim, led us around the town for nearly two hours, pointing out everything from a hand grenade sitting in a classroom to a T-72 tank abandoned in an orchard. We dutifully marked the locations of unexploded bombs, tank rounds, RPGs, and out-of-place metal objects we couldn't identify but were reticent to touch. Finally, when the midday sun had us soaked in sweat, the men said that only one object remained.

Ibrahim pushed through a wooden gate in a high wall, leading us into the isolated yard of a house on the neighborhood's main street. My paranoia kicked in, and I posted Marines outside the wall, at the gate, and inside the courtyard. If anyone hoped to ambush us, they'd better have a good plan and a lot of firepower. But Ibrahim led us through the yard to an innocuous-looking piece of metal buried nose-first in the dirt. A green and silver fin stuck up six inches above the grass.

"That's an RPG round, sir. It was fired but didn't detonate," Colbert said, as he edged back from the projectile.

"Pretty unstable," I replied. I felt like whispering, as if a loud noise might engulf us all in a ball of fire.

"Correction, sir: *very* unstable. We can't just leave it here for EOD to take care of in a week or a month. Kids live in this house. I can blow it up." Colbert looked at me coolly.

I knew he could blow it up. I also knew that doing so was, for us, expressly against the rules. We could mark ordnance, count it, and photograph it. We could not blow it up. Too many Marines were losing fingers and eyes to volatile piles of explosives. But then, this was a family's yard. Half the village had gathered outside the gate to watch the Americans work their magic. Our credibility was on the line. Not personal pride — that sort of immaturity got people killed — but the credibility of the U.S. Marines as a force for good in these people's lives. One concrete act of goodwill outweighed a thousand promises, meetings, and evaluation teams.

"Get the C-4, Colbert, and do your thing. If you blow your hand off, so help me God, I'll chop the other one off myself," I said.

"Roger that, sir."

We herded the growing crowd outside the courtyard as Sergeant Colbert and his team built a charge to detonate the RPG round. He molded a lump of plastic explosive into a disk the size of a silver dollar and inserted a blasting cap. Colbert took the C-4 in one hand and looped thirty yards of time fuse in the other. He and Sergeant Espera entered the yard and walked carefully toward the offending fin. Their helmet chin straps were snugged and their flak jackets tightly closed. When they approached the round, they dropped to their hands and knees, and then to their stomachs, crawling slowly forward and stringing the fuse behind them. No one in the platoon breathed as Colbert tucked the charge into the hole the RPG had dug in the turf. Because it had been fired, the round was armed and could explode at any time. He nestled the charge close to the body of the grenade and then tamped dirt on top to amplify the effect of the blast. Colbert and Espera reversed their approach — first crawling, then kneeling, and finally walking quickly back to the waiting platoon.

"No need to chop my hand off, sir." Colbert smiled and lit the fuse. Marines waved the Iraqis down to a crouch.

Colbert waited quietly, looking at his watch, before yelling, "Fire in the hole!" A geyser of dirt shot up over the wall, raining pebbles down into the yard and sending a dust cloud out into the street. The villagers cowered for the briefest instant before breaking into cheers. Sergeant Colbert and I walked into the courtyard, looking for the scattered bits of C-4 that would indicate an incomplete detonation. There were none. A crater marked the former resting place of the RPG round, and only tiny scraps of metal remained from the grenade itself.

Ibrahim and the owner of the house approached us. "Thank you. Thank you. Please come inside and drink tea with us. You are our guests today."

Colbert smiled wanly and deferred to me. "Sir, I have a team to take care of. You're our diplomat." He walked back to his men, who were now trading high-fives with Iraqi boys wearing wraparound sunglasses borrowed from the Marines.

I explained that we had other towns to visit and other jobs to do. Ibrahim understood and welcomed us back to Qalat Abd al Jasadi anytime. Driving out of town, I felt that we had accomplished something greater than blowing up one leftover grenade.

# 36

I T WAS TIME for the patrol's main event. I had been curious about the "amusement park" label on the map since first noticing it days before. Most Americans thought of deserts and torture chambers in Iraq, not merry-go-rounds and roller coasters. Reports that the fedayeen were operating from the grounds of the park and that the same spot might include one of Saddam's palaces only fueled my interest. Six hours of daylight remained, enough time for us to answer the battalion's initial questions and plan aggressive foot patrols for that night. But, of course, the plan changed. After we left Qalat Abd al Jasadi, the battalion ordered us back to the power plant no later than EENT, or the end of evening nautical twilight — the true darkness that arrives an hour or so after sunset. I slammed my fist on the dashboard but radioed back a calm acknowledgment. Accounting for driving time back to the power plant left less than five hours to recon the amusement park.

Rushing was not an option. To rush is to risk being sloppy and making potentially deadly mistakes. We would approach the mission as methodically as we could. Given the daylight and crowded area, I decided it would be pointless to try to sneak up on the park. Better to drive right to it, pick a safe spot, and observe it for a while before deciding on our next move.

A man-made lake nearly a mile long separated the park from the road. To enter, visitors crossed a concrete bridge near the midpoint of the lake. Since marshland bordered the amusement park to the north and south and the Tigris flowed to the west, the park was an island of sorts, separated geographically and psychologically from Baghdad. A tower dominated the park's skyline. It looked like a smaller and poorer Seattle Space Needle, a wonder of the early 1970s slowly falling into disrepair. Promenades and amphitheaters surrounded the base of the tower. The wooden frame of a roller coaster stood above the once-man-icured shrubs and palms. Everything was dusty brown, colored with peeling paint and fading murals of pirated Disney characters. Through binoculars, I imagined crowds of people and colorful balloons. I couldn't decide whether it was the most hopeful place I'd seen in Iraq or the saddest. Eventually, I settled on the latter.

The platoon spread out along the lakeshore, glassing the park with spotting scopes, binoculars, and rifle sights. I planned to watch for an hour. Gunny Wynn and I were discussing the wisdom of entering the huge park with only twenty-two Marines when a battered red Volks-wagen chugged up and stopped near our position. Ten rifles trained on it immediately. I turned to watch, but we continued our conversation.

"It's a deserted island. They can cut us off. We need to plan for that," Wynn said. He wasn't against going into the park; he just wanted to make sure we thought it through in advance.

"What about putting a sniper team up in the tower?" I asked. "They could overwatch us everywhere and coordinate air."

"Bad idea, sir. They'd be vulnerable up there, and we'd have to drop a team just to secure the base of the tower. Then we'd be down to fifteen guys. Better to stay together."

I wasn't about to contradict Wynn on sniper tactics. Before every mission, I'd float a dozen ideas, and he'd shoot down eleven of them. Then he'd suggest a dozen refinements, and I'd turn away eleven. The winnowing process helped us come up with the best plan.

"Sir, Gunny, better get over here," Doc Bryan called from his position next to the car.

A middle-aged woman sat in the driver's seat, waving both hands helplessly through the window. Behind her, I saw a man sitting impas-sively in the back. I walked toward the car and smelled the infection.

A teenage girl, about thirteen, reclined in the front passenger seat. A cast covered her leg. She smiled stoically, almost coyly, but her lips trembled, and pain shone in her eyes. Mish said her name was Suhar. She had been wounded by a bomb more than a week earlier. Iraqi doc-tors had slapped a cast on her leg, but she hadn't received any follow-up care. Her parents hoped to run the gauntlet of American checkpoints to find a hospital, but they saw us on the side of the road and decided to stop.

I looked at my watch. Four hours till we had to return to the power plant. "Doc, you've got fifteen minutes," I said.

Retrieving his med bag, Bryan sliced open the cast and peeled it back from her leg. Suhar screamed. Flesh peeled off her leg in strips, and the bones beneath were clearly broken. Green and yellow pus oozed from the holes in her skin. The smell nearly knocked me over. With the cast off, Suhar settled into choking sobs that racked her body.

I knelt in the dust next to her mother. "Mish, please ask her name."

She looked at me and said, "Mariane."

"Mariane, we will do everything we can to help Suhar."

The parents watched Doc as he worked, and I watched them. I couldn't fathom their emotional cauldron. Their child was grievously wounded, probably by Americans, but her life depended on the charity of other Americans. They had to hate us. If the tables were turned, if I were that father watching my daughter suffer, I'd be plotting the deaths of the people who'd harmed her.

I swore under my breath. Our mission was to recon the amusement park. My commanders wouldn't think kindly of us getting sidetracked to help this girl. The night before, I had rejected the personal pleas of the villagers to protect them from thieves. When the shooting orgy had erupted all around us, that decision had been confirmed as the right one. With Suhar, I faced a similar choice: stick to the mission and hope we'd be serving the greater good, or be distracted by a personal sideshow. The very concept of "greater good" was fading into fantasy. All we knew was what we saw. In training, this would have been a slam-dunk scenario — turn the girl away and focus on the mission. But the past month hadn't been training.

Suhar's parents watched with great dignity as Doc Bryan scrubbed and prodded at their little girl. When he glanced at me, I asked for an update.

"This infection will kill her. She's a heartbeat away from septic shock. Sir, we have to get her to a hospital." Doc had turned away from the car and spoke quietly. "I understand the choice you have to make, but you should know that without care, she doesn't have a chance."

Calling the battalion, I asked to speak to Dr. Aubin. Bryan took the handset from me and relayed information on Suhar's wounds. We waited while Aubin checked to see what resources were available in Baghdad.

I fought not to sound bitter. "Resources in Baghdad? How about the whole fucking U.S. military? They better give us something."

Finally, Aubin called back. "Hitman Two, there are no American aid stations set up yet for Iraqi civilians. We have locations on a few Iraqi hospitals, but none of them have any supplies. Do your best to buy her time so her parents can locate another source of care."

I was livid. Aubin was a good man. He had proven his guts and dedication ten times over at Qalat Sukkar, and I knew the situation angered him as much as it did us. He had done all he could. I thanked him and turned back to Doc Bryan, asking for options.

"I can clean and irrigate her wound, then pump her up with antibiotics and check the infection . . . for now. I can wrap her with a clean dressing. We'll give her parents a supply of dressings and antibiotics and instructions on how to use them. But without proper care, the infection will become systemic. She'll die."

"Do your best, Doc. Give them all the supplies you can spare without compromising the safety of the platoon. Let me know when you're finished."

I walked away to sit in the dust with Gunny Wynn. "Can you believe this? We're supposed to be the power here. We can't even get a doctor for a teenage girl," I said.

Wynn suggested that we give the parents directions to RCT-1's headquarters. We knew its exact location, and they had to be better equipped than we were. I agreed and bent over the hood to write out a note in clear block letters:

THIS GIRL, SUHAR, HAS BEEN WOUNDED BY AN AMERICAN BOMB. WE PROVIDED BEST MEDICAL CARE AVAILABLE AND SENT HER FAMILY TO SEEK FURTHER TREATMENT AT HQ INCHON. PLEASE RENDER ALL POSSIBLE AID. SEMPER FI. BRAVO TWO, 1ST RECON BATTALION, MC 3937 0063, 14APR1130Z2004, 1STLT N. C. FICK, USMC.

Mish gave the note to Suhar's parents, along with directions to Inchon, the call sign for RCT-1. When Doc finished cleaning and rewrapping the wound, we watched the Volkswagen speed off down the road toward Baghdad.

"If they don't get killed at a checkpoint, they'll probably just get laughed at by Inchon," Bryan said, spitting in the dust with all the disgust I felt.

It was late afternoon by the time we crept slowly across the bridge into the amusement park. Tending Suhar had cost us two hours. On the hundred-meter span across the lake, the platoon made the mental shift back to combat mode. Tenderness gave way to aggression. We turned right at the end of the bridge and made a slow counterclockwise sweep through the abandoned walkways and parking lots. As in the rest of Baghdad, looters had been a step ahead of us. Broken glass lay everywhere, along with random pieces of furniture discarded by thieves in midflight. The incongruity was surreal: Humvees passing a carousel, and Marines poking rifles into the Tilt-A-Whirl's teacups to make sure they were empty. Everything was empty. The park was not only deserted but assertively so. Doors swung on their hinges, and paper trash tumbled by in the wind. It was Hollywood movie set empty. The part of me still untouched by the war wanted to sit down at one of the picnic tables and read in the sunlight.

The platoon leapfrogged through the park, with teams alternating security and kicking down doors to search buildings. We found a movie theater, a snack bar, and administrative offices, but no signs of fedayeen. With the sun quickly sinking, I urged the Marines forward. I wanted to reach the northern tip of the park, where my map showed the large building identified to us as a "suspected regime palace." We approached it more warily than we had the other buildings but repeated the same drill of posting two teams on the perimeter and sending two teams inside. The building was a single story, sprawling along the lakefront.

I followed Sergeant Espera through the door and into a large room. The Marines moved in stacks, rushing along the walls with rifles at eye level. My weapon was a digital camera. A piano stood in the corner next to a long wooden bar. The glass cabinets had been emptied of alcohol, and broken glassware crunched under our feet. We moved through a ballroom with an inlaid floor and shattered chandeliers. Decorative ceiling panels hid recessed lighting, and unbroken windows opened onto a pool in the courtyard outside. Flashlights mounted on rifles cut beams of light through the shadows. Following a hallway, we opened a door. A king-size bed and a large bathtub filled the room. The next door revealed the same layout.

The "palace" was a hotel. It was opulent, more opulent than anything we had seen in Iraq, but certainly not one of Saddam's residences. The amusement park had been a weekend getaway spot for midlevel Ba'ath Party officials. That conclusion made a fedayeen presence seem even more likely. I snapped a dozen photographs to pass on to the battalion's intelligence officer before continuing our sweep through the park.

We moved south along the Tigris. There were fewer buildings there, only a shady field filled with picnic tables and a scenic walkway over-looking the river. We rumbled down the sidewalk, scraping past benches and an ornate railing. I looked to the right and felt a cold shot of adrenaline in my chest. Bunkers and trenches honeycombed the mud flats at the river's edge. Armored personnel carriers, large generators, and antiaircraft guns sat along the banks. Four machine guns simulta-neously swiveled and depressed to aim down at the fortifications below us. Through my binoculars, nothing moved.

Since the positions all looked deserted, I split the platoon in half to save time. Wynn took two teams down the slope to investigate the bunkers along the river, while Sergeant Lovell's team and I remained behind to check inside another building. It was a trailer, like a mobile home, and it sat separate from the rest of the park. It looked out of place. Lovell shouldered the door open, and we entered the single room. Papers cluttered the floor, but I hardly noticed at first. I stared at the maps hanging on every wall. They were Iraqi street maps of Baghdad, with the eagle crest of the regime on each sheet, and I recognized them immediately. They looked like the maps I'd been studying in the ROC. Most of the American positions in Baghdad were drawn on the sheets in red pencil. They were out of date, but only by a few days.

"Holy shit, Lovell, check this out. They know all our positions."

"Yeah, and these filing cabinets are filled with more." He kicked open a drawer, and reams of maps and papers spilled out. "Looks like we found the fedayeen headquarters."

We gathered up large armfuls of papers to take back to the intelli-gence shop, giving priority to the annotated maps and anything per-sonal — identification cards, operations orders, and whatever else we could guess at without reading Arabic. Lovell's team piled the rest of the papers on the pavement outside the trailer and doused the stack in gas-oline from a spare fuel can. It burned quickly, sending ashy flakes floating across the picnic grounds. I radioed down to Gunny Wynn to let him know we had a fire going.

"Lots of stuff down here, too — gas masks, atropine injectors, MOPP boots and gloves. Looks like they were ready for a chem attack. No signs of life, though."

When the Marines climbed back up to the Humvees, they brought Iraqi military radios and two sets of night vision goggles. The goggles were older than ours, and much more primitive, with Cyrillic writing stamped into the metal. We had heard the secretary of defense's accusations that Syria had been exporting night vision equipment to the Iraqi army during the first week of the war, and we wondered whether we'd found evidence to support his claims. I tucked the gear in with the maps, looking forward to the mission debrief.

We were racing the daylight and continued moving south to the far end of the amusement park. I called the battalion to update our position and received a pointed reminder of our expected return time — no later than EENT, less than two hours away. I wanted to finish our search of the park before returning to the power plant and hoped the southern corner would have fewer buildings to comb through. Marines walked alongside the Humvees, searching through sheds and empty offices. We reached the final hundred meters before the southern edge of the park.

Cresting a small rise on a paved path intended for golf carts, I saw a row of warehouses through the trees. They were low and windowless, with padlocked doors. There was no way we could search them and still make it back to the power plant on time. I called the battalion and requested a one-hour extension to complete our search. It was denied. We drove past, hoping they were empty, or perhaps filled with lawn mowers and other maintenance equipment for the amusement park. I photographed the outside of the warehouses and noted their location in my patrol log, adding that we hadn't searched them owing to time constraints.

Fifteen minutes before EENT, I requested permission to reenter friendly lines. We rolled slowly through the gate and stopped at Bravo Company's warehouse. As the platoon started brewing coffee and cleaning weapons, the team leaders and I walked to the ROC for debrief, lugging everything we'd collected over the past two days. We pulled chairs around a desk in the brightly lit room and cracked open cold Cokes from a cooler in the corner. After thirty-six hours on constant alert, I needed the caffeine. I summarized the information collected by the platoon, and each team leader elaborated on details specific to his team. The debriefer scribbled furious notes as we poured out the results of two days of nonstop observation. Despite the maps, the photos of the hotel, and the night vision goggles, the patrol's defining feature became our failure to search the warehouses.

The next morning, another recon platoon was diverted from its mission and found dozens of surface-to-air missiles in the buildings we'd bypassed. There were signs that others had been removed, possibly the night after we were in the park. Over the coming months, when insurgents downed Army helicopters, killing dozens of soldiers, I couldn't help but wonder if the weapons had come from the cache at the amusement park. Treating Suhar had been a costly decision. I was learning that choices in war are rarely between good and bad, but rather between bad and worse.

# 37

THE NEXT WEEK PASSED in a blur of planning, patrolling, debriefing, and more planning. Our mission statements grew broader: "Patrol in zone to disarm the populace, locate unexploded ordnance, stabilize disorder, stop looting, locate key facilities like hospitals and schools, distribute food and water, provide medical care, and show American presence." We did each of these things every day, and frequently all of them at once.

We left the power plant on Thursday morning, April 17, for a patrol north of Sadr City. In addition to all the standard tasks, our mission for the day was to locate a place to distribute four thousand gallons of fresh water the next morning. Mish was patrolling with another platoon, so Hammed Hussein joined us. Hammed was a local resident hired by the battalion as a translator. He arrived at the power plant shortly after sunrise, dressed with great dignity in a rumpled suit, probably the finest outfit in his wardrobe. Upon learning that I was the patrol leader, Hammed walked up as I studied my map and launched into a harangue against American culture and the war in Iraq.

"You should not have done this. Saddam was a bad man, but America should have waited for the Iraqi people to overthrow him themselves. In time, we would have crushed him."

"Hammed, I'm just a lieutenant," I said. "I lead patrols. I don't make policy. Either come help us or go home, but don't pick a fight with me this morning. I'm too busy."

We traveled east along a dike overlooking Sadr City. Fetid trash and pools of stinking sewage waited below for any Humvee unfortunate enough to slide off the dirt berm. We eased under fallen power lines while packs of yapping dogs ran alongside. Children playing soccer stopped to wave as we passed, and women dug for water in the foul dirt fields between apartment buildings. Men rocked on their haunches in the shade, smoking bad cigarettes and staring us down. I got the feeling that only our overwhelming force kept them from stringing us up as infidel invaders. From my admittedly narrow perspective, the climate on patrol had worsened in only a few days. Violence and looting continued to plague a city lacking even basics such as electricity and clean water. I felt as if we were under constant scrutiny by people who were less and less impressed with what they saw.

I stopped the platoon outside a collection of brick buildings three kilometers beyond Sadr City. A heavyset man with thinning hair led a crowd toward us. He introduced himself as Mr. Kadem and requested, with a ceremonial flourish, that all aid to the village be coordinated through him. I asked what sort of aid he wanted.

"We need only two things: clean water and bronze statues of George Bush."

I decided to play along. "We can help you with the water, but what will you do with statues of George Bush?"

"We will put them in our streets to show our loyalty. First, though, the Americans must help us pump the sewage which is flooding our town."

I told Mr. Kadem we could give him a hundred gallons of water immediately and would stay for an hour to provide medical care to children. He nodded and barked commands into the crowd behind him. Men surged forward, pleading for aid while pointing at small bruises and cuts or their seemingly healthy eyes, legs, and heads. They shoved the children aside.

The platoon started throwing elbows and pushing with rifle butts. For a moment, I feared a riot. Mr. Kadem restored order, and we treated a long line of kids for cuts, burns, and dehydration. With the Marines' help, a team appointed by Mr. Kadem emptied our spare water cans into the town's common cistern. Depleted of water and medical supplies, we packed up and continued east along the berm, looking for the next place to put our drop on the Iraqi sponge.

The dike ended at a paved road leading north from Baghdad. People there, a week after Baghdad's fall, had not yet seen Americans. Crowds filled the street. Open markets sold everything from fruit to stereos.

Storefronts lined the road, and above them clotheslines stretched between balconies. Every few blocks, a mosque punctuated the parade of buildings sliding past our windows. Most of the town was dusty brown, dilapidated, and forlorn, but not the mosques. Bright lights stretched to the ground in strands from the minarets, like the rigging on cruise ships. The buildings were washed a bright white, with garish murals of happy crowds and singing children. Even their yards were well tended, little islands of greenery in a sea of dust and stagnant sewage. Of everyone we saw, the men lounging near the mosques looked the toughest. According to the map, we were twenty kilometers from the power plant, and I felt every inch of it. Normally, we updated the battalion on our position every two hours, but I started sending updates every thirty minutes, just in case.

In the same spirit that had inspired us earlier in the week to roll into the neighborhood that had looked most like a Ba'athist hideout, we parked in front of the biggest and most ornate mosque. We were careful to stay outside the mosque's marked perimeter but wanted to "show American presence" and speak to someone with real authority over the people living nearby. In post-Saddam Iraq, those authority figures were the mullahs.

As expected, it took less than thirty seconds for a crowd of men to surround us. Mostly middle-aged, they didn't surge forward to touch us and practice their English as other Iraqis had done. Instead, they kept their distance and appraised us. Espera and I stood together near the front of the crowd.

"Mexican standoff," I said. As was usually the case, I left my rifle in the Humvee, wearing only a pistol on my thigh in an attempt to close the distance between occupier and occupied. I was helmetless, but not quite committed enough to remove my body armor. The rifle slung diagonally across Espera's chest loomed large in my peripheral vision.

"Sir, I'm deeply offended that you would slur my people that way," he said jokingly.

An older man, dressed in white and crowned with a turban, stepped forward and introduced himself as Mullah Mohammed of Diyala. Next to me, Espera mumbled under his breath, "Yeah, well, I'm Sergeant Tony of Los Angeles. Who gives a fuck?"

Hammed lingered behind the Humvees, trying to hide his face from the mullah. He knew we would eventually leave, but he had to live there when we were gone. I called him forward and asked Mullah Moham-med what we could do to help the people of his community. He launched into a long monologue, distilled by Hammed as a list of facts and requests: one hundred thousand people lived in the area; there had been no reliable source of fresh water for five years; there had been no electricity since the start of the war; looting was not a problem, and he knew of no fedayeen activity; he would appreciate one American sweep through the town each day. I offered to return the next day with fresh water. The mullah accepted, but only on the condition that we would bring the water to him and allow him to distribute it to the people him-self.

I didn't want to play kingmaker. At that point, our priority was to get life sustaining services to people in need, not to empower local strong-men and allow our aid to become a tool of political advantage. I didn't know whom to trust. Our only Arabic speaker was Hammed, and I wasn't sure I could even trust him. Most of the time, he cowered in the back seat of the Humvee, afraid to be seen helping the Americans. He would say whatever he had to in order to save his own skin. So I delayed the decision. I decided to consult with the colonel and Major Whitmer back at the power plant and simply told the mullah that we would re-turn in the morning to distribute water to his people. He thanked us and uttered a few words that Hammed translated as a blessing reserved for unknown strangers.

I brewed coffee in the morning, taking comfort in the simple ritual. We had dragged a cast iron stove down from one of the offices. It sat in the warehouse doorway, surrounded all day and all night by Marines on ammo cans and MRE boxes. My tin canteen cup was too hot to touch. I held it in gloved hands, blowing steam from the coffee and watching the sun rise over the fields beyond the fence.

We were ready to go, waiting only for Hammed to arrive. He insisted on walking to the power plant in the predawn darkness rather than al-lowing us to pick him up at his home. I watched Hammed come through the gate, a small figure in a jacket and tie stumbling along the rough dirt road. He waved jauntily to me but made straight for a group of Marines sitting around a coffeepot. They welcomed him warmly and pulled up another ammo can. A few minutes later, when I walked over to give them a ten-minute warning, Hammed held a canteen cup and was engrossed in a debate over the name of the youngest-ever Playboy Playmate. His criticism of American culture was already starting to waver.

The night before, during our patrol debrief, I had asked higher-ranking officers in the battalion how I should deal with Mullah Mohammed. After the initial "fuck him" response, Major Whitmer agreed that our assistance shouldn't be made a weapon in local power struggles. We were to drive into town and offer water to all comers. If the mullah didn't like it, he and whatever suicidal followers he could muster were free to try to stop us. Follow-on peacekeepers, civil affairs experts, and civilian consultants could debate who was allowed to play in the rebuilding of Iraq. That wasn't for us to decide. Our only goal was to prevent a humanitarian disaster from tearing the country apart. That meant food, water, shelter, and medical care for every single Iraqi, regardless of religion, social status, or former party affiliation. His reasoning made sense to me and became our guidance for the day.

We first drove downtown, into central Baghdad, to meet up with a water tanker at the Marines' main logistics base. From the base, we escorted the tanker north on the road we had traveled the day before. I watched the wide-eyed tanker drivers in my mirror; they hadn't been out on their own before. We wove through the same crowds thronging the outdoor vendors. The mosque's minaret was visible over the rooftops ahead of us.

"Weapon! Three o'clock." Reyes's warning came over the radio, and I looked to my right. A teenage boy cradled a rifle, leaning against a building and staring us down. When we stopped, he cocked his head a bit higher, as if in challenge. My first thought was that he was only bait. As the Marines studied the walls and rooftops around the boy, I climbed from the Humvee and walked up to him. He let me get close before setting the rifle on the ground and stepping back from it. I picked up the ancient Enfield and slid its bolt back, dropping three rounds into my palm. The gun was clean and well oiled. I turned and walked back to the Humvee, throwing the rifle in the bed. The expressionless boy watched us go. If that had been a test, we had won.

We passed the mullah's mosque and pulled off into a dirt lot on the other side of the road. The platoon set up a perimeter around the tanker. Expecting a frenzy, we strung cloth tape between the vehicles, controlling access to the water through one narrow entrance and exit. I was suspicious when no crowd gathered while we worked. After ten minutes, we still sat alone on the street corner.

"Motherfucker trumped us," Gunny Wynn said, shaking his head. "I guess we know who's boss around here."

We gathered our tape and led the tanker north a few miles to a town we had not yet visited. Alongside the road, women dug down through the trash heaps to the shallow water table. Even little girls helped to cart home buckets of muddy water. As always, the men sat in the shade, watching the women work over the tips of their cigarettes.

The road split on the north side of the town of Al Jabr, enclosing what in the United States would have been a village green or town square filled with flowers or a gazebo. In Iraq, it was a flat piece of dirt with the supreme virtue of being mostly free of trash and raw sewage. We set up our cordon with the tanker in the middle and within minutes were thronged. People streamed from every corner of the town, carrying, pushing, and dragging receptacles of all kinds: plastic buckets, antifreeze bottles, rubber bladders, even a child's wading pool. Tractors and donkeys did some of the lifting, but mostly it was done by women and girls. I watched in awe as seven-year-olds hefted five-gallon cans of water weighing forty pounds onto their heads.

Espera's team pulled security on the road, and he leaned against the quarter panel of his Humvee to watch the melee. "Goddamn, sir, if we'd had to fight the women around here instead of the men, we'd have gotten our asses kicked," he said.

I had placed Sergeant Reyes's team north of the square where the two sections of road rejoined and disappeared around a bend. We worked the northernmost American zone, and I didn't want a truck full of fedayeen to come barreling down the highway and blunder into a fight with us in the middle of a crowd of women and children. The other teams kept order among the people waiting for water. Gunny Wynn and I were talking with two Iraqi men when we heard shouting up on the road.

"Gun! He has a gun!"

"Hold your fire! He's turning around."

We ran to the pavement and saw a white Toyota Land Cruiser being stopped at gunpoint by Rudy's team. Four men inside held up their hands in surrender. Apparently, they had been traveling south when they saw the Humvee sitting in the road. They tried to do a quick U-turn and in the process threw an AK-47 out of the window of the truck.

Raising that rifle had nearly cost them their lives. Jacks saw the weapon and was about to fire his Mark-19 when the AK was dropped instead of aimed. He sighted in on the truck, ready to stitch it.

Wynn and I approached the Land Cruiser. The men inside looked well dressed and neatly groomed, traits we had noticed among the fedayeen and foreign fighters. The driver began to speak.

"We Kurdistan. Kurdistan. America friend. Come boom-boom Ba'ath Party. Boom-boom fedayeen. George Bush very good. We Kurdistan. America friend."

He thrust a folded piece of paper at me. The top bore an official-looking embossed seal, and some of the writing was in English. From what I could decipher, it was a permit issued by the Patriotic Union of Kurdistan allowing the man to carry an assault rifle.

"These guys are peshmerga," I said. I knew the Kurdish fighters were staunchly pro-American. They had been helping U.S. Special Forces fight Ansar al-Islam, a terror network based in northern Iraq. That afternoon, they were doing exactly what we'd been briefed they would — exacting revenge on the Sunni-dominated Ba'ath Party for atrocities committed against them under the Hussein regime. All the intelligence reports had a "wink-wink, nod-nod" quality. Like the Northern Alliance in Afghanistan, the peshmerga were thugs, but *our* thugs.

We were under orders to disarm the populace but also to avoid getting tangled up in other people's fights. In Sadr City, I had listened as senior officers had encouraged the revenge killings as a necessary part of Iraq's eventual stabilization. Some American units were even reported to be distributing captured weapons to anti-Ba'athist militias. Once again, grand strategy and national policy came to a head in a single decision by a small platoon.

"Give him his rifle back, Rudy, and let them go."

Rudy handed it over, saying, "My enemy's enemy is my friend."

"I never thought we'd say that," I replied. "We've spent too much time in the Middle East."

I felt dirty rearming the peshmerga and lending my tacit approval to their killing spree. But war makes for rational choices that are hard to understand in more reflective moments. I preferred to have as many proxies fighting for us as possible if that meant more killing and dying done by them and less by my Marines. With a conspiratorial wave, the men in the Land Cruiser resumed their hunt, streaking south toward Baghdad.

While escorting the water tanker back to its base, we learned that the battalion was leaving the power plant to move to a new location. I copied the grid coordinates in grease pencil on the windshield and looked at my map. It matched up with a soccer stadium near the presidential palaces in the city center.

I turned to Gunny Wynn. "Looks like we're moving downtown."

"Damn, and I was just starting to appreciate the quiet of that power plant out in the middle of nowhere. Just goes to show, things can always get worse."

I propped the radio on the dashboard and tuned in a news broadcast from London. The announcer reported thousands of Baghdad residents marching to protest the American occupation.

Wynn smiled wryly and said, "Sure am glad we worked our asses off today."

# 38

WE SPENT THE NIGHT on the cool grass of the soccer field built by Saddam's son Uday. Gunfire echoed around the stadium, and tracers passed low over the stands, but we rested easily in the company of so many other armed Americans. Reyes worked out by flipping through a deck of cards and doing pushups to correspond with the number on each. He sweated through the deck again and again. Jacks read comic books, punctuating his reading with dramatic recitals for the benefit of the platoon. They howled in appreciation and passed around cups of coffee. We felt normal again.

I sat in the grass next to Gunny Wynn while he brushed his teeth. Mullah Mohammed, the boy with the rifle, and the rampaging peshmerga already existed in another world. We had escorted the tanker back to its base and then picked our way through the city to the new coordinates we'd been given for the battalion. I believed that this was just another way station and that the platoon would be back on patrol the next morning. But Major Whitmer pulled me aside when we arrived.

"Hope you had a good day, Nate. That was your last patrol."

I thought for a second that I was being relieved. Maybe I had pushed back too hard against my CO. "Why's that, sir?"

"The division's turning most of Iraq over to the Army. We're going home."

Home. Home for me had become a Humvee cab. In its most luxurious incarnations, home was a warehouse or an abandoned building that provided some shelter from the sun and wind. Home could be a hospital in Kuwait or a hospital ship out in the Gulf. Nothing existed beyond that. The concept was too abstract. The word didn't even register.

It was April 19. The regime had fallen only ten days earlier. We'd been in San Diego ten weeks before that. Everyone expected a deployment lasting six months or a year. We knew the hard part was only beginning. Baghdad still seethed. Gunfire, explosions, crime, death, and disease defined the city. It was enough to keep every last American busy all day, every day, for the coming year. We couldn't possibly be going home.

"Maybe we're getting lucky. Straight to Kuwait. First flight home," Gunny Wynn said, as he leaned toward a side mirror on the Humvee, running an electric razor across his chin.

I stared at him.

"You're right," he said. "I don't know what I was thinking."

We left the stadium before sunrise to get as far as we could before the day grew hot. By mid-April, noon temperatures already approached one hundred degrees, and they would only get hotter with each passing day and each southbound mile. I traded places with Christeson and stood on the rear bumper of the Humvee, holding on to the upright struts and feeling the wind in my face. I wanted to enjoy one last look at Baghdad.

The city was cool and quiet as pink streaks appeared in the sky and the streetlights blinked off one by one. Dawn is the same everywhere, even in Baghdad. The frenzy of the night was over, and the frenzy of the new day hadn't yet begun. A garbage truck rumbled down a residential street, stopping as men in coveralls jumped off and emptied the cans. Some residents kept garden plots on the median in the roadway, and stooped men tended their vegetables, waving as we passed. I imagined they had been lifelong farmers who had moved to the city in old age to live with the children they couldn't keep on the farm. Lights shone from a few upper-story windows, and I wondered at the thoughts of families waking up to their tenth day of freedom. Maybe they'd look out the window and watch us going by. If they saw us, I wondered, what would they see? I couldn't know. Despite our best intentions, Iraq and its people remained alien to me.

Baghdad's veneer of routine wasn't without cracks. An Army patrol picked its way through an industrial park. Tanks manned checkpoints at regular intervals along the road. Most neighborhoods looked untouched by war, but the government buildings towering over them were shells turned black inside. Shock and awe. One highway underpass hid the burned remains of an Abrams tank, a tank retriever, and two supply trucks. Their sad story begged to be told.

At sunrise, we passed the blue clamshells of the Martyrs Monument, a tribute to the Iraqi dead in the war with Iran. Public memorials appeared to be one thing the Hussein regime had done right. This one soared above the surrounding homes, opening, closing, and changing shape with the shifting perspective of our movement. The monument's beauty, after so many weeks of mud brick and wreckage, was staggering. Near a sign for Saddam International Airport, the battalion turned south on Highway 1 and left Baghdad behind.

The sun beat down between billowing clouds. Riding with my head pitched back, I watched them swirling and changing shapes. No smoke. No jets or helicopters. No gunfire, no mortars, no turtling inside my body armor. All we needed was music. I played with the shortwave, but the choices were the BBC, Arabic talk radio, and religious chants. Six hours south of Baghdad, we pulled off the highway into a field of reddish clay. I observed the ritual of emplacing the machine guns at hundred-meter intervals and sketching a fire plan, but it was a struggle. As quickly as we'd been thrown into the war, we were being withdrawn even faster.

We dallied in the field for three days. Surely, we mused, there had to be a power plant to guard, a school to rebuild, a convoy to escort, or even a plane leaving Kuwait City with a few empty seats to fill. Anything beat roasting in the dirt and debating our future. On the second night, three combat engineers attached to the battalion were marking an Iraqi minefield along the side of the road. One of them stepped on a small antipersonnel mine. The blast tore his leg off at the knee and liquefied the eye of a Marine standing next to him. When I told the platoon about the accident, Espera shook his head. "There are a thousand ways to die," he said.

Our only consolation was the flood of Army soldiers streaming north toward Baghdad. Their columns of tanks and trucks passed without pause through the days and nights. The Fourth Infantry Division had missed the war because Turkey had vetoed an American attack through its territory. But it arrived just in time for the occupation. We empathized with the soldiers on their way to a hot and dangerous summer of peacekeeping.

On our last night in the field, I was walking the battalion's lines along the highway when an Army tanker truck pulled to a stop at the edge of the pavement. Five more swung in behind it. A second lieutenant hopped down from the cab and waved to me.

"Howdy. Can you tell me where to find the intersection with Highway 8?" he asked. He held a crumpled, hand-drawn map.

"Christ, man, you're still like fifty klicks south of it."

He looked perplexed. "Well, how's the road up there? Safe?"

"Depends. You got an escort? Heavy weapons?"

The lieutenant gave a quick nod, dismissing my question. "We're armed." It was the verbal equivalent of snapping his suspenders.

"You mean that thing?" I pointed at the pistol on his belt.

"A rifle in every truck." Defiant.

"Stay the fuck away from me. You guys have no maps, no weapons, no fucking clue where you are. I don't want to be around when you get hosed." I hated feeling that way and tried to make a joke of it, but I couldn't. Sometime in the past month, we had become veterans. And like the veterans in every war, we didn't want to be near the new guys. New guys got themselves killed.

On April 22, we drove another hundred kilometers south to what the division euphemistically called Tactical Assembly Area Paige, a former Iraqi military base on the outskirts of Ad Diwaniyah. RCT-5 had shot its way through the town a month before, and the bullet holes and shrapnel scars remained. The Marines said that Paige was biblical, not because it was down the road from Abraham's Ur, but because each day brought a new plague — heat, wind, sand, flies, mosquitoes, and sickness. Our first morning there, after waking up in a septic field surrounded by burning trash fires, Gunny Wynn stared at the Iraqis digging for water in the noxious dirt. "These motherfuckers are tough," he said. "Third world tough."

The platoon lived in a carport a hundred feet long and twenty feet wide. Concrete pillars supported a concrete roof above the concrete floor. There were no walls. The concrete absorbed so much heat during the day that it was too hot to sleep near at night. It radiated like an oven until dawn, when it began recharging for the next night. I wanted to sleep under the sky, but disease-ridden sand fleas infested every patch of ground, so I settled for wrapping up in a waterproof sleeping bag liner and sweating through the night. Sleep was intermittent anyway. Living in a field of human waste spread dysentery through the platoon. The closest I came to willing my own death in Iraq was while curled up in the dust outside a plywood latrine, too weak to swat the jellybean-size flies clustered on my head.

Rumors swirled of surveillance missions along the Saudi border or patrols into Ad Diwaniyah. Eighteen thousand Marines slowly assembled at Paige, enough for almost any mission imaginable. The Marines kept active — studying maps, prowling for intelligence around the division's headquarters, and working out with an improvised weight set of discarded Iraqi tank parts. But after three weeks, we received the order to turn over all our ammunition to other units driving north. On the division's status board, a little green card next to First Recon's name was changed to red. We were done.

Combat missions had galvanized the battalion. Without them, the pettiness of peacetime military life returned. One morning, the captain assembled our company for PT: a run around Paige followed by calisthenics. We stood in rows in the dust, wearing green shorts and tan combat boots, resigned to working out without a shower. The Marines were sullen; they resented taking orders from a leader they no longer respected.

The captain chose pushups as our first exercise. While he counted the repetitions, the whole company was supposed to echo him loudly. Instead, fifty Marines grunted silently through a set of twenty-five, mumbling numbers at the dirt. Crunches were next. The captain asked for a volunteer to lead the counting, and Gunny Wynn trotted to the front of the formation. He dropped on his back and began counting out loud. The company roared in unison, *"One . . . two . . . three . . . four!"* The Marines around us stopped to watch as they realized that a small mutiny was taking place. I smiled, staring at the sky as I curled my crossed arms to my thighs and tried to out-shout them all.

The captain summoned me that afternoon to his makeshift office in an old barracks building. I found him sitting behind a desk, wearing his full uniform instead of the trousers and T-shirt we usually wore in the heat. When he didn't invite me to sit on one of the MRE boxes strewn across the floor, I knew I was in trouble.

"Lieutenant Fick, I'm relieving Gunny Wynn for insubordination."

I started to reply, but he cut me off. "In Ar Rifa, he challenged my orders in front of the Marines," he said. I tried again to speak, but he looked down at his paperwork and said, "Dismissed."

My gut impulse was to throw my metal lieutenant's bars on the captain's desk and tell him I quit. But of course I couldn't do that. Wynn and I were a team. We felt we had a duty to protect the platoon from the caprice of the larger corps. The Marines' loyalty to Wynn was fierce, something like love. Relieving him would be a blow to their morale and to their trust in the battalion. I decided we had to put our pride aside and figure out a way to keep our jobs.

When I got back to the carport, Wynn was supervising the cleaning of the platoon's sniper rifles. He looked up when I walked over.

"Let's take a walk, Gunny."

We left the camp and started down the road that ran for a mile along Paige. I felt light without my body armor, carrying a pistol instead of my rifle. Around us, Marines scrubbed weapons, counted ammunition into piles, and repaired their vehicles for the long drive back to Kuwait.

"The CO plans to relieve you for disobeying his orders," I said.

Wynn took the news quietly and kept walking. Finally, he replied, "Bullshit. I only disobeyed his orders when they would have gotten people killed for no reason. I'll go to the colonel."

"*No.*" The word sounded harsher than I'd intended. "You need to let me deal with this."

"Sir," he protested, "these guys are attacking me when *they're* the ones who screwed up. I'm going to the colonel."

"Mike, this isn't about you," I said, trying to appeal to his sense of duty. "It's about the platoon. You're the only thing between these guys and our Marines. Listen to me: *I* will deal with it. I know it's crazy, but I have more firepower right now."

When we returned to the carport, I sat down to figure out what to say to the captain. He was a bad combat leader but not a bad person. It didn't seem right to hold poor decisions under fire against him. To a greater or lesser extent, we had all made such mistakes. But vindictive decisions after the fighting was over were another matter. I thought the captain had a grudge against Wynn.

When I went back to the captain's office, he looked up wearily.

"Sir, I feel obligated to warn you that you'll have most of your company in revolt if you relieve Gunny Wynn," I said.

This time he asked me to take a seat. To his credit, he listened while I explained that relieving Wynn over my objections meant that he no longer had faith in my judgment. If that was the case, then he should relieve me, too. When I hesitated, he waved a hand for me to continue. "Sir, we're almost on our way home," I said. "The company did its job and nobody died. Can't we just let it go and get back to our lives?"

Gunny Wynn kept his job, and I kept mine.

On a Friday afternoon in May, I gathered the platoon at the center of the carport. I had been working on a secret project for the previous week — wrangling permission from the division for a visit to the ancient city of Babylon. Colonel Ferrando pressed hard on our behalf, and almost unbelievably, it was granted. After major combat ended, the First Marine Expeditionary Force moved its headquarters to one of Saddam's palaces near the town of Hillah, seventy miles north of Ad Diwaniyah. The palace overlooked Babylon's ruins. Part of my desire came from studying the classics in college. I had tramped through crumbling cities in Greece, Italy, Spain, and North Africa. But nothing compared to joining the handful of Westerners who, in the past thirty years, had visited one of the ancient world's greatest cities. Part of it, too, was the welcome change of pace for the Marines and a chance to go home with memories of something truly good. Seeing Babylon was a way to get out from behind the gun sight.

We left Paige at seven o'clock the next morning. Iraqi vendors lined both sides of the road, hawking beer, AK bayonets, Arab porn, and crude Iraqi flags of painted canvas. We disciplined ourselves to stop only for two coolers filled with sodas and a bunch of ripe bananas. Turning north on Highway 1, the platoon accelerated. Army supply convoys lumbered along in the slow lane as we flashed past on their left. Hikers in San Diego joke about not needing to outrun mountain lions; they only have to outrun other hikers. The same principle applied on Iraq's highways. For a month or two, though, the roads were mostly safe. The war had ended, and the insurgency hadn't yet begun. Still, when I briefed the Marines about the trip, I acknowledged that some of them might think it foolish to take the risk of going sightseeing. Anyone who preferred not to come was free to stay at Paige. They all chose Babylon.

The exit toward Hillah led us through miles and miles of palm groves. Holes in the frond canopy marked where American planes had blasted Iraqi tanks. Fresh growth would soon cover the blackened patches of earth, and maybe someday tourists would poke at the rusting hulks as they do in the South Pacific and Normandy. Closer to Babylon, we noticed changes in the modest homes along the road. A stainless steel Sub-Zero refrigerator dominated the front yard of a one-room mud hut. Slabs of pink marble and two ornate wardrobes stood near another. A decrepit Datsun pickup truck held a crystal chandelier. It looked as though a palace had been looted.

We rounded a bend in the dirt road and saw a building like a science-fiction fantasy atop the only hill for miles around. Part fortress and part castle, it tapered as it climbed, squat but ornate. It shone in the sunlight, punctuated by gaping black windows. That first view of a presidential palace conjured up all the dark mysteries of Saddam's Iraq. Dinner parties with lines of black limousines, sparkling lights and music reaching out across the palm groves. I imagined hammered brass trays piled with steaming meat and vegetables, cavernous baths, and a harem. I thought also of forced labor, torture, and executions. The building exuded a bit of each of these things. An American flag hung in the highest window.

Ancient Babylon spread across the plains beneath the palace. The city had been excavated by Germans a century earlier and its treasures carted off to Berlin. Most of what remained was, like the palace, a fantasy. Saddam had reconstructed Babylon not according to any archaeological evidence, but to tickle his own fancy. Crenellated walls and soaring towers crowned the bricks of the original ruins. Once each year, the regime had held a ceremony in Babylon to celebrate Iraq's glory. Saddam himself had played the role of King Nebuchadnezzar.

We parked next to the famed Ishtar Gate, a blue portal covered with reliefs of lions, stags, and mythical creatures. I remembered only the highlights of Babylon's history — Hammurabi, the Hanging Gardens, the death of Alexander the Great — and was relieved when a distinguished older gentleman approached us. His first sentence made me laugh: "Call me Ishmael." Wearing a fedora and dark sunglasses, Ishmael had been an archaeologist at Babylon before the Ba'ath Party came to power in 1968. He carried a thick binder filled with maps and photographs and offered to take us on a tour of the site.

Ishmael shepherded us through Babylon's cobbled streets. He spoke lilting English, weaving a story of mighty kings and fallen empires. Behind him, like so many schoolkids on a field trip, trailed the platoon, covered with guns and knives, straining to hear every word. We walked down the fabled Street of Processions, past the basalt Lion of Babylon, and across the stage on which Alexander is rumored to have died. Colbert slid next to me and marveled that, in only two years, we had followed two of Alexander's most fabled campaigns — across Afghanistan and Iraq.

"Somehow I doubt I'll be remembered as 'Brad the Great,'" he said.

Ishmael mixed his history lesson with modern parallels: new beginnings, imperial hubris, the death of an old regime. He kept up a running commentary on Saddam's abuses. Six of his family members, including his only son, had been executed in the 1990s. Inside the mysteriously cool natural icehouses deep beneath the floors, he quietly expressed his hope that the Americans would kill Saddam and end his terror definitively. The fear still gripped him.

Back outside, Espera stood against a wall, with the sunlight casting sharp shadows across a stone courtyard. "Look around. This great empire rose and fell. Everything rises and falls, nations and individuals, too," he said. Lacking a cigar to point with, he leaned back on his hands. "Sometimes I think these decisions are already made; the script is already written, and we're the last to read it. Maybe the universe is like a big watch: If you can crack the formula to the universal principles, then you can figure it all out."

Colbert cut in. "Is this your goddamn lottery theory again?"

Espera ignored the exasperation and bent toward me. "Think about the lottery for a second," he continued. "You buy some tickets at 7-Eleven, and you turn on the TV that night to watch some dude read numbers off Ping-Pong balls. Well, there's nothing random about which numbers pop up." Espera said this as if it were all self-evident. Then he narrowed his eyes and got to the point. "If you could calculate the weight of the balls, the temperature and humidity of the room, the force of the little air jets, and a thousand other variables, then you could correctly predict what numbers win." He looked around with satisfaction. "Same thing here. Babylon fell. Iraq fell. The United States will someday fall. It's already written. That bullet that hit Pappy had his name on it since it was iron ore in the ground. We just couldn't see and calculate all the variables in time to save him. I'm not sure if that makes me feel better or worse."

A small crowd had gathered. Ishmael looked uncertainly at his competition. Reyes clapped Espera on the back and said, "Don't know if I agree with you, brother, but well said. Amen."

Colbert wandered off, saying, "Tony, you need to go home and get laid."

"Tell me something I don't know, white boy." Espera fell back into his own brooding, and we followed Ishmael toward the Ishtar Gate.

He carefully gathered his maps, tucking them back into the binder. Ishmael shook each of our hands, saying he hoped that Western tourists would soon flock to Babylon and help his people recapture their lost prosperity. Removing his fedora, Ishmael insisted that we didn't have to pay him but allowed that any money "would buy many things of need" for his family. Gunny Wynn was a step ahead. He had collected a few dollars from each of us and tipped Ishmael a year's wages.

We looped around a circular drive leading up the hill and parked near the palace's front door. The view was even more spectacular than I had expected. We gazed across the entire sweep of Babylon, over the palms, and past the Euphrates. The next day, another recon platoon stood in the same place and watched in horror as a Marine helicopter crashed into the river and sank, killing its four-man crew and one Marine who had jumped in to save them. But our afternoon was peaceful, and I could almost understand Saddam's delusion, from that perch, of keeping the whole country under his thumb. We crossed the threshold through wooden doors two stories high.

The entry hall seemed modeled on a cathedral, but the power conveyed to visitors was not of God, but of Saddam. We tromped across an inlaid marble floor, marveling at a chandelier nearly the size of a Humvee. Carved panels of dark wood stood inside deep alcoves in the walls, like statues of saints. Doors led to long hallways promising riches. A grand staircase rose to balconies overlooking the ground-floor rooms. Everything was marble, crystal, or mahogany. One ceiling displayed a mural showing the sweep of Iraqi history, from the Ishtar Gate to Saddam Hussein. The whole place was garish, superficially impressive like a Las Vegas hotel rather than awe-inspiring like a medieval cathedral. It represented no grand idea or human triumph. Men from the First Marine Expeditionary Force headquarters camped in the upstairs rooms, and filthy cammies floated in a marble tub where, perhaps only weeks before, Saddam had enjoyed one of his final soaks.

*       *       *

A week later, we packed up for the five-hundred-kilometer drive to Kuwait. Leaving at six P.M. to avoid the midday heat, we passed through As Samawah, where convoys had been mobbed and shot at on previous evenings. The town slept through our passage, and we saw only dogs barking under streetlights. We paralleled the Euphrates River toward Nasiriyah, and despite the warm air, I shivered when I saw its lights on the horizon. Memories of our first visit, exactly two months earlier, came surging back. As we refueled on the highway, scorpions scuttled across the pavement, casting shadows in the headlights which made them look a foot tall. I drove a long leg through the dead hours of early morning, passing near the Ar Ratawi railroad bridge and the oil fields of Rumaila. After Gunny Wynn took over, I fell asleep in the passenger seat and woke up in the sunlight of the empty Kuwaiti desert.

# PART III

# Aftermath

Anyone who looks with anguish on evils so great must acknowledge the tragedy of it all; and if anyone experiences them without anguish, his condition is even more tragic, since he remains serene by losing his humanity.

— AUGUSTINE OF HIPPO

# 39

I STROLL IN THE SUMMER SUNLIGHT at a lakeside family reunion. Young cousins splash in the water, while adults laugh over drinks. In the distance, a band plays. I approach people to join the conversations, but no one can see or hear me. I am invisible to them. Looking down at myself in confusion, I see that I wear desert camouflage and carry a rifle slung across my chest. Blood soaks my clothes.

For months after coming home, this dream woke me. Not every night, only a dozen times in all, but often enough to make sleep an act of will. Sometimes I got up and took a walk. Sometimes I did pushups on my bedroom floor until I collapsed in exhaustion. Mostly, though, I stared at the ceiling and tried to think of something, anything, else.

The homecoming story is a cliché. From the moment we arrived in Kuwait, I felt that I knew what would happen next. One Marine in a different battalion cracked almost immediately and shot another Marine in the chest during a touch football game. We took off from Kuwait City aboard a commercial airliner. The passengers cheered as the wheels left the ground. My seat was clean, the food delicious, and the stewardesses pretty. Some people talked, most slept, and I stared out the window. The pyramids at Giza slid past in the morning light. In Frankfurt, I stood at the terminal door for twenty minutes, just marveling at the green grass. We entered American airspace north of Syracuse, New York, on Tuesday, June 3, 2003, at two P.M. The pilot said, "Welcome home," and we cheered again.

When we landed at the Air Force base in Riverside, California, I walked down the stairs to the tarmac. There were the grills where the

Red Cross had cooked hamburgers for us, the hangar where we'd slept on the floor, and the television still blaring at the rows of empty chairs where we'd watched the space shuttle burn up. Outside, headlights moved on the freeway. A Tuesday evening commute. Nothing had changed.

The delusion persisted through our bus ride back to Camp Pendleton and the midnight reunion with our families on a basketball court behind the battalion's offices. I locked my weapons in the armory but kept the holster on my thigh to hide a bloodstain from the boy at Qalat Sukkar. People waved signs and cheered, and we played the returning heroes. Sergeant Patrick stood quietly, apart from the crowd, dressed in starched cammies and wearing boots for the first time in two months. He wore them, despite the pain, because he thought it was right to greet the platoon while wearing his proper uniform. We all hugged him, along with our mothers and fathers and wives and girlfriends, because he was family.

I felt lonely that night in the hotel room — no radios hissing, no stars overhead, no Marines standing watch beside me. I slept in two-hour chunks. Before dawn, I woke up and took my second shower of the night, just because I could. A dark brown face stared back from the bathroom mirror. I saw lines on my forehead I hadn't noticed before. The horseshoe still hung around my neck on its loop of parachute cord. I slipped it up and over my head for the first time since Christmas.

Delusions of normalcy continued as I settled back into my daily routine. I stopped for coffee on the way to work. I got stuck in traffic and went to the grocery store to refill my refrigerator. Life's simple conveniences kept me so grateful that I hardly thought about the war. The return felt seamless. Sometimes I imagined that the four-month interlude had been a dream I could just forget.

But bit by bit, little things dragged me back. On a Saturday afternoon, a Marine friend who had not been in Iraq invited me to go skeet shooting with him at Camp Pendleton's range. I accepted reflexively, thinking nothing of it. I noticed him looking at me as we drove up the freeway. Finally, he spoke.

"What the hell are you doing?"

I was swerving randomly under overpasses. In Iraq, that made it harder for people above to drop hand grenades into the Humvee.

"Sorry. I wasn't paying attention."

When we got to the range, I stood on the firing line with a shotgun and a bag of shells. Suddenly, I had no interest in shooting skeet. I had last fired a gun shortly before midnight on April 1, on the highway north of Al Hayy.

I sized people up on the street, looking head to toe for the telltale bulge of a pistol or a bomb. Not having a tourniquet and IV bag nearby made me vaguely uncomfortable. I ate up every scrap of news about the men still fighting but preferred not to talk about it. I cried sometimes for no reason at all. When a driver cut me off in a merge lane, I visualized, without emotion, pulling his head back and cutting his throat with my car key. On the Fourth of July, a firecracker sent me diving behind a car door, reaching for a pistol that wasn't there. I felt older than my father. And I had the dream.

I thought I was losing my mind. The only way I knew I was still sane was that I thought I might be going crazy. Surely, that awareness meant I was sane. Crazy people think they're sane. Only sane people can think they're crazy. I was reduced to taking comfort in a tautology.

After three years as a platoon commander, I was promoted to captain and chosen to become the commanding officer of the Basic Reconnaissance Course. There are a limited number of operational jobs in the Marine Corps, so my two combat deployments guaranteed me a tour behind a desk instead of an immediate return to Afghanistan or Iraq. When I'd started OCS in 1998, I'd considered making the Marines my career. After Afghanistan, the possibility had remained, only slightly diminished. After Iraq, I knew I had to leave.

Most people in my life acted as if getting out was a natural choice for me. When I'd accepted my commission, friends and relatives had asked questions such as "Last time we talked, you were at Dartmouth. What happened?" or "Do Marines get paid?" An acquaintance felt the need to console my parents, saying, "You must be so disappointed." These people now thought that I was correcting an earlier mistake, or perhaps that I'd satisfied my adolescent bravado. They thought that the job's practical hardships had driven me out — long deployments, frequent moves, low pay, and danger. But they were wrong. For me, the intangible honor and pride of being a Marine officer outweighed all the adversity.

Some of my buddies in the Corps understood that the decision was more personal. They knew that I chafed under a hierarchy that sometimes valued polished boots more than tactical competence in its leaders. They figured that we had done in four years what a previous generation of Marines had done in twenty, or maybe never. Promotion, as an officer, means more paperwork and less time with the troops. They knew that I had joined the Marines to hold a sword, not a pencil. They were right, but the real reason was even deeper.

I left the Corps because I had become a reluctant warrior. Many Marines reminded me of gladiators. They had that mysterious quality that allows some men to strap on greaves and a breastplate and wade into the gore. I respected, admired, and emulated them, but I could never be like them. I could kill when killing was called for, and I got hooked on the rush of combat as much as any man did. But I couldn't make the conscious choice to put myself in that position again and again throughout my professional life. Great Marine commanders, like all great warriors, are able to kill that which they love most — their men. It's a fundamental law of warfare. Twice I had cheated it. I couldn't tempt fate again.

The battalion traditionally held a sendoff ceremony called a "Hail & Farewell" for its departing officers. Major Benelli scheduled mine for a Friday afternoon when he knew I wouldn't be in town. It was a snub, but not one that stung, since my allegiance wasn't to the battalion; it was to the platoon.

Recon platoons are steeped in tradition, and one of the finest is the paddle party. Mine was held at Mike Wynn's house on a Friday night in August. The whole platoon was there. They put me in a chair in the center of the room and gathered around. The ceremony's roots stretch back to Viking warships. According to tradition, when a warrior left the crew to settle down and start a family, his comrades presented him with his oar as a symbol of the contribution he had made and of their own collective weakening after his departure.

The youngest Marine, Lance Corporal Christeson, held the paddle first. Gunny Wynn and I had recommended him for combat meritorious promotion from private first class to lance corporal, one of the first since the Vietnam War. The paddle passed from his hands through the whole platoon, moving in order of seniority, with each man telling a story as he held it. "Lower, Christeson. You're shooting too high." Rushing to the landing zone at Bridgeport. Task Force Sword. Ambush Alley. Espera and the ever-present cigar. Lasers in Muwaffiqiya. Horsehead.

Sydney. Boat raids. "Take the shot." The paddle passed from Gunny Wynn, the senior Marine in the platoon, to Sergeant Patrick, the man who had made it. Patrick turned the paddle around, showing it to me for the first time.

He had carved it from a four-foot block of cherry. Green, tan, and black parachute cord wrapped the handle. My captain's bars, jump wings, and ribbons adorned the blade. On the back, Rudy had inked First Recon's insignia and attached a photo of the platoon in the Kuwaiti desert on the eve of the war.

I reached out to touch it and sensed another crease in history. When my hand closed around the parachute cord, my command of the platoon ended. In their words, I was promoted from captain to mister. In mine, the most meaningful year of my life was over.

A few mornings later, I drove to work for my last day. It was a foggy, cool Southern California morning. In the parking lot, I saw my replacement, a red-haired captain named Brent Morel. We had gone to lunch together the day before and sat for two hours as I tried to put the platoon into words — Colbert's cool demeanor, Rudy's enthusiasm, Jacks's mastery of the Mark-19, Patrick's southern aphorisms. The war in Iraq hadn't ended, and I wanted Morel to know the men when he took them back for their second tour.

"Mornin', Brent."

He looked up from the waterproof bag he was sealing. "Hi, Nate. We're heading down to the beach for a fin."

"Everybody?"

"Whole platoon. Wanna come?" It was a gracious offer, but I couldn't accept it.

"They're yours now, man. Have a good one."

In the office, I collected all my gear, cleaning each piece and stuffing it into my rucksack to return to the supply warehouse. I held my rifle, thinking of Al Gharraf and the dead fedayeen. Putting my hand around the grip of my pistol, I was back at the bridge in Muwaffiqiya with tracers slicing through the dark. Brown bloodstains still mottled my flight gloves, but I shoved them into the ruck. I tried for a moment to beat Iraq's dust from its canvas but gave up. This pack would probably be retired anyway. A piece of shrapnel had torn through its outer pockets and ripped away all the snaps.

At the warehouse, I waited in a line of Marines turning in their gear.

Some were heading to new assignments, others getting out. All were quiet. Near the opposite doorway stood a group of second lieutenants, new guys with fresh haircuts. They joked and laughed, pretending not to see us. I wanted to gather them up and tell them what my father had told me as a new Marine: "Stand tall, but come home physically and psychologically intact." I knew they would clasp their hands behind them, listen respectfully, and then laugh behind the back of the crazy captain who'd forgotten that Marine lieutenants are invincible. So I walked to my car and drove home instead. They would figure it out for themselves.

A few months later, I was working in Washington, D.C., and the platoon was back in Iraq. I drove down to Virginia Beach on a Thursday morning in April to pin a Bronze Star on Shawn Patrick's chest. He had recovered from his wound and was an instructor at the Amphibious Reconnaissance School, training new recon Marines. As I passed Quantico on I-95, I listened to the national security advisor testifying before the 9/11 Commission. The symbolism struck me — passing the place where I had begun my Marine Corps career, listening to a debate over the event that had launched me into two years of combat, traveling to a ceremony to close a chapter of the story.

The phone rang. It was Cara Wynn, Mike's wife. She was breathless, speaking so fast that I could barely understand her.

"The platoon was ambushed in Fallujah. A bunch of guys were hit and flown to Germany. That's all I know right now."

While on patrol, Bravo Company had hit a sophisticated combined-arms ambush. A group of insurgents had opened fire on the convoy from behind a berm next to the road. An RPG had exploded inside the lead Humvee. One Marine had lost both his hands, and four others had been wounded. The platoon had attacked the ambushers' position, killing dozens of them.

In Virginia Beach, Sergeant Patrick stood unblinking as his commanding officer read the Bronze Star citation:

For professional achievement in the superior performance of his duties while serving in support of Operation Iraqi Freedom as Reconnaissance Team Leader, Team Two, Second Platoon, Bravo Company, First Reconnaissance Battalion, First Marine Division, from March, 2003 to May, 2003. On the night of April 1, while entering the town of

Muwaffiqiya, Iraq, Sergeant Patrick was shot in an enemy ambush. While under hostile fire from three directions, he applied a tourniquet to his wound, resumed firing, and directed his team's fire onto enemy targets, inflicting massive damage on the enemy forces. Sergeant Patrick remained in the kill zone and continued leading the Marines in his team until the enemy had been annihilated and his fellow Marines were out of harm's way. Sergeant Patrick's exceptional professional ability, initiative, and loyal dedication to duty reflect great credit upon himself and are in keeping with the highest traditions of the Marine Corps and the United States Naval Service.

We went to dinner afterward to celebrate, but we worried about our friends seven thousand miles away and wished we could be with them.

On my drive back to Washington, Cara called again. "Nate, I have some bad news."

I pulled over to the side of the road, waiting as if watching someone wind up, in slow motion, to punch me.

"Captain Morel's dead."

Brent had been shot in the chest while leading the platoon's counterattack. The Marines who fought to save him said that he had survived the golden hour. They recalled that when he died, aboard the casevac helicopter, he was so pale that his red hair had turned gray.

The new World War II Memorial in Washington had opened to visitors before its formal dedication. Still in shock over Brent's death, I drove into the city under a full moon to see it. I needed a physical connection to sacrifice. Floodlights bathed the circle of granite slabs in a warm yellow glow, much less harsh than the stark white of the Lincoln Memorial and the Washington Monument. Elms towered just beyond the circle of light.

I walked clockwise around the central fountain, reading words carved in stone and letters left behind by family and friends. Three times I ducked into shadows to hide my tears. The names and faces were different, but these were the same men. At one end of the memorial stands a wall of gold stars — four thousand of them. Each star represents one hundred Americans killed in World War II. I stood and counted eight of those four thousand stars, a minuscule slice of the wall's upper left corner. That was Afghanistan and Iraq combined. All the firefights, bombs, rockets, and helicopter crashes. Brent and Horsehead. All the heroism, blood, fear, humor, and boredom. Eight fucking stars.

I drifted after leaving the Corps. At age twenty-six, I feared I had already lived the best years of my life. Never again would I enjoy the sense of purpose and belonging that I had felt in the Marines. Also, I realized that combat had nearly unhinged me. Despite my loving family, supportive friends, and good education, the war flooded into every part of my life, carrying me along toward an unknown fate. If it could do that to me, what about my Marines? What about the guys without families, whose friends didn't try to understand, who got out of the Corps without the prospects I had? I worried that they had survived the war only to be killed in its wake.

After channeling all my energy into applying to graduate school, I got a phone call from an admissions officer: "Mr. Fick, we read your application and liked it very much. But a member of our committee read Evan Wright's story about your platoon in *Rolling Stone*. You're quoted as saying, 'The bad news is, we won't get much sleep tonight; the good news is, we get to kill people.'" She paused, as if waiting for me to disavow the quote. I was silent, and she went on. "We have a retired Army officer on our staff, and he warned me that there are people who *enjoy* killing, and they aren't nice to be around. Could you please explain your quote for me?"

"No, I cannot."

"Well, do you really feel that way?" Her tone was earnest, almost pleading.

"You mean, will I climb your clock tower and pick people off with a hunting rifle?"

It was her turn to be silent.

"No, I will not. Do I feel compelled to explain myself to you? I don't."

I was frustrated as much by respect and attempts at understanding as by unfeeling ignorance. The worst were blanket accolades and thanks from people "for what you guys did over there." Thanks for what, I wanted to ask — shooting kids, cowering in terror behind a berm, dropping artillery on people's homes? There wasn't any pride simply in being there. The pride was in our good decisions, in the things we did right. I hoped that I'd done more right than wrong, hoped that I hadn't been cavalier with people's lives. I was learning to accept that sometimes the only way to fight evil is with another evil, however good its aim.

In June, one year after coming home from Iraq, I dragged a childhood friend to the Civil War battlefield at Antietam in western Maryland. I wanted to walk the ground. Among the split-rail fences and restored cannons, I saw RPGs and fedayeen. Where would I have put my machine guns to defend the Cornfield? How would Hitman Two have assaulted the Bloody Lane?

The sun was warm on my arms, and bees buzzed through the tall grass as we meandered toward Burnside Bridge. There, on the afternoon of America's bloodiest day, troops made three unsuccessful attempts to cross Antietam Creek under withering fire. We stood at the center of the span with our hands on the stones.

"Was it a waste?" I asked.

"No," she replied. "They won, and Lincoln issued the Emancipation Proclamation. They freed the slaves, the way you freed the Afghans."

I didn't answer.

"Think about the women under the Taliban and the poor Iraqis under Saddam," she continued, seizing a chance to change the subject. "You helped do so much good for so many people. Why can't you take comfort in that?"

Staring down at the water, I measured my words, running through a justification I'd given myself a thousand times before. The good was abstract. The good didn't feel as good as the bad felt bad. It wasn't the good that kept me up at night.

"You sound so unprincipled," she said, shaking her head. "Why can't you find peace in what you and your men sacrificed so much to do? Why can't you be proud?"

I took sixty-five men to war and brought sixty-five home. I gave them everything I had. Together, we passed the test. Fear didn't beat us. I hope life improves for the people of Afghanistan and Iraq, but that's not why we did it. We fought for each other.

I am proud.

AUTHOR'S NOTE

AND

ACKNOWLEDGMENTS

Although the feelings expressed here are mine, I believe that my platoons and our wars are generally representative of the larger Marine Corps. I relied heavily on my patrol logbooks, daily journal, frequent letters home, official histories, and the recollections of my fellow Marines. All events are portrayed honestly and are, to the best of my knowledge, historically accurate.

For further reading about the Marines and the warrior ethos, I recommend Mark Helprin's *A Soldier of the Great War*, Michael Hodgins's *Reluctant Warrior*, William Manchester's *Goodbye, Darkness*, Steven Pressfield's *Gates of Fire*, Tom Ricks's *Making the Corps*, Jonathan Shay's *Odysseus in America*, E. B. Sledge's *With the Old Breed*, and James Webb's *Fields of Fire*.

A portion of this book's proceeds will be donated to veterans' organizations, including the Marine Corps Scholarship Foundation, dedicated to funding higher education for the children of Marines killed in action.

I thank my parents, Niel and Jane, and my sisters, Maureen and Stephanie, for their boundless love and support. In worrying, mailing cookies, and listening, they also served.

My fellow platoon commanders were, and are, comrades in the truest sense. Thank you to Patrick English, Vijay George, Ed Hinman, Ty Moore, Walt Messick, Brendan Sullivan, John Nash, and Jim Beal. My former commanding officer Rich Whitmer taught me more than he will ever acknowledge. Thank you, Oden Six. To Keith Marine, I can only say "Dang."

I am forever grateful to Mike Wynn, Brad Colbert, Shawn Patrick, Rudy Reyes, Steve Lovell, Tony Espera, Tim Bryan, Mike Stinetorf, Hector Leon,

Gabe Garza, Evan Stafford, Anthony "Manimal" Jacks, Walt Hasser, Nathan Christopher, James Chaffin, Harold Trombley, Teren "T" Holsey, John Christeson, Michael Brunmeier, Jason Lilley, Josh Person, Leandro "Shady" Baptista, Eric Kocher, Dan Redman, and A. J. Hull. You had my back. Semper Fidelis.

Writing a book is no more solitary than fighting a war. I thank Bradley Thayer, Jeremy Joseph, Craig Nerenberg, and Frank Russell for planting the idea. Eric Hammel encouraged it, and my agent, E. J. McCarthy, made it real. Callie Rucker Oettinger has been a tireless advocate. Honest readers sharpened the draft in countless ways. Thank you to Austin Whitman, Andrew Hilton, Mark Hotz, Abby Joseph, Jonathan May, Evan Wright, Margaret Angell, Andy Carroll, Mike Hodgins, Al Stam, and Andy Colyer. Finally, Denise Gitsham was with me from the beginning to the end. Thank you.

At Houghton Mifflin, I found people who cared as much about this book as I did. Thank you to Lori Glazer, Bridget Marmion, Larry Cooper, and Barbara Jatkola. Anne Seiwerath answered my endless questions with patience and grace, and Whitney Peeling made the project her own. I reserve my greatest thanks for my editor, Eamon Dolan. With the passion and intensity of a drill instructor, he whipped this book, and its author, into shape.

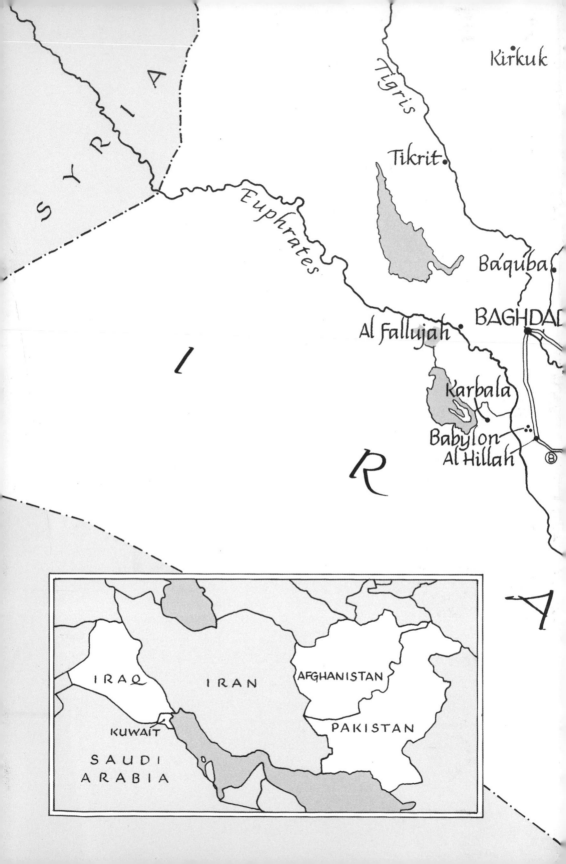

Kirkuk

*Tigris*

Tikrit

Báquba

*Euphrates*

Al Fallujah

BAGHDAD

Karbala

Babylon
Al Hillah

SYRIA

I

R

A

Ⓑ

IRAQ

IRAN

AFGHANISTAN

KUWAIT

PAKISTAN

SAUDI
ARABIA